The Great Reading Disaster

The Great Reading Disaster
Reclaiming Our Educational Birthright

Mona McNee & Alice Coleman

imprint-academic.com

Published in the UK by Imprint Academic
PO Box 200, Exeter EX5 5YX, UK

Published in the USA by Imprint Academic
Philosophy Documentation Center
PO Box 7147, Charlottesville, VA 22906-7147, USA

ISBN 9 781845 400972

A CIP catalogue record for this book is available from the
British Library and US Library of Congress

Never must we despair. Never must we give in,
but we must face facts and draw true conclusions from them.

Winston Churchill, House of Commons, 1935.

Contents

Acknowledgements

First, we acknowledge each other. We have worked closely together and now regard ourselves as equal partners in the authorship of the book. We both recognise that it would not have come to fruition without the other's contribution. But its existence also depends on many others. We owe a great debt to all those who kept the flame of learning alight during the dark decades, sometimes at the expense of losing their jobs. They are the "few" in the Educational Battle of Britain but still too many to list in full here. Their importance will be apparent from our mention of their writings and actions in the course of the book. Some, however, must be singled out for special acknowledgement.

Dr. Joyce Morris has been fighting the good fight longer than any of us. A truly scientific research worker, she showed, over half a century ago, the dire effect of the decline in phonics teaching and has been unflagging in her subsequent defence of effective English teaching in our schools. She has been honoured on both sides of the Atlantic.

John Daniels and Hunter Diack were authors of the 1954 *Royal Road Readers,* which provided a phonics lifeline during the early decades of the great whole-word tsunami and armed Mona McNee for her career in remedial teaching.

Sue Lloyd's records show how the initial teaching alphabet (i.t.a.) gave slightly above average results when used with the whole-word method but became quite outstanding when used with phonics. After Progressivism suppressed i. t. a., she devised a version using the ordinary alphabet and worked with the publisher Chris Jolly to spread the phonic message both in Britain and abroad.

Two educational psychologists are Martin Turner, who courageously publicised the disaster of the "real books " method, in Croydon and then across the country, being sacked for his honesty, and later supported phonics in the Dyslexia Institute, and Marlynne Grant, who persuaded a Gloucestershire school to adopt phonics and its excellent standards.

Dr. David Harland, a former Senior Schools Medical Officer in Norfolk, devoted much time to testing children and helped Mona McNee towards her understanding of dyslexia.

Bonnie Macmillan has pursued research in depth, exposing the myth that mixed reading methods are beneficial. She assembled 500 research reports as a basis for her *Why Schoolchildren Can't Read,* and explained the brain structures that make boys four times as prone to dyslexic illiteracy as girls in her *Why Boys are Different.*

Baroness Caroline Cox and John Marks ran a valuable information exchange group that enabled supporters of better education from all over the country to meet each other in the House of Lords. Together they produced evidence that comprehensive schools had a dumbing-down effect. John Marks has also impeccably investigated other important aspects of education and has been a leading light in the Campaign for Real Education (CRE).

Debbie Hepplewhite took on editing the Reading Reform Foundation's Newsletter when Mona McNee, its founder, felt it needed new voices, and devoted much time and energy to the RRF's campaign. Jennifer Chew, the present editor, is active within both the RRF and the CRE. As a sixth-form teacher, she carried out incisive research into poor spelling. She is gentle but persistent and extremely well-informed — always ready to answer our questions.

Joyce Watson and Rhona Johnston performed a signal service with their superb Clackmannan research project. They confirmed the many earlier proofs of phonics' superiority in a masterly way that created a public stir and, we hope, bodes well for the future.

Last but not least–quite the reverse–Nick Seaton, who set up the Campaign for Real Education and enthused its members to form an energetic campaigning body with a wide remit of constructive activities. This is now the leading fount of practical efforts to rid education of the dictatorial stranglehold of Progressivism.

What these people have in common is their motivation to ensure that every child should be able to read, and their resistance to all the pressures to accept fashionable but counterproductive non-phonic ideas.

Alice Coleman
Mona McNee

Preface

This book has had a long gestation period. It was initiated by Mona McNee in the late 1980s after her success in teaching backward children to read fluently had shown her that their problems had been artificially created in school by the use of Progressivist methods.

One study revealed that Progressivism left 33% of school leavers illiterate and a further 17% able to read only so precariously that by the time they were 20 they had not read a single book in the preceding year. Half the nation's children were being subjected to eleven years of schooling that failed to give them even the elementary basis of education that was completed by the age of seven in pre-Progressivist days. This great reading disaster was caused by the look-say method of teaching, which presented whole words and not individual letters.

Mona McNee therefore embarked upon a campaign to restore the successful phonics method that taught letters and their sounds, and how to build them up into words. If it again became the norm, as it was before World War II, the illiteracy rate would drop back to 1%, as it was then. The damage to our children's intellects, and especially those of dyslexics, is completely unnecessary.

She was crusading for what should have been self-evident but everywhere she met stonewalls of resistance. She realised that the faulty teaching techniques had achieved their dominance through concerted pressure by what Baroness Blatch later called the "Progressive Mafia". Its diktat had taken over every corner of state schooling, including educational publishers. It was perfectly possible to publish fanciful accounts of meeting aliens in UFOs but a proven practical way to reverse our educational decline was considered too fanciful even to contemplate, and the first draft of this book was repeatedly rejected.

Mona McNee suspected (wrongly) that her literary skill might be at fault and handed her typescript to Alice Coleman to edit. The result was a new structure and more background explanation of the issues at stake. The partnership coincided with the Conservative government's launch of the National Curriculum and national testing, and for a while we hoped that these would bring a dénouement that would make this book a histori-cal record instead of an active campaign.

It was not to be. The powerful Progressivist Mafia fought back, mostly in a subterranean way but still masquerading as the road to improvement. Labour's National Literacy Strategy typifies its pious promises and its fail-ure to deliver. Our observations of such ploys have been incorporated into Part III of this book, entirely as an addition to its original concept. Several battles have been won by the supporters of high standards but the war is far from being over and we hope that this book will provide further ammunition.

Both authors regret being robbed of the true meaning of the word "pro-gressive" since it was commandeered by "progressive education" and used to cast a rosy glow over what has really been a regressive decline. The whole progressive ideology is an "ism" and so, in this book, we write of "Progressivism" and "Progressivists" with a capital "P", in the hope that the adjective "progressive" can be reclaimed for its traditional use.

The Progressivist mystique alleges that there is a profound professional complexity in the teaching of reading. There is not. The claim is only a cover-up to excuse Progressivism's high failure rate and Part IV of this book will explain a straightforward alternative. This is not merely a return to traditional phonics, excellent though that was, but is better described as "traditional-plus". Mona McNee's reading scheme, *Step by Step*, adds many refinements to simplify and accelerate the process of becoming a reader. It was originally intended to help strugglers damaged by Progressivist teaching but its simplification has made it easy for parents to teach their three- and four-year-olds to read and thus "school-proof" them before they are exposed to school muddlement and possibly handicapped by lifelong illiteracy.

Because Progressivist publishers rejected the phonics-based *Step by Step*, Mona McNee printed it privately and relied on the recommendations of satisfied users to sell it. Their enthusiasm proved very positive. Recently, a publisher did take it on but printed only 2000 copies and sold them in a desultory way, claiming there was no demand. Shortly after this, *Step by Step* was mentioned by John Clare, the Education Editor of the Daily Telegraph, and nearly 700 more orders poured in. Sales have reached almost 21,000 copies and now, interestingly, the proportion of children able to read *before* starting school has risen to 20%.

Besides teaching pre-school children and school strugglers, the scheme has proved its worth in *preventing* illiteracy when used from the very beginning of school life and also in *rescuing* illiterate adults.

Our aim for the present book is to reach parents, teachers, school gover-nors and everyone concerned with education, so that they can understand what has been behind Progressivism's great reading disaster and see how to take avoiding action. We have included practical ways of outflanking illiteracy and completely banishing it within a fairly short time.

The term "phonics" is one of several names used for what has been the successful way of teaching reading ever since the invention of the alphabet over 3000 years ago. When it was the sole method, it did not need a special name and was often colloquially referred to as *the ABCs.* But when the whole-word alternative appeared, the term *phonetics* was adopted to signify linking letters to their sounds. This was subsequently reserved for the written symbols of the International Phonetic Alphabet and the shorter *phonics* took its place to refer to the teaching method. This is used in Parts I and II of this book.

In the 1990s, however, the term *analytic phonics* was coined for an inferior method that still gave priority to whole words with only an unsystematic reference to letters, so again a distinctive term was needed for true phonics. "Analytic" means breaking words down, whereas traditional phonics means building up, i.e. synthesizing letters into words, so the term *synthetic phonics* was born. This is used in Parts III and IV.

In early 2006, the Secretary of State for Education and Skills, Ruth Kelly, issued an edict that schools must use the phonic method but there seems little evidence that its implications are properly understood or that any serious re-training programme for teachers is being put in place. The Progressivists now have a sixty-year history of foiling opposition by the advocates of phonics and so we believe that the explanations and recommendations in this book are needed just as much as ever.

PART I

UNDERSTANDING
THE GREAT READING DISASTER

Chapter One

Schools for Scandal

In 1987 a *World in Action* programme revealed that six million adult Britons could not read. The problem was least among old people and worst among school leavers, of whom 25% were so illiterate that they floundered even when simply faced with forms to fill in. These were only the hard core. There was a further large problem of those deemed literate when leaving school but whose grasp of the printed word was so rudimentary that it slipped away from them within a very few years. These were termed functional illiterates, who could not decipher items such as fire instructions on which their lives might depend.

So, it emerged, at a time of unprecedented educational provision and expenditure, that at least half of the supposed beneficiaries were being deprived of that most basic element of learning: the ability to read. Schools for scandal indeed!

In the decade following that great educational shock there was enormous public concern and attempts to raise standards, including the wholesale prescriptions of the National Curriculum, but the problem has remained severe. A 1997 study showed that hard-core school-leavers' illiteracy had risen to 33% and other research highlighted the additional seriousness of functional illiteracy. The Basic Skills Agency estimated that total adult illiteracy had grown to nine million.

There were two lessons to be learned from these dismal facts. The first is that the great sledgehammer of the National Curriculum had failed to crack the fundamental nut, which was incompetence in the teaching of reading. Ability to read is the foundation of almost all education. Fluent readers have the wherewithal to educate themselves in due course but nonreaders remain at the mercy of the system's inefficiency. If the Conservative government's drive to raise standards had addressed *only* teaching to read, its failure would have been more obvious, giving a sharper incentive for a better approach and greater achievement. We need a deeper insight into what went wrong in order to apply a more effective remedy.

The second lesson is that such insight has always existed; the remedy has always been known. Old people are rarely illiterate because *their* teachers knew how to promote literacy effectively. They were skilled in the *phonic method* of relating letters to sounds and building up successive letter-sounds into words. This was the normal approach before World War II and it produced virtually universal reading ability.

For example, when Alice Coleman taught 1200 secondary modern school pupils during the 1940s, only one, a brain-damaged child, was unable to read. That was an illiteracy rate of 0.01%. Today, on average, at least 30 of those children would be in special schools for the learning disabled and a further 300 would be illiterate, with many more destined to lapse into illiteracy soon after leaving school. At that time, Kent's 24 special schools for backward children did not exist and the secondary moderns took all, except for the blind and profoundly deaf, and a few going to grammar or independent schools.

Critics of phonics will probably leap to protest that Alice Coleman must have been teaching in an affluent leafy suburb, but this was not so. It was a working-class area of Thameside with mainly blue-collar employment in cement, rubber and paper factories. Furthermore, every child had experienced between four and six years of wartime disturbances to their education, including evacuation to safer areas, winter schooling reduced by an hour to avoid travelling in the blackout, frequent lesson interruptions to rush down into the air-raid shelters and numerous nights disturbed by air-raid warnings. The school itself had been bombed. Those children were indeed disadvantaged but not by their teachers. They could read.

If abandoning phonics has wrought so much havoc among potentially normal readers, how much worse has it been for the genuinely disabled? This was where Mona McNee came into the picture and was so aghast that it inspired her to give up teaching in a grammar school and devote herself to remedial work.

She rediscovered the lost efficacy of phonics teaching when faced with the most challenging of tasks: introducing her Down's Syndrome son to the skills that eventually made him a fluent reader. Tim had been fortunate in his infant school, where he learned by the phonics method, relating letters to sounds. He was taught the sounds of the alphabet and by the age of seven he could decipher and spell three-letter words such as "run" and "fox".

He was then placed in an ESN (educationally sub-normal) school with specially qualified staff, who should have been able to accelerate his learning but actually brought it to a complete standstill. They regarded traditional phonics as politically incorrect and substituted the Progressivist system with its *look-say* reading methodology. This disregarded the sounds of letters and was based on the purely visual recognition of the appearance of words as wholes, which gave it the alternative name of the *whole word* method. As Progressivism began, progress stopped. Tim stagnated on Ladybird Book 2 for two years but the teachers' message to Mona McNee remained "Don't interfere. You will muddle him."

For two long years she stood by, wondering why his good start had been followed by a failure to go on learning. Then she attended a parents' meeting and saw, on the classroom wall, something done by every child except her own. She talked to the teacher, a specialist with good discipline, but received no hope, and went out to her car and sat and sobbed.

"Well", she thought, "for all their qualifications they have taught him *nothing* and I can't do worse than that." She had never tried to teach anyone to read and did not even remember learning to read herself, but by the grace of God she came across the Royal Road Readers, which were phonics-based and introduced words in a graded order of difficulty. They were very good for children who already knew their letters and sounds. She started with Book 1, Part 1, Page 1, and steadily plodded through the lot: exercises, stories and companion books. She did not know if Tim would ever really learn and after reading Pearl Buck's account of her daughter's attempts, was ready to quit at any time if he became distressed. All she knew was that he had not reached the limit of his potential and so she kept going.

Looking back now, when she teaches with a liberal use of games, she realises that Tim did it the hard way with no light relief. Every morning they worked for 20 minutes before school and continued through the holidays. In eighteen months he reached the end of Book 9 and could read! At school he was *still* sitting with Ladybird Book 2 and she had to *tell* his teachers that he was literate. They tested him and found that it was true.

Now he reads whatever he wants: the Observer Aircraft book, the names of countries which he can find in the atlas, and words such as "reconnaissance", which he understands. He once asked what "skit" meant and as his mother began to explain, he said, "Oh, you mean parody." He can read a map to navigate on car trips and can find his own television programmes. Like many with reading problems, he sticks to non-fiction and is particularly interested in history. On the genealogical tree of the Royal Family he would do well on Mastermind.

His life today would be very different if he had not learned to read. But Mona McNee asks herself, "Why, oh why, did I wait two years? I saw for myself that someone well able to learn was simply not being taught by his qualified teachers."

She then investigated the pattern of reading disability in her extended family. Of twelve children who started school after World War II eight had dyslexic difficulties but Tim was the only one with a low IQ. Her niece's dyslexic son was bright and articulate, and his teachers did not even realise that he had literacy problems. This post-war situation contrasted with that of the earlier period. A check back through every branch of the family, including in-laws, great uncles, etc., revealed not one unable to read, write and spell. There was no way in which the post-war failure could be related to a poor home background.

Mona McNee began talking about reading failure and found many people whose children had literacy problems. So when she moved out of London she decided to change from grammar-school work to the teaching of reading and in 1975 took on the bottom 20 of a 120-child intake year in a Norfolk middle school. The teacher she replaced at the beginning of the summer term was better in terms of class control, a happy classroom atmosphere, craftwork, etc., and was also trained and experienced in teaching reading. Yet it seemed that the children made more progress in one term with Mona McNee's phonics than in her predecessor's two terms with the whole word method, and their reading records proved that this was true.

Each child has a reading age (RA), ascertained by checking how far he or she can progress through a list of words or sentences graded according to the average ability of each chronological age (CA). In a year the RA should advance twelve months by simple maturation and the remedial teacher's task is to help children add extra months to catch up.

During her predecessor's two terms the class caught up by an average of 2.3 months but six had not caught up at all and had actually slipped back further in relation to their CA. During Mona McNee's one term, by contrast, no child lost ground and the average catch-up gain was 10.6 months. The termly rate of progress was therefore nine times as fast as before, despite the fact that her term was broken up by sports days, trips out, etc. She knew that the accelerated progress could not be due to her personally and had to spring from the difference in the method used: phonics instead of look-say.

She continued remedial work for five more years and realised that most of her pupils would not have needed remedial teaching at all if they had been taught by her methods from the start, in their infant schools. She was not in an inner-city school with special difficulties stemming from problem estates, nor were the children coming from homes where English was not spoken. The three first schools that supplied most of the intake were adequate or good in respects other than reading and the children were bright enough to catch up, given the opportunity. The only explanation for their poor reading attainment seemed to be the method of teaching. The schools themselves were creating the reading problems and necessitating the cost of remedial teachers.

The crux of the problem is the difference between the successful *phonics* method and the fashionable *whole word* method with its various derivatives. Teacher training focuses on the latter and therefore Mona McNee's lack of reading training proved a bonus. She was reaching back naturally into the skills and drills of common sense and also her experience with Tim, and finding that they worked, as they always do. Over the course of time she found ways of refining the phonic method for maximum efficiency and after she had encountered the Reading Reform Foundation, established in USA in 1961 as a way of reaching a wider circle of like-minded people, she worked with help from a small group to set up a UK Chapter in 1989.

It is some slight consolation to parents to learn that they are not alone and need not agonise in isolation. They can stop blaming themselves and recognise that the fault lies with the schools. With few exceptions, poor learning results from poor teaching, even with dylexics.

Poor teaching, in turn, is due to the way education students are trained and brainwashed into accepting ineffective whole-word methods as the only option. Their minds have been closed against the better phonics alternative, which they have heard mentioned only in a miasma of smear and sneer. Progressivism has progressively displaced the old tried and trusted methods and progressively caused a decline in educational standards.

When this book was first envisaged, its aim was to *expose* the Great Reading Disaster and formulate *policies* for its cure. However, during its gestation period events have overtaken us. The lone voices protesting against the tide of educational decline, with its rip current of reading failure, have been joined by others and there has been a great deal of exposure with an abundance of policy statements. But even though these have been backed up by massive public expenditure and educational upheaval, there is little improvement to show for them. Change is still in the hands of the same "experts" that presided over the decline and whose "solution" has been to call for massive extra funding, partly to be spent on smaller classes.

More money and smaller classes are facile but spurious solutions. They have been constantly applied for decades and constantly followed by falling standards. The response to the exposure of scandal remains a woeful lack of insight into its cause, and hence into its cure also. Our present aim, therefore is to promote *understanding* of the real reasons for the decline, so that action can be oriented in the right direction.

We also recognise that policy statements are often no more than sound bites or spin and not geared to any practical measures that could truly salvage the situation. Even if the policies themselves are on target, they are not an automatic guide to getting matters rectified in practice. We need specific *strategies* that can be efficiently applied in the classroom if policy is to be translated into bona fide achievement. Thus understanding and strategy have replaced exposure and policy as the aims of this book.

Part I, *Understanding the Great Reading Disaster,* consists of four chapters. The present one introduces the problem and is followed in Chapter 2 by a clarification of the two contrasted approaches to literacy: traditional phonics and the Progressivist whole-word approach. It compares the two and explains why phonics is so much more efficacious. Chapter 3 is a broader critique of Progressivism as a whole and with Chapter 2 sets the terms of the discussion, paving the way for the evidence in Chapter 4. This charts the decline, which began earlier than is usually realised. It never allowed a real recovery from the effects of World War II.

Part II, *The Watchdogs That Failed*, explains why the disastrous trend was so long protected and how official support for it was backed up by suppression of criticism. The agencies responsible are treated individually in Chapters 6 to 13 and an overview of motivation follows in Chapter 14. Part II deals with the period up to the 1988 Education Act, when the government had recognised the decline and initiated an attempt to tackle it.

Part III deals with *The Struggle For Reform*, covering the period up to the present. The aim was to move back to high standards but Chapter 15 shows how a Progressivist backlash has largely continued to misdirect both the reforms and the testing of their results, limiting their success by deliberate obfuscation. Even some of the brightest achievements have now been reversed. Chapters 16 to 18 summarise three great problems still posing a challenge—teaching method, testing and discipline, while a fourth, the immense cost of education, follows in Chapter 19 and shows how improved standards would themselves bring large economies.

Part IV, *The Way Ahead* focuses on practical solutions directly related to the teaching of reading. Chapter 20 explains how parents can teach their children to read before they go to school and thus avoid having their minds confused by the whole word method and its derivatives. The method set out here is Mona McNee's self-published *Step By Step*, that has been used by numerous parents, whose satisfaction with it has led to widespread recommendations and the sale of 21,000 copies. It includes a basic phonics workbook plus information on reading games and other useful material. It also enables parents to question teachers and recognise the signs of any counterproductive methods that need to be outflanked.

And it is not only parents and children but the teachers themselves that we hope to help. Those who wish to break away from the blinkers imposed by their training will find Chapter 20 of value in the basic task of developing literacy. The phonics method can reduce their workload, including the present onerous lesson preparation and testing procedure, and also give them a greater sense of achievement and job satisfaction. The children, too, would enjoy more school satisfaction.

Chapter 21 outlines a protocol for simpler, cheaper and more effective testing after two school years, to relieve the burden on teachers and allow more time for actual teaching. Chapter 22 makes some recommendations for improving discipline.

Chapter 23 summarises the overall message, and outlines the various types of productive action needed to restore phonics to its rightful and rational place in our schools.

Chapter Two

Phonics v The Whole-Word Method

The Great Reading Disaster was caused by abandoning traditional phonics in the teaching of reading and espousing the Progressivist whole-word, or look-say, method. We shall support this statement with copious evidence of decline, but first we must clarify what the two approaches actually are. Today, as the phonics concept filters back into favour as "synthetic phonics", some schools are claiming to use it with little success; they say it still produces non-readers. Such claims greatly confuse the issue. The teachers have not been trained in phonics and do not understand it. They believe they are practising it when they are really doing little more than nod towards it from a stance still firmly rooted in look-say.

This means that we cannot discuss the *effect* of the two approaches unless we first define and explain them, and that is the present chapter's role. Both methods are said by their practitioners to harness the child's natural way of learning, but whereas phonics usefully mobilises the left side of the brain, look-say harmfully depends on the right side.

The Two Sides of the Brain

As the brain evolved through the animal kingdom, its main function was to process sense data into meaningful information. It is known that new-born babies are confronted with huge arrays of sense impressions that they gradually learn to sort out, but this process has had to be observed indirectly as babies cannot explain what they are experiencing. Direct evidence is obtainable from people who have been blind from birth and then receive the gift of sight at an age when they have command of language. They describe what they see as a meaningless jumble of coloured patches, which are not automatically identified as separate objects or as parts of the same object. Things they know well by touch have gradually to be translated for sight recognition, and the perception of shapes has to be progressively extended. The brain then constructs *gestalts* (from the German word "Gestalt" meaning "shape, form or appearance"). Gestalt psychology is concerned with a system of thought that regards all mental phenomena as being arranged in patterns or structures perceived as wholes and not merely as the sums of their parts.

Thus, sounds, which can be quite meaningless in themselves, are assembled into the significant patterns, or gestalts, that constitute words and this fact was seized on by Progressivist theorists to assert that whole words are the natural units to present to learner readers. Children, they argued, should learn to read complete words from their overall shapes and not by building up letter sequences. They should not relate the appearance of the word to its component sounds but look at its shape and be told what it says — hence the synonymous terms "look-say" and "whole word".

This theory, or more correctly this untested hypothesis, is wrong, for three major reasons. One is that infant speech learners do not begin with whole words but with an extensive babble of sounds, which they only gradually, and at first imperfectly, fit together to form spoken words. The natural counterpart in reading is to learn with the letters that represent sounds and gradually fit them together to perceive written words.

The second reason is that the whole-word method relies upon visual sensing only, whereas the phonic method combines both visual and auditory evidence. It is now known that the auditory aspect plays a larger part in learning to read than the visual, even for many who are very hard of hearing, so the whole-word method's dependence on the visual alone knocks away a major prop that supports learning to read.

The third reason is that the human brain has evolved further, beyond the gestalt-synthesising of sense data, and is no longer symmetrical. Its right side continues to serve the gestalt function of pattern-recognition but the left side has developed in association with the growth of language and that part of it operates in a different way. It perceives things in linear sequences, sound following sound to make words, words following words to make meanings, meaning ordered into sentences, and sentences arranged to create logic. The brain's left side may be described as linear, linguistic and logical — a nice alliterative mnemonic that applies just as much to the written as to the spoken word.

Thus, in relation to the word "cat", the right brain harbours the visual image of the animal but the left brain deals with the sound and letter sequence c — a — t. The phonic principle recognises this and asserts that children need to learn reading as a linear sequence of letters and sounds built up into a logical order to form words. This is in harmony with the natural working of the left brain's mechanism for speech and verbal processes. It goes *with* the grain.

The look-say tenet of starting with whole words argues that just as we see a house as a unit and not as individual bricks, tiles, windows, etc., so we should learn to read by comprehending word shapes as units and not by itemising the sequence of letters as if they were individual building bricks. This was made to sound very plausible but it is a completely false analogy. Its promoters did not remember their babyhood *learning* to assemble houses as visual units, nor did they take account of the fact that perception through pattern-recognition is the role of the right brain. For most people, verbal ability does not reside in the right side and trying to force it there by look-say goes *against* the grain.

The whole word approach does extend a little into the left brain but only into the visual sector at the back, which has remained symmetrical, and not into the asymmetrical language sector further forward.

Some children, especially girls, are blessed with good connections between the two brain hemispheres and can spontaneously translate their pattern-learning into the linear-logical mode. Others, especially boys, have less good connections and are perplexed. This can help to precipitate the problems of dyslexia.

Catering For Differences

Children experience things in different ways and both methods try to cater for this range. They disagree, however, on what the different experiencing consists of.

Phonics teaching recognises that children learn through their senses and individuals may find different senses more useful. The aim therefore is to make learning to read a *multi-sensory* experience, to ensure that any particular sense preference is served and also that all the senses are stimulated to reinforce each other.

The whole word method defines experience as *learning by doing* and also believes that children should *discover* things for themselves, even the highly sophisticated art of reading. Because everyone is different, it advocates *mixed methods*: whole-word and even whole-sentence patterns, clues from illustrations and other kinds of guessing, being read to, variously termed paired reading, shared reading, readalong and reading apprenticeship, and even a small genuflection to phonics in an unsystematic, incomplete way that emasculates its value. They hope that every child is suited to one of these but in reality the eclectic mix proves muddling while the discovery method carries the risk of non-discovery and a sense of failure.

The Phonic Method

Information comes to us through our senses and learning is assisted when the meaning of each sense image is comprehensible and the evidence from one sense is confirmed by that from the others. In the case of reading, the visual information provided by a clearly formed letter is reinforced by the auditory information of its sound: "tee says tuh". The sounds are not only heard but also spoken, evoking the kinaesthetic sense involved in mouth and throat movements, or even repetitive chanting in unison. Large-scale muscular feeling and kinaesthetic movement are brought into play by getting the children to draw the form of each letter in the air, with their arms fully extended. This is then reduced to a smaller scale, with tactile experience added, in tracing out the shape of a letter with a finger while having its parts explained: where to begin, which direction to follow and where to end. Further reinforcement comes from learning the correct way to grasp a pencil and write the letter. Colour may be used to help distinguish the vowels from the consonants in the early stages.

One letter is dealt with at a time with a certain amount of repetition. Some children need more than others but the multi-sensory approach makes the repetition varied.

The beginning stage is very simple. The alphabet is taught in a carefully selected order, so that successive letters reinforce earlier ones with the differences clearly explained. One possibility is to begin with "c". Then "á" is introduced as "c" with a short straight ending and "d" as "c" with a tall straight ending. For "o", the "c" is made into a complete ring, while "g" is "á" with a tail. The letter "b" is left till much later, when "d" has been well learned, as separating these two letters minimizes the risk of the mirror-writing that confuses the two, and is a particular pitfall that traps dyslexics.

Right from the start children learn that letters follow from left to right, and their sounds follow in the same sequence, to merge into a word. Even with the first three letters, c−á−t, they can learn to read "cat" − really read it by sounding out successive letters. Their sense of progress and achievement is sustained as the next three letters enable them to read and write "dog". Even at this early stage they can learn that changing just one letter changes the word, e.g. from "cat" to "cot", and a little later that the letters in "pins" can be rearranged to make "nips", "pips", "snip" and "spin". These distinctions make them alert to decipher letters accurately and in the correct sequence, to get each word exactly right.

This lucid, logical method teaches the whole alphabet, and even if there is only one new letter each day, it has almost all children reading any three-letter word with a short vowel in eleven weeks in Reception classes. Then there follow letter groups with straightforward sound combinations as in "rest", "sand" or "stump". Next come vowel and consonant pairs (digraphs) that create single sounds such as "oo", "ch" and "th", going on to other conventions such as adding a final "e" to convert a short vowel to a long vowel. The steady explanation of more letter groups and spelling rules is accompanied by a gradual speeding up in sounding out, until the synthesis of letters become automatic and there is virtually instant reading on sight. With more than one daily reading lesson from the start, the children learn to read even more quickly.

The aim is to instil early confidence in the logic and readability of English. The rules are taught in an order that leaves only some 10% of all words failing to conform. Many exceptions are words of foreign origin, which the child does not need until much later while those met earlier are seen and remembered as curious deviations from normal spelling. They are all phonic in part and maintaining the method minimizes the part that is deviation.

All children, apart from the blind, profoundly deaf and brain-damaged, can learn to read within two years, while still in the infant school. Reading schemes should not go on forever and after two years children should be capable of choosing their own books. The main job of learning to read is over and the teacher can then concentrate on expanding vocabulary and teaching grammar, punctuation and, later, style. Thus, the phonic method is geared to succeed at every stage. Later on, it is not exactly simple as there are many nuances related to the child's successive needs, but it is still *systematic,* and easier for the child to work at and for the teacher to absorb and apply.

It also embodies a second anti-fail mechanism. It can keep the whole class together. All the children face the teacher's desk, which leaves less opportunity for them to distract each other and they are all taught each stage together, so that no-one suffers the dismay of being left behind. Nor do the quicker ones have a sense of marking time as they can practise with more varied material at the stage they have reached, leaving the teacher free to help the slower ones. It is like a sheep-dog keeping the whole flock moving in the same direction, even though there are leader sheep and stragglers.

The Whole Word Method and Its Derivatives

While the phonic method is pragmatic, the whole word method is doctrinaire. The doctrine of *learning by doing* has been used to denigrate formal instruction as a strait-jacket that cramps spontaneity and natural development. It is asserted that children should not be subjected to rote learning or spelling and tables drills. They should not be regimented in rows facing the teacher but allowed to sit in informal groupings with more freedom to talk and move about the classroom. They should not even be provided with lined paper, as lines might constrain their free expression in sprawling letters.

These freedoms reinforced the greater permissiveness that children were meeting from birth. It was spearheaded by Dr. Spock on baby care and continued in schools as the child-centred doctrine. Early advice to "interest" the child became transmuted, in the 1962 Plowden Report, to "children's own interests should direct attention to many fields of knowledge and the teacher is alert to provide material, books or experiments for the development of their ideas." Child initiative was to be pre-eminent, even though in the same breath the Report commented, ". . . there is only a limited range of material within the capacity of primary school children."

Overloading the teacher further is the doctrine of an *individual programme* for each child, to afford the experience needed for discovering things for themselves instead of being told. It is no wonder that teachers cannot cope with such big classes as their predecessors.

This is the ethos of whole-word promotion. The phonic method was discarded as too formal, and learning by doing was paralleled as "learning to read by actually reading". The look-say concept claims that the quick way to read before actually learning to do so, is to be told what certain words are in order to recognise and say them from their overall shapes. This breaches the doctrine that children should not be instructed but look-say is inconsistent in other ways as well. Recognising whole-word shapes fitted the trendy gestalt concept and also seemed superior because it went straight to *meaning* instead of getting bogged down, as alleged, in mere letter symbols. The words used initially are chosen for their distinctive outlines: long or short, and variously accidented by upper and lower extenders in different places. Here are some favourite examples. Can you read them?

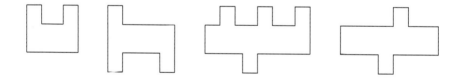

Fig. 2.1: Schonell's examples of distinctive word shapes using upper and lower extenders as clues. See the end of the chapter for the solutions

Children and parents are at first delighted by this apparent evidence of rapid learning but there is a limit to how many words have sufficiently different shapes for unequivocal recognition. In any case, words in capitals do not offer clues from extenders. As more words are presented, muddlement sets in but this is where the discovery method is supposed to take effect. Children are supposed to "catch on" to the realisation that words are made up of letters that follow certain rules but the rules are withheld from them and they are not even informed that there is a code to crack. Margaret Meek, in *Learning to Read* (1982), firmly stated that they must *not* have instruction in deciphering letters, sounds or words.

Being kept in the dark like this does not help young children make one of the great leaps of civilisation and grasp the principle of the alphabet. It is now thought certain, as summarised by Dafna Yalon in her 2003 book, *Graphology Across Cultures,* that just *one* intellect in the whole of human history was able to create such an invention, and it is possible to trace how every other alphabetic writing system has been derived from this single flash of creativity. Even the Chinese, for all their brilliance, did not develop anything more advanced than whole-word ideographic designs, and when infants are presented with words as if they were ideograms, it is not surprising that they do not discern the alphabetic principle.

Those who do catch on, perhaps with phonics help from Granny, outstrip the defeated ones and the class becomes spread out over a wide range of attainment, which intensifies the need for individual programmes. There is no way to keep the class together, so stragglers and non-starters develop a sense of failure.

To absolve teachers from blame, there has arisen the myth that the non-readers are *not yet ready to read* and must be left to catch on naturally. Reading readiness is said to occur at any age up to seven and only if it has not happened by then should remedial help be given, *if* it is available. This can waste two whole years at the very age that is the optimum school period for learning to read and it can seriously damage the children's self-confidence. Meanwhile, they go on being given books to practise a skill that cannot be practised until it has been taught and learned in the first place.

Although blind to the merits of phonics, whole-word theorists have diversified their own methods to try to broaden the basis for success. *Flash cards* are a drilling system, in which words are repeatedly held up and named until the children can "read" them. Because of confusion among similarly shaped words, this may take a long time — in one case it needed 500 showings to produce mastery of just one word. With so many individual programmes to attend to, the teachers cannot pursue much of a vocabulary with the slow learners, who remain effectively non-readers. Monotonous flash-card drill is far worse than the boredom that whole-word experts allege for phonics. There is little sense of progress after only about 30 words.

Sometimes the whole-word method is expanded into the whole-sentence method in the hope that a more coherent meaning may help children to learn better. With repetition they may indeed be able to recite a whole small story book, but by the rote learning that whole-word enthusiasts despise and without being able to read any of the same words in other contexts.

The whole-sentence method was further inflated by Frank Smith's *real books* concept. This contended that school readers are too narrow and boring to hold children's interest (often true) and should be replaced by ordinary books. "Reading is learned by reading," wrote Jeff Hynds, a British supporter of real books. "You have to behave as if you were a reader . . . reading exercises to develop particular skills do not help." Instead, unskilled, uninstructed children have to look at texts being read to them and absorb reading ability by a kind of osmosis. This is a vain hope. Other names for real books are the *storybook method,* the *apprenticeship* method, and the *holistic/wholistic/whole language* approach.

Real books is the most extreme of all the whole word methods and has done serious additional harm since its debut in 1985. It abandons even the single-word shapes in basic whole-word approach, so children do not acquire so much as a small reading vocabulary. It advocates using any book, to stimulate interest, and is also called *emergent reading,* on the claim that all the stimulation will cause the ability to emerge in some untaught way. It does not. Instead there is increasing frustration and unless there is a genuine remedial rescue, children may develop a lifelong aversion to books.

In 1990 the Children's Book Circle granted Jill Bennett its Eleanor Farjeon Award for being an "inspirational source for change". As a real books expert she believed that "the natural way to learn is through stories — sheer enjoyment will do the rest." But the rest proves to be non-reading. One little girl brought to Mona McNee for remedial lessons had been so demoralised by unremitting failure through a year of the storybook method that she began to cry as soon as her mother picked up a book.

Other ways of exploiting the value of meaning attempt to intrigue children with what a text *might* mean, by inviting them to discuss possibilities, i.e. to hazard guesses. They must consider illustrations as clues to what the words or stories might be, and this is claimed as an incentive to cross the reading barrier (without being given a technique for doing so). To encourage such guesswork, approximate answers are praised as acceptable, some of which, such as "pony" instead of "horse", can only confuse in reading terms. Being allowed to skip words or simply being told words they cannot guess are other incitements to inaccuracy.

Guessing is a bad habit that makes it difficult for a child to settle down to master the careful coding needed for true reading and the damage is compounded by whole–word's acceptance of errors. It is considered justified by the rush for meaning and misses the pleasure of fitting a jigsaw of letters together into a word and getting it right by oneself.

When children do not progress, they may be left to "practise" on the same old book in the hope that light will dawn—a kind of *"look-and don't say"*, which generates boredom, frustration, depression and disruptive behaviour. A feature of much education today is lack of discipline with violence towards teachers and classmates—extremely rare during the phonic era when children were successfully taught to become literate.

To help defuse a strained atmosphere, children are allowed to work together in *paired reading,* and to discuss the text, as a means of language development. But there is no guarantee that their conversation devotes attention to the reading task. In our experience there is more work being done when the class is silent.

Sometimes activity involves *colouring* pictures. This is simply a nursery pursuit that detracts time from what could have been actually teaching reading. It seems meant to arouse interest, as is Margaret Meek's recommendation to choose stories that *have a shape.* What does this mean? Comic strips that make guesswork easier?

Many of these approaches are described as broadening or enriching *language experience,* "much more than" the mere mechanics of reading. However, they are much less than phonics teaching. They distract attention from the basic task and prolong the need for it throughout school life and on into adulthood. They necessitate long-drawn-out reading schemes and materials for successive age groups, which are vastly more expensive than the simple phonics materials needed for only two years. Now, whenever we come across the words "broad", "rich" or "much more than", we think, "Off we go, up into the clouds, feet not touching the ground."

Simplicity is alien to the whole-word approach. Instead, it prides itself on *the complexity* of its mixed methods, mostly devised to offset the inadequacy of the basic method. Sometimes phonics is claimed as part of the mix, but it is a very attenuated kind, for example, first letter and guess the rest. Betty Root, former head of Reading University's Reading Centre, denounced phonics as too abstract for children, despite the fact that one can observe it working well for them. She castigated it as too complex, then boasted of the complexity of whole-word methods, and then used the latter complexity to excuse teachers for failing to teach reading properly.

The same smokescreen was exemplified by Vera Southgate's 1981 Schools Council Project, *Extending Beginning Reading.* "Each decade our knowledge of reading is enriched by contributions from the psychology of learning, linguistics, language learning and other studies, and, consequently, the more the complexity of the process is realised, the more difficult does it become to define reading." How much energy goes into defining it abstrusely instead of teaching it effectively?

Rachel Pinder went still further and denied that reading can ever be actually taught. Yet even three and four-year-olds can master it if given straightforward phonics teaching.

Complexity used to be given as a reason for discouraging parents' concern. "Don't interfere. You'll muddle him." But then a U-turn *blamed* them for their children's lack of reading readiness and urged them to undertake *readalong*, i.e. reading to them to fire their interest in learning for themselves. Most children *are* ready but cannot learn when denied instruction. And the truly unready may have illiterate parents unable to provide readalong.

Comparison of Phonics and Whole Word

The contrast between the two approaches could not be greater. Well taught phonics is intensive and achieves virtually universal success within the first two years, whereas whole word is more spaced out with non-reading activities, takes longer and often does not succeed at all. Each year, according to the Basic Skills Agency, it unleashes up to 300,000 illiterates into adulthood. The phonic method is straightforward and systematic, while whole word uses complex elaboration with inconsistencies between theory and practice. Phonics provides the essential auditory basis; look-say withholds it. Phonics imparts a sense of achievement and school satisfaction, but whole word, with its penumbra of mixed methods, creates much confusion, dissatisfaction and a sense of failure. Phonics bestows a strategy for tackling unknown words, while look-say leaves children at a loss with words that they have not been specifically taught. Phonics is safe for all children but look-say harms the emotional balance of many that it fails and is disastrous for dyslexics. Phonics reduces the teacher's workload; whole word overburdens it. Phonics boosts teachers' morale; whole word undermines it.

Whole word also has the disadvantage of relying on out-dated scientific conclusions. An old study of eye movements during reading appeared to reveal pauses that enabled each word to be taken in as a whole, but recent measurements with more refined equipment prove that no matter how speedy the reading, the eye does scan every letter in sequence. This confirms, yet again, that letters and not whole words are the essential cues.

Alice Coleman proved this in a train passing a station at just the right speed for her to see the name-board but not read it. She could decipher only the first two letters, "RU". The whole word reached her retina but that was insufficient. The reading process clearly began at the left and decoded just as much of the linear sequence as the speed of the train allowed.

Not everyone can arrange for a train to travel at just the speed needed to generate this proof but there is a simpler everyday route to similar evidence. Try reading when daylight is fading and see what happens when the word shapes are still visible but the individual letters cannot be made out. Must you switch on the light then, to see the letters, or can you continue reading until it is too dark to see even the shapes? It needs only a brief encounter with text at twilight to show the fallacy in thinking that word shapes suffice.

The plain fact is that all the evidence of scientific tests proves that phonics is effective. No such evidence exists for look-say, etc., and cannot exist because it is not effective, except for a brief false dawn when it enables a small number of sight words to be mastered.

Phonics is clearly the better method and so, on the assumption that quality must be paid for, people may react with "Yes, but we could never afford it." Yet here it is cheaper to buy the best. The cost of the whole-word *Oxford Reading Tree* scheme approaches £7000 for an eleven-stage programme for each pupil intake, whereas Mona McNee' sold her *Step by Step* for only £5 and it could last a teacher for years. All her other materials cost £80 and, if desired, could be made even more cheaply from paper, cereal-boxes, etc., and still serve successive classes. Higher standards and lower cost both stem from the phonics method, and a further saving arises from the fact that schools would no longer be paying for remedial teachers to try to pick up the pieces after widespread failure has been created.

To conclude the comparison, we quote from a 1990 article by Kevin Cassidy, head of St. Clare Primary School in Handsworth, *A-Plus is for the Alphabet*. At that time he was so persecuted by look-say zealots that he felt it necessary to shelter behind a pseudonym.

> I am the head of a primary school in the heart of the Midlands in a particularly deprived area . . . By the age of seven all [my pupils] are reading. Our methods work, we are oversubscribed, and our teaching of reading is based firmly on the early introduction of phonetics[1]

> There is growing evidence that the fundamental teaching of basic skills, not least in the teaching of reading, is not as firmly rooted in reality in some schools as it should be. The phonetic method seems presently not even worthy of consideration by the experts but I would insist that the teaching of phonetic regularities and irregularities should be at the base of any reading system.

> It is most frequently the case in schools that when a child fails as a reader, the special needs teacher will revert to the phonetic method to retrieve the situation. If this is so, why is the earlier teaching of phonetics not seen as having a value in reducing reading problems in the first place?

> The current interest appears to focus mainly on "look-say" or "real books" approaches. Schools are encouraged by advisers, teacher trainers, and other experts, who have no ultimate responsibility for the results of their advice, to pursue the latest cherished Holy Grail of the latest trend.

---

[1]   Phonic teaching used to be called phonetic teaching but subsequently the term "phonetics" was reserved for the international phonetic alphabet.

When I recently gave a talk to a group of educators in London, half of them walked out, disturbed at the challenge to the current beliefs. The ones who stayed behind were those who accepted that reading is a skill that needs to be taught, not just absorbed.

One experienced head teacher told me that reading schemes and phonetic approaches should be thrown in the dustbin. Perplexed by this methodology, I asked how any tangible assessment of children's individual progress could be made in such an unstructured environment. The answer he offered in all seriousness was that it would be obvious from the look of excitement on their faces!

Judging reading ability from facial expression rather than from actual ability to read is all part of the woolly thinking that typifies the whole-word dogma. It is totally bogus. Children who are happy at six while not learning to read will not be happy at sixteen as illiterates.

Why then has education persisted so blindly and so long with an expensive method that has so much wrong with it? This is something we need to understand if we are to avoid continuing in the same old deeply gouged rut. The context will be explored further in the next chapter with a broader analysis of Progressivism as a whole.

Solution to Figure 2.1

These word shapes are supposed to be a sure guide to reading the words, "look", "jump", "elephant" and "aeroplane".

Chapter Three

Progressivism

Early Origins

Progressive education *(modern methods)* is defined in the Encyclopaedia Britannica as "a reaction against the alleged narrowness and formalism of traditional education". It was introduced on the one hand as something new, assuring its supporters that it was a go-ahead avant garde, but on the other hand as having ancient roots going back to Plato, Quintilian, St. Augustine, Francis Bacon and Dean Colet, the founder of St. Paul's School in 1510. It seems to have claimed everything good about the past and blamed everything bad on traditionalism. Its view of the latter is completely unlike the mainstream traditional schooling known to both Mona McNee and Alice Coleman, who speak from first-hand pre-Progressivist experience of both learning and teaching in schools as widely located as London, Kent, Norfolk, Staffordshire, Merseyside and Glamorgan.

British Progressivism was partly a genuine concern for pupils' welfare, to protect them from the dire but atypical ills pictured in *David Copperfield*. The new doctrine was presented with beautifully expressed warmth and a seductive rationalism that won enthusiastic recruits and its appeal should not be underestimated. It is well illustrated in Rachel Pinder's 1987 book, *Why Teachers Don't Teach Like They Used To*.

A primary school head with experience of secondary and adult teaching also, Rachel Pinder seemed well qualified to present the Progressivist case—but then she declared that it is impossible to teach children to read. One can only give them support while they teach themselves (or fail to do so). No wonder there is such a high illiteracy rate! How can Progressivists be so ignorant of centuries of success by tutors and schools, and of today's high achievement by phonics teachers, even in the least promising areas?

This gives us fair warning. With Progressivism it is essential to look beyond the glitzy shop window and inspect the quality of the goods themselves. By their fruits ye shall know them and not by their rosy eagerness.

Jean-Jacques Rousseau, 1712–1778

The first outline of Progressivist education was in a 1762 novel, *Emile*, by the French philosopher, Jean-Jacques Rousseau, noted for fine writing and wise ideas, and also for highly unsound ones, e.g. attacking science and art as corrupting influences, condemning urban life as vicious, and urging a simple back-to-nature existence. His work was marred by lapses into phantasmagoria, which escalated into delusions verging on paranoia. His *Du Contrat Social* urged handing over all individual rights to a community authority.

Emile introduced the *child-centred* concept of education, arguing that a child's wholly good nature should not be warped by discipline, although Emile himself hardly had such freedom. The first of four educational stages, babyhood, during mastery of speech, should be for physical and sense-organ development: *learning by doing*. In the second stage, up to age 12, the child's *interest* should be captured by games and amusements — the *play-way* — and he should not be taxed by scholarly instruction. From 12 to 15 would be the stage of learning, not from books, but from the "book of the world" — the same learning-by-doing principle but including knowledge gained independently in concrete situations: the *discovery method*. Only after 15 would Emile learn of morals, ethics, religion and history, and be allowed contact with other people. He would have had a tutor to himself, which seems related to the present demand for ever smaller classes. And boys should be educated to be men, *not for employability*.

Rousseau did not practise what he preached with his own five illegitimate children. Instead, he took them from their mother at birth and deposited them at the door of a foundlings' hospital. His educational ideas seem just plucked out of the air but they nevertheless proved influential, and inspired a succession of experimental schools, including the Montessori, which stresses kindergarten learning through activity, though not lax discipline. Rousseau's influence culminated in the twentieth century when Progressive education came to dominate much of the English-speaking world.

The Illuminati and Hegel

Rousseau's concept of the social contract was embraced by the *Illuminati*, a secret society founded in Ingolstadt University, Bavaria, in 1776. Behind an overt concern with intellectual freedom it had a hidden political agenda, which did not stop at just handing over individual rights to a local community but aimed to work slowly over the generations towards world domination. An important early step in the process would be the corruption of education, to bring successive generations of children into the submissive fold, and this was to be done in a deceptively genial way:

Some of the Illuminati's documents came into the hands of the Bavarian government, which promptly banned it. There were later unconfirmed rumours of its revival, but naturally its members would have ensured that any such continuation would have been in an unidentifiable form. Some of its power-seeking tentacles have been traced by Anthony C. Sutton (1986), who found that they included G.W.F. Hegel, the German philosopher (1770–1831). Sutton wrote,

> For Hegel, the State is absolute. The State requires complete obedience from the individual citizen. The individual does not exist for himself in these so-called organic systems but only to perform a role in the operation of the State.

These sinister undertones can be recognised where Hegel said, *"Unity must ultimately subordinate them to itself"* but he usually wrapped them up in apparently benign aspirations. He said of the organic unity of society,

> There should be such community between the members that all our conflict and competition should only lead to a better distribution of functions between them and improve the life of society as a whole.

Hegel eventually used his power-seeking urge to propel himself into the type of eminence that led the writer of his entry in *Chambers Encyclopaedia* to say he might well have been considered the "philosophical dictator of Germany". And he is believed to have had a strong influence upon John Dewey, the Father of Progressive Education.

Related Ideas

Related ideas came from the gradual nineteenth-century erosion of a God-centred ethos in favour of man-centred thinking. Darwin's *Origin of Species* undermined the literal interpretation of Genesis and was seen by some as disproof of God's role at the centre of our lives. Fabians, socialists, communists, psychologists and humanists all claimed to be able to make a better world in their own image, and grasped the importance of using education to mould society. They did not bother to obtain an explicit political consensus, parental agreement or any kind of permission, but contrived to introduce the child-centred principle as the school-age equivalent of man-centred. This came about only gradually because those who cared about religion set up their own church schools. The association of these "isms" with total power-seeking is exposed in R.L. Martin's book, *Fabian Freeway*.

Gestalt Psychology

A late nineteenth-century influence, *Gestalt Psychology*, arose in Austria and southern Germany as a reaction against north German psychologists' introspective identification of personality elements. Gestalt means shape or form but in psychology it is defined as "pattern" or "configuration". It is based on the fact that the whole is more than the sum of the parts. Max Wertheimer, its leader, replaced introspection with phenomenology and refuted the claim that only the objective methods of natural science produced genuine knowledge. He reasoned that it is human thinking about scientific results that creates certainty. Experience is not merely logical but also intentional and directed, and involves abstractions such as classes, meanings and essences, while conversely some directly observable phenomena may be optical illusions. True knowledge was held to consist, not of "fallible" chains of logical argument, but of descriptions of *a priori* knowledge gained by the intuitive experience of the transcendental self. When this mode of thinking entered the Progressivist stream, it seems to have brought an antipathy to objective facts. *Issues rather than facts* became the preoccupation.

Progressivism intuitively declared that the relevant gestalt in learning to read was the whole word. It argued that just as we understand a *tree* as a whole, rather than as a collection of leaves, branches, etc., so we should grasp the *word* "tree" as a whole, rather than as a collection of letters. This failed to recognise that while the tree's visual image is a unit *pattern* appreciated by the right brain from any angle, the written word "tree" is a letter sequence, perceived linearly by the left brain. It also ignored that letters themselves are gestalts of individual strokes. It later advocated more complex gestalts: whole sentences, stories and books, and whole language. This starting with wholes is a *top-down* approach.

John Dewey, 1859–1952

Progressivism's gestalt strand merged with its child-centred strand in USA, where practical rules were laid down by the philosopher John Dewey, whose work was analysed by Anthony O'Hear in 1991. Dewey was an adherent of the school of thought known as *Pragmatism,* which asserted that no object, idea or knowledge had any value apart from its practical consequences. From this he developed the idea that education must be *relevant,* later a Progressivist watchword. Child-centred education meant the pupils should not have to learn anything unless they could immediately understand its relevance, and this principle swept away what was regarded as the dead hand of pre-existing knowledge and culture. There was no need to burden children with a mass of facts that they could not perceive as related to their own experience and, more particularly, were not *interested* in.

Relevance would help children work things out for themselves—the discovery method. This would seem to mean that vast numbers of pupils should be endlessly re-inventing many varieties of the wheel in the absence of established information, but in practice it produced nothing so useful, nor was it intended to. The value was perceived to lie in their efforts, regardless of whether their actual findings were right or wrong. For these little research workers, from the age of three onward, the important thing was *the process* not *the product*. No-one seemed to feel that deliberately leaving children ignorant in this way was a dumbing down that could damage them in adulthood, and no-one seemed to recall that useful findings have often emerged from apparently irrelevant aspects of learning.

But children have short attention spans. They cannot work in blind faith and need to know that their efforts are achieving something; otherwise they are discouraged. So if they achieve only errors, that implants a sense of failure. To overcome this, Progressivism urged teachers to give constant praise, regardless of whether the products were true or false. No-one must feel inferior; "all must have prizes". The last phrase was adopted as the title of a penetrating book by Melanie Phillips on the plight of British education. She particularly attacked the idea of *cultural relativism* used to shroud inaccuracy on the caring pretext that everyone's ideas are as valid as every-one else's and must be equally honoured.

This is egalitarianism gone mad: it means teachers are to lie to children. As well as keeping them ignorant through the doctrine of relevance, they are encouraged to believe that any false knowledge they glean is the truth. How can such a dishonest system be dignified as education? Children's self-esteem would be better protected by equipping them with the skills to deserve the praise they need, which is exactly what phonics does.

Concern for process not product led to the slogan that children were being trained to *think for themselves*. Combined with the emphasis of caring praise, rather than concern for truth, it led on to *hostility to testing*. Process would be very difficult, if not impossible, to test while product, which *would* lend itself to testing, was considered unimportant. Moreover, test-marking would involve differentiation and that would undo all the solicitous work of awarding equal praise. Thus, in spite of his pragmatic emphasis, Dewey deprived himself of the test scores that would have provided feedback on the practical consequences of his methods.

Progressivism's caring facade urged that children should not be mere units in a class but left free to pursue their own needs as they arose. As with Rousseau, child nature was considered essentially good, needing an untrammelled environment to allow the goodness to develop naturally. The child was equated with the flower bud, already holding all its potential for full blossoming, which had only to be drawn out. The very word "education", it was alleged, meant just this *drawing out* of inner potential. The child mind did not need information fed in; that would be stuffing it with dull, irrelevant facts, as the old formal teaching was said to do.

Inevitably, Dewey's child-centred discovery method necessitated *smaller classes,* which entailed greater expense. His Progressivist school in

Chicago gradually reduced the pupil-teacher ratio to about four children to each teacher or aide, and it was the resulting high cost that led the University to ask him to leave. Insistence upon small classes became a general feature of Progressivism. British class sizes have been greatly reduced and funding greatly increased but there are still complaints of too many children per teacher and too little money. Such dissatisfaction seems an indelible feature of Progressivist education.

Dewey's discovery method, based on relevant experiences in small classes, was set in the context of Hegel's philosophy of the *connectedness* of all things: nature, society, and the individual. He regarded all kinds of boundaries as artificial divisions in what should be a continuous whole, and therefore urged the abolition of traditional school subjects in favour of *cross-curricular projects* that would demonstrate the interlocking nature of reality.

In pursuit of connectedness, Dewey felt that the individual mind should not be differentiated from the social group. He abominated the development of a separate inner personality, which he took as a sign of social divisiveness.

> What is called inner is simply that which does not connect with others — which is not capable of free and full communication. What is termed spiritual culture has usually been futile, with something rotten about it, just because it has been conceived as a thing that a man might have internally — and therefore exclusively. (1916).

Thus he wrote off all unusual mental talent and distinctive genius, believing that the only worthwhile culture was that which could be shared with the greatest number of others — a lowest common denominator. He called for education to be organised as *group work,* with constant dialogue within the group, to develop co-operative problem-solving and decision-making in a common mode. Ideally, groups should also relate to other groups to promote collective similarity. This was another reason for rejecting tests. They would distinguish an elite and he preferred to blur distinctions and embrace *multiculturalism.*

Deweyism is inherently self-contradictory. For all his talk of child-centredness, he really aimed to sacrifice children's individuality to the group — social engineering related to Hegelism and also to his own leftist political stance, which stressed equality, often a means of levelling down. While he derided the traditional authority he wanted to replace, he did not hesitate to incorporate a more intense authority of his own. He extended the concept of a *democratic community* from the political arena to the classroom, demoting the teacher from being an older, wiser expert on the curriculum to being a mere *facilitator* to arrange the learning that the child democracy decided. He asserted that children derive most benefit from programmes that they themselves have discussed and negotiated. This did not encourage genuine thinking for oneself, as the individual had to bend to the ideas of the majority, and the majority might also have been bent to the will of the dominant child, not necessarily the brightest or the wisest.

It seems no coincidence that although Dewey's Progressivist doctrine took root in USA in the 1920s, it did not grip British education seriously until the 1945–51 Labour government introduced more leftist policies than the UK had previously experienced. It began, not only with publicity for the doctrine but also with an increase in the number of Progressivist appointees in the various tiers of the educational establishment.

Dewey also bequeathed another legacy; the role of the educational guru. Teachers who had worked diligently for years to turn out large numbers of literate pupils became as nothing in comparison with Progressivist ideologues, who became world figures. Guru status was enviable and the respect it accrued from pontification became an end in itself. These power-ful people had a vested interest in supporting the Progressivism that exalted them.

Progressivism as a Grandiose New Paradigm

Education evolves as teachers find better ways of helping children to learn but Progressivism went beyond evolution to revolution. It did not build upon antecedents but overturned them and has been called a completely new paradigm. The dictionary defines "paradigm" as "pattern or model" but it is not used for small-scale phenomena. It means a novel perception of some aspect of existence that compels a complete break with what has hitherto been the conventional wisdom. Columbus's discovery of the New World revolutionised the contemporary view of the shape and size of the earth. Copernicus's records of planetary motions introduced an entirely different perspective on the earth's place in the universe. Pasteur's work on microbes transformed our medical understanding.

These examples were based on factual evidence but there is another class of new paradigm founded on purely mental constructs. Unlike the changes in perception that *followed* new facts, these *began* with visionary ideas and led to coercive efforts to put them into practice. Communism was one such sweeping change of mind-set. Modern Movement architec-ture was another and so was Progressivism. The problems they caused were never acknowledged by their instigators, who applied a great deal of compulsion to try to make them as permanent as the truly objective ones. Communism survived as long as it did by creating a system of fear, com-bined with a blanket travel ban to prevent observation of healthier social conditions elsewhere. Modernist architecture has been able to dominate because of authoritarian planning control and a blind determination to blame tenants and not building design for the appalling misery of problem estates. Progressivism likewise began with a claim to benefit society but it, too, developed a power structure that refused to see the damage being done.

Objective new paradigms are open to criticism and ready to be disproved if there is contrary evidence but that is the last thing permitted by the fabricated ones. Progressivism closed off objective scrutiny by banning testing. Ostensibly this was to spare children the distress of failure but the hidden agenda was that it might reveal a failure of Progressivism itself and that was not to be tolerated. Existing tests were also a danger to be eliminated. The eleven-plus was abolished and General and Higher Schools Certificates were watered down to O-Levels and A-Levels, and later GCSE. Failure was disguised as an F-grade pass and A-Levels were weakened by coursework, which may be a cheats' charter.

Thus for a long time, the evidence of the Progressivist paradigm's failure was brushed aside. However, there was a great deal of research that produced many telling statistics supporting phonics methods and condemning look-say, and these will be exemplified in the next chapter. Meanwhile we present a critique of the main points of the Progressivist manifesto in terms of logic rather than statistics.

a) Education Means To Draw Out
Progressivism's dictum that "education" means to draw out what is already present in the child contains two fallacies. The first is a false derivation. The word does not come from the Latin "educere", to lead or draw out, as that is a third conjugation verb, which would have given the derived noun "eduction", without the "a". The "a" indicates a first conjugation verb, "educare", with just the opposite meaning, "to nurse, nourish or feed in". Jennifer Chew, who exposed this long-standing error in an article in the Reading Reform Foundation's Newsletter, quoted a neat example from Lewis and Short's *A Latin Dictionary*: "Educit obstetrix, educat nutrix", translated as "the midwife brings forth; the nurse brings up". The nurse would be a wet nurse, providing the baby with milk. And so education really means feeding children with the milk of knowledge and not trying to milk it out of them.

b) Non-Didactic Teaching
Gaffe though it was, the drawing-out concept led to some very real consequences, through the dogma of *non-didactic teaching*. "Didactic" means "intended to instruct", i.e, "teaching". So didactic teaching translates as teaching-type teaching, which is a tautology, and non-didactic teaching means non-teaching teaching, which is an oxymoron.

Despite the clumsiness of "non-didactic", Progressivists do mean something by it. They prescribe that teachers should not deliver knowledge because "children are not sausage skins waiting to be filled." True enough, they are not, but they do have minds needing to be furnished and talents needing to be honed. Their fulfilment is not already there within them and bound to unfold without adult aid. We know that feral children, growing up in the wild, forfeit much of their humanity and remain ineducable. Even lesser neglect produces severe problems. One boy, left largely to the company of dogs, walked on all fours and spoke only dog language. Leaving it to nature is not enough; a didactic approach is at least partly necessary.

In didactic classrooms, the children sit in rows facing the front or, with younger ones, in a squared horseshoe with a space for activities. These layouts allow all the children to focus on the teacher, who can more easily present the systematic and coherent knowledge, cultural traditions, civilised values and practical skills that human beings need.

Progressivism finds this too impersonal and regimented, and advocates a warmer, more individual approach, with small groups of children seated to face each other around tables. The teacher communicates more personally within each group in turn and adapts to children's different needs. When working with one group there must be self-help co-operative work in the other groups, which is said to encourage maturity.

The non-didactic approach sounds caring but it has several practical disadvantages. It grossly overloads the teacher, whose preparation is multiplied by having to think out how each child is to be occupied for a whole day, especially if, as is recommended, each group is doing something different. The decisions involve an early morning start to furnish each group's workspace with appropriate materials and a late finish to cope with all the clearing up. The teaching itself is repetitious, group by group, or else enormously diverse if each group's different interests are catered for, and then there is record-keeping, to log each child's experience as a guide to his or her future work. Such a programme is very burdensome and it is not surprising that teachers feel stressed.

The children, too, are penalised. Despite the aim of individual attention, each one receives very little. Simple arithmetic shows that the school day divided down into time per pupil allows only a few minutes each. Contrast that with whole-class teaching, where each child receives the teacher's attention for much longer. No matter that it is simultaneously directed to all the others; each one benefits from the same stream of carefully structured material. Group work is then used only where appropriate and not as a blanket approach.

In Progressivist classes children work with children most of the time and psychological research reveals that this is counterproductive. In families with a low ratio of adults to children, the latter's mental development is held back, compared with those in families with a higher adult ratio. The effect of many children can potentially be offset by the influence of uncles, aunts, grandparents, god-parents, etc., but the greatest common factor in the emergence of gifted children is the undivided attention of mothers who are aged over 35 and therefore more experienced and knowledgeable, just as didactic teachers are expected to be.

Two independent American research projects on gifted children both proved that the great majority of them are the first or only children of older mothers, and there is large-scale corroboration in the American *Who's Who,* where 75% of those listed fall into this category, despite the absence of a peerage based on primogeniture. A second, smaller, gifted group consists of youngest children born sufficiently long after the nearest sibling to have been the only pre-school child in the home, receiving the same sort of attention as the firstborn. Innate intelligence need not be exceptional to benefit from this advantage. Position in the family was a stronger influence than any other factor, including IQ.

Didactic teaching is the closest school approach to a high adult ratio, whereas Progressivism creates the many-sibling pattern of children interacting mostly with other children. Rachel Pinder even extols the fact that groups share their findings with other groups so that they go on learning from each other instead of from systematic teaching by an adult expert. Since too much child-to-child interaction seems to result in "dumbing down", it is not surprising that public examination standards have fallen.

Apart from the child-to-child emphasis there is another reason why this classroom layout causes dumbing down. For much of the time the children are not actually working. Several research investigations have observed the effect upon the proportion of the class time spent non-constructively, and have found a huge wastage, ranging from 33% to 75%.

This all contributes to the fact that non-didactic Progressivists have produced millions of lifelong illiterates denied access to knowledge through reading, whereas didactic phonicists make virtually all pupils fluent readers by the age of seven.

c) Cultural Relativism and Process Not Product

Progressivists are unabashed by the charge that they deny pupils access to knowledge. Knowledge is something that they scorn. They first set up an Aunt Sally image of traditional education as a relentless conveyor belt forcing dry facts into children's minds, and then criticise it as if saying something profound about traditional teaching itself.

They dismiss knowledge on the basis of cultural relativism, the view that nothing is really objective. Ideas and conclusions are not right or wrong but merely different and they all have their own validity. Different cultures, e.g. standard English versus sloppy, ungrammatical and obscene street speech, cannot be compared in terms of better or worse; each is valid in its own way. The claim that some ideas are superior or inferior, good or bad, true or false, right or wrong, are *value judgements* and "value" is not valuable but biased. One should be tolerant, not judgemental.

The logical answer is "Yes, so *you* cannot be objective either. *You* are making value judgements. *Your* ideas are not superior, good, true or right, so there is no reason to believe them." But here Progressivism breaks its own rules. It defends its own stance as right and condemns traditional teaching as wrong. It makes the value judgement that correct spelling and punctuation are elitist and bad, whereas the language of crude television programmes has "vitality" and should be preferred to the classics for English literature syllabuses.

Alice Coleman once attended a Schools Council conference called to debate adoption of her *graphicacy concept* (akin to literacy and numeracy in her own field of maps and other visual-spatial learning). The Schools Council displayed its idea of excellence in the form of a school newspaper full of errors. When criticised, the official replied that if the mistakes had been corrected, it would not have been the children's own work. Correction would have made it bad, wrong, false and inferior — a monumental value judgement. Alice Coleman was thankful that the conference rejected Schools Council sponsorship of graphicacy, as she felt that would have tainted it. Later it was adopted by the Associated Examining Board on its merits, without the kind of ginger group employed to boost Progressivism.

Cultural relativism poses as kindness and superior psychology, saying that constant correction damages pupils' self-esteem and may warp them for life. They need encouragement and praise, which should not be held back by judgemental carping. It is the process of learning that matters, not the product. In any case different products are all held equally valid.

The term *constant* correction is a give-away. It would certainly be necessary for Progressively taught children who are allowed to develop deplorable standards right across the board. But it is not necessary in traditional education which introduces knowledge and skills in structured steps that enable most children to get most things right. Traditional teachers know that work may be partly right and partly wrong; they praise the former and explain the improvement needed for the latter. This helps build self-esteem and also adds another vital life skill: ability to accept and act on criticism without feeling devastated by it.

Constant unearned praise is known by psychologists to promote vanity, which is usually a bad foundation for life, especially in deprived areas where home influence may not offset the harm of Progressivist schooling. Teachers may compound the local disadvantages by low expectations of achievement, and blame scapegoats such as poverty, unemployment, social class or poor parenting, while traditionalists use didactic phonics to overcome these handicaps.

d) Hostility to Testing

Progressivism denounces testing as a harsh, judgemental source of stress inflicted on children. It is rarely very stressful in traditional schooling where small but frequent tests act as an inoculation. Psychologists have found a little stress can be helpful. It is test-free Progressivism that has led to the suicides of Oxford high-fliers who fear examination failure.

The hidden agenda, perhaps unconscious even in fully convinced Progressivists, is that tests could reveal low standards and reflect upon professional competence, which is therefore never checked. Various plausible anti-test arguments have appeared in the press and elsewhere, not least because the process-not-product maxim makes testing unfair.

Another ploy claims standards have always been poor and dredges up criticisms made in 1858, 1938, etc. This is the "Roman soldier fallacy". If a centurion wrote home complaining of British rain, it does *not* prove the weather was wetter then than now, but merely that we had a damper climate than Rome. Similarly, the 1858 Newcastle Report's comment that many children could not read or write must be taken in the context of no universal free education; they were illiterate because they were without schooling, whereas today's illiteracy occurs despite a dozen years in school. The 1938 Spens Report stated that many grammar- school or even university graduates could not express themselves in good English, but that refers to lapses below the high standards of that time, quite unlike today's gross inadequacies.

Some of the faults attributed to traditional teaching are in fact features of early Progressivism. Rachel Pinder castigates the *Janet and John* reading books as boring, but at the time their "Look! Look ! Janet. Look! Look! John." was considered an improvement on interesting stories precisely because their repetition was essential for whole-word familiarisation.

A further tactic designed to confuse the standards issue is to pick holes in the traditionalists' so-called *golden age,* but who so-called it? Not the traditionalists who simply recall that standards were much higher before Progressivism took over. In Alice Coleman's Thameside school, where only one pupil in 1200 was illiterate, there was a big spelling problem due to gaps in wartime schooling, but it proved perfectly amenable to her programme for spelling improvement in every class. Today's spelling, which it is felt demeaning to correct, is much worse. Whereas traditional teachers were alert to improving good standards still further, Progressivists are content with low ones and do not want them checked. If anyone is claiming a golden age, it is the self-satisfied Progressivists.

e) Lack of Discipline

Even beyond cultural relativism is moral relativism. The doctrine of natural goodness has a corollary in the injunction that children should not be punished. In its extreme form this means letting them get away with anything and everything, and doing exactly as they wish. One of Alice Coleman's colleagues visited his son's school with a family message and was directed to the maths class. However, the boy was not there and the teacher explained that he had not felt like maths and preferred to be out on the playing field kicking a ball about. Of course, such extreme over-permissiveness is not typical, but nor is it rare.

Progressivists justify such licence by asserting that self-discipline is more desirable than discipline from outside, but this is just a sound-bite unrelated to reality. Children learn self-discipline from the experience of orderly behaviour required of them, and without such a model, backed up by moral teaching, they find it very difficult to get themselves together in a self-disciplined way. Disruptive and violent behaviour has multiplied in schools during the Progressivist era. One 1977 Inspector's report noted that fighting among pupils had broken out several times in the course of a single lesson.

Active campaigning against punishment was the aim of STOPP (Society of Teachers Opposed to Physical Punishment), which produced a report on the "child-beating" policies of 2119 schools. Entitled *The Violent 81%*, this document usefully exposed abuses but went over the top in assuming that even a moderate, last-resort caning was vicious sadism. Corporal punishment was abolished in state schools in 1986 and that has often proved the final straw in promoting disciplinary breakdown, which rebounded on teachers and left them helpless.

It is surprising that psychologists remain silent on this issue, as one of their most fundamental classifications, introversion/extraversion, yields firm evidence that different personalities have different punishment needs. Head scans reveal that introverts have a great deal of brain activity going on, which corresponds to a mental life rich enough to absorb and act upon admonitions without needing physical reinforcement. Extraverts are much more outgoing, often with too little brain activity to make admonitions stick. They learn by doing, or in this context, by being done to. From the physical sensation of a smack or caning they can learn to make the behavioural adjustments that they cannot learn from mere words. Extraverts are not traumatised by moderate physical punishment applied as a logical response to bad behaviour, but introverts are more sensitive. The introversion-extraversion scale is a continuum, and it is only extreme extraverts who might need, after other methods fail, to be caned. The woman who wrote to the press boasting that she had never spanked her children, and dogmatizing that everyone else should copy, ought to be thanking her luck in having relatively introverted offspring and being spared the problems of highly extraverted ones.

Too little punishment lets bad behaviour escalate into hooliganism and crime, and it is more cruel to condemn children to a criminal record than to nip it in the bud with a judicious smack. "Spare the rod and spoil the child" emerged from the wisdom of Solomon and is reflected in today's adage, "Better a small confrontation now than a big one later". US psychologists find that over-compassionate permissiveness is a form of moral neglect, and advise "tough love" to show children that their parents' concern for them must include enough discipline to prevent their ruining their lives. This also a responsibility for teachers.

f) The Evil of Having an Inner Life

Progressivism's views on introversion and extraversion are very old-fashioned. Back in the Victorian age of sterner discipline, children were moulded as far as possible into orderliness and conformity. Extraverts benefited from this discipline and were more likely to be stable, while introverts were sometimes over-moulded to the point of distress and instability. These were the patients observed by the psychiatrists of the time.

Naturally, the doctors did not see stable introverts or extraverts, or even unstable extraverts whose outgoing reactions landed them in prisons, not mental hospitals. This lack of a cross-section led to the misconception that introversion was defective while extraversion was healthy. Dewey adopted this idea; hence his denigration of a separate inner life as undesirable.

Psychology has since moved on, as looser discipline left more introverts unstressed and able to lead stable and fulfilled lives. Extraverts, however, have been left more undisciplined and psychiatrists have had to deal with them in prisons. This has created a shift in perceptions, leading to the idea that it is usually the extraverts who are the baddies.

Progressivism has not moved in step with psychology and still has practices designed to eradicate the supposed evil of a personal inner life. This dated attitude flies in the face of further evidence that introversion is not a remediable disability but a perfectly normal condition of much of the population. Indeed, it is largely genetic, though partly modifiable by nurture. Introverts have a rich inner life to attend to, with an absorbing intellectual or cultural agenda, so they do not want to be constantly socialising. They are good learners who may become great thinkers, academics, research workers, writers, etc. The nation needs them and should not try to snuff out their talents by unremitting immersion in social engineering of group-work.

Conversely, extraverts, who are more dependent on outside interests, should not be exclusively reinforced in their outgoing stance. They need a balancing input of concentration, etc., to strengthen their inner life and help them control antisocial tendencies. Schools should recognise differences and provide for both these aspects of personality.

g) Social Engineering Through Group Work

Progressivism sees it as self-evident that children should be equal and alike, and therefore stipulates that they must be kept in perpetual mental contact and communication through co-operative work. Small groups facing inward around tables are to function as microcosms of society. Working together is supposed to prepare them for the interaction that democracy needs. Sharing activities and solving problems jointly is intended as an initiation into societal duty and there may also be overt socialist political indoctrination. By contrast, traditional teachers were trained not to reveal their own political leanings, as impartiality was thought essential for the flowering of individual freedom. Progressivism's different ideal urges politics, termed "citizenship", as a valid part of the curriculum.

Working in small groups as an introduction to democracy was followed up by enlarged groups in team teaching, where two or more classes worked with two or more teachers. To facilitate this wider communication, school buildings were designed on the *pod principle*. Individual classrooms had incomplete dividing walls, with gaps that carried noise distraction from one room to the next. Or there might be several classes going on in different parts of the same hall. These layouts put disruptive behaviour on more public display than in self-contained rooms, and hence more likely to be imitated, which did not help discipline.

Alice Coleman was once allocated a pod room for a sixth-form conference workshop scheduled to go on till 4. 30. At four o'clock the gap in the wall was invaded by a horde of children set on streaming through to an exit beyond. She instinctively advanced towards them with arms outstretched, saying "Out! Out!" and back they retreated. The teachers were astonished that they obeyed her, which revealed how far discipline had become a lost art.

Paradoxically the drive for equality and similarity did not make use of the bonding influence of school uniforms. They were thought too formal as well as undemocratically dividing school from school. This attitude led to some highly insensitive school mergers, followed by hooliganism as rival gangs clashed. The notorious Ridings School in Halifax was an example, where expulsions for violence soared.

h) No Streaming or Selection
The equality ideal, plus the hostility to testing that would have revealed inequality, led to the view that school classes, like society at large, should span the full range of abilities to be a preparation for life. Streaming by IQ was anathema and mixed-ability classes were advocated on the argument that everyone would have something to contribute. For example, less bright children would probably be more practical and good at sport, while the brighter ones would be more logical. Their collaboration would nudge the backward ones forward and safeguard the quicker ones from intellectual arrogance by giving them experience of what the slower ones had to offer. This was supposed to be another facet of introduction to democracy.

It was a plausible theory but it did not work in practice. Nature does not always bestow gifts with even-handedness, and some bright children are good all-rounders while some less bright ones may be disadvantaged on all fronts. The latter came to feel intensely inferior in the constant presence of cleverer ones and, as there are so many non-readers, their distress is widespread. It sometimes turns into a keen resentment of the able ones, who are targeted by gangs of bullies. Some bullies' victims have been seriously injured or even killed and some have committed suicide. So much for school democracy!

Long ago in USA the persecution of gifted children had become so standard that they habitually concealed their ability. This was well known, so there was no excuse for British schools to follow suit, but the usual blind eye was turned to serve the Progressivist cause.

Mixed-ability classes held bright children back, as teachers had too little time to develop their full potential. Nor did the system prevent intellectual arrogance. Able pupils in constant inescapable contact with the mediocre were bored to tears by the dragging pace suited to the average. And if they were also taunted and bullied they had all the more reason to despise the others. Arrogance is far less likely in classes streamed to give plenty of pace and competition, away from constant awareness of others' lesser capabilities.

Similar observations apply to non-selection, which is non-streaming at whole-school level. Grammar, technical and secondary modern schools, as well as single sex schools were all merged into co-educational comprehensives. Today's examination league tables show that comprehensives' standards are generally lower than those of the remaining selective and single-sex schools, not only grammars but also secondary moderns, so any gain from this social engineering is not academic excellence. Nor is the academic sacrifice offset by social benefits; this was illustrated by a detailed study of Kent schools made by Andrew Ewart Smith in 1997.

Smith analysed the incidence and cost of three years of theft/burglary, criminal damage and fire in each of 763 state schools and found that the 58% with at least one of these problems were generally larger than the 42% free from them. Affected primary schools averaged 11% larger and secondary schools 18% larger. This was not a simple matter of more pupils committing more offences, because the number of antisocial incidents increased disproportionately faster than the number on roll. Co-educational secondary schools had 40% more crimes per 1000 pupils than boys' secondaries and 51% more than girls', while comprehensive secondaries were 44% worse than non-comprehensives.

So Progressivist tenets of large schools, co-education and non-selection have proved socially adverse. Instead of democratisation, there has been criminalisation. The whole is indeed more than the sum of the parts but in the negative sense of "more means worse". What a pity that the drive for smaller classes was not matched by a drive for smaller schools.

Kent, unusually, had retained some grammar schools but in most local authorities the anti-streaming, anti-selection dogma had totally deprived bright children of fast-track classes or schools. However, there was a new kind of selection in the form of special schools for the least bright. Formerly Kent had only three special schools: two small ones for children in long-stay hospitals and the Royal National School for the Deaf. By the 1980s there were 24 more, for the severely backward 3% of children. They were not always effective. As Mona McNee well knows, the Kent special school attended by her son did no more than provide him with a parking desk.

i) The Interconnectedness of Knowledge
Progressivism abhors divisions, not only among people but among school subjects and sought to dismantle the supposedly divisive traditional subject structure. The first step was to introduce the *cross-curricular project*, which was already established when Alice Coleman began her teaching career. However, she was soon disgusted by the Board of Education's promotional booklet intended to increase its use. The exemplar illustration came from the school of a fellow student where officialdom had ordered the *staff* to produce the project; it was not the children's work. Her reaction was that if no genuine children's project was considered worthy of inclusion, there must be something faulty about the whole concept.

Later teaching experience convinced her that projects take up a great deal of time in relation to their learning value. This thought recurred when reading Rachel Pinder on a local environment project which covered roughly the same ground as Alice Coleman's local geography lessons but took much longer. For the latter's lessons, the children studied her papier-mâché model at twelve inches to the mile with a vertical interval that clearly showed slopes and the cliffs of chalk and clay pits along the Thames. Later classes repainted land uses on the model: factories, shops, houses, parks, main roads, railways, etc. They brought in samples of factory wares as well as splendid flint echinoderm fossils from the pits. Pollution was observed as cement-dust coating roofs, decreasing with distance from the works (which had secretly been asked to maximize dust effluent and create fog over the Thames to help foil German bombers).

Projects escalated into *integrated days,* or even *integrated weeks,* in which the children worked through assignments they themselves decided. Rachel Pinder set out eleven advantages in this. Children are not interrupted by lesson bells but work at their own pace, spending more time on aspects that interest them. They take more responsibility for their learning and become more motivated. They learn to organise materials and equipment, read labels to discover what is stocked where, help themselves to what is needed and replace it afterwards. This engenders responsibility for the classroom and legitimises walking about, which obviates fidgeting. They also find the integrated tasks more realistic than practising skills through textbook exercises.

Advantages for teachers are not having to distribute lesson materials, as the children help themselves, and hence there is time to spur constructive imagination, provide information and help with difficult tasks. Another benefit is more detailed record keeping.

Bur many teachers find detailed records a burden, not a benefit. They involve noting which children have covered which topics and what omissions each one needs to make up in future. This involves intensive, time-consuming preparation and monitoring, especially as essentials may be interrupted by pupils wanting to pursue a particular item to create a dance, drama or book. Teachers eventually resisted having pupils work in the classroom through breaks, as they needed a break themselves. It is not surprising that they had to become mere "facilitators" and some have totally abdicated from a genuine teaching role.

These processes created a retreat from the allegedly artificial traditional subjects, which were often abandoned except for external examinations. Even there, cross-curricular influences appeared, in the guise of new subjects such as media studies. But dismembering established fields of learning is not justified by brain studies. Traditional subjects are not just arbitrary artefacts but related to specific brain areas. Damage in one area creates a blind spot for nouns (grammar), which have to be referred to by circumlocutions. Damage in another area may rob the individual of a sense of place and direction (geography). Traditional subjects became established because they work with the brain's structure, building on natural foundations.

Progressivism defined "natural" as "self-educating". For example, they felt that the brain's grammatical tendency would cause children to speak well by mere imitation, but those without good speech models failed to do so. Neverthless, Progressivists disparaged grammar as elitist and it ceased to be taught. Natural expression, as in the Schools Council error-ridden newspaper, was not to be interfered with. One art lecturer said children should not be taught the rules of perspective as these interfere with natural artistic vitality.

But education, like medicine, *is* interference with nature. Otherwise, why would we need it at all? Traditionalists distinguish natural aptitudes from their educated counterparts. We can learn naturally to find our way round our locality but this skill is enhanced into much wider significance when we learn to read maps. Verbal ability can be educated into literacy, numerical ability into numeracy, spatial ability into graphicacy and social ability into oral articulacy and emotional intelligence. Traditionalists begin the last by teaching good manners and then gradually worked up to complex relationships, but raw Progressivism allows all that to be left to nature and favours early sex education. Then some pupils apply it as learning by doing and we hear of rapes committed by pre-teenagers.

j) Child-Centred Education

It is difficult to know what child-centred education is. In the 1944 Education Act it aspired to provide opportunities to develop the full potential of each child's abilities and aptitudes. But the differences offered by the grammar, technical and secondary modern schools created for this purpose were swept away by comprehensivisation.

For Rousseau child-centredness meant a personal tutor for each child but the same approach for all. There was no question of an academic child being allowed to learn from books. Dewey also worked towards a high staff ratio, which might have exceeded even his 1:4 if its cost had not become intolerable to the funder. He, too, imposed a social engineering system that was the same for all, regardless of individual differences.

It also means "interest the child", familiar to good traditional teachers but converted by Progressivism into the *play way*, with games, trips and amusements, and the reduction of work to what children saw as relevant. This seems a poor preparation for the working world where one must take the rough with the smooth and not pick out only what appeals. Rousseau's disregard of employability has led, for far too many children, to twelve years of training for unemployability.

Child-centredness sometimes means developing children's ability to *think for themselves* and *question everything*. This sounds high-minded and is not at odds with "issues not facts". It does not aid acquisition of a unifying body of knowledge and culture, which Progressivism considers no loss, but the lack of a common culture is rather divisive, which offends another Progressivist principle. However, such inconsistencies can be taken in the stride of theorists who believe everything is equally valid.

Alice Coleman found that "thinking for oneself" was not the same as *thinking clearly*. One year she found that her Canadian students attempted to assimilate what they heard and ask questions to deepen their understanding before pursuing possible alternatives. But many British students thought that trotting out an instant challenge was thinking for themselves. The challenges were mostly routine topic headings, such as, "What about the political or economic aspects?" At first she patiently explained, but then realised that the best answer was, "Well, what about them?" This revealed a complete hollow behind the façade and gave her a foothold for beginning to undo the harm this Progressivist dogma had wrought.

"Child-centred" can be the opposite of *subject centred*, thus involving learning through projects, etc. It can also mean operating projects democratically demanded by children. Acting on the claim that children work better on topics chosen by themselves can leave huge gaps in their education, so the teacher must be crafty enough to manipulate them into asking for what would be good for them. This is not always possible.

Another interpretation is emphasis on child leadership and denial of the teacher's role as an older, wiser source of knowledge and culture, replacing it with the role of a service facilitator. This, together with an abdication from discipline in many schools has led to a loss of respect for the teaching profession and an increasing number of physical assaults by pupils. Teachers used to feel fulfilled in their work and proud of their profession but many find that difficult at present. Even those with a true vocation and real achievement may suffer this side effect of the rule of the Progressivist majority.

This takes us on to the purpose of this book: the teaching of reading. The remaining topics in this critique are specifically concerned with the Progressivist tenets that have defeated literacy and created so many reluctant pupils.

k) The Gestalt Dogmas

Gestalt theory in teaching to read is based on the common misconception that the way we do things as adults is also the way children learn. Gestaltists look at a word, seem to see it whole, assume that is how they learned it and urge that every child should learn that way too.

They neglect their own concept that there can be misleading optical illusions and fail to recognise that the perceptual fallacy of whole-word reading is one of them. K. Rayner has presented the modern findings that adults still read words by their letter sequence from left to right but do it so rapidly that they *seem* to be reading them as single units simultaneously.

Forcing children to read whole words by the look-say method is like telling young piano learners to play a piece in the correct tempo, without being taught the individual notes or the significance of their stave position. We can see that it would be ridiculous to place a sheet of piano music in front of complete beginners, let them hear what it sounds like, and tell them to learn to play by playing, but this is an exact analogy with showing children a page of print, reading its sounds to them and expecting them to learn to read by reading. It is cruel to inflict such frustration on children and the cruelty is not restricted to childhood. It is even more cruel and humiliating when it leaves people illiterate for life.

l) No Rote Learning or Boring Repetition

Look-say claims to be kind because it avoids the boring rote learning and repetitious drilling said to be involved in phonics, i.e. learning the alphabet and building up words. This is a judgemental condemnation that is simply untrue. It is look-say that is boring and repetitious, and phonics that gives children an early sense of progress and mastery.

There are 26 English letters, plus digraphs such as "oo", "au", "eer", "ch" and "ng", making up a total of 52 sounds. This limits the number of letter-sound relationships, and even after just a few of them have been learned, they can be blended into words, so a constructive element is present from the start.

Contrast that with the long-winded effort of learning whole words from their shape, unexplained by their letter content. There are well over half a million English words but even if we restrict children to the 850 commonest ones specified in Basic English, there would still be 17 times as many units to be learned by rote as with phonics. The first few words may be easy to recognise on sight because they are chosen for their distinctive outline shapes but such distinctiveness is not unlimited. Words with just one letter different may look the same shape to a child who has not been taught letters, e.g. "cat", "cot", "cut" or "eat".

It gets harder. Flashcards are shown repeatedly in the hope that children will register the fine differences but they are mostly beaten by the similarities. Adding to the word-stock becomes more laborious, while some memorised words are forgotten. Without letter clues the child may fasten on others, such as a smear on the card or the place of a word in a story learned by heart, but this is not progress. The same word in a different context may still baffle. What could be more boring than endlessly repeated trials with a low success rate?

The "merits" of look-say came from a faulty experiment, exposed by Rudolf Flesch in *Why Johnny Can't Read*, in 1955. Two sets of children were given 20 test words after six months' teaching. The look-say group scored ten and the phonics group only six. Flesch explained that the look-say group had romped through all 20 and got half wrong, while the phonics group slowly built up words and got all they attempted right. They were like young pianists, placing accuracy before speed. A similar test six months later would have shown they had picked up speed and got all 20 right while the look-say group would still have had many errors. Phonics-taught children draw increasingly ahead from then on. And today's improved phonics methods have them ahead in less than six months.

Phonics lays firm foundations for the future; look-say is a get-rich-quick scheme whose bubble soon bursts. Unfortunately, Rudolf Flesch's evidence was wilfully ignored by the Progressivist establishment, determined not to be perceived as wrong.

m) Reading for Meaning and not Mechanical Letter Assembly
The claim that phonics learners pursue a mechanical exercise while look-say learners read for meaning is also contrary to the evidence and again reminds us of Progressivists' ignorance about phonics. This is not

the teachers' fault but stems from a concerted training-college policy to condemn it and never mention how it actually works.

It is true that a word has meaning in itself and young look-say learners can read it straight off – *if* it happens to be one of the few sight words they have been taught. If it is something else, they have no idea of its meaning or pronunciation. Young phonics learners do not read words straight off but try to build them up letter by letter. This makes them halting in mid-word, which is used to imply that phonics is mechanical, while look-say learners' halting in mid-sentence is somehow overlooked.

Phonics' initial strivings are not mechanical but the application of logic. This is rewarding to children as they are mastering words by their own efforts, using the strategy of letter-sound correspondence. This strategy is transferable to completely new words, with help from more spelling rules as they advance. The halting phase is temporary and they become fluent readers, taking the mechanics for granted and going straight to meaning.

Look-say halting is not temporary; it has to recur with every new word because there is no strategy (apart from guessing) for tackling the unknown, and the limited size of the sight vocabulary means that a vast number of unknown words are lying in wait. These unfortunate children fall further and further behind their phonics-trained peers. "Process not product" is a thoroughly apt description. Look-say locks pupils into a process that they can never fully master, while phonics children have a wonderful product – the ability to read.

But, it may be argued, quite a proportion of those in look-say schools do learn to read, so how do they achieve it? That may seem a great mystery. One strand in the solution is that some children who are deprived of the alphabet for reading may still be taught it for writing and are enabled to "catch on" by transferring it to the reading task. But many others learn only because they are taught by the phonic method, out of school.

Another strand used by some look-say teachers is *onset and rime* – a mere nod in the direction of phonics. The "onset" uses the alphabet to pick out a word's initial letter or letter pair as a clue for guessing. But many words begin with the same letter, so the guess may be quite inaccurate. For example, "The dog got wet" is straightforward for phonics readers but presents pitfalls for look-say readers. The initial "g" may lead them to guess "go" and they read "The dog go went". This is hardly reading for meaning. The "rime" element takes sets of the last two or three letters to be identified because they rhyme. Tracing all the letters in a logical sequence throughout the word is still anathema and the guessing gets worse with longer words.

n) Writing with Creativity

It is claimed look-say pupils write more creatively because they are not held back by the mechanics of decoding letters. Perhaps this parallels "creative accounting". Some of the creative spelling and syntax is so imagina-tive that it is hard to puzzle out any meaning at all. It may be Dewey's instant relevance but it lacks long-term relevance to employability.

In reality, those who lack the basic mechanics find it harder to devote their minds to creative tasks, whereas those who have been taught to mas-ter the basics effortlessly can concentrate better on creativity. Strong evi-dence on this point emerged from the research on the *initial teaching alphabet*, to be discussed in Chapter 4.

Progressivism also introduced the concept of *emergent writing*, to paral-lel the idea that reading could be picked up by osmosis without being taught. Children are encouraged to scribble in the hope that actual writing would emerge. This sounds like the idea of letting a thousand monkeys loose on typewriters for eternity to see whether one of their random efforts might be the same as *The Encyclopaedia Britannica*.

Emergent writing is another claim of learning by doing, which says that just as one learns wood carving by carving wood, so one learns writing by writing. The fallacy is seen as soon as one extends the analogy to learning dentistry by drilling teeth or surgery by cutting people up. Fortunately, these ways of acquiring expertise are outlawed as unethical, and practice is deferred until there has been a great deal of theoretical learning. A sur-geon who let a work-experience boy just hold a clamp during an operation was immediately disciplined.

There are in fact two kinds of skill. Purely physical skills like walking, swimming or riding a bicycle, have to be learned by doing them, but prior instruction is essential for those that involve more mental understanding, and both reading and writing are of that type.

Learning by doing and discovery are two Progressivist basics that are imperfectly understood. To clarify them we draw on the science of gra-phology. Handwriting experts have shown that different ways of absorb-ing knowledge are related to variations in the speed of brain activity, which are shown in different letter formations made at different speeds. There are five main gradations and some adults have mental resources that spread across two or more.

Psychologists relate intelligence level to mental speed but graphologists have found that this is not the whole story. Each speed is related to a differ-ent way of receiving and processing information and supports different kinds of contributions to society. This is a genuine case for not distinguish-ing superior or inferior *types* because each can have better or worse levels of achievement within it. One Nobel Prize winner had the second slowest mental speed.

Practical thinking is the slowest and depends heavily on sense data. Learning by doing is natural for these children. They have an excellent sense of their bodies, which gives them good hand-eye co-ordination, manual dexterity and aptitude for sport. They have good potential for dealing with materials, equipment and machines, and may be suitable for city technical colleges. However, learning by doing should be restricted to practical subjects and even for these, many will need prior instruction before they can "do" effectively.

The second category, *methodical thinkers*, have a mental speed between that of the slow learners-by-doing and the quicker ones suited to the discovery method. They are missed out by Progressivism, even though they are the majority at school age. They are best suited to the didactic methods that Progressivism bans. They are good at taking in information delivered to them but their brains need time to process and file it, after which they have good memories for it. They may appear a bit dull in class, as they are not ready to answer questions on what has just been taught, but they often do better than expected in examinations, which fit their deferred time-scale more effectively. They are best with logical material that does not require too much complex analysis and so they may shine at number work and computer work. A Nobel Prize winner in this category had worked methodically through a systematic sequence of chemical syntheses and lighted upon a very important organic compound.

The third group consists of medium-quick minds with the spare mental time to probe beyond information received and *investigate* further for themselves. They are also likely to have an *analytical* bent capable of re-arranging information into a clearer order. The discovery principle fits them very well but there are limits. Children should not be expected to discover everything for themselves and certainly not that great invention, the alphabet and its role in learning to read. But once they have been taught, they can be encouraged to read as much as possible and use reference books and libraries to soak up information.

Fourthly there is another group overlooked by Progressivists—pupils with such *keen comprehension* that they seem to absorb knowledge instantaneously. If they are dragged down to the average working speed, they have so much unengaged mental time that they can be thoroughly bored. They need to be stretched to avoid becoming mentally lazy, not only by extra work but also by constructive criticism, identifying their occasional leap to a false conclusion. They need exercises requiring them to slow down for checking and analysis, which helps to make their intelligence useful as well as just high-scoring.

In Progressivist classes they always seem to be able to cope with the work, so they are left under-stretched while the teacher attends to the less able. Keen comprehenders do best when streamed with other fast brains and also with investigative analysers who help them tackle the art of improving the knowledge they absorb.

Finally, there are rare ultra-fast thinkers, who are *one jump ahead*. Even while receiving information they are already working out how to exploit it. This is "cunning", which may be either positive or negative. They need challenges that reveal their initiatives and ensure that they are ethical and not purely self-seeking. If they become resentful of being deprived of reading and other skills, they can be very cunning in avenging themselves.

Conclusion

The differences in human nature noted in this chapter cast fresh light on what constructive child-centred education should be. Traditional teaching appears to have all or most of the solutions: didactic presentation, streaming, selection, better discipline with an open mind about physical punishment for extreme extraverts, subject-based material to fit the structure of the brain and, above all, phonics teaching to utilise the linear, logical left brain, without neglecting the right brain's pattern insight in other aspects of education.

Furthermore, by developing the ability to read and write fluently, beyond the need for undue effort in the mechanics, phonics teaching releases children's minds to concentrate on the content of what they are producing, and hence to be more freely creative at an earlier age than look-say pupils who are always struggling with the unknown.

Now that Chapters 2 and 3 have explained the look-say background of reading problems and the wider issues inherent in the Progressivist movement as a whole, the time has come to outline the course of events responsible for the educational crisis that we have called *the explosion of illiteracy*. Chapter 4 will now provide the hard evidence for the existence of a severe decline in standards during the Progressivist period ever since World War II.

Chapter Four

The Explosion of Illiteracy

The last two chapters explained traditional teaching with its phonics foundation and Progressivism with its lack of foundation, as the background for appreciating the *evidence* of educational decline. We shall now show that in what we call the *upwave period,* up to World War II, traditional methods created rising standards, while in the later *downwave period,* Progressivism created falling standards. The early downwave, up to the mid-1960s, was an *ambiguous phase,* when the Progressivist decline was masked by the efforts of those still teaching phonics but subsequently Progressivism was dominant and the decline was unmistakable for those with open eyes. This was the *cover-up phase,* when Progressivists used effective spin techniques to impose their image of success and delayed any reform attempt until the 1988 Education Act. This chapter deals with the facts. The mechanisms behind them follow in Part II.

The Upwave

Before W.E. Forster's 1870 Education Act established compulsory education from 1880, there was already a strong trend towards universal literacy, traced by E. G. West (1965). Over the forty years up to 1858, the population grew by 68% but the number of children at school grew four times as fast, by 271%. Each age group was better educated than its predecessor; 1865 navy returns showed that whereas 89% of seamen and 94% of petty officers could read, the figure for boy recruits was 99%. By 1880, some 95% of 15-year olds were literate as compared with today's 50-60%.

Before 1891, education was not free; parents paid. West showed that the largest group of fee-payers consisted of working-class parents, with the Church providing the next largest number of places. There were also some "voluntary aided" schools with an official subsidy. Literacy was greatest in urban areas (now the inner city), where school-founding initiatives could draw upon a dense population to share the cost and this is in stark contrast with today, when it is often alleged that social conditions in these same areas are the cause of low literacy attainment there.

Forster intended his Education Act to help only the 5% still without schooling, largely in rural areas. He did not mean to create a vast near-monopoly of state education. That came about when the Board of Education set up Board Schools with a much greater capacity than was needed and then filled their places by reducing their fees and becoming partly tax-funded. Their subsidies undermined competition from the existing independent schools and forced most of them out of business. West compared this massive state intervention to a scenario of assisting a few starving families by ordering free food for all.

No danger was perceived in this near-monopoly because British civilisation was then on the upgrade. The school leaving age was 13 and classes were larger, so far fewer teachers were then needed and consequently they were of a high calibre, especially the women, who had few other career opportunities. And as more educated children passed into parenthood, the next generation came from more literate homes and standards continued to rise. The only reversal occurred in World War I, after which Cyril Burt's testing suggested that 10% of urban pupils were backward readers. This is a much lower percentage than at present and was also related to a more stringent definition of backwardness than now. The performance of this 10% would probably qualify most of them as average on today's scale.

A striking testimonial for UK education came in 1928 from Robert Saudek, a Czech who worked mainly in the UK and USA, and whose fluency in five languages made him a sought-after speaker in European universities. His wide international experience convinced him that British educational standards were the best. A gifted experimentalist, he made detailed studies of how children learned to write. He compared the old looped writing with the new "linked script" or "joined-up print" that was introduced by the Board of Education in 1922 and gradually adopted by schools in the later 1920s and 1930s. He established that when nine-year-olds changed to the simpler style, their writing speed increased by 75% and even 13-year-olds, well practised in the old script, showed a 34% gain. The new style was neat and it freed children from much laborious penmanship and gave more time for actual learning, which was a further boost to educational standards. It also helped learning to read by reinforcing the same written forms that the children saw in print.

It is a pity that no national reading test was conducted at the educational peak of the late 1930s but no doubt the satisfactory upwave conditions precluded any perceived need for it. The most authoritative comment comes from the Board of Education's 1931 *Report of the Consultative Committee on the Primary School* (the *Hadow Report*), which observed that only a few children needed systematic reading instruction after the age of seven. This seems the origin of the statistic that there was less than a 1% illiteracy rate, a figure which should be borne in mind as a comparator for those observed later, during the downwave.

The Downwave 1: The Ambiguous Period 1945-1965

The upwave was broken by World War II, when teaching time was seriously curtailed by shorter school hours in winter to avoid the blackout; gaps due to air-raid alerts; school closures to repair bomb damage; mass evacuation from vulnerable areas; and problems in finding school premises in reception areas. After the war there was great concern about lowered standards and in 1948 the Ministry of Education commissioned a sample survey by Dr. Joyce Morris of the National Foundation for Educational Research (NFER).

NFER confirmed the disquiet about standards. Far from there being only a few backward children older than seven, some 30% of 15-year-old school leavers were found backward or, even worse, semi-literate or illiterate. This was a sudden large deterioration but, as that age group had spent six years of their schooling in wartime conditions, it was hoped that ongoing peacetime education would soon make the scandal a thing of the past.

That hope was dashed by a 1952 NFER survey, which showed a similar percentage of backward, semi-literate and illiterate school leavers, who had had fewer wartime years at school and should have done better. Clearly, post-war education was not rectifying matters. An appalling 19% of seven-year-olds had hardly even begun to read, despite only peacetime years in school, and 45% more still needed reading instruction, a total of 64%. And nearly half of them (30%) were still backward when leaving school at fifteen. Despite eight more years of schooling they had not been equipped with the vital skill of reading. Once established, backwardness was tending to persist.

Inertia was again illustrated by Joyce Morris's 1956 and 1957 tests of 100 children at age ten and again at age eleven. They were not deprived and should have easily mastered four simple words that the *Hadow Report* said were known by seven-year-olds in 1930. Surprisingly many failed to identify them and, even worse, showed little ability to profit from their mistakes. A year later, many remained baffled by the same words (Table 4.1).

These children had not suffered wartime problems, so clearly post-war education was not up to pre-war standards. Joyce Morris wanted to discover why. She followed up some of them until they left school in 1961 and analysed a large range of their personal traits and home and school conditions. The chief factor was the schools' standards, which depended first on the head and secondly on the staff. Children who made a poor start continued in severe difficulty. Only about one in eight who were backward in the second year ever caught up to average and at least half remained extremely poor readers all their school lives. There was something lacking in the post-war teaching of reading, which placed a great responsibility on teachers to ensure a good start before discouragement set in.

Table 4.1: Kent Study of 100 Children (Joyce Morris)

Test Word	Percentage Unable to Read	
	1956 (Age 10)	1957 (Age 11)
Find	34	11
Past	37	19
Empty	50	26
Inviting	67	34

What constituted a good teacher? Various tests distinguished how poor and good readers deployed their reading skills. Almost a quarter of poor readers could not name all the letters of the alphabet and nearly half had an imperfect knowledge of their sounds. Almost all had a rather muddled idea of whether to attack words from the left or the right side, and 38% either merely guessed at what the words might be or did not even try to tackle them. They had an extremely limited ability to analyse or build up words from their phonic elements. All these tendencies were consistent with whole-word teaching.

The good readers, by contrast, worked out the sound of each part of the word and then assembled the sounds and syllables to pronounce a result that sounded right in accordance with their previous experience. This was compatible with phonics learning.

This study of methods did not reveal a totally clear-cut difference, as the contrast was blurred where methods were mixed. Nevertheless, it showed that where the phonic element was getting through it created good readers, while its failure to get through created poor ones. The poor readers who then received phonics help in word-building were the ones who made the best progress during the study period. The research clearly indicated that "good teachers" were those who used the successful phonics method.

Morris's work was a strong early warning on the danger of the whole-word method, and if it had been heeded at the time, the great educational crash would have been averted. Her warning was based on facts derived from testing, so the Progressivists, who discredited both facts and testing, continued to turn a deaf ear and reading failure persisted.

Meanwhile, traditionalists were exploring how to make the already effective phonics method even better. One outstanding project was the *initial teaching alphabet (i.t.a.)*, which was tested in one of the largest and most scientific of all educational research programmes ever, and proved exceptionally successful, producing fluent readers in a very short time, with positive knock-on effects in other aspects of education.

Irregularities in English spelling are no reason for jettisoning the successful phonics method but they can be something of an obstacle in learning to read. To obviate this, Sir James Pitman, in 1959, proposed a simplified alphabet. He knew that there would be entrenched opposition to any fundamental tampering with established spelling, so he stressed that his system was for use during the learning period only and would give place to the standard alphabet once the initial skill had been acquired. To make this reassurance doubly sure, he called his system the *initial teaching alphabet.* It equated one written symbol with one sound, i.e. 44 letter symbols for 44 of the sounds in the English language (Fig. 4.1). The eighteen new letters were carefully devised to make the subsequent transition to traditional orthography (t.o.) as easy as possible.

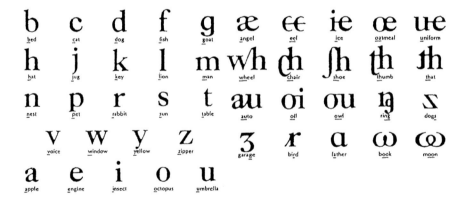

Fig. 4.1. The initial teaching alphabet.

Some of the extra symbols were consonants made to resemble the digraphs that would replace them after the transition, e.g. "ch", "sh", "th", "wh" and "ng". Long vowels, which are frequently spelt by adding "e" to the end of the syllable, were formed by adding "e" immediately after the corresponding short vowels. Thus, long "a", as in "plain", "play" and "plate", was always spelt as "ae" with the two letters combined into a single symbol. "C" and "k" were both retained to avoid creating an unnecessary difference from t.o., and capital letters were left until after the transition, which is why the name "i.t.a." was always in lower-case letters.

The launching of "i.t.a." was very thorough and 73 Directors of Education offered support at a 1960 press conference. A major experiment was set up under the impartial leadership of John Downing of London University's Institute of Education, with impeccable sponsorship including the Education Minister, and an expert committee was formed to ensure the rectitude of the meticulous large-scale observations needed for conclusive results.

The i.t.a. Foundation was established to convince people of the system's merits by pub-lishing information and materials, and setting up teachers' workshops and a panel of experienced speakers. A parallel organisation, the i.t.a. Federation, was more directly concerned with classroom practices.

The Downing research began with controlled experiments to compare the progress of children learning through i.t.a. and through t.o. The two groups were chosen from termly intakes over the period 1961-1964 and there was careful matching for age, sex, socio-economic class and intelligence. No child had received any pre-school instruction; all were starting from scratch. Both groups used the same *Janet and John* readers.

The i.t.a. learners progressed significantly faster. After one year 20.6% had reached at least Book IV, compared with 3.3% of the t.o. group, and this lead was sustained. After seven terms, 78.1% of i.t.a. children had passed beyond Book V, the proficiency milestone that ensured reading ability for life, but only 37.8% of the t.o. pupils had reached that level. Some 45% of the latter were still on Books I, II or III, which meant that they were likely to remain backward readers, or even non-readers, permanently, whereas the figure for i.t.a. was much lower at 15.1%. This important finding revealed that two-thirds of pupils left illiterate or semi-literate could have escaped that fate if they had been taught by i.t.a.

However, the 15.1% where i.t.a. failed requires an explanation, as it is far worse than the 1% illiteracy rate established by the 1931 Hadow Report, and also worse than the 10% found backward after World War I. Hindsight reveals an unfortunate reason.

Downing's research did not gather information on whether teachers were using phonics, whole word or mixed methods. The i.t.a. was regarded as a *medium of instruction,* not a method, and could be used with either or both of the phonics and whole-word approaches. Later it emerged that i.t.a. had improved both methods but when used with the whole-word system it was less effective in absolute terms than with phonics. The 15.1% were being held back by the whole-word component and not by i.t.a.

The i.t.a. learners performed twice as well on reading isolated words with no contextual clues. They were less dependent on guessing and generally used the word-building strategies associated with phonics. After seven terms they were 6.6% better than the t.o. group for reading speed, 43.8% better for comprehension and 81.2% better for accuracy. In fact, they were simply much better readers, although it seems that many of those who had been subjected to the whole-word method had been able use the straightforward logic of the i.t.a. alphabet to perceive the phonic principle that they were not being taught.

The chief early doubt about i.t.a. concerned the possible difficulty of transition to t.o. However, Downing found that there was only a slight temporary setback, soon more than made up. Many teachers reported that the change was normally smooth, effortless and hardly noticed by the children. This applied even to the least able, who needed to make the change rather later.

In spelling, the i.t.a. group was 12.2% better in the first year and 21.0% better in the fourth. Those classed as low achievers showed little or no spelling superiority at first, because they were tested in t.o. while still on i.t.a. but they pulled ahead after the transition. Madeleine A. Piers found that their advantage was well maintained at the secondary school stage and it seemed that, because their first learning experience was logical and consistent, they noticed and remembered the oddities of irregular spelling.

Even before the first research results, i.t.a. schools noted such impressive gains in reading and writing that many more i.t.a. classes were formed. Two years after the launch, 8,800 children were learning, or had learned, in this medium and demand was outstripping the supply of books and materials. In Oldham, i.t.a.'s greater ease of learning led to its use for four-year-olds and it became a remedial tool at all ages, reinforcing the general conclusion that its use with phonics from scratch would make most or all remedial work unnecessary. At its peak it was used in 10% of British primary schools and spread overseas to other English-speaking countries, as well as for beginners in English as a foreign language.

The overall evidence of success may be supplemented by the experience of an individual teacher. Sue Lloyd's school in Lowestoft used i.t.a. as a medium in conjunction with look-say and achieved only a mediocre score but then she introduced a little phonics and found that the score increased. This led her to add more phonics gradually, year by year, until her class's average reading quotient stabilised at 8 to 14 points higher, depending on the children's ability. Others schools adopted phonics with i.t.a. more quickly and eventually achieved marked improvements in reading ability within a single year. Not surprisingly, i.t.a. teachers became great devotees of the Pitman alphabet.

Yet this superbly researched and successful medium fell victim to the unresearched and unsuccessful t.o. whole-word method! Something very strange was going on.

The Downwave 2: The Cover-Up Period

In the mid-sixties the march of the whole-word method overtook the improvements that had masked it and the average itself began to decline. This has led many people to believe that the decline did not begin until then but in reality it stemmed from increasing reading failure from 1945 on, as the whole-word approach was progressively becoming dominant.

Why did that dominance take two decades to develop? At the end of World War II, phonics teachers filled the whole professional range of 45 years from certification at age 20 to retirement at age 65. It was expected that about half would have retired by 1967-68. However, the number of new teachers was increased to cater for the post-war baby boom and also for two pledges in the 1944 Education Act: raising the leaving age to 15 and reducing class sizes. So traditionalists were outnumbered a few years earlier than expected.

There continued to be many researches into the growth of illiteracy and these have been detailed by Bonnie Macmillan in her 1997 book, *Why Schoolchildren Can't Read*. We shall mention only a few, to give the flavour of the facts that were consistently ignored by those who could have taken constructive action.

In 1965, nationwide testing of seven-year-olds was conducted by the National Child Development Study (NCDS), as part of a lifelong observation programme of 11,000 children born in the first week of March, 1958. Although they had completed infant school, 37% still needed infant-style help with reading and 10% had barely embarked upon acquiring the skill. The lowest social class had 48% poor readers — an excuse for teachers to believe that this group was unteachable.

Two West Midlands studies of seven-year-olds, in 1961 and 1967 respectively, showed that 25% of the first group had not even started to read — a bad enough figure but vastly outdistanced by 40% in the second group, six years later. The rapidly continuing decline is consistent with the advent of progressively more teachers in the younger age group that had been trained to use the ineffective look-say method.

The Inner London Education Authority (ILEA) tested 26,200 children at age eight in 1968 and again at age eleven in 1971. The first results were seized upon to blame social class rather than poor teaching, as 17.7% of children with semi-skilled fathers were poor readers as compared with 25.9% of those with unskilled fathers. However, class can hardly be blamed for the fact that more of these same children (22.0% and 28.0% respectively) had become poor readers three years later. The schools themselves must be held responsible for three years of education that had actually made these children more backward.

G.E. Bookbinder in Aberdeen conducted a test of 2500 eight and eleven-year-olds in both 1962 and 1972. Possibly the first set aged eleven had been less subject to look-say, but ten years later, this was less likely and standards had fallen. Those with professional and managerial fathers had escaped the decline but the children of the unskilled and semi-skilled showed a marked overall deterioration. This reinforced the trend towards blaming the home for backwardness. No thought was given to the possibility that the more educated parents may have been supplying the phonics understanding that the schools were withholding, whereas decline among the other social classes was all the schools' own work.

In a 1970 NFER book, *The Roots of Reading,* B. Cane and J. Smithers commented on twelve disadvantaged localities designated as "educational priority areas". They found that classes which were more formally organised and had phonics teaching, had higher reading standards than those in permissive schools where teachers opposed phonics and waited for reading readiness to occur. This made it clear that social class was not the main factor.

NFER tested further samples in 1970 and 1971, and found that the percentage of illiterates and semi-literates had increased from 32.5 to 35.8. By then there were some 19,000 children in Educationally Sub-Normal Schools (later termed Special Schools) and, if those had been included, the figures would have been worse.

Another 1971 study picked out four educational priority areas and found that, even excluding immigrant families, between 17.5% and 35.8% were actual or virtual non-readers. The next year A. H. Halsey said that reading standards were poor throughout. Yet despite the mounting evidence, the Progressivist camp still closed its eyes to the existence of deterioration, although one of its leaders, Vera Southgate did go as far as admitting that there had been a "declining interest" in reading in infant classes.

The year 1972 was full of potential. NFER published a report, *The Trends of Reading Standards,* which attracted the attention of the Education Minister, Margaret Thatcher. Determined to tackle the problem, she set up a Committee of Inquiry into the teaching of reading, chaired by Alan Bullock. Unfortunately, the Bullock Committee was beguiled by Progressivists and while professing an open mind and paying lip-service to phonics, also contrived to ridicule it and support the dominant whole-word stance. Its Report did nothing to improve reading. Quite the reverse. In 1987 the Adult Literacy and Basic Skills Unit (ALBSU) tested 23-year-olds who had been pre-Bullock infants and found an adult illiteracy rate of 10% but when, in 1990 it tested 16 to 20-year-olds who had been post-Bullock infants, it found the rate had jumped to 25%, with a further 10%, probably the semi-literates, who had a serious spelling problem.

Bullock's conclusions were disastrously mistaken but his report did not appear until 1975, after a change of government, so Margaret Thatcher's keen mind was not brought to bear on it officially and there was no criticism from her Labour successor. Bullock, despite a note of dissent by Stuart Froome, proved more influential than the research evidence and the cover-up continued.

While Bullock was deliberating, there was growing concern about the galloping increase in the number of illiterates who had passed out of the school system and into the adult population. In 1973 D. Moyle estimated that there were as many as one million and in 1975 the precursor of ALBSU was set up to rescue them through well publicised evening classes. It has been largely unsuccessful, because it has favoured the same ineffective look-say, whole-word technique that had already misfired with children. Its own statistics indicate that after it had been operating for twelve years, the number of adult illiterates had increased to six million, and after 22 years, to nine million.

Standards and Statistics

All the foregoing evidence, and much more, pointed in the same direction of decline. No post-war result was anywhere near the low 1% illiteracy rate of the 1930s and the overall picture was an increasing failure to equip children with one of the most essential skills needed in modern life. The term "explosion of illiteracy" is no exaggeration.

Reading attainment can be expressed as *reading age* (RA) but this varies in significance according to the child's actual *chronological age* (CA). Thus RA8 denotes average reading ability in an eight-year-old, advanced reading in a seven-year-old and sadly backward reading in a ten-year-old. The RA suffices for class records where each child's CA is known but not for wider comparisons. To allow for CAs and simplify comparisons, the concept of a *reading quotient (RQ)* was devised. Reading age is divided by chronological age and multiplied by 100 to give percentiles, on the same principle as the IQ. The formula is:

$$\frac{RA}{CA} \times 100 = RQ$$

The average child's RQ works out at 100; higher figures denote above-average reading and lower ones indicate lagging behind. Those who progress at a constant rate keep the same RQ over time, as their reading age increases proportionally to their chronological age, while those who benefit from remedial teaching show an upward jump in their RQs.

Average RQs (ARQs) can be calculated for whole classes, schools and local education authorities. Any rise or fall in ARQ figures reflects improvement or decline, so this statistic can assess the achievement of teachers and institutions. If traced over time for the same class it can show whether teachers or methods are helping children to catch up or condemning them to lag still further. ARQs could have settled the question of decline right from the start of the downwave before large-scale damage had set in and as long ago as 1980 Mona McNee was urging that this neglected statistic should be used countrywide.

However, the idea fell on stony ground and its rejection was more sinister than just a refusal to listen. Progressivists did not believe in testing and could shut their minds to it but they must have known that standardised tests would not blinker everyone else, so they re-interpreted the tests in ways that avoided giving results that were comparable over time.

Initially, RQ 85 or below meant backwardness, but as the whole-word method spread, backward readers multiplied. It would have been logical to admit that the look-say method was flawed and revert to phonics but whole-word bureaucrats were so addicted to Progressivist ideology that they adopted cover-up ploys. They moved the goalposts.

The first ploy came in 1950 when the Labour Minister of Education redefined the backwardness threshold as 80 instead of 85. Children with RQs of 81 to 85 were just as backward as before but were henceforth classed as normal, so teachers were no longer concerned about them. This was no small deception. Five points may not sound much but it reclassified as normal some two-thirds of pupils who were previously deemed backward. Those who had gained only eight or nine months RA in 24 months at school were no longer thought to have a problem. This made the figures look good but did not help children learn to read.

If backwardness had not increased, this change of definition would have conveyed a huge but spurious improvement but as it *had* increased, the redefinition merely disguised the decline, suggesting that there had been little deterioration and shielding the establishment from blame. The effect of the change was not explained to the public, and young teachers, too, were deceived. Without the experience to realise that unprecedented numbers were having serious reading problems, they were launched into the routine response of "Don't worry; he'll catch on", a delay that made remediation harder.

Another displaced goalpost was the ARQ average. The average child's standard had been 100 but the 1970s decline meant that the average had fallen to 97. This should have been a further danger signal justifying the abandonment of the whole-word method, but again a cover-up ploy was adopted. The new mean of 97 was re-rated as 100, giving an impression of no change. The alteration sabotaged the possibility of any true comparison of standards over time and the decline continued to be masked.

This adjustment affected more than just the average; it had an automatic knock-on effect throughout the whole range of ratings. Every score had a correspondingly debased significance. Thus, what had been below-average scores of 97.1 to 99.9 were now pronounced above average, while the backwardness threshold of RQ 80 was a step worse than it had been and much worse than the original threshold of RQ 85. This debasement further distorted teachers' capacity for recognising poor progress and seeking remedial action.

The situation was further confused by the existence of many different tests, each with its own average. In 1979, Her Majesty's Inspectors found no fewer than 35. New tests and new averages for old ones had multiplied out of step with each other and become thoroughly out of joint, both over time and across local authority boundaries. They created a baffling jigsaw puzzle that was too difficult to fit together, and there was probably a temptation for officials to select those tests that made their local results look better.

The distortion produced by diverse averages can be illustrated by a 1979 NFER reading test devised with the publishers, Nelson, and applied for separate use in England and Scotland. The Scots were more averse to the whole-word method than the English but instead of letting the difference show, NFER calibrated the tests independently for each country. Thus, if a young Scot and a young Englishman aged between 7 years 9 months and 8 years 2 months both returned 40 correct answers, Jock was rated at RQ 92 and Johnny at RQ 95. For RQ 70, Johnny needed only six or seven correct answers to be considered equal to Jock with twelve or thirteen correct. This is sheer nonsense and shows how seriously test results can be made to mislead. Other test defects will be explained in Chapter 17.

Some authorities left everyone in the dark by not testing at all and some tested but kept the results secret. Even those which published them cited only a single ARQ, which did not give the information about individual schools needed by parents. Inspectors' reports on schools withheld specific ARQs and gave only subjective opinions of above or below average. And as the downwave average might equal upwave backwardness, their comments had little value.

For example, Addingham School, Bradford, was rated above average in 1986 and *The Times* reported this as "Ten out of ten". The teachers celebrated with wine; the children had buns. But the inspectors' report gave no clue as to the actual reading standard and as the school would not release the figure, one suspects it was not outstanding. If it was under ARQ 110 it would have been greatly surpassed by other schools, and if only ARQ 102 or 103, it would have been a state of near backwardness.

A run of Norfolk figures illustrates the comparability problem. In 1976, the county ARQ was 99.3 and six years of attempts to improve it saw only a modest rise to 103.3, still near-backwardness, falling to 102.9 in 1983. There were no results for individual schools, so the cause of this small rise is unknown. If it reflected better results in just a few schools adopting the phonic method, it could have supported a truly constructive strategy. But perhaps because of Mona McNee's probing, the county changed the test. In 1989 she was told the average was 100.85, based on a sample only. There was no recognition of declining standards.

For all these reasons the percentiles and ARQs obtained during the downwave, and particularly during its cover-up period, substantially underestimated the seriousness of the situation. However, ALBSU highlighted the blinkers imposed by the doctored scales in a 1980 study, which showed that 36% of 14-year-olds did not read any books. The figure for boys was higher at 40% but even among girls, nearly one-third were also illiterate or semi-literate to an extent that put books beyond their intellectual reach. This was a severe indictment of the value of their schooling and confirmed that the damage inflicted in the infant school stood little chance of later repair. What humiliation and misery all those years of compulsory school attendance must have meted out to failed readers!

Even worse was the illiteracy rate among young adults, half of whom had not read a single book during the preceding year. It seemed that many pupils classed as satisfactory while still at school had gained only such a tenuous grip on reading that they subsequently lapsed into virtual illiteracy. Our huge and costly school system was actually failing 50%.

ARQ measurement has been abused but with proper safeguards (see Part IV) it could be an excellent way to keep checks on reading standards. The following examples show how well it charts the benefits accruing with a change from whole word to phonics teaching.

Woods Loke School in Lowestoft had an ARQ of 102, the same as Suffolk as a whole, but as it gradually adopted phonics it steadily raised its standard and thereafter remained in the 110-116 range. Church Voluntary-Aided School near Accrington benefited from the Woods Loke example and raised its ARQ from 102 to 115 in only three years. Holland House School, Edgware, raised the ARQ of its very first phonics intake to 123 after two infant years and its second cohort profited even more rapidly, reaching 135 in just a single year. Specific ARQs like these are far more meaningful than inspectors' vague opinions.

ARQ figures were usually divided into four bands, "good", "mediocre", "poor" and "bad", with boundaries at 110, 90 and 75, though the slippage in standards meant that each band was over-rated. Table 4.2 gives figures for the early 1980s, showing percentages of children in each band for the whole country (despite inconsistent tests) and for Norfolk, seemingly above average. But both compare very unfavourably with those in the next three columns, for the three phonics schools mentioned above. Those were in no way favoured by local circumstances and all had had undistinguished records earlier, when using look-say. They had not changed staff or catchment areas but only their method of teaching reading and it was as a result of introducing phonics that they soared into the upper bands.

Table 4.2: Percentages of Seven-Year-Olds in Each ARQ Band

Band	National	Norfolk	Phonic Schools		
Good (110 and over)	26.4	33.3	73.0	82.0	75.0
Mediocre (90-109)	49.4	49.6	24.0	18.0	20.0
Poor (75-90)	19.8	15.2	3.0	—	5.0
Bad (74 and under)	4.4	1.9	—	—	—

The poor and bad figures show that schools were failing one child in four nationally, and one in six in "above-average" Norfolk. The three phonics schools were failing none, as the few "poor" children were recent transfers from whole-word schools, still catching up.

The nation and Norfolk were allowing half their pupils to fall into the mediocre class and many of these must have subsequently become part of the 50% unable to read books. Only one quarter and one third of the nation and county, respectively, were deemed good. This was massive under-achievement. The phonic schools had three-quarters of their well-taught pupils ranked as good and this impressive figure would have been possible in all schools if phonics had become the normal practice. Fluent reading would have been achieved by virtually all children by age seven and the downwave would have been reversed. However, those who tried to reverse it were almost always comprehensively baulked by the Progressivist higher echelons of the state educational system.

Real Books

The 1980s brought winds of change in thinking about education and more people acknowledged the fact of declining standards. It became clear that Progressivism had had a good run for the taxpayers' money and had been found wanting. In other fields of national life, also, there was radical reappraisal and there it was not restricted to mere opinion but accompanied by action. Nationalised industries were privatised; the undemocratic power of the trades unions was cut down; and council flats were less high-rise. There was a real hope for a remedy to attack education's feet of clay.

Ideas were not wanting but instead of resorting to the successful methods of traditional teaching, the local authorities allowed themselves to be beguiled by untested innovations. Phonics was still dismissed as "old hat" and its value was brushed aside. The Progressivist activists were still looked to as the "experts", and they introduced an even greater non-phonic extreme — *real books*.

The real books concept had been introduced in North America by the theorist, Frank Smith, who seems never to have taught a child to read, and also by Kenneth and Yetta Goodman, who were against *any* form of reading instruction. They preached the value of parents reading to children in a cosy way that involved them in the *apprenticeship* of "pretend reading" and supposedly gave them the experience of what it was like to be a reader. This, it was argued, would let them soak up ability to read for themselves by a process of *osmosis*. It was also described as *emergent reading* and its chief value was said to be that it did not need a graded vocabulary or the boring repetition of sight words to accustom children to their shape. Instead, it could be used with books of any degree of difficulty, provided that the children could enjoy them. Alternative terms were the *storybook* method or *holistic* method.

Henrietta Dombey of Brighton Polytechnic claimed to have brought the real books approach to Britain in 1982 but it really took off in 1985 with Liz Waterland's *Read With Me*. Previously there had been sight recognition of repeated whole words, stretching to repeated whole short sentences and also whole short story books, which non-readers appeared to read fluently even if holding them upside down. But real books discarded the dullness of repetition in favour of interesting, non-repetitive material, which deprived children of even a small sight-word vocabulary. Liz Waterland plunged even deeper into the dogma that reading must be caught, not taught.

Her own pupils could cope with real books but she omitted to mention that they had learned their letters at age three and four in nursery school and were thus equipped with the phonic knowledge that could facilitate mastery of real books. For those who lacked any such foundation, the real books method was a disaster.

The real-books concept was pure fallacy. It did *not* help children to read but triggered a sudden worsening of the already appalling non-reader rate. Only teachers who had been brainwashed into accepting a high non-reader rate from look-say could have entertained its nonsensical thesis for one moment, let alone flock to Frank Smith's regal lecture tours. Probably the high incidence of failure had pre-disposed them to believe that anything new could hardly be worse and might well be better. But it was indeed worse and from 1985 led to an even steeper rise in illiteracy wherever it was used.

The Raglan School in the London Borough of Bromley adopted the real-books method when its teachers were indoctrinated by Jeff Hynds in an in-service course at Thames Polytechnic, now the University of Greenwich. By 1987 the school's reading attainment had fallen so low that parents were alarmed and signed a petition protesting against it. An inspection was promptly ordered and revealed abysmal standards. One third of infant leavers were as much as two years behind, which meant that they had not really started learning to read at all. Councillors were dismayed that their professional teachers had not detected the decline before the parents and demanded an early return to basic skills. They also banned any further Thames in-service courses for the Borough's primary schools and although Jeff Hynds blustered that this was misguided, he subsequently left the institution.

As Bromley was shaking off the shackles of real books, Croydon was introducing it. After three years the number of children needing remedial treatment had soared and Martin Turner, an educational psychologist, wrote a frank report: *Croydon Assessment of Reading at Age Seven*. The Borough's 1985 record had been bad enough but by 1990 there were 29 of its 70 schools with an illiteracy rate of worse than 30%. Table 4.3 gives a few examples. One school halved its illiteracy rate by changing to phonics and that led Turner to join the ranks of phonics advocates.

Table 4.3: Illiteracy Percentages in Selected Croydon Schools

Schools Changing to Real Books	Before	After
A	15	48
B	19	30
C	21	63
D	22	44

Martin Turner collected results from nine other authorities, and eight of them reported a rapid decline in standards after adopting the real-books method. His report, *Sponsored Reading Failure*, showed how the education system itself was responsible for crippling so many children's mental development.

John MacGregor, the Secretary of State for Education, asked NFER to ascertain how far the decline had spread nationally and the 116 local education authorities were approached for information. Of these, 21 did not even bother to respond and 36 replied that that they had not tested any seven-year-olds during the preceding decade. Roughly half had conducted tests but over a quarter had no results capable of answering the question. Only 26 authorities could give a proper answer and 19 of these (73%) reported a decline.

These 19 were brushed aside by whole-word and real-books supporters as being only an unrepresentative 17% of all local authorities, which implied that every one of those keeping no check had not suffered a decline. That assumption was soon disproved when John Clare, education correspondent of the *Daily Telegraph,* identified 30 authorities with falling standards. The emerging picture was one of widespread ongoing decline.

Education authorities are not always the most objective source of information. Tower Hamlets glowingly commended its Culloden Primary School for an equally glowing series of BBC programmes, yet its reading standards were abysmal. Once they were unmasked, they were attributed to the children's low intelligence, but Martin Turner subsequently proved that their IQs were somewhat above average, despite being in a deprived inner-city area. It was bad teaching that was at fault. Liz Lightfoot, then the education correspondent of *The Mail on Sunday,* followed up with incisive articles and the next Secretary of State for Education, Kenneth Clarke, ordered an inspection, which produced a highly critical report. Ironically, many of the practices that the report condemned had actually been recommended in recent Inspectors' publications.

While reading standards were slipping so disastrously in many state schools, private schools retained a strong incentive to adhere to the successful phonic method, and their achievement attracted more parents to afford their fees. The independents' 5.8% of the child population had risen to 7.3% by 1989 and showed the direction in which public confidence was tending to go.

A 1991 Gallup Poll carried out for the *Daily Telegraph* revealed that nearly three-quarters of the population had by then come to believe that the quality of education had fallen. The 25% that still had faith in the state system was the lowest percentage of any European country. The figure for Denmark, Finland and Switzerland was 77%.

All the evidence pointed to a catastrophic growth in reading failure that progressively worsened over the decades from 1945. Why, during all that time, did it escape the attention of our educational watchdogs and become so rampant? Part II of this book will show that it was the watchdogs themselves that were engineering the decline.

PART II

THE WATCHDOGS THAT FAILED

Chapter Five

Watchdogs Galore

From time to time it is suggested that our rickety education system needs a watchdog to guard the nation's interests. One idea is for an ombudsman who would investigate complaints and see justice done but this seems to embody a fatal flaw. An ombudsman cannot take action until after the damage has taken place and the real need is for a preventive mechanism that ensures children are not harmed in the first place.

The recurrent call for a watchdog implies that education has never had one. That is quite untrue. Watchdogs accumulated, tier upon tier, and worked reasonably well during the upwave period. During the downwave, however, they were seduced into Progressivism with its deluded prescription of look-say, while the new watchdogs instituted during that period were Progressivist from the start.

The first educational watchdogs were the teachers, charged with expanding the spread of literacy. Their number constantly multiplied, with the 1870 Education Act introducing compulsory schooling in 1880, the raising of the school-leaving age to 14 in 1918, 15 in 1944, and 16 in 1972, the enlargement of sixth forms, the reduction of class sizes, the appointment of remedial staff, the expansion of further and higher education and the advent of adult literacy classes. By the 1980s there were 457,000 school teachers, including heads, in state schools alone, and such a formidable workforce *ought* to have been capable of keeping illiteracy at bay.

Head teachers were second-tier watchdogs. Initially they taught the children and also supervised apprentices: pupil teachers aged 13 to 18. These would subsequently become assistant teachers and the most promising went for two years of college training to obtain a certificate qualifying them to train other pupil teachers.

The teacher-training colleges were a further tier, which expanded to train all teachers and then, in the name of better standards, lengthened their courses from two years to three in 1973, with an increasing proportion of students staying on for a fourth year.

Watching the school watchdogs from 1839 was Her Majesty's Inspectorate (HMI). Its members were not then drawn from the teaching profession but were other educated and widely respected men of integrity, such as ministers of religion, whose reports, letters to the press, articles and speeches drew attention to further educational needs. Their role was to test pupils and assess each school's attainment level which, during the period of payment by results (1862–1897), determined the level of grants. The downwave saw the addition of a large number of local education authority inspectors, styled advisers.

The 116 local education authorities (LEAs) consisted of officers controlling many aspects of funding and were also the paymasters of auxiliary watchdogs such as advisers and psychologists. In turn, they themselves were supposedly watched by elected councillors on education committees, although the latter tended to regard the officers as the experts.

Schools were also supervised by Boards of Governors including local councillors. These became highly politicised as councillors became increasingly aligned with the national parties but this was eventually considered to have gone too far and council representation was reduced in favour of more parent governors.

Central government also oversaw education through a Privy Council committee controlling HMIs. It was upgraded as the Board of Education in 1899, Ministry of Education in 1944 and Department of Education and Science in 1979. Then, since poor schooling was failing employers, it merged with the Employment Department in 1997 as the Department for Education and Employment, and in 2001 became the Department for Education and Skills.   Governments have also created prestige watchdogs in the form of Committees of Enquiry and Select Committees to consider specific aspects of education. These had to report and wind themselves up but some recommended permanent quangos to succeed them, as yet another watchdog tier with a wide range of functions, some of them cluttering up education with counterproductive activities.

The driving force behind some of these watchdog tiers was a number of charismatic and ambitious Progressivist gurus, whose writ seemed to run the breathless path of sacred doctrine. Their influence has been immense and teachers grappling with the problems of Progressivism have naturally turned to them for reassurance on existing methods and insight into new ones, all unaware that these people were themselves the architects of the problems. The gurus, who usually commanded the eminence of a training college or university post, self-confidently carried all before them, and the last thing they wanted was to risk evidence of failure by tests of what their dogmas had achieved in practice. Their own self-importance seemed to have a higher priority than a realistic appreciation of children's educational welfare, although lip service to the latter has been a key theme attracting their disciples.

The Progressivist orthodoxy spread its influence to the publishing houses, which responded by boycotting phonics-based reading schemes as well as books giving credence to traditional realities. This became necessary for their commercial survival as they had to produce what the schools wanted to buy. Even the press, with all its pride in being an independent watchdog, became infected with the same reluctance to give space to any departures from the all-pervading Progressivist convention, and this was particularly true of educational journals or supplements. Letters to the editor were systematically ignored if they did not adhere to the Progressivist line. Broadcasting fell under the same spell. The BBC team that spent nearly a year filming the wonders of Progressivist education at Culloden Primary School in East London produced six programmes that completely concealed the appalling rate of illiteracy there.

The voluntary sector also had its institutions, such as teachers' unions and learned societies, which reflected and supported the prevailing educational fashions. Other bodies, originally for other purposes, were taken over by Progressivist zealots. However, some kept alive the small flame of phonic realism.

Teachers, heads, training institutions with their gurus, LEAs, civil servants, ministers, official committees, quangos, publishers, the media, and voluntary bodies, all seemed to have become tarred with the same Progressivist brush. Independent voices were ignored to the point of suppression. How could this happen in what claims to be a free country? This will be explored by looking at each tier of watchdogs in turn.

The 1988 Education Act sprang from an eventual realisation that all was not well with British education and the remedy was seen as a National Curriculum that would facilitate systematic tests. This was accompanied by new watchdogs to oversee standards and testing. With the coming of the Labour government in 1997 there was a call for yet another watchdog in the form of a General Teaching Council after the model of the General Medical Council, which is empowered to strike doctors off the register if they are guilty of incompetence or other professional misconduct. The GMC strikes off about a dozen doctors each year and we wonder how a General Teaching Council would cope with the 15,000 teachers who were declared incompetent by the Chief Inspector in 1993.

Another problem is that the most likely candidates for appointment to such a Council would be the currently influential "experts" of Progressivist persuasion. Its establishment would simply be another coup for Progressivism, helping to keep the education system in bondage for a further period.

Part II addresses the conditions of the cover-up period of the downwave before the recognition of low standards had progressed far enough to result in the 1988 Education Act and the struggle for reform. That phase is reserved for Part III.

Chapter Six

Teachers

The whole structure of education rests upon the teachers and their prime task is to teach children to read. If they fail to do so, their pupils are so mentally maimed that they can hardly benefit from the remainder of their school life and are robbed of potential for self-education in adulthood. Such teachers are surely to be blamed, yet we must remember that they, too, are victims of the Progressivist dogma. Mona McNee likes to say, "We love the teachers but we hate the teaching."

Modern primary school teachers have a hard row to hoe. They have been trained to reject the quick, straightforward and successful phonic method and struggle with the long-drawn-out and problem-ridden complexities of the whole-word technique. They have been brainwashed into relinquishing a calm, orderly classroom in favour of having individuals and groups milling around in a multitude of activities. They are burdened with repeating every stage of activity as different children become ripe for it at different times, and they are forbidden the economy of effort to be gained from introducing work to the whole class together. They are expected not only to have eyes in the back of their heads but also multiple antennae sensitive enough to perceive what each child is doing at every moment and to slot all this information into the overall context of each one's progress and future needs. They also have to keep records of all this diversity.

Is it any wonder that teachers are under stress and that ways have had to be found of easing the burden? The tragedy is that the proposed easements have mostly exacerbated the harm done by Progressivism in the first place.

Smaller Classes

Class size has been massively reduced. Nineteenth-century classes of up to 80 gave way to up to 50 in the first half of the twentieth century. Alice Coleman's fellow students in the 1940s had classes of that size and she knew that her own school was fortunate in having only 39–40. The 1944 Education Act promised primary classes of 40 and secondary classes of 30, while the fall in the birth rate after 1975 prompted smaller classes rather than fewer teachers. Even when the number dropped to 20-25, there were still complaints that this was too many. Envious eyes were cast upon private schools, some with classes of 15-20, which was mistakenly considered the reason why they do better by their pupils than state schools.

The overall teacher-pupil ratio has continued to fall but there have also been more out-of-class roles such as careers advisers, field-centre staff and remedial teachers, so actual class size crept up a little. Primary classes of 30 came to be regarded as at danger level and at least one union recommended sending "excess children" home.

Smaller classes were still considered the royal road to improved standards by David Blunkett when he became the Secretary of State for education in 1997. He, like many others, would not believe the factual evidence proving that this idea is a myth.

First there is evidence over time. The second half of the twentieth century saw two parallel trends: falling class sizes and falling standards. This does not prove that smaller classes *caused* lower standards but it *does* prove that they did not prevent the decline and still less created the improvement still blindly claimed for them.

Secondly, there is evidence over space—a comparison of 61,000 primary-school classes across the country. Each local authority had to report what percentage of their primary and secondary classes exceeded the 30-child limit and these figures could be compared with test results. For the London Boroughs, there was a clear association between the two. The higher the percentage of classes exceeding 30, the higher the results and vice versa. The worst results came from authorities with very few "over-large" classes. A similar trend also applied at the secondary school level—further evidence that refuted the alleged link between small classes and high standards.

Indeed, there was such a clear reverse link that a causational element could be suspected. It seems probable that where there are more children in the classroom, Progressivist methods are intolerably burdensome and induce a return to whole-class teaching, which in turn sparks off the improvement that eludes small classes. It means rearranging desks to let all the children face the front instead of sitting round tables where half of them have their backs to the teacher.

The myth that small classes are beneficial needs to be discarded along with other unsubstantiated tenets of Progressivism. While it persists it will continue to do harm. When Blunkett, as Secretary of State for Education, decided that smaller classes should take precedence over parental choice of school, he was dictating that "excess" children excluded from good schools must join poorer ones with spare places. This widened the damage to educational standards.

Low Standards

Another response to Progressivist pressures was simply to accept low attainment as normal. This was not true of all teachers but as those trained in look-say came to dominate the school scene, the memory of better literacy levels was lost. High attainment had no place in the Progressivist creed of equality. Literacy, as the *product* of reading lessons, was not important; the emphasis was on making the *process* meaningful and fun. This did not appear to the indoctrinated teachers as the sacrifice of standards that it actually was.

Consequently the many slow readers or non-starters were regarded as nothing to worry about. Parents were assured that their children were "not yet ready to read" but would eventually "catch on". Many never did but the occasional sudden grasp of the few was enough to convince teachers that all might do so.

An example of "catching on" was provided by Alice Coleman's nephew, Eric, who was a confused non-reader at seven, although he was intelligent enough to know every country on a world map. Despite receiving remedial teaching, he was making no progress, probably because the remedial teacher was using the same ineffectual look-say that had failed him originally. However, his five-year-old sister was learning so rapidly with i.t.a. that his mother decided to teach him herself over the summer holiday. The result was dramatic. Eric promptly became a compulsive reader and high achiever, going on to a marine engineering degree and a successful career. The teacher probably thought he had "caught on" spontaneously but the real switch was the phonic method. A parent who had left school at the then normal age of 14, had accomplished in six weeks what teachers with seven or eight more extra school and college years had failed to achieve in two years.

Many teachers were at such a loss to explain to worried parents that they fell back on professional mystique. They had been so brainwashed by their training that they did not question their faith in the look-say dogma and believed that parents should not question it either. Geoffrey Saunders, the head of the infamous Culloden School, expressed this attitude by saying,

> The way we teach nowadays is very different from when many of the parents were at school. They often don't understand that their children are learning but in a more exciting and palatable way.

This explained nothing and reflected the general stance that it was all too complex to go into. The sensible response would be a challenge, "Well, explain it to me", but many parents felt too cowed to be assertive. Others found themselves having to do battle in defence of their children. "My daughter being taught look-say has a traumatic time. "Meaningful and fun?" Ha ha! Tears, tantrums and despair, night after night."

Homework

"Night after night" refers to homework. After a long period of demanding that the teaching of reading should be left to the professionals and kept free from parental interference, a new form of relief from pressure was discovered — exporting the work to the home. Parents were now *supposed* to be involved.

Infants had to take a small book home each night so that parents could help them practise reading. To equip them to give such help, they were introduced to the whole-word method, which constrained them to tell their children what the words were, over and over again. Slowly and painfully, rote learning was enforced, and when the child could parrot the whole story (sometimes with the book closed), the next book was produced and the whole miserable effort began all over again.

This process without the product of actual reading convinced many parents that learning to read really was difficult, which alleviated criticism of teachers. Others, and probably grandparents too, remembered their own phonic learning and proceeded to *teach* their children rather than just hopefully help them to catch on. Some decided that they could do better than the school and undertook responsibility for home education. Others engaged private tutors, either to supplement schooling or on a full-time basis in co-operation with other parents. Those who could, made considerable sacrifices to send their children to private schools. Such externalizations of reading from the state schools were highly beneficial to the pupils concerned but did nothing to help teachers understand the error of their ways.

Shifting the Blame to Parents

From recruiting parent help, it was only a small step to blaming parents for their children's illiteracy. In 1991 the National Association of Head Teachers (NAHT) said that *only* 5% of school starters could already read, while 80% were not even ready to begin. The General Secretary, David Hart, asserted that most children should learn to read *before* going to school. Had the Progressivist ideology totally divorced teachers from the basic concept of their role? The answer, in relation to reading, seemed to be an unfortunate "Yes".

Leaving aside the implication that untrained parents should impart the skill that defeats trained teachers, there is no doubt that some school-starters have been so neglected that they cannot respond easily, even to traditional teaching. Some parents do not talk to their babies and toddlers, and stuff dummies into their mouths to rob them of freedom to articulate. The nursery department of Havelock Primary School on Tyneside estimated that half its three-year-olds were retarded at the 18-month developmental stage, capable only of disjointed words and unaware of what books were.

By age five, they were like three or four-year-olds and some had not even made the full two years of natural growth expected for the intervening two years.

It was said that children with such backward communication lacked familiarity with the speech sounds needed to match the written letters if they were to crack the phonic code. This aspect went unnoticed by look-say teachers who had no truck with sounds or letters but they *were* concerned with the handicap imposed by a small vocabulary and restricted understanding. They blamed parents for being feckless and irresponsible, and let themselves off the hook by declaring that such children were not yet ready to read. Now children are entering reception classes at four, those who cannot speak properly are grossly disadvantaged from the start.

Failing parents were made the scapegoats for failing teachers but no-one seems to have asked how nine million parents left illiterate by their schools could possibly teach their children what they had not been taught themselves.

This prompts the question of who actually *did* teach children to read. One tranche, possibly 10%, was successfully taught in private schools, which resisted the whole-word method. The generally quoted figure for independent schooling was a little over 7% but many parents who could not afford fees throughout their children's school lives, nevertheless contrived to do so for the important first few years. Of the 90% attending state schools we had NAHT's 1991 figure of 5% of school starters already taught to read at home, and the ALBSU figure of 50% remaining totally or functionally illiterate. This left 45% of state pupils (or 40% of all pupils) who appeared to have been taught to read in state schools, but had they really?

We suspect that many children were rescued by family or friends, as with Mona McNee's son Tim and Alice Coleman's nephew Eric, or through private tutoring. Mona McNee alone has taught some 360 dyslexics to read but their parents tell her that teachers are so sensitive about having their competence questioned that they keep quiet about the tutoring for fear that their children may be marked out adversely at school. So teachers continue to believe that their own efforts have enabled the 45% to catch on and are rarely confronted with evidence of how others have succeeded where they themselves failed.

One parent who asked whether she should teach her child letter sounds or engage a private tutor, received a sharp answer from the teacher, "Definitely not! That will only confuse him." She was advised to give him a picture and let him write down his thoughts about it, but after a week he had made only zigzag scribbles. The teacher was delighted. "That's very good . . . That's the beginning of the process." Process, yes, but the product was still way out of sight and the mother's anxiety was unabated.

There were also some dedicated phonics teachers who kept the torch of successful reading alight, though perhaps only on a concealed, under-the-counter basis. But their number declined as Progressivist pressure increased. Some were treated very shabbily. One, for example, was sacked for unprofessional conduct. Her crime? She insisted on teaching children to read with phonics rather than holding them back in illiteracy by using the prescribed whole-word method.

Low Expectations

Blaming parents became habitual in many inner cities where comprehensive schooling was parallelled by comprehensive redevelopment in Modern-Movement blocks of flats, making it difficult for parents to keep tabs on their children or for neighbours to lend a hand. This led to anti-social behaviour, delinquency and crime. Utopian social engineering promised that these estates would enhance community life but they dismally did not. Instead, they destroyed the pre-existing neighbourly spirit and created the desolation of anonymity, as was scientifically established in Alice Coleman's book, *Utopia on Trial*.

Traditional housing provided role models and a code of behaviour that helped socialise children but in Modernist estates it all fell back on the nuclear family — often a single parent. Such pressures downgraded parental skills. Those who with proper neighbour support could have been outstanding were rarely more than just good. Good ones were reduced to being average, mediocre ones to being bad, and bad ones appalling.

Yes, parenting could be poor but officialdom was ultimately to blame. Tenants were the victims of misguided planning. Families who moved out to traditional residential areas soon found a spontaneous easing of their role. Similarly, tenants in nine estates where Alice Coleman was empowered to replace most of the harmful design features by harmless ones, also rapidly formed a natural community structure with a profound beneficial effect upon children's behaviour. One headmistress wrote to say that since the design of her catchment estate had been improved, the children were much calmer and easier to teach.

So teachers, like tenants, were victims of Modernist architecture and would also benefit from *the relevant type* of estate design improvement. The damage done by mistaken design is now proven in all continents except Antarctica, which has no Modernist buildings.

Traditional housing was unpopular with the planners who sponsored Modernist design guides in the same way that traditional phonics was rejected by educationists who had invested their prestige in the whole-word method. Both groups promulgated the idea that social class, poverty and unemployment were the cause of anti-social behaviour in the estates and reading inability in the classroom. This myth needs to be laid to rest.

Much socio-economic research is based on what is easy to investigate. Population Census data are easily transferred to computers for working in comfort at one's own desk. Not for these people the trudging round 50 km^2 of inner London that let Alice Coleman's team observe which designs attracted litter, graffiti and vandalism, etc. Their horizons are circumscribed by what is recorded in the Census and since the real causes are not recorded there, the findings do not cohere well and have given rise to the mystique of complexity.

This failure stems from a lack of what Edward de Bono termed "lateral thinking". His analogy is that if you dig for truth in the wrong place there is nothing to be gained by digging ever deeper. The need is to move to a different place where true insight may be waiting. Moving out from Census-digging to explore design proved fruitful lateral thinking, while persisting with derivatives of look-say is an unfruitful rejection of the phonics treasure-site.

The concept of socio-economic factors as causes is what Richard Dawkins calls a *meme,* i.e. an idea with a tenacious life of its own regardless of its accuracy. It a kind of mental gene, blindly reproducing itself. Unemployment is not the *cause* of poor learning but its *effect.* School leavers who are illiterate find their employment potential much reduced.

The socio-economic meme leads to grave social injustice. High unemployment and other problems in certain areas have given teachers low expectations of *all* the children there. It is believed that nothing much can be expected of them so the aim is to keep them amused rather than attempt the task of making them literate. The play-way rules supreme and the disadvantage of illiteracy is added to the pre-existing ones.

Social class has changed greatly since the early twentieth century. Poverty was much more intense; the minimal dole was not topped up by housing and heating benefit or supplementary income. And unemployment had few escape routes; fourteen-year-old school leavers had no option of staying on in education or joining youth schemes. So why were the children of those areas not unteachable? Why was Britain an educational world leader?

Alice Coleman can testify from personal experience that socio-economic factors were not associated with low educational achievement. Her working class father was unemployed in an area officially classed as "distressed" but the local schools were excellent. She remembers giving her first lesson at the age of seven, when, uniquely, her teacher was called to a staff meeting (possibly because the head had died). Told to preside over reading, she occupied the teacher's high chair and summoned successive groups out to the front to take turns in reading aloud. The only problem was that they were all so keen to read that they did not want to make way for the next group, and she had to learn, there and then, the art of teacher assertiveness. The groups were graded by ability in a class spanning two age-years, but even the youngest six-year-old could read. Teacher expectations were high and sustained by the phonics method.

During the downwave, there were still some inner-city schools that shone despite local conditions. Phonics and high expectations had a redemptive effect that defied the socio-economic meme. Stanley Craig of the Vicarage School in Newham, a poor area in London's East End, had many Asian pupils unversed in English, but his use of phonics led to such high standards that his school was rated among the 10% best in 1988. Similar successes occurred wherever inner-city teachers did not invite defeat by using look-say.

Remedial Teaching

Remedial teaching barely existed during the upwave, as backward children were not too retarded to attend ordinary schools. During the downwave, however, many pupils lagged beyond the help of look-say teachers and were labelled as educationally sub-normal (ESN). They were segregated into special ESN schools, like the 24 in Kent taking about 3% of the total school roll. Tim McNee attended one of these and was slotted among other low achievers from a wide area, so on leaving school he had no local friends, as he would have done in the days when effective methods would have allowed him to attend a local school.

Despite exporting their ESN children, ordinary schools still found the teaching of reading an uphill struggle and special remedial teachers were appointed to help the slow ones catch up, either individually or in small groups. But there never seemed enough staff to meet the ever-increasing need. The special schools and the remedial teachers in ordinary schools came to absorb more and more of the education budget. In Norfolk it was 10% of the county total and still rising when Mona McNee moved away. And despite all this expenditure there were still numerous pupils left illiterate at school-leaving age.

Why was the remedial effort so often ineffective? Simply because most remedial teachers were using the same counterproductive methods as most infant teachers. Some who used phonics, like Mona McNee, successfully rescued whole-word victims but their successes were overwhelmed by the tidal wave of new illiterates. How much better it would have been to give all infant teachers a short course in genuine phonics teaching, to let them *prevent* the problem rather than creating it and necessitating an expensive cure.

Discipline

From their birth, babies are learning. Waving their arms gives them a first under-standing of reach and distance. Touching and tasting inform them about softness and hardness, cold and warmth, wetness and dryness, sweetness and bitterness, etc. Listening helps them to discipline their babble into intelligible sounds. Crawling teaches them the practical effects of left and right, and how to support themselves with their arms. If they are denied any such natural stages they are left with damaging gaps in their knowledge.

In the 1980s many Japanese school starters were falling flat and sustaining facial injuries. This was traced to the use of baby walkers — harnesses in which they were hung up to exercise their legs and go straight into walking without preliminary crawling. The harnesses were useful space savers in small Japanese houses but they denied the babies experience of supporting themselves on all fours. At school they had space to run — and to fall — but did not know how to use their hands to break the impact, so they fell like logs.

Progressivists and traditionalists draw diametrically opposite lessons from early learning. The former see the crux as unfettered naturalness — process not product — and apply it as unfettered permissiveness. For traditionalists the moral is consistency — the product of the process. Children learn that the world is a consistent place. The cot is not snug and warm one night and prickly as a hedgehog the next. Without stable consistency, the world would be bewildering; one would never know what to expect or how to behave. So, too, with discipline. Children need rules, limits, regularity and routine, if they are not to become confused. In fact, this kind of disciplining is also natural; a baby is soon taught not to poke its mother's eyes.

Psychologists confirm that the healthiest influence is not the degree of permissiveness or strictness, but the degree of consistency. Even the earliest learning involves testing the limits and it carries over from the physical to the social environment. The more consistent the discipline, the more easily children learn the limits.

Over-permissiveness is now recognised as a form of neglect. Children need to be taught not to have all their own way and to exercise courtesy and consideration. Learning respect, deference and tact are part of one's education for getting along in life, and require explicit instruction as well as imitation of loving parents. Fortunate is the school where the children come from such homes and wise is the school that builds an orderly ethos on that foundation.

Some school starters come from homes where parents do not educate their higher nature by means of consistent discipline. It is difficult to do so in problem estates, where some pre-school children are completely unsocialised. It is many years since teachers first complained of five-year-olds attacking them with scissors and chairs. Nevertheless, it is hypocritical to grumble about parents passing their disciplinary problems to infant schools when these, in the name of child-centred freedom, do not tackle the problem themselves but pass it on the junior schools and thence to secondaries and in some cases to colleges, the police and the prisons. At each stage the children grow bigger and also more daring in the ways they test ill-defined limits. The parents start the rot but over-permissive schools do not stop it. They feed it and even initiate it; the parents see their children's behaviour deteriorating when they start school. Some teachers keep the peace temporarily by giving in to pupils' demands but that creates worse problems in the long run. And when those pupils become parents, the prospect for the next generation is exacerbated.

Years ago a polytechnic vice-principal emigrated to Australia after being attacked by a student with a knife. That was then an isolated incident but there has since been worse violence perpetrated by more children and at increasingly younger ages. Some teachers are so frayed by the constant battle for discipline in a sea of multifarious activities that they are even more willing to settle for the play way as a means of appeasement. They may argue that noise is evidence of a happy classroom with essential social interaction going on.

Apart from over-permissiveness, indiscipline may also stem from the look-say's failure to teach reading. Phonics-taught children enjoy considerable school satisfaction as they successively master letters, words and spelling rules, and come to read fluently. Reading becomes an enjoyable activity that occupies quite a lot of their leisure time and they also find uses for writing. Their mastery enhances their self-esteem, which continues to be gently boosted as the ability to read underpins the rest of their schooling.

By contrast, illiterates and semi-literates lack school satisfaction and feel humiliated by failure. They cannot read as a pastime and seek other activities, perhaps crafts or sports, or perhaps retaliation by needling teachers. They may exploit the child-led curriculum by pushing for more non-reading aspects, or test the limits with insolence, bad language and disobedience. They may bully classmates, attack teachers, play truant or tread the slippery slope from graffiti to vandalism to burglary, mugging and arson. Or, since sex lessons seem more comprehensible, they may experiment in that direction. Both children and staff have been sex victims.

It is not only non-coping extraverts who take refuge in crime. Although non-coping introverts are more likely to succumb to mental illness, a few may be so demoralised by ostracism that they are easily recruited by gangs that offer brotherhood in wrong-doing. One such boy murdered a school-fellow with a seventeen-inch knife at the instigation of a Triad gang that had assuaged his feelings of lonely insignificance.

Downwave reading failure reduced career options and led to criminal behaviour as a substitute. The British Dyslexia Association estimated that dyslexics are 14% of the population and other figures go up to 20%, but two studies of prisoners identified dyslexics as 45% and 52%. This is an unrepresentative concentration and non-dyslexic illiterates increase the percentage further. An American study found that over 80% of convicts were non-readers.

Clearly, illiteracy is an important factor leading to crime, which implies that teachers who failed to teach reading properly had a strong input into the escalating crime rate. Their faulty methods not only created poor readers but also funnelled many of them into jail. This may seem a harsh judgement but remedial action is simple. Conversion to phonics is a straightforward cure that could be applied immediately with the coming year's school intake, and also with remedial teaching for backward readers of every age.

Even worse for teachers in bad schools was a progressive erosion of disciplinary sanctions. From 1986 the cane was no longer available as a longstop to deter bad behaviour, and assaults by teachers were redefined to include even the lightest touch. As a result, problem children and their parents have been quick to sue and demand financial compensation. But how could teachers control rampaging children when they could not even hold them or put them out of the classroom?

The only remaining sanction was exclusion, either temporary suspension or permanent expulsion. The numbers of both ran up into four figures, with large annual increases. Yet even those drastic measures did not solve the situation, as on appeal some schools had to take back even the most violent pupils, regardless of the effect upon their child and staff victims.

New York has lessons for us. In 1957–58, some 600 unruly pupils were expelled because it was thought safer to let them roam the streets than remain in school to prey on other children. Social deterioration continued and the crime record became appalling. One year, 1000 of the murdered bodies in the city could not even be identified.

But then Professor James Wilson devised the idea of *zero tolerance*, applied by the police from 1993. They no longer gave priority to the most serious crimes while leaving lesser offences to escalate, but argued that if the latter were nipped in the bud, the future supply of serious offenders would be cut off at source. Within four years the crime rate had been reversed down to that of 30 years earlier. The murder rate was halved, robberies were 40% down and car-theft reduced by one-third. Major as well as minor offenders got the message. The problems were still immense but the improvement was unprecedented and ongoing, as also in other cities where zero tolerance was tried. Wilson said,

> The city was in a genuinely desperate condition. It had a million people on welfare. It had a school system that was close to collapse. It had a hospital system it couldn't sustain. It had a workforce it couldn't pay for. The streets were filthy; criminals were rampant . . . Well, that's all changed . . . the middle classes are moving back. It feels safer and smells cleaner.

If zero tolerance deters those already criminalised, how much more would it affect four-year-old school starters? If orderly traditional classrooms replaced disorderly Progressivist ones, and if school satisfaction created by phonics replaced all the dissatisfactions of illiteracy, then indiscipline would be nipped in a very much younger bud. During the upwave, serious crime in the UK was less than 3% of its present rate and better teaching could reduce it again. It would not fall right back until the Modernist estates were redesigned to facilitate better child-rearing but at least the large educational multiplier effect would be cut out.

Teacher Absence and Turnover

For all these reasons, teacher morale fell to a low ebb. Persistent stress without hope of alleviation wreaks havoc on body and mind, and illness can be a relief, justifying absence for even the most dedicated. Sick leave figures showed that stress illnesses were commoner among teachers than any other profession. One study identified the average annual loss per worker as six working days in industry, ten in the public sector and 14 in teaching. This actually underestimated the problem, as teachers also had the relief of longer holidays.

Rhodes Boyson, a former successful headmaster and Education Minister, said,

> In many schools all discipline has broken down. If you are a teacher down to teach 4C on a Friday afternoon and the class is out of control, you are not going to be there.

It is in such schools that the major part of teacher absence was concentrated and their sub-standard education was made worse by the resulting lack of teacher continuity. These were schools to escape from and few teachers remained there for long. A survey of 855 schools, including 688 primaries, was carried out by the six main teachers' unions and an increasing staff turnover was reported. In London the average primary school had fewer than one-third of its teachers surviving in post for as long as five years, and in some schools staff comings and goings meant that some children had three class teachers in the same year.

A quarter of London's primaries had at least one teacher short, as vacancies were difficult to fill. Schools were clutching at the chance of *any* staff, no matter how unsuitable, and 28% of heads said that they had a mismatch between staff members' teaching duties and their qualifications. They did not say that even some suitably qualified teachers were incompetent, though doubtless that was the case, as we shall see in Chapter 7.

Pamela Robinson and Alan Smithers of Manchester University studied over 18,000 staff leavers in 1988 (Table 6.1). Only 4.2% had reached retirement age and even that was 60, not 65. Although the biggest single group went to other UK teaching posts, it was outnumbered by those who did not. The second largest group, premature retirers, was over five times as numerous as those who persisted till 60.

Moreover, the escape trend was intensifying. In 1989 it was reported that the number leaving on health grounds had risen from 2551 to 4041 in just two years. In any case, after three or four years training at public expense, few teachers repaid the investment in them by making the classroom their lifelong career. Teaching had ceased to be a magnetic vocation for the majority and was frequently a repelling experience. Some emigrants, however, rediscovered professional satisfaction in overseas schools where Progressivism had not cast its blight.

Table 6.1: Staff Destinations (1989)

Destination	No. of Teachers	Percentage
Other UK teaching posts	8648	47.9
Early retirement/ill health	3948	21.9
Normal age retirement	752	4.2
Educational administration/ training	752	4.2
Other employment and training	1692	9.4
Gone abroad	564	3.1
Family reasons	564	3.1
Moving from the area	188	1.0
Other	940	5.2
Total	**18,948**	**100.0**

Recruitment Problems

Despite staff shortages over much of the downwave, it was always assumed that there would be enough capable people to meet the various educational expansions but this was not so. People are all different and the qualities that make a good teacher are not universal — no matter how much

Progressivist egalitarianism regards everyone as equal and interchangeable.

Apart from the black hole of vacancies, many teachers were not up to the job. Training colleges had to deliver as many as possible and issued certificates to all, regardless of suitability. Some students applied for reasons such as long holidays and job security or the respite of a four-year course to defer joblessness. Once in post, they ranged from excellent to hopeless, but it was almost impossible to dismiss incompetents.

Some were attracted to teaching for immoral reasons — the ugly question of child abuse. Some offenders have been charged but unfortunately there have also been false allegations by malicious trouble-makers.

Lack of Respect for the Teaching Profession

Teachers used to be held in high regard, both because they did their best to live as exemplars for society and also because they provided a good education and inculcated orderly behaviour. Many still do so but during the downwave increasing numbers did not, forfeiting respect for themselves and also creating contempt for the profession as a whole.

Progressivists believed that their ideology offered the best of all possible worlds and were convinced that their whole-word methodology was the super-highway to literacy. It was usually unwittingly and not deliberately that they brought about the erosion of professional status, yet in retrospect we perceive a chain of causation from theory to effect. The erosion began in small ways. For example, insistence on equality meant that the teacher should not be above the children either literally or metaphorically. The high chair and the dais that gave a raised view over the class were abolished in favour of having everyone democratically down on the same floor level. This erased the psychological advantage of having the class look up to the teacher. Later the equality was extended to having the children call the staff by their first names.

Many teachers retreated from the role-model concept in other ways. They became ill-kempt and scruffy in the name of informality but then blamed low salaries for the fact that many pupils were much better dressed. They stopped eating lunch with the pupils and robbed them of good table manners and cultured discussion; the noise level shot up. They coarsened their speech to avoid standard English and one was even reported as urging his class to shout out obscenities. Their behaviour became more lax and in one case children peered through a classroom window to watch two teachers engaging in sexual intercourse.

Teachers also alienated public regard by sending children home instead of absorbing them into larger classes and also by going on strike. The National Union of Teachers frankly struck for a pay rise, regardless of how they were victimising the children, but that offended many members' sense of professional responsibility and they transferred to other unions.

Children who were told that *they* determined the relevance of what was taught, or were humiliated by being left illiterate, or who developed through indiscipline into bullies or victims, or who endured years of boring ineptitude disguised as professional mystique, or who defied compulsory education by playing truant, all grew up into adults with a low opinion of teachers. Some then defended their own children with hostility or even violence towards school staff.

The situations described here were worst-case scenarios before 1988 but they were far from rare. Some or all of these conditions affected many schools. Teachers who continued to do a good job still commanded respect but the perception of teachers in general declined.

Two general comments are needed to conclude this chapter. The first is that, however unwittingly, teachers have robbed at least half of their charges of vital self-esteem, and it is appropriate to quote George Bernard Shaw's comment on this subject in *Candida*:

> It is easy — terribly easy — to shake a man's faith in himself. To take advantage of that to break a man's spirit is devil's work.

And when that devil's work is applied to children's education, it is intellectual abuse, which like physical abuse, sexual abuse and emotional abuse, can damage them for life.

Secondly, it is not our aim to undermine the self-esteem of the teachers themselves. In their defence it must be remembered that they were driven into becoming steadily less free agents, as other tiers of watchdogs tyrannically imposed modern methods. It was against their will that many teachers were forced to abandon traditional methods, while vastly more were never taught them. The bad currency of the whole word and its derivatives was, and still is, presented to them at college as the full and exclusive horizon of the teaching of reading.

Chapter 7

Teacher Training

Why was the great surge of reading failure on such a monumental scale? Why did teachers not realise that the whole-word method was misdirected and opt for the effective phonics method instead? Some did, but most persisted in the same misguided rut. The reason for this perpetual sleep-walking was that their training had indoctrinated them into accepting the *righteousness* of the whole-word method with a kind of religious-cult zeal. The real villains were not the victimised teachers who carried out the intellectual child abuse but the training establishments that had brainwashed them into doing so.

The early training colleges had neither the wish nor the opportunity to espouse unrealistic methodology. Their students had already served five-year apprenticeships as pupil-teachers and were well versed in classroom realities. The staff, too, had been high-achieving teachers before being promoted to training status and were well equipped to give demonstration lessons for observation by their students.

Even after the pupil-teaching system ceased and students went straight to college from sixth forms, the academic qualification of four Higher School Certificate passes was not enough. They had to have demonstrated classroom potential by serving an observation and teaching stint in a local school before submitting their college applications. School practice was also a strong feature of the training itself: twelve weeks in the two-year course, divided among four different schools. At Furzedown College, where Alice Coleman trained in 1941–43, one afternoon a week for a term was spent helping in a nursery and those intending to teach seniors also had to observe in an infant reception class for a week.

No student was left ignorant of the phonic method, although look-and-say, as it was then called, was mentioned as a device for irregularly spelt words and the sentence method was referred to as an idea but not a serious technique.

An Occasion Ripe For Change

Sporadic attempts were made to popularise the whole-word method in Britain but, despite a favourable mention in the 1931 Hadow Report, they all proved abortive until three events conspired to produce a climate that welcomed radical change after World War II.

The first was the effect of six years of war in reducing educational standards. Compared with the abysmal standards of the late twentieth century they were still high but they nevertheless meant that the further decline due to look-say did not stand out in such stark contrast as it would have done during the crest of the upwave.

Secondly, the war created a public demand for widespread improvements. The 1945 Labour election landslide brought massive nationalisation, planning machinery, the National Health Service, and a spirit of welcome for educational experiment.

The third factor, which determined the *direction* taken by all this eagerness was the rise of a charismatic guru capable of eliciting great heights of enthusiasm for his educational philosophy. If the initial teaching alphabet had been available to fill this vacuum of expectancy, it might have brought a change for the better. But it did not come until later when look-say was too well established to dislodge. The great guru had already been enthroned as *the* expert and his name was Frederick (Fred) Schonell.

Professor Schonell

Schonell was the British Dewey, who integrated the early trends and launched an effective movement. He was a psychologist from Western Australia who came to Britain in 1928 to acquire a Ph.D. in educational psychology at London's Institute of Education. Such was his impact that in 1931 he became an educational psychology lecturer at Goldsmith's, one of the more prestigious training colleges, and the very next year received an honorary D.Litt. from the School of International Studies in Geneva. A knighthood followed.

He produced a useful little book entitled *Essentials in Teaching and Testing Spelling*, which listed the words each school age-group should know. Alice Coleman used it in the 1940s to upgrade the spelling in her Thameside school by setting targets for each class. However, as her campaign succeeded, it became clear that even children with IQs below 80 could easily manage the words deemed appropriate for those a year older. This was her first experience of the "dumbing down" that did not expect enough of children. She later concluded it reflected the fact that Western Australia's children do not start school until they are six and would quite logically be a year behind Britain's five-year-old starters.

Another example of dumbing down was the concept, also originating with Schonell, of children being *not yet ready to read*. This has been paralleled by the work of the Swiss psychologist, Jean Piaget, who investigated children's cognitive development and proposed four stages. Stage III, from age seven to twelve, was claimed as the first age for logic operations, and Schonell regarded seven as the right age for reading readiness. But we all know children can be logical much younger than this and Piaget's time-scale is now seen as faulty. The reason has been traced to the complex formulation of his test questions, which left children puzzled. If they had been framed more simply, younger children could easily have given the right logical answers. But Piaget was very influential, like Schonell, who also believed that five-year-olds who floundered did so because of their age and not because of the obstacles imposed by the whole-word approach.

Schonell's "strongest plea" was not to hurry the child by expecting too much too soon. He argued that a slower, broader approach would repay doubly later on. He saw no problem in non-reading seven-year-olds, who would surely learn at eight or nine, or even ten, though he did say that the longer the reading disability continued, the harder it would be to treat. It has been pointed out that Rudolf Steiner schools do not embark upon the teaching of reading until age seven and this seems to have no ill-effect. But that is significantly different from Schonell's concept. Steiner children do not *fail* at five or six, because the question of reading has not yet arisen, but Schonell knew bright ones would pull ahead and less bright ones lag far behind, and that *is* failure with all its emotional upsets.

We now know that many children *are* ready to read at the age of three or four and if taught phonically at home they are already effective readers before they go to school.

Schonell claimed that his book *The Psychology and Teaching of Reading* was scientifically based on well planned, carefully executed research. But the nature of that research seems quite peripheral to the fundamental question, which is: "*When children in matched groups are taught by different methods, which method produced the best readers with the fewest problems?*"

For example, he noted a comparison of five-year-olds' spoken vocabularies with the words used in their reading books, made by A.C. and P.E. Vernon, who found that the two were different and opined that they should be the same. This is hardly scientific and seems to say that reading should be banned from enlarging children's vocabularies. Another item cited is the need to use 18-point type for small children, gradually reducing it to 12-point for older ones — useful background but not evidence supporting the whole word method.

When he did address the basic question, it was in an unsubstantiated pronouncement that reading failure was usually due to prematurely plunging children into what he called an over-analytic method (phonics) using abstract symbols (letters) before they understood what words and sentences meant in spoken English and could therefore see the purpose [Dewey's relevance] of the operations confronting them. This seems to be a basic misunderstanding of the child's mind.

Young children acquire knowledge by accretion, accumulating small items suited to the time-scale of their short attention spans. Alice Coleman had a strong reminder of this when introducing a small girl to colourful land use maps, in which she seemed most interested. The first map had a clear contrast of colour combinations showing different land uses in its two halves but this point fell on deaf ears as the child did not yet know what the individual colours meant, let alone their combinations. Nevertheless, she studied the map with great absorption and then announced that she had found 29 churches with spires!

It is such small, disconnected beginnings that gradually and naturally add up to a broader understanding. This is a bottom-up approach. Trying to force a broad, top-down perspective as a pre-requisite for detailed work can prove a time-wasting delay. While Schonell-method children are slowly becoming ready to read (or often not ready), they could have already become fluent readers if taught phonically.

Letters *are* abstract symbols but so are words, and much more complex ones. If "plunging in" to the former demands too much, plunging in to the latter demands even more. It disregards the educational principle of going from the simple to the complex—the bottom-up approach. Schonell was not wholly against phonics, but believed it should come later and through an indirect, unconscious process of osmosis during experience with whole words. He seemed unaware of the alternative of explicit teaching and rapid mastery.

Yet he was not narrow-minded. Kathleen Clarke, one of his psychology students after he became Professor of Education in Swansea in 1942, told Alice Coleman of his liberal-mindedness in referring to fringe subjects as the antecedents of the true sciences. At this she made a scathing aside, a little too audibly. Schonell heard and sternly admonished the class never to condemn from a basis of ignorance. To drive the lesson home, he set a vacation assignment, asking each student to investigate and report on a topic such as astrology or phrenology. Kathleen Clarke was allocated graphology and embarked with scorn but as her knowledge grew so did her respect. She discovered that the subject was falsely denigrated and went on to become a graphologist herself. Her skill in handwriting analysis proved to be a valuable asset both personally and in her hospital career, where she was responsible for the welfare of nurses.

Schonell's attitude in such matters impressed people with his insight and open-mindedness, and helped create the charisma that attracted a devoted following. But why was he not equally open-minded to the superiority of the phonic method?

A first reason was that his career was largely devoted to the study of retarded children. He and his wife Eleanor wrote several books on various aspects of backwardness, for example, *Backwardness in the Basic Subjects*

(1942). He seems to have been so focused on learners with problems that he did not realise he was missing the full potential of others.

Secondly, he seemed unfamiliar with true phonics. When he exemplified children's realisation of the phonic principle, it was in terms of syllables, not letters. He mentioned their dawning recognition that the word "p-at" shared a sound with "th-at". Syllabaries are fine for languages with few syllables, such as Japanese with 47, but English has thousands. True, that is fewer than the number of words but still much more daunting for a young child than the 26 letters and handful of digraphs needed for real phonics.

So in the confidence of phonic ignorance, Schonell increased his sway and a vicious circle set in. Look-say steadily produced more backward readers, so more teachers turned to him as the great guru of delayed literacy. His stature waxed and his writ ran wider. There was an enthusiastic rush to leap on his bandwagon and those who wished to inherit his mantle sought posts in the training colleges, where lectureships largely carried an automatic authority and influence. Furthermore, Schonell's prestige made him something of a kingmaker in the college sphere.

Looking back we can see that the 1950s brought a significant educational decline but it was not apparent at the time. Schonell retired in 1961 and died in 1969. Before then Progressivism's aversion to objective testing had perpetuated the whole-word in-group and drawn more colleges into its fold.

The Colonisation of Training Colleges

Extra teachers were needed in large numbers after the end of World War II to meet the three expansion pledges in the 1944 Education Act: the raising of the leaving age, smaller classes and more grammar school places. There was also the further element of the bulge in the birth rate, when men returned from the war theatres and family formation resumed. Furthermore, full employment, family allowances and cradle-to-grave welfare encouraged earlier marriages and larger families. Infant intakes became much larger and the expansion spread up through the primary range and later into the secondary schools. An idea of the scale of the extra demand is indicated by the building of 38 new primary schools in Kent alone between 1948 and 1958. The number of extra teachers needed nationwide was immense.

Existing training establishments were enlarged and new "emergency colleges" were founded to train mature students in one year and help fill teaching vacancies quickly. All required new lecturers and it seemed natural to appoint keen young Progressivists alert to the trends of the day. The whole-word method gained a foothold and was served up as the staple diet to students. The phonics alternative ceased to be even mentioned, especially in the new colleges with no continuity of staff who understood its value. Despite the enormous proven success of i.t.a., it seemed no college espoused it, apart from its headquarters in the London Institute of Education, which itself later became a keen centre of Progressivism.

The bulge passed through the school system but rather than cut down the colleges, the need for teachers was increased by again raising the school leaving age, to 16 in 1972. The following year the colleges' future was further protected by increasing the training period from two years to three, with an optional fourth year to qualify for a B. Ed. degree. Later, the three-year course also carried a degree award.

Some staff were recruited straight from university to lecture to intending students without having had any school-teaching experience themselves. It was reasoned that the longer course involved more academic work and justified having more subject lecturers, distinct from those responsible for training. This was plausible but sucked in a higher proportion of staff who were in no position to challenge Progressivist dogmas and the whole-word method. Some of them actually became the most active whole-word protagonists,

Eventually the growing unemployment that began in the mid-1970s brought a fall in the birth rate that created great educational over-provision. In Kent alone there were 50,000 excess school places and school closures set in. Training provision was affected in turn and some college closures were inescapable. It was decided to close many older colleges and retain the new ones, on the argument that the latter had better building conditions, but this further reduced those places where traditionalism might be lingering.

The Progressivist downwave affected the whole English-speaking world. Look-say was one of its great drivers with a rationale of rejecting the irregularity of our spelling. Languages with a simpler correspondence between letters and sounds had no reason to depart from phonics and their educational standards did not slip in the same way.

"A prophet is not without honour, save in his own country", so it was not surprising that Britain's Schonell came from Australia. Nor, considering North America's long headstart in Progressivism, was it surprising that the next dominant influences here were Kenneth and Yetta Goodman from USA and Frank Smith from Canada. The adage is not completely true; Goodman and Smith were also honoured in America.

Kenneth Goodman

Kenneth Goodman, an avowed Progressivist and comprehensive-school promoter, was Professor of Language, Reading and Culture in the University of Arizona. In USA the Progressivism he inherited was some 25 years further down the road than that in Britain and from his first literacy project in 1967, he helped it plunge still further. It could no longer be presented as an innocent hope for an untried method, so its defects had to be wrapped up in high-flown language to convince everyone that teaching to read was very complex and difficult. Goodman asserted that it was not a mere method but a philosophy, and not just educational but social and political as well, with the political Right as the enemy.

The philosophy was named *psycholinguistics*, or *whole language*, and Goodman liked to be called "the whole language guru". He joked that he did not found whole language; it found him. This pun allowed him to imply that it arose spontaneously from classroom experience and must therefore be natural and right.

It would not have arisen spontaneously from teachers who understood phonics but by then there were few who had escaped whole-word indoctrination. This restricted "natural" choice of the indoctrinated was not natural to the workings of the brain.

Psycholinguistics is an unproven hypothesis, which parallels the negative aspects of Progressivism in the whole-word method but applies them to spoken language with devastating side-effects upon written language. It has been analysed and exposed in John Honey's 1997 book, *Language is Power: The Story of Standard English and Its Enemies*.

Goodman's tenets embrace Progressivism's false egalitarianism, claiming that all languages are equal in their adaptation to the needs of the communities that speak them. It alleges that no language is more primitive or advanced than any other, and the same applies to their diverse dialects. No matter that some have vastly richer vocabularies and nuances of meaning, or have streamlined away needless inflections; all are of identical value.

The term *whole language* is based on the idea that we speak in the context of information and not in an isolated vacuum. This is a truism that does not need such ponderous elaboration as Goodman gave it and it overlooks a fundamental point. Using a language in which we are fluent is not the same as acquiring it initially. Goodman was free with Progressivist advice to teach children and not subjects, but he did not understand the child mind sufficiently to know the difference between learning to read and using an accomplished reading skill. He aimed to impose the whole gamut of language use upon beginners.

> Language is best learned not by specifically teaching it but by supporting it in a full range of genres.

However, the full range was not genuinely full. Behind a façade of respect for all, he urged that pupils should be denied standard English, which he considered a "myth". Instead, they should be locked into their own dialects and the "rich innovativeness" of local slang. In fact, he was in favour of Babel, the denial of a common tongue. Yet while advocating the fossilisation of ethnic and social differences, he also railed against their effect when lack of standard English denied access to jobs. He failed to understand that standard speech, like ability to read, is a passport to a wider, richer life. We should not be surprised by his self-contradiction. There are many inconsistencies inherent in Progressivism and, as whole language is more extreme than whole word, its internal incompatibilities are more exaggerated.

The most audacious incongruity was Goodman's claim to be scientific, while dismissing the accepted scientific canons that safeguard what can be accepted as true. He quoted John Dewey rather than proven evidence, using the unacceptable ploy of *argumentum ad hominem,* or name-dropping. He disagreed with standardised tests that could have produced proof or disproof, because they conflicted with his own opinionated criteria, which he would not submit to a proper trial. Perhaps he unconsciously feared exposure and substituted mere assertion, preferring a head count of those satisfied with mass failure to the firm testimony of phonics' successes. Worst of all, he bragged, "for me research is never neutral". True research is always neutral; one must always be ready to jettison pre-conceived ideas if the results of an investigation disprove them.

Frank Smith

Frank Smith burst into print two years after Schonell's death with *Understanding Reading* (1971) and quickly became an international guru. His books appeared on the reading lists of all UK teacher-training establishments and were ordered for their libraries in batches of 20 copies, to indoctrinate students. Knowledge of phonics was carefully withheld so the students had no comparator to assist critical analysis of his ideas.

How he achieved his eminence is not clear, as he had no experience in the teaching of reading. His background was in philosophy and he studied linguistics at Harvard. English by birth, he lived abroad and in 1980 joined the Department of Curriculum in the Ontario Institute for Studies in Education. He seemed unaware that views based on adult reading fluency were not applicable to children's learning and appeared not to care whether his ideas were workable. He declared,

> Children cannot be taught to read. A teacher's responsibility is not to teach children to read but to make it possible for them to learn to read.

He asserted in a high-flown way that phonics was a mere method, while all other approaches — whole word, paired reading, language experience, whole language and psycho-linguistics — were a philosophy, with which a mere method could not be compared. It certainly *can* be compared in terms of effectiveness in teaching children to read, but that would have offended Smith's aversion to both teaching and testing.

He understood *nothing* about phonics, as was apparent from his sarcastic claim that "ho" could be pronounced in totally different ways: "hot", "hope", "hook", "hoot", "house", "hoist", "horse", "horizon", "honey", "hour" and "honest". But "ho" is not taught in phonics, which distinguishes "h" as a consonant and then "o" and its digraphs as different vowel sounds (Table 7.1).

Table 7.1: Phonemes Incorporating The Letter "o"

"o"	Short "o" in "hot" and with a silent "h" in "honest"
"o"	Unstressed "o" in "horizon"
"o−e"	Long "o" in "hope", made long by the final "e"
"oi"	A diphthong in "hoist"
"or"	A digraph in "horse"
"oo"	Short and long sounds in "hook" and "hoot"
"ou"	A diphthong in house and, with a silent "h", in hour"
"one"	In "honey", "none", etc.

The same spirit of gross ignorance typifies his negative commandments, which were noted in his writings by Gary Scott Miller of British Columbia and shown here in Table 7.2.

Table 7.2: Smith's Negative Commandments

1. Don't aim for early mastery of the rules of reading.
2. Don't ensure that phonic skills are learned and used.
3. Don't teach letters or words one at a time.
4. Don't make word-perfect reading a prime objective.
5. Don't discourage guessing.
6. Don't insist that children read carefully.
7. Don't correct errors immediately.
8. Don't identify and treat problem readers as early as possible.
9. Don't use every opportunity during reading instruction to improve spelling and writing instruction.
10. Don't insist on the best possible spoken English.

Miller said that these don'ts made him feel like an experienced brain surgeon being criticised by an ignorant second-year medical student. Smith's book was entitled *Reading Without Nonsense* but it could hardly be more nonsensical itself, giving a strong impression that his aim was *not* to get children reading. This self-appointed guardian of literacy also wrote a 1989 article entitled *Overselling Literacy*, which claimed,

> Literacy doesn't generate finer feelings or higher values. People who can't read or write, think just as well out of school as people who can. Literacy won't guarantee anyone a job.

This declaration of literacy's unimportance came strangely from one who had set himself up as its guru, to acquire fame and fortune by cajoling teachers to embrace his recipe — and his only — for helping pupils to become literate. If this was not the height of hypocrisy, it was the depth of self-deception, and neither quality fitted him to prescribe for the development of children's minds. What a pity that someone with such a crippled outlook won adherents in education, where clear thinking is a central need.

We first comment on three aspects of Smith's statement and then outline how his illiteracy recipe has unlocked disasters far beyond his limited purview.

a) Literacy does not generate finer feelings or higher values.   This contains a soupçon of truth. Finer feelings need to be nourished at an early age to prevent permanent disregard of the nobler things of life. But with even a small foundation, reading can open up thought and emotion to appreciate and espouse higher values that might never occur to one except through print. Smith was indulging in one of Thouless's 38 kinds of crooked thinking — pretending that part of an issue was the whole. Another defect was an implicit assumption that the converse was also true, i.e. that illiteracy does not generate coarser feelings and lower values, which is again true in part. Not all illiterates fall into criminality but the *probability* of their doing so is vastly greater than for literates.

b) People who can't read or write can think just as well out of school as people who can.   This is ironic! Does he mean illiterates would be no more crippled in their thinking than himself? True literacy gives access to a wealth of fact and understanding that helps people think in a much better informed way.

c) Literacy won't guarantee anyone a job.   This, too, is a half-truth or quarter-truth but nevertheless the *chance* of a job is much greater for literates and so is career choice. Smith's limited perspectives prevented him from examining the converse, that illiteracy guarantees a much greater *chance* of unemployment. Susan Elkin wrote:

> If you can speak or write English with clarity and accuracy in a way which can be generally understood throughout the English-speaking world you will, almost certainly, do better in life than someone who can't.

British children have a head-start, as English is their mother tongue, but this advantage is thrown away by gurus who impose methods that turn them into illiterates. Smith considered literacy and illiteracy as simple opposites but there is more to it than that. Innate intelligence can be nurtured by stimulation, and reading and writing actually increase the IQ.

They help the brain to develop normally while reading failure inhibits full development. Smith also neglected the weight of emotional baggage created by failure: humiliation, frustration, resentment, anger, retaliation, lack of self-esteem, inability to cope with various adversities, and acceptance of victim status with all the maltreatment that it tends to attract. Illiteracy leads to multiple forms of stress.

Stress is an appalling health hazard for those who lack the confidence and skill to cope with it. It floods the brain with cortisol, causing neurological burn-out and brain-cell death through diseases such as Alzheimer's, with its total loss of identity in the late stages.

Dr. Dharma Singh Khalsa, President of the Alzheimer's Prevention Foundation amassed a great deal of clinical experience on the prevention, arrest and reversal of decline in various kinds of senility and his book, *Brain Longevity* (1997), set out the evidence on how to keep the brain healthy throughout the whole of life. He showed that, just as lack of stimulation causes parts of infants' brains to atrophy, so there is a counterpart in middle and old age. Among his measures for safeguarding the brain, he emphasised "use it or lose it" and regarded reading and writing as among the most effective processes for brain health.

> Reading, many neurological researchers believe, is uniquely beneficial for the brain. Much reading matter, of course, is intellectually enriching, but the mere act of reading, regardless of content, is highly beneficial. Reading requires active engagement of the mind and imagination, and it powerfully stimulates both hemispheres of the brain as well as the limbic system.

So, because of the broad age group that the look-say and whole language gurus have affected, we now face a growing disaster in the field of health. *Another case of Alzheimer's? Do we blame Frank Smith?*

The outrageous ideas of these international gurus spread infectiously through British training colleges, spawning a ramifying network of support. It seemed that each establishment had its own mini-guru trying to outdo the masters. It would be tedious to explore their repetitious refrain in detail, so we comment on just two.

The Reading Reading and Language Research Centre

The first "Reading" in this name refers to the town of Reading and the second one to the educational skill. Betty Root was its Director for many years but did not prevent the centre from being infectiously look-say, and as thousands of students were attracted there, it must have been responsible for a great deal of phonics phobia.

Bridie Raban, a Reading lecturer, and Cliff Moon, a primary school teacher, wrote a whole-word propaganda book, *A Question of Reading*. It cited Frank Smith's books as essential reading and reasserted all the false claims and self-contradictions of the language experience creed. It pontificated that reading needs to be developed on the run, as attention to letters would slow children's efforts to derive meaning. But it countenanced much greater slowing by getting them to guess beforehand what a given word sequence *might* be saying. Constant discussion of what one *might* be going to read before actually reading it seems a bigger brake on progress than pausing over a few letters in a graded scheme. Another self-contradiction urged that "success breeds success", while also advocating that children should repeatedly fail by risking mistakes in the word-guessing game.

Phonics teaching works for all, but these ignorant authors stated that they knew of no one method that could always succeed. They nevertheless advocated all the inadequate methods and said, "If we persevere long enough . . . we might begin to point in the direction of some of the answers." This admission of weak incompetence did not deter them from posing as experts. As was de rigueur, they denigrated testing, and in a quite preposterous fashion. "Every reading test tests something different and none tests reading." And "Reading Age tests will be unreliable guides . . . even useless." Certainly, such tests are not perfect, as we shall show in Chapter 17, but that should stimulate their improvement, not their abolition.

Moon and Raban admitted that many children failed to read but presented their own methodology as if it brought no failures. They did not even mention the great dyslexia epidemic that had broken out in the wake of the whole-word method (see Chapter 11) and gave no help for its prevention and cure. That the book sold well in the contemporary Progressivist ethos was made the sole criterion of success.

London University Institute of Education: Margaret Meek

Mrs. Meek, a whole-language guru in London's Institute of Education, turned a blind eye to that Institute's renowned research on the initial teaching alphabet and in 1982 produced *Learning to Read,* a book that regurgitated all the look-say nonsense. "Above all", she declared, "[children] should not have special instruction in deciphering letters, sounds or words." Instead she urged that they should guess — a process she dressed up as "predict". She dismissed reading tests by arguing that children should not be tested as if they were washing powder, which is argument by false analogy — another of Thouless's types of crooked thinking. She also averred that dyslexic difficulty was simply a label invented by middle class parents to cloak their children's reading failure with a semblance of respectability.

She ignored the implications of her own assertions. "A good teacher makes more difference than any method" implied that the 50% of children left illiterate or semi-literate had bad teachers. "Teachers who want to teach the child to read can do so" meant that half did not want to, and that those who had some children succeed and some fail were picking and choosing which ones they would consign to illiteracy's dustbin. She was writing rubbish and made no attempt to ascertain the method used by wholly successful teachers.

One of her former students, Judith Graham, described how Margaret Meek trained her classes to teach reading. She began by asking them what they thought children ought to do in order to read. Back came the answers: know the alphabet and the sounds the letters make, learn about sylla-bles—all the right things. But Margaret Meek swept them all away and produced the toughest bit of William Faulkner she could find, asking the students to read it and say what they had been doing. Judith Graham wrote:

> I kept reading it through, even though I didn't understand much; I scanned it and got an impression. I had to keep re-reading and going back to see what on earth was going on. I had no difficulty with the words—just the mean-ings! The rest of the one-year course was spent persuading students that the model of reading they had thus jointly constructed was the model that begin-ning readers needed to use too.

Meek rejected the students' common sense in favour of disastrous ideas based on adults' study of a very difficult passage. How could she possibly think that little children's minds were just like theirs? This, again, was the crooked thinking of false analogy.

Equally unacceptable was "Any significant research I have done rests on having treated anecdotes as evidence." But relying on anecdotes lets unscientific workers select facts supporting their prejudices and reject those that do not. It is vital to test the full range of facts systematically and establish whether the pros or cons are stronger. Of course, anecdotes are often useful triggers for initiating research or, after obtaining real evi-dence, to serve as *illustrative* material helping to communicate the facts more crisply.

A brief mention may be made of the New Zealander, Ted Glynn of Otago University, who encapsulated the guessing-game technique in an acronym, PPP for Pause, Prompt, Praise. This was operated by pausing for children to hazard a mistaken guess, prompting them with a helpful hint, or the answer, and then praising them, regardless of whether they got it right or wrong, which did not teach them the difference.

Student Selection

How do the colleges select applicants for student places? The logical answer is that they should pick the best qualified and turn down those who would be a bad example to pupils. But there are any number of anec-dotes suggesting that this may not happen, such as a taxi-driver's complaint that his child's teacher was instructing him in her own poor spelling and also many good teachers' criticisms of grossly inefficient colleagues.

Anecdotes have not triggered any large objective research investigation, and it might well be difficult to get admissions tutors to acknowledge that they have acted in this dumbing-down way, but we are able to cite a small-scale test that was devised by Annis Garfield.

In the 1980s there was a severe teacher shortage and the Department of Education and Science pleaded for recruits, especially for mature graduates to switch into the education field. The TASC project (Teaching as a Career) was attractively publicised and the Central Office of Information declared there were unlimited opportunities. Annis Garfield, who had many teacher relatives, decided to respond, and seemed to fit all the requirements.

- Her first-class Cambridge degree in classics showed that she had a fine mind, like many of the most memorable teachers of the past.
- She had worked in law and a variety of voluntary fields, as well as serving 13 years as an O-Level and A-Level marker for the Oxford and Cambridge Board. This fitted the official assertion that outside experience in other jobs would be of "great value".
- She had two children aged 10 and 12, and had also privately tutored backward children to help them defeat illiteracy. This fitted the official statement that experience with children would be "a huge asset".

Classics might not be in high demand but Annis Garfield was well equipped to teach English, which her examining work had shown to be appallingly neglected. Some examples of the spelling, punctuation and syntax errors that she had encountered may be quoted:

> Squeler say alot of thing to reasure the other Animal mind excuser about what was writen of the sided of the van estc
>
> Snoball tell's the animal's
>
> mean't
>
> say's,
>
> see's
>
> lady macbeth is trying to cover up the big sin her and her husband done
>
> The battle went pretty well beans nobody expected it.

During the next three years Annis Garfield applied to a range of training institutions but was rejected by them all. Why was that, when she seemed just what central government wanted? There were clues that her high standards offended the sloppiness of the training staff. Mostly they did not even offer her an interview but when she went to one that did, with neat hair and dress, she found the interviewers looking thoroughly scruffy. Her views on good English literature were beaten down in favour of choosing second-class trash to be read purely for amusement, while anti-racist overtones were evident. Perhaps her worst crime was her belief that phonics teaching, which had helped her remedial pupils, should be used from the start to *prevent* reading failure.

After repeated rejections she phoned one college for an explanation and was told that she could compensate for her "inappropriate" degree by studying craft, and having a year's hands-on experience in a primary school. That could not be as a teacher, which was forbidden to the unqualified, but as a playground assistant or a dinner lady.

Her next step is intriguing—testing whether the advice she had been given would, in fact, win her a place. She submitted a bogus application littered with spelling mistakes, grammatical errors and meaningless jargon. It purported to come from a 41-year-old black dinner lady named Sharon Shrill, and won a rapid acceptance from the college! It seems an extreme interpretation of egalitarianism to consider that the ill-educated Sharon Shrill would be suitable for taking charge of young minds.

Annis Garfield's experience confirmed what had long been suspected. At least one college was averse to recruiting trainees with the best qualifications for work in schools and preferred those with a poor command of English and other inappropriate traits. Teachers with a true sense of vocation are fully justified in criticising the Sharon Shrills among their colleagues, who are keeping standards low and bringing the whole profession into disrepute.

Do we really need training establishments that are detracting from real education instead of constructively contributing to it. Would it not be better for trainees to learn on the job in the best schools?

Tailpiece

It would be quite satisfying to expose training staff to the same bafflement that they engender in failed readers. Could they learn one of the Arabic languages without knowing its letters or even that it should be written from right to left? Of course, this is mere day-dreaming but there might, one day, be an opportunity for a simpler test.

We could coin a new word (as Alice Coleman has done a few times in her career) and decide to write it according to the extreme look-say rules promoted by the training colleges. Letters and their sounds are considered irrelevant so we might decide that "rzlxjq" looks quite nice and here is the shape one is expected to read it by. It is distinctive but unreadable and unpronounceable:

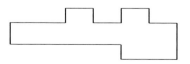

The gurus would demand to hear it and be told its meaning, but they produce illiterate school-leavers who will encounter a huge number of words without access to this information, and it is only fair to give them first-hand experience of what that is like. They may well say that this challenge is ridiculous and, if so, they will have picked upon the right word to describe the illogic that they themselves impose upon vast numbers of people.

How did the gurus manage to pull the wool over teacher's eyes for half a century? And when the failure of their methods became clear, why did they concede that letter decoding could be allowed only *after* children had learned to read by the whole-word method? And, most vitally, *why is their writ still acceptable in so many quarters?*

Chapter 8

Head Teachers

Teachers may be brainwashed by their training into whole-word adherence but class-room experience and the guidance of wise heads should have been able to convince them that something was amiss and that better practices should prevail. Unfortunately, this salutary antidote was often lacking, as many heads had themselves been indoctrinated.

Head teachers can profoundly influence their schools. This may be for the better; those who introduce phonics and discipline can stimulate a great leap forward. Or it may be for the worse, as in the case of the Lambeth despot whose entire staff resigned within a few weeks of her arrival, as also did their replacements in the following term.

One ploy used to exclude traditionalists from headships was deceptively reasonable. It was insistence that any new head must have a degree. Because the great university expansion came a little later than Progressivism, traditional phonics teachers lacked honorifics and were almost automatically excluded from appointment as heads. No matter that as college students they had been far more strictly selected for intelligence and character than most of today's undergraduates; no matter that they had proved excellent teachers with easy good discipline and 100% achievement of pupils' literacy; they were still passed over in favour of younger graduates who could present themselves as being up-to-date.

The practice of appointing younger, Progressivist heads coincided with the cult of youth and soon habituated selection committees to the idea that the slightly older traditionalists must be past it. It was a grave injustice to their generation to deny them due promotion and also a grave injustice to the pupils brought under the heel of Progressivism.

Yet even some members of the favoured generation have resorted to bluffing their way into headships with falsified qualifications. Their dishonesty was not necessarily detected at the time of their appointment but some were unmasked later when using their positions as heads to engage in further fraudulent practices.

The Daily Mail reported that selection committees, often mainly school governors, were remiss in not checking applicants' credentials. In 1990 a policeman at the Staffordshire police headquarters told Alice Coleman that he knew of three teachers who had previously been convicted of sex offences. He longed to warn parents but was not allowed to do so. That rule was now changed and a black list was compiled but even in 2006 it emerged that 90 people with paedophile leanings had been appointed to teaching posts. This loophole is to be closed but even so, there is no way to alert the committees to criminals as yet uncaught, some of whom, particularly child abusers, have continued undetected for many years.

Some selection committee members went beyond being hoodwinked and actively connived to select predetermined candidates, with pre-interview coaching sessions to ensure that the chosen ones could satisfy other members' prejudices. The head who refused to allow pupils to attend the ballet *Romeo and Juliet* because it was a heterosexual love story, proved to be the live-in lesbian partner of the Chairman of Governors who had appointed her. Perhaps she won the post on her merits but perhaps nepotism was not dead.

New heads brought new-broom measures that often changed the whole school ethos. Their own Progressivist classroom experience had taught them how hard it was to avoid illiteracy or how frustrating it was to teach older ones who could not read fluently, so low standards might be part of their normal expectation. They, too, had been brainwashed into regarding phonics as hopelessly old-fashioned and fuddy-duddy, so they were naturally ready to oust it. Worse still, their ears were deafened to class teachers' defence of its merits by the financial inducements they were offered to eradicate it. Ronald Threadgall, of the Initial Teaching Alphabet Federation, said that the main factor in the eclipse of i.t.a. was the arrival of new heads who had been promised extra funding if they banned it.

Some heads were not allowed to appoint applicants who were the most capable even within the limits of Progressivism but were forced by selection committees to accept people according to non-educational criteria. Others just jogged along in an undistinguished manner, ignorant of how much better their staff could have been and unwilling to recognise teaching problems or provide help. One father reported to the Reading Reform Foundation that the headmaster at his six-year-old twins' school had a notice to parents on his door:

If you have come to complain about our reading scheme, KEEP OUT!

It was the National Association of Head Teachers (NAHT) that introduced the preposterous principle of expecting school starters to have been already taught to read. This is actually not a bad idea, as children who learn by phonics at home are school-proofed against the disastrous effect of whole-word teaching. But coming from heads it was a feeble abrogation of responsibility, which compares unfavourably with teachers' attitudes during the upwave.

At the beginning of the nineteenth century, few people could read but by its end almost all could do so, thanks to the efforts of competent teachers and tutors. Many down-wave heads not only failed to emulate them but seemed unwilling even to consider doing so.

NAHT denied that schools contributed to falling standards and blamed contemporary society for concentrating on instant gratification and not valuing perseverance. Did they never ponder where this social ethos came from? Half a century of engineering children into the play-way instead of the work ethic could hardly have failed to produce such an effect.

Another excuse for reading failure was the impossibility of teaching emotionally disturbed children. However, that seems an inverted view of cause and effect. Inability to read, with all its erosion of self-confidence and self-esteem, is often the *origin* of emotional problems but even if there are other causes, reading failure is an additional, exacerbating stress. Proof that illiteracy is cause and not effect comes from many instances of emotional disturbance being cured when school strugglers have been taught to read by phonics tutors.

As older heads sympathetic to phonics and traditionalism retired, younger heads were left even more monolithically in support of Progressivism and its look-say methodology. It took 40 years to produce the first six million adult illiterates but only another ten to increase the total to nine million. The annual rate had doubled.

Heads, like class teachers, had been brainwashed at college to reject the phonic method entirely, not on its merits, which were concealed from them, but on purely doctrinaire grounds. So instead of being able to act as wise counsellors when teachers were befogged by ineffective approaches, they had been programmed to reinforce the harm done and even to help drive enlightened teachers out of their schools. Furthermore, both class teachers and head teachers were made to toe the look-say line by the next tier of watchdogs — the school inspectors.

Chapter 9

The Inspectorate

The next tier of watchdogs also had a lot to answer for. While it was the training institutions that indoctrinated inexperienced students with unsubstantiated dogmas, the Inspectorate rejected its golden opportunity to wean teachers into practical realities and instead used its influence to reinforce the disastrous methodology. In this sphere, too, the downwave seems to have brought a perversion of power not present in the upwave.

Her Majesty's Inspectorate (HMI) was always a powerful body and the Chief Inspector's post was described as probably the most powerful in the whole educational establishment. Its power was reinforced by the introduction of payment by results in 1862, whereby the HMIs tested the children to determine each school's grant. Testing ceased in 1885, in favour of more general assessments and the block grant system followed in 1897.

The HMIs began to by-pass results to consider teaching methods instead but eventually did justice to neither. With the coming of the downwave, their attention to attainment became feebler and their concentration on techniques became stronger. Preferences related to the teaching of reading covered the whole gamut of the whole-word method and its derivatives, and also language development through picture-guessing.

Sheila Lawlor commented that though the Inspectorate's publications did not make this stance explicit, the HMIs were keen protagonists of Progressivist doctrines in practice. They exercised control by reporting favourably on those who conformed to "correct" methods and adversely on those who did not. Devising novel methodological slants was respected as a mark of distinction so some inspectors fell over themselves to advance new and untested ideas, to the despair of phonics teachers, who felt they were being railroaded into rubbish.

As the declining standards of the downwave created progressively more difficulties for teachers, it seemed that extra in-service help was needed. No matter that the training period had been increased by 50% and in many cases by 100%, teachers could no longer be as self-reliant as during the upwave. One response to this growing need for support was to duplicate the role of the central HMI by providing separate groups of inspectors at local authority level. These were usually known as advisers.

Even sensible inspectors became tarred with the Progressivist brush. One phonics teacher reported that a sympathetic adviser was impressed by the achievement this method made possible but when challenged to speak out in its favour, said it would cost him his job if he did not go along with his colleagues' whole-word precepts.

Besides conforming themselves, inspectors and advisers also forced heads and teachers to conform. Regardless of whether their pupils were making good progress, they were judged by the inspectors on the basis of correct or incorrect methodology, and those getting good results with phonics were warned that they would be debarred from promotion unless they toed the doctrinal line. They were left in no doubt that phonics was considered apostasy.

A case reported by Liz Lightfoot, then of the Mail on Sunday, was the berating of an experienced head by a 29-year-old adviser. The offence was the use of the Letterland reading scheme. Its phonic content is quite minimal but, even so, the adviser castigated it as beyond the pale. The head had to steal the Progressivists' child-centred argument and respond that different methods had to be retained to suit different children.

Inspectors' antics would have been ludicrous if they had not been so sinister. King Edward VI School, Stratford-on-Avon, was an example of excellence ignored in favour of dogma. Among the country's best schools, three quarters of its pupils went to university. The HMIs found the boys well motivated, well behaved, receptive and high-achieving, but they also heavily criticised deficiencies related to not following Progressivist imperatives. They complained that the teaching was old-fashioned, the teachers dominated the classes and the boys were cowed by too much listening. The school did not prepare properly for either employment or higher education!

Inspectors claimed to champion cowed pupils but they did not hesitate to brow-beat hapless teachers. In his eight years as a Wiltshire County Councillor, Fred Naylor realised that local advisers dictated how the curriculum was taught and if probationer teachers did not fall into line, it was made clear to them that their careers would not prosper.

As elsewhere in education, the greater the inspectors' confidence in untested trendy methods, the greater their reluctance to accept objective evidence revealing that the trendiness was wrong-footed. Their ratings of schools became vaguer and more subjective, and even where the authority had test results, they did not mention them in their reports.

In 1989, when low standards had become widely recognised, the Inspectorate produced an apparently germane, but very unfocused, report: Reading Policy and Practice at Ages 5–14. It was based on seven primary and ten secondary schools, far too few to be representative, despite claiming to represent rural, suburban and inner-city areas. Only one sentence touched upon standards - the vague statement that reading fluency was at least satisfactory and pupils' attitude to reading was positive. One wonders whether the sample schools were selected to conceal the huge national problem of illiteracy and paint a defensively rosy picture instead. There was no precise definition of "satisfactory" or "positive", and no objective citation of average reading quotients (ARQs), so comments remained platitudinous, e.g. "lower-achieving pupils were the least keen readers."

The Report sparked more interest where it promised to address the effect of different teaching methods but this part, too, proved disappointingly vague. It mentioned that some schools had been moving away from graded schemes towards an apprenticeship approach based on shared reading, i.e. real books, but there was not the slightest perception of the abysmal results of that method. Apprenticeship difficulties were seen as persistent, in which case most schools returned to graded books but it seemed to have escaped the inspectors' notice that the use of graded schemes throughout might have precluded the more persistent problems. Or perhaps not. There were no specific comments on the types of graded scheme used but they seem to have been largely whole-word-based.

Of two commended schools, one included unobtrusive structures such as recognising initial phonic blends and the other had more phonics but there was no acknowledgement that it was the merits of phonics that had put them in the lead. On the contrary, mixed methods were thought beneficial, though learning to read was considered very laborious. One eight-year-old was mentioned as having found it hard to read his favourite story, The Three Little Pigs. He was quoted as saying, "I cracked it in the end by reading and reading", which sounds suspiciously like learning to recite it parrot-fashion. Difficulties were still much in evidence in Year 6 and one giveaway phrase concerned library books borrowed but not necessarily read.

The conclusions of this report speak for themselves. Initial reading was considered well taught but produced some persistently backward pupils not always receiving adequate help. The most effective methods (not specified) were not all used in every school and advanced reading skills were not coherently developed. Literature teaching was all right but not sure of matching up to the National Curriculum, and competent teachers did better than others. Schools often needed clearer reading policies and assessment methods, and the quantity and quality of school library stocks was variable.

These comments illustrate the Inspectorate's vague over-generalisations and lack of specific assistance for teachers of reading. Part IV of the present book aims to give much more realistic help. Meanwhile it is clear that the Inspectorate, as it existed during the downwave, was in serious need of reform.

Chapter 10

Local Education Authorities

"He who pays the piper calls the tune."

The LEAs were the immediate paymasters in state education, disbursing funds from both local and central sources. Education made the largest demand upon local tax revenue, usually absorbing over one-third of the total and even over one-half. And this was only a minor part, as more than 80% came from the national exchequer, so LEAs were the biggest business in local officialdom with a wide range of powers. They controlled up to 40 services, from school meals to student grants, and their concentration of power made them a natural magnet for Progressivists. Many authorities exercised their role responsibly but not all.

The LEAs were educational planners, deciding the number, size and type of school and the broad nature of educational provision. They formulated policies on which subjects should be offered, how children should be taught and how schools should be run. They had ways of enforcing their policies and if their ethos was Progressivist, they could ruthlessly implement the ideology rather than aim for high standards.

They could appoint Progressivist advisers willing to threaten teachers with no promotion unless they toed the desired line. One London Borough Councillor, Edward Lister, observed that local inspectors, who were continuously embroiled in the same narrow ideas as their LEAs, were more likely to "go native" than the national HMIs, who saw varied standards over a wider area.

LEAs also controlled staff appointments through their political representatives on selection committees, and many heads had to accept unsuitable teachers instead of those that would best complement the existing staff team. Heads could also be kept on track by councillors and their allies on school governing boards.

LEAs also decided which children should go to which schools. Some allocated pupils to suit egalitarian social engineering, which was then furthered in mixed ability classes. Remote lip service was paid to the idea of meeting each child's best interests but in practice many were treated as pawns to be moved into positions that suited Progressivist ideology.

Parents' wishes were foiled, not only by the action of certain LEAs but also by the inaction of many more—their failure to provide useful information on the standards achieved by individual schools. Features such as new buildings, large playing fields, non-academic activities and the head's pleasant persona could all be displayed to impress parents but not whether their children would be properly taught to read.

The Inner London Education Authority

After the 1870 Education Act, London was a unified LEA. As the capital grew, it merged with neighbouring areas but each added borough retained some independence, including responsibility for education. The original LEA became the ILEA (Inner London Education Authority), consisting of eleven boroughs plus the Cities of London and Westminster. By 1982, it had nearly 2000 real estate properties, some of which were just left as wasteland and some of which it did not even realise it owned, which says little for its efficiency.

John Bowis, MP for Battersea, reported on its condition in *ILEA: The Closing Chapter* (1988). He showed that its inefficiency was matched by gross over-spending. Its figure of £2085 per pupil was much less than today's peak but nevertheless much more than the range from £1015 to £1355 for 88 of the 94 LEAs investigated. Its high expenditure might have been justified if it had bought high achievement but it did not. Kent, spending less than half as much, ranked 22nd for A-Level results but ILEA ranked 86th.

Much of the extra outlay went on administrative staff, who were two and a half times as many per pupil as in the average LEA. Yet these people neglected some blindingly obvious tasks. One survey showed vacancies for 29 mathematics and 21 science teachers and also surplus staff of 37 and 26 in these two subjects respectively. But instead of solving the shortfalls by redeployment, this large administrative workforce left many children untaught.

ILEA denied that its combined high-cost, low-attainment record was the worst in the country, which was easy to say at a time when testing was beyond the pale. Even then, however, O-Level and A-Level results placed it regularly within the bottom 10%. When ARQs at age 7+ became available, its infant schools were seen to have the same abysmal standard. Its 7+ ARQ was 89, as compared with 102 for the rest of England and Wales, and it was that 89 that brought the overall average down to 100. As explained in Chapter 4, a downwave reading age of 89 was the equivalent of backwardness during the upwave and that low level was ILEA's average. Moreover, the drag imposed by its appalling results allowed other authorities to believe that their 102 was above average, whereas 110 was needed to escape actual backwardness and 115 to equal the phonics average.

Despite claiming acceptable standards, ILEA also excused low ones as due to inner-city problems. When objective tests revealed the dire state of Culloden School, which the BBC had presented as a model of excellence, ILEA sheltered behind a plea that low IQs made inner-city children hard to teach. Yet the Culloden children's average intelligence quotient proved to be somewhat above the national average; their plight was purely the result of their being dumbed down by ILEA's mistaken teaching methods.

Another case of dumbing down was a sixth-former who gained just one mediocre A-Level in a class where all the rest, including the teachers, had little interest in learning. Later, as a mature student, he obtained Class 2.1 Honours in Philosophy at University College London, showing that his potential had been grossly neglected in his ILEA school.

A frequent excuse was that many inner-city pupils could not speak English but this is not a valid argument. In one ILEA school where the head insisted on phonics, a whole intake of non-English-speaking starters became above-average readers in two years.

Unfortunately, many capable and devoted ILEA teachers could not fulfil their potential because Progressivist social engineering took pride of place. Reading was seen as less important than eradication of sexism and the Childeric School in Lewisham actually forced boys aged seven to wear skirts, carry handbags and play with dolls. Marriage and heterosexism were targeted, e,g, by rewriting Goldilocks to replace the father, mother and child family by Mummy Bear, Friend and Baby Bear. Other children's books were chosen for their homosexual message and physical education was decried as a relic of militarism.

Above all, Progressivist contempt for "right-wing" politics led to the practice of indoctrinating children with extreme left-wing ideology. A clique from the Revolutionary Left formed the Inner London Teachers' Association (ILTA), with an office in an ILEA school and a magazine, *Teaching London Kids*, written by teachers with extremist views. It incited anti-white racial hostility, anti-imperialism and the abolition of capitalism to democratise society. "When I think of Thatcherism," it proclaimed, "I think of a system that exploits ignorance." Yet what could exploit ignorance more than Progressivism's leftist dogmas imposed on illiterate children deprived of the ability to shape independent views through reading?

Unsurprisingly, many families tried to save their children from these shortcomings by sending them to independent schools or to state schools in better boroughs nearby. This great escape involved no fewer than 45% of inner London pupils but its scale was disguised by an ingress of children from equally bad adjoining areas, such as Brent and Haringey, who came to those ILEA schools perceived as better than their own local ones.

ILEA families were also denied access to most local voluntary-aided schools with their high standards, as virtually all such schools in London were so threatened by left-wing power that they went to the expense of moving out to the shires in order to survive.

When it was proposed to abolish the ILEA and make its thirteen areas educationally independent, its "virtues" were extolled by a Haringey teacher who opposed its abolition. But she recoiled from the idea of merging Haringey into it, as she preferred to be a big fish in a small pond while wanting to deny ILEA staff the same opportunity.

Norfolk Education Authority

Progressivism was worst in left-wing authorities but its hidden political agenda also colonised Conservative ones. This happened in Norfolk where, from 1972, Mona McNee campaigned for phonics teaching. Her unusual success as a remedial teacher, using phonics, should have won a responsive hearing for her argument that if all infants were taught phonics from the start, it would prevent illiteracy and save the county the extra 10% that had to be added to the education budget for remedial work. But, despite all the evidence of phonics' advantages, her pleas fell on deaf ears, because the watchdog posts were solidly occupied by Progressivist officials and the elected members trusted them when they represented her facts as mere trouble-making. Consequently she met stonewall resistance.

Her offer to teach the three Rs in a reception class received no acknowledgement from the Area Education Officer. And when she applied for an advertised infant-school post, he said that teachers would complain if she were appointed to any local school, as her crusade to improve reading had made her unpopular.

Someone from the West Suffolk Teachers' Centre did write but only to recommend Frank Smith's "excellent" *Understanding Reading*, which was precisely what she was criticising. Three first-school heads debarred her from working with their children. They denied having any "faulty learning" to remediate and refused to visit Woods Loke School where Sue Lloyd had eliminated illiteracy with the super-phonic i.t.a. method. Suffolk LEA was also too disaffected to check whether the benefit of earlier learning at Woods Loke was raising O-level results.

Mona McNee tackled teacher training by writing to Charles Cripps at Cambridge University's Institute of Education, explaining that the worst problem for remedial teachers was look-say's conditioning of children to guess words, which made them resistant to detailed letter decoding. Cripps, speaking later at the Norwich Teachers' Centre said that no current teachers taught spelling but otherwise ignored the issue.

An important aspect of her campaign was to question the cover-up of reading standards. Norfolk, with an ARQ a little above the bogus average of 100, was pronounced admirable and everyone seemed to want to ignore the stream of illiterates coming to Mona McNee for help and to enjoy the glory reflected in the self-congratulation fed to the Eastern Daily Press: "Norfolk pupils top the class." "The county's teachers earn a gold star." One head claimed results were improving each year when really they were just fluctuating within a point or two of the same mediocre level. All turned a blind eye to the proof that changing to phonics brought a rapid gain of at least ten points, followed by a sustained high level.

Church schools and the Norwich Diocesan Council felt confident that the Christian majority on their school governing bodies would preclude any takeover by an adverse monopoly influence. They could not accept that a Progressivist monopoly was already in place and that governors were trusting its officials while ignoring pupils' poor attainment.

But governors seemed just as impervious. One refused to read an explanatory package, saying that figures meant nothing and what mattered was what was really happening, i.e. that children were learning to read jolly well with existing methods. He shut his mind to the fact that Mona McNee was having to rescue illiterates from his own school.

Inspectors were equally unresponsive. Asking to meet an HMI produced only a blank and when repeated evoked the reply, "HMI Mr Howarth is unable to accede to your request." Nor would a senior language adviser. Inspectors fell back on the cliché, "there is no one way to teach reading". But there is one highly successful way — phonics — which they were suppressing in favour of Frank Smith's failed approach. They covered up their neglect by refusing to produce attainment figures in their reports on the schools they inspected.

It was hoped that County Councillors would examine the facts and figures objectively but they, too, trusted their Progressivist officials as being the "experts". Mrs Roualle, the Education Committee chairman, made, but then cancelled, an appointment to discuss the problem and passed the buck to the Deputy Chief Education Officer, advising Mona McNee to raise the matter in a professional, i.e. Progressivist, circle such as a teachers' centre.

One councillor did get as far as looking at her remedial teacher's reading records but the figures achieved only a severe reprimand for breaching confidentiality. Another councillor advised leaving a statement in each member's place at a meeting and this was done. But the statements were whipped away before the meeting opened and Mrs. Roualle said that was because the topic was to be raised at the next meeting. It was not. The Director of Education complained that putting documents at each councillor's place was "not protocol".

The Education Committee also ignored its own budgetary evidence that standards were slipping so badly that in 1983-84 the number of remedial teachers had to be more than doubled, from 18 to 42 full-time equivalents. Discussion of this proof was evaded by placing the item late on the agenda, after the meeting's time had run out.

Going from the Education Committee to the Leader of the whole County Council again failed to arouse concern, and once more the buck was passed to Progressivist officials. Responses escalated from "your letter has been noted" to increasing levels of sarcasm, "your interesting views", but the facts were still not taken seriously.

Nor was any credence given to the 1983 findings of the United States Federal Government that look-say methods were the cause of falling standards. That cut no ice with Norfolk's ingrown authority and nor did the official US statement that phonics teaching would leave no child illiterate.

Saddest of all was the attitude of Councillor Mrs. Gillian Shephard, later a Member of Parliament and Secretary of State for Education and Science. As a teacher of French, she ought to have understood the phonic principle of letter-sound relationships but she proved just as locked into look-say Progressivism as the rest. Someone closely connected with her had learned to read from ILEA instruction, so that was that.

When asked why reading attainment figures were not presented, she replied with an evasive sidestep, saying that the results were "treated with some reservation because of the nature of the tests and it is not intended that they should be given the credibility that you infer" [sic, for "imply"]. This is typical Progressivist distrust of testing and facts. It is true, as we shall show in Chapter 17, that some reading tests are not too accurate for individuals, but the errors cancel out for school and county averages, which would be far more reliable than the total lack of test information that Gillian Shephard favoured.

When her attention was drawn to the 233% increase in remedial teaching at an extra cost of nearly £300,000, she merely sent a postcard in acknowledgement. Total county spending on special needs rose to £5.6 million in 1984-85 and to £20 million seven years later, but the LEA would not see that their methods were actually creating the special needs, quite unnecessarily.

A suggestion that Gillian Shephard should ascertain the ARQ figures of Norfolk's best and worst schools in order to compare their teaching methods evoked the reply, "You are always so specific in your statements about reading levels." Would she have preferred vagueness? "You might find some satisfaction in raising your suggestion with a professional body like NAHT. I am quite sure they would give you an up-to-date view of the professional opinion of reading standards." She seemed too blinkered to know that NAHT's view was resentment that only 5% of school starters could already read and indignation that schools should be expected to teach reading at all.

Why did Gillian Shephard recommend the failers and stave off someone who was really teaching illiterates to read? Why, when the Annual Survey of Attainment was rushed through a Schools Sub-Committee meeting in two minutes, did she describe it as a full discussion? Was it because, as a teacher herself, she had been indoctrinated in the way described in our chapter on teachers and was too bigoted to have an open mind towards the serious problems of educational decline?

The Conservative government at Westminster took a less complacent view of educational standards and encouraged LEAs to organise workshops on possible improvements. Norfolk scheduled one on "Reading" and Mona McNee asked to take part. The topic was then changed to the broader and vaguer one of "Primary Schools" and her application was disregarded. So, too, was one of her deepest concerns, dyslexia, which was dismissed in the belief that no such thing existed.

Other LEAs were also gripped in the stranglehold of Progressivism, to a greater or lesser degree than Norfolk, which has been used as an example because of our access to a complete record of its reactions, presented here as a skeletal account. It illustrates how thoroughly support for look-say had infiltrated every aspect of education to create a hidebound and monolithic narrow-mindedness. As a remedial teacher, Mona McNee had remained open-minded in order to embrace what worked best to rescue illiterate children from their look-say rut and turn their lives around from failure to success. Others seemed to care less about the plight of the children and more about preserving the illusion of their own spurious rightness.

Chapter 11

Central Government

The dual strand of officialdom and elected members also existed at national level. The officials were the civil servants with permanent tenure, who could accumulate expertise and climb the career ladder, knowing that they would outlast the term of office of any Minister or Government. This attracted the power-hungry, who created a watchdog for Progressivism instead of for excellence. They ceased to be public servants and became covert public masters.

An attempt to expose this conspiracy was to ridicule it on television in *Yes, Minister* and *Yes, Prime Minister*. These revealed officials' dismay when the Minister's policy ran counter to their own and also their secret conferring on how to manipulate him back on to the "correct" rails. The Minister always yielded, unaware that the overt reasons masked more devious aims.

Alas! The series' verisimilitude was so farcical that viewers did not take it seriously. Some Ministers, however, were keenly aware and when William Waldegrave signed a prize copy of *Yes, Minister*, he also wrote, "It is all true." Margaret Thatcher readily accepted Alice Coleman's account of similar tactics in the Department of the Environment, and a former MP, Christopher Gill, wrote to the press of

> . . . a deeply engrained belief that the man in Whitehall knows best and an extreme reluctance on the part of the Mandarins to listen to outsiders who really know what they are talking about, especially when the advice offered conflicts with the received departmental wisdom.

In education, the received wisdom was Progressivism. Some Ministers, who lacked a mind open to evidence, took the slightest suggestion that they had been misled as an insult to their intelligence, which simply reinforced their counterproductive conditioning.

Non-ministerial MPs were further from the chalk-face of educational decline than local councillors but also more likely to receive pleas from parents and hence more aware of the problems. As a result, reform was eventually promoted by central and not local government.

John Dewey, the father of Progressivism, was a left-wing moderniser and his legacy has remained with the political Left. This bias has been repeatedly made clear from Progressivists' bitter denunciation of traditionalism as "right-wing", an automatic term of abuse.

Traditionalism v. Progressivism broadly parallels Conservative v Socialist/Labour politics. It does not apply to all party members but only to government tendencies. Basically, the Right aims to conserve the good aspects of the nation's traditions and build on them, restricting innovation to the reform of abuses. The Left believes that advancement depends upon a clean sweep of tradition in order to modernise across the board.

The 1945 Labour Government did not tackle education directly. Its priorities were to create centralised control in other ways: government bulk buying of all imports, retention of food rationing, nationalising coal, steel, rail transport and medical provision, and putting a brake on land-use initiatives by comprehensive planning. Education appeared untouched but Progressivism was in tune with Labour's modernising drive and allowed to flourish.

The Conservative Government of 1951 was more alert to educational problems, though not to their true causes, and set up three Committees of Inquiry, respectively on maladjusted, secondary and primary children. All were hijacked by Progressivism.

The Underwood Report, 1955

Entitled *The Problems of the Maladjusted Child,* the Underwood Report confused cause and effect, claiming that emotional disturbance was producing non-readers. This excuse was balm to ineffective teachers and trainers, as it blamed parents and exonerated the schools. No-one asked why emotional disturbance was reaching plague proportions in peacetime when it had not done so in the more difficult wartime conditions. Nor would they heed the opposite explanation that emotional problems were often the *result* of the humiliation of illiteracy. No-one investigated whether such disturbance was commoner in whole-word than phonics classes nor was attention given to the fact that Underwood's hypothesis did nothing to ameliorate the situation whereas phonics teaching did. Non-readers rescued by phonics could regain self-esteem and cast off emotional distress, as Mona McNee often observed with her remedial pupils.

The Newsom Report, 1963

As Progressivism spread, there were more illiterate school leavers and the Newsom Committee was briefed to enquire into *The Education of the Less Able Child, 13-16.* It found that backwardness at this age affected 50% of pupils and therefore entitled its report *Half Our Future.* It urged remedial action before they left school — which could not be more than a patch-up job. Pupils do not become backward readers in their teens; their problems originate in the infant schools. The real need is for *prevention* then to obviate the need for *intervention* later.

The Plowden Report, 1967

The Committee *To Consider Primary Education in All Its Aspects* offered hope of introducing prevention, but did not deliver. Lady Plowden's appointment exemplifies a basic error often made in choosing heads for such enquiries. Her qualification was administrative skill in chairmanship and as she had been neither a pupil nor a teacher in a state primary, she depended heavily on the views of Progressivist colleagues. Traditionalist witnesses received short shrift. The report, *Children and Their Primary Schools,* was not produced until the next Labour Government came in and it proved to be in tune with leftist attitudes.

As part of the Progressivist cover-up, the report claimed that there had been a dramatic advance in reading, which was quite untrue but diverted attention away from illiteracy and its look-say cause. It embraced Progressivist recommendations, urging that the uniqueness of each child necessitated separate individual treatment as *"the essential process on which all educational strategy and tactics must be based."* This was welcomed then but imposed a heavy burden upon teachers and was heavily criticised later. In 1995, Nigel Hastings commented:

> Established tenets that had successfully guided the course of education, in some cases for hundreds of years, were overturned and cast aside. A whole body of new and untried precepts was introduced and teachers who had devoted their lives to instructing the young found that they were faced with a grim choice: change your teaching methods or be frozen out. Don't teach them to spell—this will come naturally with time. Don't teach them to read or write; these are mere tricks that they will learn effortlessly in due course. Don't teach the multiplication tables; you will bore them and they won't want to come to school.

In fact, "Don't teach." The classroom with orderly rows of desks facing the teacher was no more. The Plowden Report was the British origin of calling the teacher a facilitator, who had to move among groups of children seated round small tables and do what (s)he could to minister to their varied needs, one child at a time, trying to be heard above all their voices as they "collaborated" with each other.

Another change was to sit the children on the floor, crowded together where they could poke each other, fiddle with the plaits of the girl in front and break toys by leaning on them. Out was the careful choice of right-sized chairs to promote good posture. These were often wastefully destroyed and expensively replaced by carpeting to sit on. The expense was also a toll on health. Floor-sitting can be spine-twisting and there has been a rise in back problems. Carpets can harbour dust and mites, and may have been a factor in the asthma epidemic.

The Plowdenist classroom arrangement was also a great time-waster. Various studies have shown that it distracts children from working for one-third to three-quarters of the time, which would necessitate a corresponding increase in school years to cover the same ground as with the traditional row arrangement. Furthermore, children need opportunities to work alone without always depending on the group, and that is made easier by the row layout.

In 1991, George Walden described the basic concept of the Plowden report as teaching children *not to learn,* on the pretext that they did not need to. Instead, they were to *discover* and *create,* and above all choose what they wanted to do, rather than having more experienced elders map out a valuable learning path for them. This youthful self-guidance was supposed to produce mature, responsible adults but it did not. Walden described the outcome of decades of this "amiable institutionalised indolence" as follows:

> ... when they can see that nearly a third of our children can't read or do simple sums at seven, when for many our school system has become a sort of running remedial process, and when they can see the vacuous-minded, sullen, resentful—in a word, Plowdenised—youngsters around us ... people have started to wonder how we got ourselves into this clownish educational posture (teachers standing on their heads to avoid teaching) and how we get out of it.

Progressivists were undismayed by this outcome; they still averred that only the process mattered, not the product. And children working independently without a constant group consensus would be egocentric and antisocial. But enjoining children to be more creative seems to have led many to be just the opposite—more destructive and vandalistic.

Plowdenism was only the same as the Progressivism that was already established and starting to make the educational decline more obvious. Nevertheless, the Report did additional harm because it gave Progressivist methods an official sanction of respectable status.

In 1964, the Labour government set up a quango, the Schools Council, which became a Progressivist extreme. The Prime Minister, Harold Wilson, declared a glowing faith in the new education with the phrase, "the white heat of technology", which he saw as a universal "fix".

The Bullock Report, 1975

The next Conservative Minister of Education, Margaret Thatcher, perceived that the key cause of the illiteracy explosion was poor reading instruction and in 1972 she set up a Committee of Inquiry specifically on the teaching of reading. Unfortunately, its apparently ideal chairman, Sir Alan Bullock, was less than ideal in practice. As the head of an Oxford College he should have brought a great intellect to the task and as Chairman of the Schools Council he should have understood the educational level of infants. But his Schools Council colleagues seem to have infected him with Progressivist ardour, even to the extent of changing the Committee's remit from the focused topic of *Learning to Read* to one with a broader scope, *A Language for Life*, which submerged its original purpose. It was eventually published in 1975 after another change of government to Labour, so there was no critical appraisal of it or even a rebuke for the unauthorised change of remit.

The Report contrived to appear impartial but actually gave biased support to the crippling look-say status quo. Its first 76 pages were concerned with preliminary infra-structure, including alleged results of testing. One lie was that for the past 23 years only 3% to 4% of school leavers were illiterate — a figure far below the research finding that had led to the Committee's creation. It suggested spurious stability instead of the actual sharp decline. There was no excuse for a well-funded Committee not to ascertain the true facts, especially as it was then a decade since greater illiteracy had ceased to be masked by upwave teachers still in post.

The Bullock Report also concealed the facts in other ways and helped make the whole-word method even more widespread. Actual reading was not addressed until Part III, where spelling was presented as a serious problem:

> . . in one study the researchers [B. Berdiansky, B. Cronnel and J. Koehler] examined the 6,092 two-syllable words among the 9,000 words in the comprehension vocabularies of six to nine-year-old children. They recorded 211 different spellings for phonemes [sounds] in these words, and these required 166 rules to govern their use. Over 10% of the words had to be left aside as exceptions.

These figures make mountains out of molehills by counting many letter blends or syllables as separate phonemes. Margaret Bishop, in her intriguing *The ABCs and All Their Tricks* (1986) has fewer, 186, but even many of those are not needed in true phonics. For example, "sl", "spl" and "st" are not different phonemes but simple blends of different letter sounds. Consequently, mention of 166 rules is a gross exaggeration. Progressivists seem to enjoy inventing pseudo-phonics in order to argue, falsely, that the phonics approach is too complex to be contemplated for use in schools.

There seemed to be three possible solutions to the spelling difficulties that the Bullock Committee noted but the Report missed a golden opportunity to analyze them properly.

a) Spelling Reform
The Committee could have proposed improving reading through spelling reform. This has been done in countries with less irregular spelling than ours, so Bullock could have made headway with it especially as the times were ripe for it.

Sir James Pitman's initial teaching alphabet, then at its height in 10% of schools, had already demonstrated how 44 English phonemes could each be represented by a single letter symbol (grapheme). And the interest shown in the George Bernard Shaw competition for an improved alphabet might have elicited practical support if its adjudicators had not killed it by selecting a scheme that did not retain a single existing letter.

English has advantages that have made it the leading international language: a huge vocabulary, few burdensome inflections and our national linguistic talent for understanding broken English. Its spelling remains the obstacle and if it were streamlined the benefit would be worldwide. However, the Bullock Committee rejected this option as being too complex to handle, even to the extent of making a few minor recommendations such as substituting "f" for "ph", as in American scientific terms, for example "sulfate" for "sulphate".

b) Traditional Phonics

In the past traditional phonics served us well and helped make English the world leader in the literacy league. Traditional spelling may be second best to a reformed alphabet but given the demise of i.t.a., it is the best we have. Unfortunately, Bullock did not recommend it but presented an alleged "balanced" survey of different methods, which was far from impartial.

One biased argument was an insinuation that phonics had ongoing problems. This is mistaken. In the days when phonics prevailed, the problems were so few that the UK's illiteracy rate was only 1%. And the subsequent growth of problems was wholly due to Progressivism's suppression of phonics, despite its demonstrable success.

Another obfuscation was the claim that phonics was still used in 97% of British schools and must therefore be responsible for the problems. The same table (11.1) showed that look-say was also used in 97% and should have been equally blamed but was not. It was also implied that the two were evenly matched but the training colleges' sedulous avoidance of phonics meant that it could not figure as largely as their favoured look-say. Whatever was passing for it must have been too poor or fragmentary to have had a genuine phonics effect.

Table 11.1: Bullock's Estimate Of Method Frequencies

Method	Percentage of Schools
Look and Say (word recognition)	97
Phonics 1 (letter sounds, digraphs, diphthongs)	97
Phonics 2 (syllables)	70
Sentence Method	51

Any phonics still in use would have had little chance against so much look-say, on the Gresham's-law principle that bad teaching drives out good. Look-say's sloppy emphasis on guessing would have conditioned pupils against carefully relating each letter to its sound. The division into Phonics 1 and Phonics 2 is also suspicious. Was "syllables" a different beginning or a second stage ignored by 27% of those using the first stage? And what can one make of the large overlap between phonics and the sentence method, which neglects even individual words, let alone letters. This table is muddled and reflects the muddling effect of mixed methods.

Bullock paid initial lip service to phonics and then denigrated it. He dredged up a hoary old chestnut, showing that a weird assemblage of letters could be pronounced in an equally weird way. Thus "calmbost" would be pronounced "chemist", because

c— can be hard as in "candle"

a— can be short "e" as in "many"

l— is not pronounced in "calm"

b—is not pronounced in "lambing"

o— is pronounced short "i" as in "women"

It was argued that deciphering "calmbost" placed adults in the position of beginners, who do not know the rules. True, but systematic phonics teaches the rules in a logical order with a graded word sequence to match. This "calmbost" argument was one of Thouless's 38 kinds of crooked thinking—taking some to mean all. If all words were baffling, there would be nothing striking about it. The existence of a minority of difficult spellings was used to obscure the fact that 90% are not, and the real teasers are rarely met by beginners.

Bullock also confused reading and writing. For reading it is easy to learn that "ai", "ay" and "a—consonant—e" are all pronounced long "a" but writing takes more effort to pick the right alternative. This requires attention to spelling. The report alleged that there are so many spelling permutations that if children had to work through them all with each unfamiliar word, they would never learn to read. This is rubbish. Knowing the letters and the common rules narrows the choice, often entirely obviating uncertainty, and fluent readers are constantly seeing correct spellings in print.

c) Abandoning Phonics

Besides pretending that it had no bias against phonics, the Bullock Report tried to conceal its prejudice in favour of the whole-word method. It professed neutrality, asserting that *no one method, medium, approach, device or philosophy held the key to the process of learning how to read.* It also denigrated phonics by asserting that teaching "kuh-a-tuh" says "cat" is incorrect and would have to be unlearnt! That is nonsense.

The Committee claimed that teaching letter blends such as "bl" would, if tested, prove more effective than "b" and "l" separately but during its three-year life it made no attempt to arrange such a test. Mere supposition sufficed, and Bullock alleged that "to endorse one [method] at the expense of the others is no more helpful today than it has proved in the past."

This methodological "breadth" illustrated how the over-permissive society had been engineered into believing unproven ideas and ignoring hard facts such as the way systematic phonics *always* brought reading fluency when it was uncontaminated by the muddling effect of the whole-word method. So even if Bullock did not overtly advocate look-say, he effectively gave it the victory by recommending mixed methods. By campaigning against the clear-cut evidence, the Report garbled public understanding of what phonics really is.

Despite its vast verbiage, the Report seemed too complaisant to study the illiteracy problem in depth. "We should not be so unrealistic as to believe that every child should be a competent reader on leaving infant school." This tolerance was a recipe for victimising children. If they are fit to attend infant school, i.e. not blind, profoundly deaf or brain-damaged, they should all be reading fluently by seven. The first two school years are the best for learning to read and now children join reception classes at age four, they could all become readers by six.

The Report's claim that only 3 or 4% of leavers were illiterate combined with its statement that it did not expect all children to be readers by the critical age of seven indicated that it was offering little or no scope for improvement. But as ALBSU proved, it did have a negative influence, with significantly worse illiteracy among adults who had been infant pupils after its publication than among those who left infant school before it appeared.

The most realistic part of the Report was the "Note of Dissent" by Stuart Froome. He disagreed that there was no reliable way to compare past and present standards, and said that the Committee had complacently ignored the evidence presented to it on this point. He deplored teachers' failure to correct children's mistakes, supposedly because to do so would interrupt their creativity. He recounted how his own experience as a primary school headmaster led him to find that greater competence in spelling, punctuation and grammar *enhanced* creativity. He also disagreed with the denigration of reading tests, which he considered necessary, and dissented from the Committee's belief that mixed-ability classes were best for English teaching. He cast doubt on the Progressivist belief that reading and writing can be absorbed as naturally as listening and speaking, which had been an argument used to support the discovery method, and he emphasised the Report's own recognition that much so-called research on topic or project work had little practical value.

Unfortunately he began his Note of Dissent by saying that he agreed with the Report's main recommendations, which seems to have drawn the teeth of his criticisms.

James Callaghan, Labour Prime Minister in the late 1970s, *did* perceive that something was wrong with education and launched the "Great Debate". Progressivists dominated the discussions and the exercise amounted to nothing more than a talking shop.

The Tizard Report, 1972 and the Warnock Report, 1978

The foregoing reports did not stem the rise of illiteracy and it now seemed that the commonest element in learning disability was *dyslexia*. This term originated in Germany in 1883 to denote severe difficulty in reading due to brain injuries in adults who had previously been competent readers. The Oxford English Dictionary's definition is "A difficulty in reading due to affection of the brain; specifically word blindness."

During the downwave, dyslexia stopped being a rare medical curiosity in adults and became a frequent diagnosis in illiterate or severely backward children, so the term passed into general use, and the Tizard was Committee set up to investigate it. This was a golden opportunity to study the dyslexia "epidemic" and its cause and to establish the best way of dealing with its reading problems. Unfortunately the Committee ducked its responsibility and produced only a superficial eight-page report, which muddled dyslexia with other conditions. It said the term should be dropped in favour of an unspecified "specific learning disability", a self-contradiction echoing Schonell's advice never to trust a diagnosis of dyslexia.

The Tizard Report said that some dyslexics could be very intelligent in other ways, but nevertheless implied that the word was just a middle-class parents' "respectable" excuse — a fancy word to mask being not too bright or simply lazy. It advocated finding the best remedial approach but made no attempt to do so and merely advised more instruction, which would only have been more time wasted on the very methods that had already failed.

Tizard's "Don't call it dyslexia" was an unhealthy attitude, not paralleled elsewhere. No-one says, "Don't call it measles". Diagnosis is the first step towards effective action and, if the Committee had investigated properly, a solution could have been found much earlier. It might have contacted the Orton Dyslexia Society in USA, which established a brain bank from bodies bequeathed for medical research at the Beth Israel Hospital in Boston, Massachusetts. Harvard neurologists discovered anatomical abnormalities in the links between dyslexics' two brain hemispheres and W. E. Drake published the findings in the *Journal of Learning Disability* in 1968. "Dyslexia" became a stigma instead of a name for a treatable condition. Implying that even the concept was controversial prevented further understanding. It became unmentionable so that if the possibility crossed a parent's mind, the reaction was, "Oh no! I'm not having *my* child dyslexic." Action was postponed as parents hoped against hope that "(s)he'll catch on", and precious time was lost. We now know that the earlier dyslexia is tackled, the more easily illiteracy is prevented but Tizard advocated *delaying* remedial action till age seven or eight.

The Warnock Report considered children with both physical and mental disabilities. It, too, paid little attention to dyslexia, with just three brief mentions, one of which again gave the impression that only parent power lent it any substance.

The British Dyslexia Association

Despite the official denials of its existence, dyslexic illiteracy continued to multiply and inspired the foundation of the British Dyslexia Association (BDA) as a charity dedicated to helping the afflicted lead satisfying lives in spite of being illiterate. It also ran courses for teachers on "Learning to Read". Similar organisations were set up in Scotland and Ireland.

Parents of dyslexics were referred to the 1981 Education Act, which stipulated that children with learning problems must be identified and provided for, but as the true nature of their trouble was not understood, this legislative concern just labelled them as backward and offered no effective remedial assistance. The BDA performed a great service by naming talented people who could be retrospectively seen as dyslexic, including giants such as Leonardo da Vinci. Einstein's brain has also revealed dyslexic features.

Some dyslexics offset their written weakness with spoken excellence, e.g. the actresses Susan Hampshire, Beryl Reid and Ruth Madoc. Susan Hampshire's courageous confession of reading disability in her 1981 book, *Susan's Story*, was a tremendous help in bringing the problems out of hiding.

Others used political oratory, e.g. George Washington and Lloyd George, and the oral gift led some of them to publish, e.g. Winston Churchill and Hans Christian Andersen, whose styles sound well when read aloud and are easy to follow. The latter's poor spelling meant that his manuscripts had to be re-written. However, these men are not practical models for today's dyslexics because they learned to read by the phonics method and were not illiterate.

Many dyslexics have taken up work with materials and machines or in sport or business, e.g. the inventor Thomas Edison, the sculptor Auguste Rodin, the racing driver Jackie Stewart, the Olympic champions, Duncan Goodhew (swimming) and Steven Redgrave (rowing), and Richard Branson (entrepreneur). General Patton, Nelson Rockefeller, and many more successful people were dyslexics. There may be special talent in the right brain's visual-spatial fields, such as mechanics, engineering, art, carpentry, designing, architecture and building. Many succeed in self-employment, e.g. running a building firm while the wife does the books. Such achievements are ways of cocking a snook at society: "See! You thought I was a dumb cluck but here I am with a fine house and a successful business. I'm just as good as you are."

Parents were advised not to criticise their children's failings, to avoid emotional stress, but the BDA did not seek treatment to *prevent* failure and distress. When told of Mona McNee's evidence that word-blindness could often be cured fairly quickly, the BDA seemed reluctant to believe that anyone else could know more about dyslexia than itself and did not pursue the opportunity. Today it is not entirely unaware of it but its main thrust is still to help in other ways. Of course, if dyslexic illiteracy shrank back to its pre-Progressivist range, there would be no reason for the BDA's existence. By contrast, The Dyslexic Institute, set up for the purpose of teaching, does recognise phonics as a remedy.

As the official Reports did nothing to illuminate the dyslexia situation, we include an unofficial statement: *The McNee Report.*

The McNee Report: The Dyslexic Illiteracy Epidemic

This report is based on Mona McNee's experience of teaching nearly 360 dyslexics to read, after their teachers had given them up as intractably illiterate. In every case she got them reading and many became highly fluent. This was possible because she explored the causes of the disability and proposed a cure, which she tested in practice and became 100% certain that it worked. Her thesis also explains why dyslexic illiteracy suddenly proliferated from extreme rarity to such a high frequency that it resulted in the foundation of the BDA.

The dyslexic illiteracy epidemic has resembled the invasion of a powerful new virus infecting many of the population's most vulnerable members – children – who are then badly disadvantaged for the whole remainder of their lives. But dyslexia is not a virus nor is its potential for illiteracy necessarily lifelong. Illiteracy can be both prevented and cured.

a) Causative Factors
A *genetic* explanation emerged from research by Drake, who established that dyslexic's brains differ from those of non-dylexics. Animal brains have evolved with two virtually symmetrical hemispheres but with the advent of language, greater asymmetry set in. The left side of the brain deals with linear linguistic logic while the right perceives patterns. Thus the word "book" is stored in the left brain but the visual image of a book is in the right brain. This is clearly seen in strokes. If the left hemisphere is

afflicted the patient probably loses the power of speech, but if the right side suffers, speech is retained.

The right brain remains in charge of non-linear pattern-recognition processes, such as map-reading, art, musical harmony, humour, perceiving the meaning of body language, understanding machines and materials, and having insight into architectural space requirements. In some people it relates ideas that linear logic does not juxtapose, to give original new insights. However, right brain creativity needs left-brain logic to vet whether these insights are constructive or just insupportably fanciful. This necessitates good connections between the two hemispheres, which dyslexics may lack.

A paucity of links between the two hemispheres is a common abnormality in dyslexics' brains. This explains why they appear to learn something one day, forget it the next but remember it the day after, depending on which side of the brain is active at the time. Einstein had many abnormal links and other dyslexic differences are still being explored. For example, the fast-processing part of the visual system may have fewer neurones, which makes dyslexics slow to process letters. Or there may be small neurones in the fast-processing part of the auditory system, which can cause mishearing of words, e,g, "aminal" for "animal", and misinterpretation of spoken instructions. The 1990s decade of concerted brain research identified several genes related to dyslexia and there may be more. They show that the condition is genetic, as previously inferred from its repeated incidence in the same families. It is about four times as common in boys as in girls.

The dyslexic sex-ratio arises from a difference in brain structure, which is explained by Bonnie Macmillan in her book, *Why Boys Are Different*. The anatomical link between the two brain hemispheres, the corpus callosum, is rather thin in the male and much thicker in females, with more cross-routes. This enables boys to retain longer concentration on issues related to one side or other, without incurring distractions from the other side, but it also makes it more difficult for them to transfer the right-brain approach of whole-word shapes over to the left-brain letter sequence of actual reading. Many more girls are able to make such transfers, needing less help to do so than boys, and consequently female dyslexia is only 20% of total dyslexia.

This accounts for the predominance of males among dyslexics and also for the fact that boys, with a greater illiteracy rate, have lagged behind girls in national tests. Proof that this is caused by the look-say/whole-word method is its reversibility when that method is abandoned. The gender-lag disappears when boys are taught to read by the phonics method, and some of them then shoot ahead of girls. They are no longer identified as dyslexic. All the undermining sense of failure and

the various anti-social reactions that dyslexia provokes, have been manu-
factured by Progressivism's wrong-headed teaching techniques.

There is also a *congenital hypothesis,* which suggests that the *degree* of
dyslexia may be influenced by pre-natal conditions. It gains support from
the fact that dyslexics are often left-handed, as also are premature babies.
A speculative idea is that as the language area in the left hemisphere is the
brain's most highly evolved part, it would be the last to mature before
birth. So babies who do not go full term may have a greater probability of
right-brain influence, including left-handedness. Similarly, the links
between the hemispheres may not have developed fully in the premature.
Dyslexic genes would increase the risk.

An environmental hypothesis springs from the dyslexia epidemic's sudden arrival and vast post-1950 increase. If it is largely genetic, it should
pass down the generations in roughly equal frequencies. It was mentioned
earlier that Mona McNee explored its occurrence in her own family and
found that all were fluent readers with no learning difficulties, as far back
as she could trace, but the picture changed abruptly in her son's
post-World War II generation, when eight out of twelve family members
were dyslexic. This sharp change coincided with the onset of dyslexia
throughout the nation, which strongly suggests that there was an environmental cause.

We therefore find three explanations: clear anatomical evidence that
dyslexia is genetic, possible evidence that it may be partly congenital, and
strong epidemiological evidence that its potential for reading problems is
a response to an environmental trigger.

Mona McNee set about resolving the paradox of how dyslexic illiterates
could have inherited their condition from literate and apparently non-dyslexic parents. She postulated that the genetic basis gives only a *latent*
potential for word-blindness (possibly affected by uterine conditions),
and that there must be some environmental *activating* factor able to make it
manifest as illiteracy. There was no activating factor during the upwave,
as the phonics method directly addressed the left side of the brain where
reading ability is located. It was not until look-say inappropriately recast a
left-brain activity into a right-brain mechanism, by emphasising word
shapes and pictures instead of letters, that activation became common.

However, the fact that the rise of dyslexia *coincided* with phonics-starva-
tion does not, of itself, prove that the latter caused the former. Firm proof
involves demonstrating that removal of the alleged cause also removes the
effect. Mona McNee tackled this stage of research by teaching phonics to
dyslexics, to see if it dispelled their word-blindness. It did, and often in
short order. Very mild cases needed only one elementary instruction,
"Start on the left, *this* side, and read from left to right" — a fact which
Progressivist teachers may fail to mention. With more severe cases, the

rescue took longer but Mona McNee was in great demand for private tuition and has now, without fail, restored their lost educational birthright to nearly 360. Nor has she been alone in this success. The proof is constantly repeated in schools that use systematic phonics and thus *prevent* the activation of dyslexic illiteracy.

Mona McNee cured word-blindness but not genetic dyslexia. The dyslexics were transformed into carriers and did not remain sufferers themselves. If they had been taught phonics first, they would not even realise they were dyslexic. Alice Coleman had not the slightest suspicion until she collaborated on this chapter and recognised dyslexic symptoms in herself. They were not activated into illiteracy because she was taught phonics by a capable teacher and could read fluently at age five. Ironically, a head who helped to convince Tizard that dyslexia did not exist, ran a school where the phonics method prevented its activation.

b) Dyslexic Characteristics at the Pre-School Stage

Mona McNee defines dyslexia as a *latent inborn potential for muddlement*, chiefly in respect of direction. The earlier it is identified, the easier it is to control and thus prevent illiteracy. There is a pre-school test using a dot pattern but parents can recognise it from the child's everyday behaviour. Degrees of dyslexia vary and pre-school signs differ from child to child, as well as from day to day in the same child. Some occur in non-dyslexics. No single criterion suffices; there should be at least five or six, to be certain that the diagnosis is correct.

- *Late Talking*. Lack of left-brain dominance means that 60% of dyslexics are slow to talk. Speech therapy may help but should not be allowed to mask the dyslexia.
- *Shoes on The Wrong Foot*. The two brain hemispheres are not fully related, so dyslexics confuse left and right. Others learn quickly when the mistake is pointed out but dyslexics go on repeating it, despite the discomfort.
- *T-Shirt Back to Front*. Reversals affect other directions, not only right-left. Back door may be confused with front, above with below and before with behind.
- *Buttons Done Up Wrongly*. Vertical confusion, with buttons done up with a "spare".
- *Clumsy Movement*. Children usually learn right from left when crawling, so crawling deprivation is bad for dyslexics.
- *Poor Co-ordination*. Clumsiness continues, e.g. being slow to catch a ball.
- *Good at Lego*. Right-brain dominance often makes a child good with shapes, patterns and manipulation.
- *Saying the Wrong Word*. The left language centre may not work properly and the verbal watchdog is sometimes off-duty. Children may say

"blue" instead of "red" and call people by the wrong names without realising it. Spoonerisms such as "par cark" or "begs and acon" may be another manifestation.

- *Patterns of Forgetfulness.* The child may alternately remember and forget something. Information may be absorbed by one half of the brain and the imperfect connection between the halves makes it inaccessible when the other half takes over. Though this mechanism is only an inference, on-off memory is a useful dyslexic indicator. Older dyslexic children should use a diary as a memory-jogger.
- *Family History.* Given a dyslexic relative, parents should watch for signs. But as dyslexia may be latent in phonics-taught relations, it is important to note the foregoing features. Left-handedness in the child or in family members may be a signal.

In any case, earlier treatment is more effective, so it is better to have a false alarm at age four than to wait until the problem is harder to put right. As we shall explain in Part IV, one important safeguard is to teach pre-school children to read, using phonics.

c) Dyslexic Troubles in School
Reading failure is the worst problem and the later it is recognised, the harder it is to rectify. Parents rarely catch it early enough because they do not know what milestones to expect. If the child lags behind the following stages, there is reason for disquiet.

With a good phonics lesson daily, children know all 26 letters and sounds after a few weeks in school. They can tackle three-letter words with short vowels and regular consonant pronunciation and after eleven weeks they can read all such words. By the end of the first term they notice letters in words around the town and read phonic words such as "stop" and "hospital". By age seven, and possibly six now they start school at four, they should be able to read whatever interests them, stumped only by oddly spelt words not in their vocabulary.

Dyslexia is hard to observe directly. Word-blind children may see words as blurred blobs or shimmering up and down the page, difficult to bring into focus. They do not realise this is abnormal so they cannot complain explicitly. A sensitive teacher may advise eye or ear tests, but these do not make the jumbled mass clearer. One costly approach is the use of special coloured lenses. There are also flat coloured overlays produced at £1 each by the Irlen Institute or Pentacles, which cut the glare of black on white and help about 20% of sufferers. Another approach is to help the hearing problems often associated with dyslexia.

Far more dyslexics can be helped by explaining, as whole-word teachers do not, that words are composed of a left-to-right sequence of letters representing successive sounds that are built up, i.e. blended, into the sound of the word as a whole. Mona McNee cleared one dyslexic's blockage in 45 minutes by letting her into this simple secret.

Beginners need to deal with one letter at a time and not with a large jumbled mass on the same page. Similarly, as two and three-letter words are introduced, there should be plenty of space all round them.

Dyslexics who do learn to read in some fashion, despite whole-word obstacles, can easily lose their place on the page and have difficulty finding it again. It may be hard for them to trace words correctly along a line or move down from one line to the next. They may not see letters in the right order and therefore mispronounce words, e.g. "merains" instead of "remains". Susan Hampshire once read a road sign as "auction" instead of "caution". Dyslexics who are struggling with the whole-word method may omit, insert or repeat words and phrases, and the effort of trying to identify them and keep track may be so intense that even if they read a passage correctly, they cannot spare attention for understanding its meaning or reading it with expression.

Gurus who insist on look-say and whole language allege that the phonics approach generates mechanical reading with no appreciation of meaning. As usual, this claim is diametrically opposite to the truth. Phonics makes the mechanics of reading easy, leaving the attention free to be devoted to the meaning. It is the dyslexic illiteracy problem activated by non-phonic methods that makes reading a mechanical effort and impedes understanding of what is being read.

Dyslexia can be further exacerbated in schools that do not offer books which make pupils avid to read. Enid Blyton's stories had this magical appeal but were outlawed by the politically correct clique. It is good they are now making a comeback. Recently, a dyslexic found a Harry Potter book and simply could not put it down. That is a splendid way to improve one's reading skill, far more effective than the dull repetitiousness of whole-word readers.

Clear clues to dyslexia appear in children's handwriting. The following list of mistakes may be made by any child exposed to whole-word teaching but if they persist after being pointed out, dyslexia is indicated. Another sign is slowness in copying from the board, and you can appreciate half of that problem if you have to copy a passage in an unknown language that necessitates constant pausing to check the unfamiliar letter sequences. You can then appreciate the other half if you do it in Chinese or some other language not using recognisable Roman letters, so that you have to keep pausing even more to work out how to draw the meaningless strokes.

- *Reversals or Inversions of Letters and/or Figures.* Dyslexics may see shapes but not their orientation. Uncertainty of up and down may confuse "n" with "u", while left-right confusion leads to writing characters back-to-front. Some children recognise the problem with "b" and "d" and solve it by always using "B" and "D" capitals, even in mid-word, so if these are the only needless capitals, dyslexia is a real possibility. Reversed individual numerals look odd and digits may be transposed: e.g. 21 for 12.

- *Letter Pair Reversals.* Dyslexics may transpose any two letters but especially pairs containing "l" or "r" with a vowel, e.g. "paly" for "play", "brid" for "bird", "sprak" for "spark" and "hoilday" for "holiday".
- *Whole Word Reversals.* Dyslexics may begin a word with its end letter and copy the rest in reverse, give or take a few deviations. Common reversals are "on/no" and "saw/was", while "of/for/from/off" are all confused together.
- *Mirror Writing.* If a word or passage has both the form and order of the letters reversed, the result can be read when held up to a mirror.
- *Reversal of Word Order.* Regardless of muddled letters, whole words may be placed in the wrong order, e.g. "Once a time upon" instead of "Once upon a time."
- *Repetition or Omission.* The letters "l" and "r" are particularly likely to be repeated or omitted but there may be other cases, e.g. "rember" for "remember".
- *Omission or Misplacement of i-dots, t-bars or Capitals.* For example, an "i" may be crossed instead a "t".
- *Confusion of Letters with Somewhat Similar Sounds.* Hearing problems may lead to confusion of similar sounds such as "f", "v" and "th" and the substitution of one for another, e.g. "fink", "wiv", or aping bad local speech.
- *Poor Page Arrangement.* Dyslexics find it hard to keep their writing on the line or the left margin an even width. Some tend to begin each line further to the right.
- *Non-Normal Stroke Direction.* It is instructive to watch dyslexics write. Lacking knowledge of letters as "too abstract", they accept that words are the units to perceive but are still expected to draw letter shapes when writing. So they see words as patterns to be copied, with no reason to start in any particular place. They may begin at the right and trace the outline backward, or start at the bottom of a tail and draw it upward.

Their difficulty in making transfers between the brain hemispheres give them poor concentration which means they must expend great effort. They grip their pens rigidly and exert heavy pressure on the paper and this, together with other demands, drains their energy.

Their illiteracy has multiple knock-on effects. It impedes development of their intelligence, which is now known to be only partly genetic and capable of being enhanced by stimulation, especially reading, so dyslexics miss out on realising their full potential. Poor reading is also a handicap in the study of most subjects and causes many dyslexics to lose all interest in

school. This creates severe frustration and loss of self-esteem, often leading to emotional disturbance and school phobia.

They may also attract social misery: taunts and abuse from bullies. Some
may escape by truanting and some try to recover self-esteem by projecting
a striking appearance as Mr. BIG in a macho gang, with way-out dress and
hair-styles, tattoos, flesh-piercing decorations, multi-studded leather jack-
ets, powerful motorbikes, and all the freaky trends. They may reject the
influence of parents and teachers, and respond to peer pressure, exacerbated by inability to escape into the solitary pleasure of reading. They
complain of nothing to do and since their efforts to avoid boredom cost
money, they may take to crime to support their lifestyle. They may also try
to boost their self-image by bullying others.

c) Dyslexia Troubles After School.

Illiteracy is a barrier to success in many walks of life. It has been suggested
that dyslexics benefit from being illiterate, as that fosters creative right
brain talents, which would not mature if they could read. This idea is quite
mistaken. Literate dyslexics who have those talents do not lose them and
can enhance them if they can enter more fully into normal society. Reading
would give a wider range of career options, e.g. as a Rolls-Royce designer
rather than a back-street garage mechanic. They would have greater
choice without worrying, "Shall I need to write?" Some gifted dyslexics
stay at the bottom of the pyramid, taking orders from their "betters", who
reach higher levels simply because they can read.

Moreover, some dyslexics cannot find a job at all. Although they might
well be good employees, they are constantly passed over if their inability
to read has tagged them with a poor school record. They are forced to
remain on the dole and may lapse into crime. It is reported that some 60%
of juvenile delinquents are dyslexic and the percentage may well be higher
among adult criminals. In USA a full 80% of prison convicts are illiterate.
The protagonists of the wrong kind of teaching reading have a lot to
answer for.

Furthermore, other dyslexics have left-brain talents to which they are
denied access if they cannot read. Alice Coleman was able to develop
right-brain map reading skill but without fluent reading she could never
have progressed to map, book and estate design and all the academic abilities needed in her career as a university professor.

Skill in reading is the educational birthright of every child in an
advanced society with universal schooling. Progressivism and the
whole-word method have stolen that birthright and we desperately need
to reclaim it.

d) Dyslexia Statistics

The total number of dyslexics is enormous, though an exact figure is difficult to reach. Schonell, before his volte-face that denied dyslexia existed, claimed a total of 50,000 school-children. BDA figures range from 35,000 to 65,000, i,e, up to 10% of the school population. Paul Marston of the Daily Telegraph estimated a total of about 70,000 severe dyslexics and several times that number with a milder handicap.

Percentage estimates vary from figures as low as 1%, 2% or 4% excluding mild dyslexia. But even a mild condition can be converted into a serious problem if the teaching method is wrong. Howarth's figure of 10% was accepted as probable by various others while a later BDA estimate raised it to 17%. Margaret Newton of the former Dyslexia Unit at Aston University thought it was over 20%.

Mona McNee attempted to check by counting all the children within a 300m radius of her home and seeing how many were dyslexic. That, together with her remedial teaching experience, convinced her that 10% was a minimum and Margaret Newton's 20% more likely to be the true level. As about 80% of dyslexics are boys, this could mean that one boy in six and one girl in 25 are affected, which goes a long way towards explaining why, in a whole-word age, boys have been faring worse than girls in the examination league tables.Even the maximum estimate of 20% dyslexic is completely out of scale with the figure of up to 60% for the dyslexic proportion among juvenile and adult criminals. The school's failure to make them literate and employable is a major contributor to the breakdown of society.

Dyslexic problems persist throughout adult life. Probably the majority of the nine million adult illiterates estimated by ALBSU in 1997, plus many more subsequently, are in that unenviable position because their genetic predisposition was activated into a needless illiteracy by the defective teaching methods imposed by Progressivism. The McNee Report should be read in conjunction with Chapter 20, which is a guide to the most effective phonic method for avoiding dyslexia activation.

Meanwhile the question of dyslexic illiteracy has taken a new twist. We have passed out of the Tizard-Warnock phase of denial that it exists but have now entered a phase of opposite denial — that there was never a time when it did not exist. The unacceptable illiteracy rate has been now developing over sixty years, which is longer than the professional life of all active teachers and also of many retired ones, so very few still alive have had personal experience of the 99% literacy rate that existed in pre-Progressivist days. Whereas the onset of dyslexic illiteracy was blamed on parents' reluctance to admit their children's low ability, its present epidemic proportions are clung to by teachers as an excuse for their failure to give all pupils their educational birthright of literacy.

We do not ask teachers to blame themselves but to look at how they were so brain-washed at college that it is difficult for them to turn an open mind towards ideas they were mesmerised into despising. If they continue to gainsay proven phonics truth in favour of whole-word dogmas without foundation, further vast numbers of children will suffer.

This chapter's title is "Central Government". The McNee report is outside that sphere but its findings should have been elucidated by the Tizard and Warnock Committees, and it remains vital for the ruling party to take note and take action.

The Pattern of Special Reports

While on the topic of central government reports, we look at their pattern over time. During the upwave, Committees were set up to report on specific aspects of education about once per decade. Their themes were proactive, to create advances. During the downwave, however, the briefs were reactive. Their themes were dictated by the problems that followed in the wake of Progressivism and as the problems multiplied, so did the Inquiries. Between 1954, when look-say had begun to bite, and 1989, there were 34 such investigations — roughly one per annum. We have considered only those relevant to reading failure.

When Margaret Thatcher became Prime Minister in 1979, she wanted to rescue education from decline but had first to attend to problems such as inflation, the unbridled power of the unions and the invasion of the Falkland Islands. Not until 1988 was there was an Education Act to begin the rescue. Progressivism was so entrenched that headway was difficult and there ensued a struggle for reform, discussed in Part III. Meanwhile, this chapter ends with an account of two quangos appointed by Central Government as additional watchdogs.

The Schools Council 1964–1988

The Schools Council was a quango set up to unify most of the work previously done by the Secondary Schools Examinations Council and the Ministry of Education's Curriculum Study Group. Its early years coincided with the Plowden Committee's sessions and it, too, was infected by Progressivist convictions. It stated its raison d'être as follows:

> The objects of the Schools Council for the Curriculum and Examinations are to uphold and interpret the principle that each school should have the fullest measure of responsibility for its own work, with its own curriculum and teaching methods based on the needs of its own pupils and evolved by its own staff, and to seek, through co-operative study of common problems, to assist all who have individually or jointly responsibilities for, or in connection with, the schools' curricula and examinations to co-ordinate their actions in harmony with this principle.

This piously promised freedom but in practice each school was forced to recast all aspects of its functioning. Woe betide those who found their state satisfactory, with no need to overturn it, and even more, those who wanted to use this mirage of freedom to embrace i.t.a. or other phonics. A pervasive meme was "Question everything; take nothing for granted", but this did not apply to Progressivism, which was never to be questioned and always taken for granted.

The Schools Council cost £1.2 million per annum in its early years and also imposed upon LEAs the expense of maintaining Teachers' Centres in addition to schools. It claimed to be carrying out research but there were no genuine investigations backed up by properly quantified tests. Instead there were mere compilations of opinions. For example, its curriculum recommendations for each school subject were a direct negation of its high-flown lip service to the ideal of each school's independence.

The Schools Council maintained its hegemony for 24 years, long after it had became a byword for promoting bad education. Mention was made earlier of its display of a school newspaper, thickly peppered with misspellings, etc., and while sanctioning these handicaps the Council also claimed to be ensuring that school leavers were qualified for employment. It did not listen to employers' protests against poor standards. It promoted poor discipline. It proudly showed a film made in a school, which was a perfect model of what a film should never be. The children had not been taught to speak well and mumbled inaudibly with their backs to the camera. There was a great deal of confused background noise and children thought nothing of walking across the foreground between the camera and the action being filmed. There was no class control nor any attempt to inculcate considerate behaviour, but doubtless this was acceptable to the Schools Council precisely because the children's conduct was "natural", i.e. uneducated.

The Basic Skills Agency

While the Schools Council was concerned with school-age children, illiterate adults were to be served by a potentially constructive quango, set up as a succession of autonomous units of the National Institute of Adult Continuing Education. This saved having to establish a new agency. Its first incarnation, the *Adult Literacy Resource Agency*, was created by the Labour government in 1975. In 1978 it became the *Adult Literacy Unit* for two years, and in 1980 the Conservative government changed its name to the *Adult Literacy and Basic Skills Unit* (ALBSU), which continued without fixed term on a three-year rolling programme. In 1991 it received separate legal status as both a company limited by guarantee and a charity with Princess Anne as its patron. It was generously funded to pursue four main aims:

- To promote the importance, and increase knowledge of, basic skills and encourage an increase in take up of provision.
- To initiate and support the development of basic skills provision.
- To improve effectiveness of basic skills programmes and training.
- To improve the efficiency of our central services and support and make the most effective use of the expertise of the staff.

ALBSU had five major branches, termed programmes:

- Consultancy and advisory services
- Development project sponsorship
- Publication of many booklets
- Staff training
- Research

Possibly ALBSU's best research was its estimate of six million illiterate adults in 1987 rising to nine million in 1997 — proof of its own failure to reduce the problem. In 1976 there were 52,522 adult literacy students rising to 177,040 in 1994, of whom 56,194 were learning English as a foreign language. This huge number could have facilitated splendid scientific trials of the efficacy of different teaching methods, especially as the voluntary staff had to take a City and Guilds training course. Different groups could have used different methods to see how each technique fared in different areas: inner city, suburb and rural villages, and hence test whether method or environment was more influential in promoting or preventing illiteracy. This would have been in line with its aim of increasing effectiveness but unfortunately, ALBSU had been captured by Progressivists, and snared into the same old ineffective methods.

In 1995 Mona McNee volunteered, and found that the "training" was focused on political correctness to avoid offending through sexism, racism, ageism and all the other isms. Desks facing the blackboard had to be rearranged in a circle and Progressivism held sway. The tutor knew far less about teaching people to read than Mona did. She repeatedly tried to interest ALBSU in genuine research but the Director, Alan Wells, merely paid a little lip service to phonics and continued the mixed methods so confusing to learners. The Chairman, Lord Moser, had a strong Progressivist pedigree of appointments and refused to support phonics.

ALBSU vaunted its learning opportunities on television but said nothing about its success, if any. Its activities seem more imaginative than practical. For example, it dreamed up an immense catalogue of 787 publications, presumably for sale to its volunteers.

In 1995 the name "Adult" was dropped and ALBSU became the *Basic Skills Agency* (BSA). Its remit was extended to allow it to work with children, which seemed adding ineffective Progressivist remediation to ineffective Progressivist initial teaching. There was no attempt to discover why phonics schools did not turn out illiterates needing its attention.

Considering its high profile and ample funding, BSA's minimal effect in reducing illiteracy has been a national tragedy. It could have done far more with far less if it had promoted reading with phonics in its publications, television time and training programmes. However, it seems much too rigid to change and the best solution might well be to stop wasting money and terminate its existence.

Chapter 12

Publishers and
The Media

We have seen how whole-word and whole-language gurus spread their creed to indoctrinate students and infect all the spheres of education that they subsequently colonised. There is a further group of watchdogs that *could* have seen through the smokescreen and reached the public directly: the realm of publishing and the media. Newspapers do not hesitate to criticise the government and, together with books, magazines and broadcasting, are potentially independent critics that could have posed a serious challenge to Progressivism. Once again, however, the Progressivist octopus proved adept at throwing out one tentacle after another to smother any warnings of danger.

Publishers

Anyone can have ideas; anyone can write books. But unless they are published, they are stillborn. The educational downwave could not have taken root without the backing of the publishers who proliferated whole-word material and squeezed out phonics. But while publishers can in theory issue any book, those that do not meet demand do not recoup their investment and the firm suffers. No matter how good the book is educationally, if it fails commercially, it blocks future production of its type.

As the whole-word method engineered its virtual monopoly, publishers found that phonics became an unprofitable minority taste. Despite it long history of sensible mainstream success, it began to be seen as a relic of the past. And though whole-word was untested and had previously been only an occasional failed eccentricity, it was now jumping out of its dubious past to win a reputation with publishers as the spearhead of the future.

A first lure was the profit to be made from the reading schemes of gurus in a virtually captive market — the schools increasingly staffed by teachers conditioned at college to regard the whole-word approach as the sole choice and likely to choose authors whose names were familiar to them from their student days.

Secondly, there was the extra profitability of schemes whose imperfect methods extended reading instruction through many years and hooked schools into buying successive books in the same series.

A third strand of profitability was that much material was designed to be consumable. Learning-by-doing meant using workbooks with spaces for children to fill in with busywork: colouring, cutting, drawing and a bit of writing. This necessitated the purchase of new workbooks each year.

When schools complain of no money for books, it rings strangely in the ears of retired teachers, who had far less and kept books in good condition to be used by class after class. The publishers' test of a reading scheme is the bottom line—how well it sells. But a true educational test is how quickly, effectively and economically it teaches children to read. Shekels for publishers and savings for schools can be diametrically opposed aims and, alas, the Progressivist big battalions have been on the side of conspicuous spending.

Publishers can easily overlook lack of educational value because Progressivist authors resist testing. In 1986, Mona McNee pleaded for pre-testing of four proposed whole-word schemes to establish how well they worked. This would have needed a two-year pilot study in, say, 20 schools to obtain each one's average reading quotient (ARQ) at age seven. All the publishers shrugged the idea off. One said that a trial would take *four* years and be too costly—an admission of the scheme's slowness. Another said, "We would not insult our authors by suggesting further tests." "Further" is a nice touch, obscuring how whole-word authors regard even first tests as anathema and offer no objective performance rating.

Pharmaceutical companies must carefully test for harmful side-effects and even then things can go wrong, as with thalidomide. Surely children's minds are as precious as their bodies and we should be entitled to facts, figures and proof instead of mere blurb along the lines of "Our soap powder washes whiter." Schemes should be labelled with the ARQ reached in two years of proper trials. Anything under ARQ 110 is below the upwave average and effectively substandard—equivalent to a government health warning: "This scheme can damage your educational health." ARQs above 110 would show at least some merits.

Alternatively, parents might prefer to know how far a scheme promotes an average reading age in advance of chronological age. Mona McNee's scheme in a reception class in Knowsley, third worst in the LEA league tables, not only increased the ARQ by the one year of age maturation but also added an extra nine months. Parents are happy when their child's reading age is ahead.

Apart from user testing, there are other quality criteria that can be checked by merely inspecting schemes and seeing whether they are oriented towards phonics or look-say. For phonics, note whether *letters with their sounds* are introduced at the outset and the sounds *blended* together as soon as possible. Children shown how to construct a word from the first three letters, c — a — t, have a satisfying sense of achievement to spur them on. Beyond letter sounds and blending, comes *grading*. For example, words where all letters keep their own sounds, as in "cat", "hand", "crust" and "hospital", should precede digraphs such as "ch" or "ng", where two letters combine to form a different sound. Primers and ensuing storybooks should introduce new words in order of difficulty, to expand reading foundations cumulatively, with a logical gradation that eases and speeds the learning path.

To assess whole-word schemes, one has to identify the obstacles that turn the learning path into a cul-de-sac: *word-shapes, sight vocabulary, word guessing, difficult words at the start, any advice to discuss what the text might say instead of reading what it does say, real books,* and *even the slightest suggestion of "learning to read by reading"*. If these schemes lay any claim to phonics, assess its efficacy in terms of the three criteria, letters/sounds, blending and grading, and also when they first appear. If they are deferred until after the whole-word method has instilled the guessing habit, the children's ability to settle down to careful decoding of letters and blends will have been impaired. Phonics should come first, fast and only.

Another criterion is how lavishly the scheme is illustrated. Colourful pictures have been promoted as a selling point but they should be just the opposite. They add to the scheme's cost and detract from the child's concentration on words. Reading should engage the child's left brain-hemisphere with its linear logic, as this directs blood-flow to the cells concerned and bathes them in nourishment. Pictures, by contrast, are the province of the pattern-recognising right brain. They direct attention and blood-flow away from the side involved in reading, which is a misdirection that substitutes guessing for the essential processes of decoding and blending. Though some uses of pictures can be constructive, most are not, certainly not those intended as a clue to guessing. The ratio of illustrations to words might form a *distraction index* for judging each scheme.

Another check is to note how far the scheme deflects the child's efforts into *non-literate activities*. Colouring pictures and drawing should be for the art lesson, to help develop graphicacy — the education of right-brain potentialities. In reading lessons it contributes nothing to the mastery of the skill but deflects attention away from it, wasting time, delaying progress and preventing the stimulus that progress could have brought. Such activities confuse literacy with graphicacy and turn learning to read into an obstacle race.

Reading Schemes 1945–1988

The descent into look-say was triggered by Schonell's book, *The Psychology and Teaching of Reading* (1945). Re-issued and later revised, this book remained in print for 30 years and popularised the following basic flaws.

1. Start with whole words.

2. Learn their shape.

3. If children cannot start to read this way, they are not ready.

4. Keep parents out.

5. Don't call dyslexia by its name.

6. There is no one way to teach reading.

From 1945 Schonell's ideas became dominant and a large part of their acceptance was due to the ready availability of his reading scheme, *Happy Venture* (1939). The paper shortage during World War II meant schools had to make do with books already in stock and when replenishing after the war, the prevailing fresh-start ethos impelled them to seek something new. *Happy Venture* was both new and available.

Another scheme that seized much of the whole-word market was *Janet and John*, from USA (1949). It offered both a whole-word and a phonics version but the latter was still largely whole word with a little phonics tacked on. Both stressed repetition to impress words on the child's memory and "Look, look Janet! Look, look John!" became their unofficial hallmark. A recent revival boasts of being exciting but is actually dull, using mundane story lines to maximise repetition. One nine-page plot is that Father buys John a blue cap and Mother buys him a brown one so he gives the blue one to Janet. The word "cap" occurs 19 times.

To defend such uninspired fare, there arose a policy of denigrating really gripping stories such as Enid Blyton's, which, for those who could read a little, were immensely successful in letting children lose themselves in a narrative and develop a love of books for life. They were condemned as politically incorrect and driven out of the market.

The *Janet and John* series has a heavy pictorial bias and its first advice to parents is "Look at the pages of pictures together, talking about the pictures." These give an expensive appearance but detract from educational value by activating the wrong side of the brain.

The scheme first lists the whole alphabet for the children to learn to recite. This negates the whole-word's claim of going straight to meaning. It then devotes a page to each letter in turn. The letter is drawn in a large double outline to be coloured in, to impress its shape on the child's memory. But as crayon strokes can be applied in any direction, these letters afford less scope for memorising letter form than the phonics approach, which provides a few instances of the letter drawn in dotted lines for the

child to pencil over, thus reinforcing the visual impression with a kinaesthetic experience of line direction and helps writing as well as reading.

The upper parts of the alphabet pages carry four highly coloured pictures that attract far more attention than the small labels printed beside
them. Each depicted object has a name beginning with that page's letter
but this is only a first-letter-and-guess approach and there is no attempt to
pursue letter-sound correspondences throughout the word. The "a" page,
for example, has pictures labelled "animal", "ant", "apple" and "axe",
with a confusing array of spelling rules: the "–le" suffix, letter doubling,
silent "e" and extra syllables, all of which phonics would introduce with a
logically graded and properly explained sequence of rules. But the
whole-word approach disdains spelling rules and chooses its vocabulary
for distinctiveness of word shape and the alleged interests of children.
The lower part of each page has six unlabelled line drawings for the children to identify and colour those that begin with the relevant letter. The
"a" page includes an aeroplane and it defies the imagination how children
who have learnt only the short "a" can identify that word as starting with
that letter. And on the next page, also without explanation, is an "a" with
another different pronunciation in "ball".

The Gaggs

As Progressivism spread throughout the state school system, the flow of
look-say books increased to a flood, which drowned out phonics by the
sheer mass of its zealotry. Some were books promoting the gospel of the
whole word; others were reading schemes.

In 1955, Newnes Educational published J.C. and M.E. Gagg's *Teaching
Children to Read*. This pair had no insight into the weaknesses of the
whole-word method and made an intellectual virtue of "the complicated
process of teaching reading". If it really is complicated (and when one
reaches metaphor, inference, etc., it can be), it is all the more important to
make the beginning stages clear and simple. But an initial sight vocabulary, including "bicycle", "aeroplane", "kitchen", "trolley-bus" and
"laugh", which the Gaggs said were chosen for "vivid meaning", is neither
clear nor simple. These heterogeneous spellings did nothing to help children develop a reading strategy. The blurb cited vital preparatory work
such as talking about pictures and choosing books. Letters and sounds
were not mentioned till two-thirds of the way through and grading was
omitted altogether.

The Gaggs complained that phonics primers concentrated on sounds
and short words, caring little for meaning, with *dozens* of words on the
same page. They did not realise that this showed phonics' greater efficacy,
unlocking dozens of words for the child. They assumed children would
read them without knowing their meaning, but children expect words to

have meaning and being able to read them is a first step towards understanding.

The Gaggs even claimed that "the old phonics approach ensured that reading was only mechanical" but how could it possibly do that? It was this kind of unproved anti-phonics assertion that helped keep phonics as a last resort for remedial work rather than forming the initial core needed for effective learning to read.

An Overview of Downwave Schemes

Progressivists ingratiated themselves with publishers as authors, advisers and experts, recommending their own and each others' books and schemes to students and teachers, and denigrating those based on phonics. Schonell himself had not abandoned testing but, as often happens, his followers became more extreme than the master, and convinced themselves that a noble purpose was served by not putting the whole-word method under the microscope. Blinkering themselves, they made their publishers equally blind to the need for objective testing and created a blanket ban on information as to how badly reading standards were declining. The new thinking was accepted on an all-pervasive scale.

So whole-word primers were what teachers ordered and publishers provided, losing interest in the shrinking demand for phonics primers. Increasingly it was whole-word authors who reaped the profit and prestige, and that reinforced their misguided dedication.

We have looked at 40 reading schemes issued during the Progressivist downwave from 1945 to 1988, and found that the phonics-based ones were not only in the minority but also suffered pressures to prevent their succeeding.

From 1922 the *Beacon Readers* gave stalwart service in enabling 99% of children to become readers before leaving infant school. Their success could not be impugned but in the whole-word era they came to be regarded as old hat and despite a 1946 attempt to update them, their sales gradually faded away.

The 1954 *Royal Road* scheme by Daniels and Diack was used by Mona McNee to teach her son, Tim. It assumed children already knew their letters and began with three-letter words. It was excellently graded and economical as well as effective, as both the books and the materials were reusable. Mona McNee used hers for 20 years before developing her own *Step By Step* scheme. However, zealots do not appreciate excellence and *Royal Road* had an uphill struggle, losing the battle in 1974. One disgusting episode occurred after Daniels had been speaking to an audience of teachers. As he departed, several of them physically attacked him and left him badly shaken.

Two phonics products were not complete schemes. Stott's 1962 *Programmed Learning Kit* was phonic games and Jones's 1967 Colour Story Reading consisted only of readers, without a primer. Reid's scheme had three variants: *Link Up* with Low in 1973 and *Letter Links* (1973) and *R and D* (1979), both with Donaldson. Wilkinson and Rogerson's *Sure Fire Phonics* (1984) was partly infected by the whole-word method, to the extent of not grading its words in order of difficulty.

Joyce Morris's *Language in Action* (1975) also fell upon stony state-sector ground, though it was welcomed by independent schools. Its phonic method, far more than small classes, would have been the vital factor underpinning their high attainment levels. Donald Moyle's *Language Patterns* (1981) was largely phonic and at first commanded considerable attention, as he was a leading member of the United Kingdom Reading Association. However, like other downwave phonics schemes, it soon began to be frozen out.

The phonics schemes were a mere handful among the many based on whole word or mixed methods. Some of those were repetitiously dull; others tried to add a bit of sparkle. The *Sainsbury Series* started with "sizzling SAUSAGES" as sight words, introducing both capitals and lower-case to children who could not yet identify a single letter. And as they had to recognise words from their shapes, they would expect to see "sausages" thereafter as a large oblong without the clue of a g-tail. It would be tedious to comment on all the whole-word and mixed-method schemes, so we have selected just three.

Ladybird Keywords (1964)

William Murray's *Ladybird Keywords* consisted of a teachers' manual and 36 books, three at each of twelve levels. It has been the biggest seller ever in Britain, and has been directly available to parents in shops and supermarkets.It is woefully short on phonics. Its Levels 1-3 contain over 300 cases of the letter "e" that do not denote its short sound, yet when Level 4 gets around to teaching letters, only the short "e" is mentioned. This was typical of whole-word experts dipping a toe into the phonics lake. They plumbed only an inch or so but convinced themselves it was the full depth. Ladybird's first level was not graded and included words such as "one", "two", "three", "magician", "was", "saw", "beard" and "window". This disregard of phonics gives the child a sense of there being absolutely no logic in spelling. It is a bar to reading, not an invitation.

Ladybird asserted, "One of the best ways of helping children to read is to read to them and with them." We know this mantra with its high failure rate, but the publishers said that they had neither the time nor the staff to produce figures on the scheme's educational success.

The Oxford Reading Tree (1986)

This Oxford University Press scheme is highly complex and ambitious, spanning eleven levels at a cost of nearly £7000 for a class of 30. It is a day's march even to work through its catalogue. Nevertheless, it became one of the best sellers, said to be in 70% of schools, and its popularity coincided with a further marked drop in literacy.

Part of its attraction is its high-tech aura, with videos and computer software. These help to occupy children while teachers attend to other groups. Stage 1 has picture stories without a word of text, and does nothing to prepare the left-brain for reading. It is simply a delay that rakes in its price. Stage 2 is whole word. Phonics is first mentioned in Stage 3, but only as initial letters without the sound-blending needed for real reading. Other phonic elements are further delayed and made much harder to master by long training in the word-guessing habit. This appears to show that phonics is too abstract for children—a teacher-manufactured problem that does not exist when letters and sounds are taught at the start.

One misguided aim is to get children to listen to a story while following it in a book to puzzle out how the printed words are related to those they are hearing—far too complex a multi-task for non-readers. In any case the story-telling is too fast for the children to keep pace visually, so they simply enjoy listening and neglect what they are supposed to be seeing. This exemplifies how aspects of the *Oxford Reading Tree* are not what they claim but simply distractions from the actual business of learning to read. It takes many years to complete and is accompanied by storybooks written by the OUP's authors. These, together with five successive workbooks, flash cards, etc., contribute to the high cost.

It may be compared with Mona McNee's single workbook, priced at £5, which completed the reading task within two years and let the class progress to children's classics and English literature instead of being fed for many years on stories written for those still learning to read. It can also be consulted on the Internet:

http://www.catphonics.pwp.blueyonder.co.uk.

Ginn 360

This colourful and costly American "complete reading and language development programme from pre-reading to age 12+" claims to be "probably the most thoroughly researched reading scheme ever". However, the quality of the research is poor. The 16,000 teachers and advisers asked to evaluate it would automatically have been whole-word protagonists, so the results are not couched scientifically. Any real improvement would have been blazoned as a quantitative reduction in illiteracy but the best the publishers can find for their blurb is a purely qualitative opinion: "the amazing interest shown by the children", "children really want to read these books" and a head teacher's confidence in the scheme's *theoretical* basis and its ability to identify [not remedy] learning problems at an early stage. The brochure emphasises three supposedly helpful methods, which in practice hinder rather than help: contextual comprehension, now known to be only a prop used by poor readers, phonemic awareness and analytic phonics instead of the highly effective synthetic phonics (see Chapter 16). Its brochure also admits that the scheme may be too expensive for schools to afford initially.

Books

In 1945 the whole-word method was new and untested in Britain, and launched on a tide of hope without strong opposition. Yet clear counter-evidence *did* exist in USA, where compulsory education, the upwave and the downwave were all earlier than in the UK, as also was recognition of falling standards. A remarkable attempt to stem the monolithic decline was Rudolf Flesch's 1955 *Why Johnny Can't Read,* published by Harper-Row. It struck such a chord with the public that it was nine months on the best-seller list but even this impact was defeated, as the great choir of whole-word voices swamped the voice of phonic reason.

Progressivists can be very patient in outlasting the impact of awkward facts and also in preparing the ground against any future attempt. So when Rudolf Flesch returned to the fray in 1981, with his *Why Johnny Still Can't Read,* Harper-Row had learnt how to smother it. They barely publicised it in USA and not at all in Britain, where it sold only seven copies in 14 months — to people who happened to know of it and spontaneously requested it. What a fate for another potential best-seller!

It emerged that Flesch's contract denied him any say in advertising and the purpose of accepting the book was to suppress it. Harper-Row had profitable whole-word sales which Flesch's book could have undermined. If they had allowed him to find another publisher, it could have competed, but accepting it kept it from anyone else and crushed its important debunking effect. One truly feels for its author, who was denied royalties for all his hard work and, more vitally, debarred from promoting his message for the salvation of America's hi-jacked education system.

Other American phonics books also had a hard time, and the same blanket opposition spread to the UK. Jean Augur, working in the British Dyslexia Association, produced a splendid volume entitled, *This Book Doesn't Make Sens . . . Cens . . . Sns . . . Scens . . . Sense,* but it could not find a publisher and she had to produce it privately in 1981.

Mona McNee's first draft of the present book, in 1987, was sent to over 30 publishers, who all rejected it and it became clear that the stumbling block was its independence from the prevailing whole-word doctrine. Oliver and Boyd said they did "not wish to publish a book which takes such an extreme position and claims to offer a complete remedy . . ." There was no insight that a possible complete remedy should be explored not deplored, and no understanding that a *positive* extreme should be welcomed more than the firm's current *negative* whole-word extreme. Again it was clear that fear of competition with existing sales carried more weight than concern for children's educational welfare.

Newspapers

Newspapers, unlike reading-scheme publishers, did not need to be committed to a single viewpoint and although they might be slanted towards editorial policy and reader preference, they were not penalised by publishing articles that opened up wider horizons. They prided themselves on their critical insight, probing the weaknesses of government and everything else. When Progressivism was in its colonising phase, they supported criticism of traditional education, but when it became dominant, they did not, in turn, subject the whole-word approach to the criticism it deserved, or keep the phonics case simmering with an occasional viewpoint article, as one might expect.

In practice, such articles were extremely rare. The whole-word fiat seemed to dominate here too, as the posts of reporters, columnists and education editors fell to those who felt it imperative to deny space to opposing views. This is indefensible—equivalent to a democracy giving tolerance to autocrats and then finding that nothing must depart from the party line. Such was the whole-word experts' desire to crush, that other views were banned.

Educational columns or supplements need to keep readers informed of developments such as the whole-word method but they should also have recognised an even greater responsibility for presenting a balanced picture. They should not have used whole-word opinions as a veto on the alternatives. But some of them seemed unable to distinguish between mere opinions and hard scientific evidence, ignoring phonics' verification in a wide range of tests by different independent researchers. The whole-word method, by contrast, has never been verified and has prevailed only because opinion supporting it came with monolithic unanimity from those who had infiltrated important educational positions.

Phonics has never been disproved by scientific evidence and its supporters should have been allowed their say, no matter how much they were outnumbered by the trendy worshippers at the whole-word shrine.

During the downwave, educational journalists virtually never cut through their self-interest to allow phonics an occasional hearing. For example, *Junior Education* accepted a favourable review by Cliff Moon and Bridie Raban of Frank Smith's *Reading* but debarred a balancing assessment from a phonics supporter. Ten years later (1981) this journal did publicise Jean Augur's *This Book Doesn't Make Sens . . . Cens . . . Sns . . . Scens . . . Sense* , but failed to follow up what she wrote:

> If all the children in reception classes were taught in this [multi-sensory] way, the children who would normally read would not *suffer but the child at risk would stand a better chance of reading earlier.*

The Times was noted for its voluminous *Educational Supplement,* commended by Lord Joseph for its wide range of opinions on topical issues. However, on some issues its range was decidedly pinched and it carefully did not sully itself with phonics. Though supportive of change, innovation and modern ideas, it left a glaring gap on the subject of the USA Government's initiatives to restore phonics. This merited front-page treatment and sustained interest, so not telling teachers of the transatlantic trend amounted to censorship. Even worse, while withholding that news, the *Supplement's* USA correspondent, Bill Norris, denigrated the American Education Secretary, William Bennett, which again illustrates the smokescreen unleashed to protect the whole-word approach.

The Daily Telegraph is a paper whose readers probably favour some aspects of tradition and might have been sympathetic to the phonics case, had they met it. But John Izbicki, its long-serving education correspondent, seemed to accept the contemporary trend completely. If he had given both sides, *with figures,* we might well have climbed out of the pit years earlier.

Local newspapers professing an interest in education were similarly influenced into one-sidedness. *The Eastern Daily Press* printed several letters from Mona McNee but rejected her attempt to warn teachers of the hazards of four new reading schemes and the need to establish what ARQ level they could accomplish by age seven. This vital information for children's educational welfare was not considered a matter of public interest.

In those dark days, newspapers seemed to leave no crevice for light to penetrate and if a small gleam accidentally appeared, it was quickly doused. Freedom of the press was also freedom to suppress, and consequently teachers and the general public read only one side of the case, which the educational results showed to be the wrong side.

Broadcasting

Radio is an excellent medium for serious talks in which a theme can be developed without the distraction of pictures flitting hither and thither every few seconds. But reading has both visual and auditory components, so television, with sight as well as sound, could have offered to *teach* reading to those benighted by the whole-word method at school.

The BBC, for long the sole television agency, could have produced invaluable programmes using phonics to teach the true art of reading. The young child's short attention span needs varied repetition to reinforce learning and that could have been provided in daily ten minute slots, in "Watch with Mother" for pre-school children and in "Children's Hour" for school starters — saving vast numbers of young Britons from the misery of illiteracy.

A great opportunity was missed but the BBC *appeared* to grasp phonics by using the American *Sesame Street* programme, which was not helpful. USA's earlier educational decline led to an earlier demand for action and one much publicised project was "Headstart", to teach reading to pre-school children in deprived areas, with *Sesame Street* on television to boost local classes. But Headstart still left too many illiterates, which is no surprise, as it had very little phonic content. Its accredited teachers were mainly trained in the whole-word method, which was no better for pre-school five-year-olds than for six-year-old first graders. The name *Sesame Street* came from the fairy-tale incantation, "Open Sesame", and symbolized opening the gateway to literacy. But in practice it was just another smokescreen to obfuscate phonics. Superficially it seemed to satisfy the phonics need, as it introduced letters but they were not so much taught as bandied about, and even then only initial letters.

A fluent reader can glance round a street scene and pick out any letter on shop fronts or street signs. But such scenes have far too much detail for beginners, who cannot pursue a given letter without being diverted by other items. Nor do they know what to reject, especially letter groups not yet learned, which crowd together in street words and conceal the one they seek. The *Sesame Street* scene was too full and changed too rapidly. Quick panning and zooming were not conducive to easy learning and leave children lagging.

Sounds are as important as letters in reading and *Sesame Street* had auditory snags too. Its American accent is not best for British learners, especially when distorted by puppet-speak with its artificial mouth movements. Lip-reading is impossible, which disadvantages the many children with impaired hearing in these high decibel days. Blending letter sounds into words is also essential but *Sesame Street* was lazy in that respect as well.

For children a letter to be learned is a new experience. They need to see it in clear isolation from any visual distractions and large enough for their young eyes to absorb its details. Television could show a single letter on a plain background and associate it with its sound, keeping to short vowels and regular consonants in the early stages. After being shown and sounded, a letter can be animated to write itself, with no obscuring hand in the way. The correct writing direction can be shown and repeated several times at a suitably slow pace that allows children to follow it with a finger on the screen.

For well over half a century of Progressivism the constructive possibilities of phonics were ignored. During the downwave, publishers and the media were absorbed into the ranks of failed watchdogs in relation to that most fundamental element of education — teaching to read. The superiority of the phonics method has always been known but the influences organised to suppress that knowledge seemed overwhelming.

Chapter 13

Voluntary Organizations

Individuals have yet more freedom than the media to reject harmful trends and form associations to promote their views. But once founded, such associations risk being infiltrated and hijacked by those of an opposite persuasion. This chapter discusses three types: of organization: unions, societies for professional expertise in teaching English, and societies of people who are alert to the educational decline and campaigning to resist and reverse it.

The Unions

The unions focus upon teachers' welfare: pay, status and legal protection. The approximate membership figures cited here were the latest available at the time of writing.

The first ones were the National Union of Teachers (NUT, 1870), now with 232,000 members, the Association of Assistant Mistresses (AAM, 1884) and the Association of Assistant Masters in Secondary Schools (AMA, 1892). The last two merged in 1978 as the Assistant Masters and Mistresses Association (AMMA) and as further education multiplied, changed its name in 1993 to the Association of Teachers and Lecturers (ATL), with 160,000 members. The National Association of Head Teachers (NAHT, 1897) has 385,000 primary-school head members. The Headmasters' Conference serves independent schools.

The growth of the grammar schools triggered separate unions: the National Association of Schoolmasters (NAS) and the Union of Women Teachers (UWT), which merged as the NAS/UWT after co-education became the norm. Membership increased as comprehensive-school teachers joined and the school-leaving age was raised, together with a drive for more sixth-formers. It now stands at 212,000.

In 1970 the NUT began to call strikes but many members disliked robbing children of school time and formed a separate Professional Association of Teachers (PAT), with 40,000 members. PAT was the only union to address the illiteracy problem, in a 1992 booklet, *The Teaching of Reading*.

However, the whole-word method was not identified as the cause of failure and the booklet supported the misguided idea of "no one way to teach reading."

Further education-college staff were attracted not only to ATL but also to the National Association of Teachers in Further and Higher Education (NATFHE), with 66,000 members. Although further education has filtered out 16-year-old school-leavers, both the ATL and NATFHE lecturers still found that their student intakes had serious reading and spelling problems, left entrenched by eleven years of schooling and hard to remedy. Even the 46,000-strong Association of University Teachers (AUT) now reports a need for remedial English and Mathematics in the newest universities.

The educational ethos has always been to accept the intake's condition and *never* criticise the feeder schools for the lack of basics. This may make for short-term peace but also long-term disaster for many children. Infant teachers neither accepted that the buck stopped with them nor passed it back to their training staff but instead blamed the child/family/home, which did nothing to increase efficiency.

Increased control and assistance in education led to more unions: the Association of Educational Psychologists (AEP) with 2,200 members, the National Association of Governors and Managers (NAGM) with 35,000 and the Society of Education Officers (SEO) with 900.

The combined union membership of nearly 1,200,000 is a powerful force. And as its teacher members were trained, persuaded, coerced or just carried along by the tide of Progressivist opinion, the unions also became vehicles for promoting the downwave.

In any case, unions exist for the benefit of their members, so teachers are the workers to be protected, while children are just the raw material to be processed. The false claims of Progressivism seemed an assurance that pupils' interests were being served and the real hurt to children was overlooked. So, too, was the hurt to the teachers themselves.

It was forgotten that traditional teachers had an easier and more rewarding job. In primary schools they prepared a single programme for an orderly class, achieving high success and enjoying unquestioned status and respect in the community. Progressivism robbed them of all that and imposed a need for multiple programmes in a less manageable classroom. Success declined, stress increased and the community's respect was often forfeited. In secondary schools the problem was often trying to make bricks without the straw of literacy, numeracy and knowledge that the primaries should have been providing, and also trying to maintain discipline among the many educationally alienated adolescents.

The unions did not truly help the teachers they served, because they lacked insight into the underlying realities and relied upon reactive tactics. As the teachers' lot worsened, they tended to become more militant, and when the 1980s government resolved to remedy the decline, they were in a frame of mind to complain and go on strike rather than co-operate.

Educational Societies

Professional societies are concerned with children's education but most were formed or expanded during the downwave, with its bogus views on what was beneficial. Just one dates from the upwave: *British Early Child-hood Education* (BECE, 1923) now with 6000 members. It focused on schooling up to age eight and as upwave teaching was firmly phonics based there was no concern with method and it still offers no support for phonics.

The early downwave, in 1946, saw the advent of the National Foundation for Educational Research (NFER), a company that undertook scientific investigations for paying clients. Its leading light was Dr. Joyce Morris, whose impeccable research into reading standards has been outlined in Chapter 4. She has remained a staunch champion of phonics but as whole-word dominance escalated, NFER could no longer find clients willing to fund research into reading methods. It ought to be commissioned to monitor all new reading schemes in the way that drugs are tested before coming into general use. Schemes failing to maintain ARQs of at least 110 for the first two school years, should not go on the market.

In 1961, the United Kingdom Reading Association (UKRA) was founded as a branch of the 1956 International Reading Association (IRA) in USA. The IRA tended to protect the whole-word approach and resist the influence of Rudolf Flesch's splendid pro-phonics book, *Why Johnny Can't Read*. UKRA, by contrast, was not systematically against phonics. Its concern was for "the teaching and learning of language, literacy and communications" and its distinguished founders included John Downing of the i.t.a. research project and Joyce Morris of NFER. However, some members favoured look-say and their brickbats so dismayed Charles Fries, the pro-phonics American guest speaker at UKRA's first annual conference that he would not publish his paper in the Conference Proceedings.

UKRA aimed for "balance", including counterproductive mixed methods but on the plus side it criticised teacher training and pleaded for explicit instruction on how to teach reading. A 1973 paper by Joyce Morris was entitled *How Can You Teach What You Don't Know?* Her 1985 research into the distressing linguistic ignorance among students and teachers was confirmed by Hunter and Cash in 1987, and also in USA. The Association's Special Interest Group on Linguistics in Teacher Education had 50 keen members by 1998, keeping in touch with developments and urging more publicity for real research, including the fundamental need for phonics letter-decoding skills. It is unfortunate that the true meaning of "linguistics" was distorted by Kenneth Goodman's term, "psycholinguistics".

In 2003 UKRA changed its name to UKLA, the United Kingdom Literacy Association, which better reflects the breadth of its interest. Its current membership includes 162 libraries, 112 schools and 491 individuals. It produces three publications: *Reading; The Journal of Research in Reading;* and *Language and Literacy News.* Its annual conference is well attended and the Proceedings are published in book form.

The 99 by 99 Group aimed to get 99% of pupils reading well by 1999. This was not achieved and the name was changed to the National Literacy Trust. UKRA saw it as a sympathetic and useful link. It ran an expensive but rather unsuccessful experiment in London's Docklands using computers and is now combined with Reading is Fundamental, a group that simply distributes books. This is a warm-hearted desire to *do* something but it misses the point. Handing out books does not make children readers. The prime need comes before that, teaching them *how* to read. The Trust is also concerned to improve school-leavers reading — a bit late in the day after eleven (now twelve), barren years in school.

The 1966 National Association for the Care and Rehabilitation of Offenders (NACRO) understood the link between illiteracy and descent into crime, but did not urge better teaching as a preventive. Despite an approach by Mona McNee, it would not challenge the received wisdom. It contacted Alice Coleman on criminogenic housing design, repeatedly offering help but totally ignoring her points. At one conference NACRO staff were so impervious to reason that a senior police officer commented to Alice Coleman that the police had no respect for them. Yet NACRO still receives government funding. Does it feel that keeping a supply of offenders outweighs the desirability of reducing crime, as that would also reduce its own fiefdom?

The 1978 Warnock Report on learning disabilities inspired the founding of BILD, the British Institute for Learning Disabilities, which aimed for quality lifestyles for the disabled. Despite its 1500 members and 16 staff, plus 500 firms and 200 other supporting organisations, there is little or no news of achievement. The National Association of Special Education Needs (NASEN) has 9,500 members.

The British Dyslexia Association (BDA) was geared for early identification of dyslexics, to offer help before they became badly damaged. Jean Augur, who worked there, wrote that if all children were taught by the phonics method, dyslexics would learn to read along with the rest. However, the BDA gave this only a nod and never seriously tried to stop the harmful teaching. It now has 8000 members but, sadly, it concentrates on intervention and not prevention.

Volunteer Reading Help (VRH) was founded in 1973 to serve 13 inner London LEAs, with later branches elsewhere. "Volunteers befriend and encourage children chosen by their teachers in regular one-to-one sessions, by talking, reading and playing games together, so that their confidence is gradually built up and they are lured into reading." This exemplifies the way the concept of "help" diverts effort into activities associated with reading but sidesteps the core need, i.e. *teaching* children to read for themselves. Effective teaching would boost their confidence far more than "help" as a crutch that stands aside from imparting real competence. Volunteers, too, would get more satisfaction if they were trained to *teach* phonics and see their protégés actually become readers instead of merely being lured into a vague willingness to do so.

VRH has 1100 volunteers, trained at 21 centres. The training urges non-discrimination on grounds of gender, marital status, social class, colour, race, ethnic origin, creed or disability. Nevertheless, Mona McNee was rejected for her hard-of-hearing disability, despite her success in teaching infants. The training also advocates guessing — just what causes the problem.

The British Educational Research Association (BERA, 1974) has about 900 members but seems never to have investigated the value of phonics. The National Association for Primary Education (NAPE, 1980) is fairly well known with 1150 members, but did not tackle the illiteracy problem and, again, had no interest in supporting phonics.

LATE, a 1980 London group, developed into NATE, the National Association for the Teaching of English, with over 5,000 members, including 80 firms. It has three publications: *English in Education, NATENEWS* and *The English and Media Magazine.* As a keen supporter of whole language, it is a strong opponent of phonics. Its position papers on key issues began with *The Grammar Book* by Brian Slough et al. (1997). Priced at £45, it was commended in the high-flown complexity of Progressivist language. It stressed that grammar teaching should not be prescriptive or decontextualised but related to children's own speech. In plain words this means that children with debased speech should have their wrongness reinforced by egalitarianism. NATE's whole ethos seems to want children to run before they can walk, in this case by appreciating the abstractions of English style from the outset instead of at a more advanced stage after they are well grounded in the basics.

ILEA's Centre for Language in Primary Education (CLPE) was taken over by the Borough of Southwark to publish books and support whole language. The Local Education Authorities Research Group, 1984, has had little emerging from it. The College of Preceptors, now the College of Teachers, published *Education Today* and in 1992 did print letters from Jennifer Chew and Mona McNee noting flaws in an earlier article but did not follow up. The National Literary Association (NLA) also promotes literacy without focusing on *how* to read.

Campaigning Societies

In contrast to the numerous groups hitching on to the Progressivist band-wagon, there are a few with objective scientific evidence in mind and these have made positive advances.

For some years Baroness Cox and John Marks organised a monthly meeting in the House of Lords for enlightened people from all over the country. The purpose was information exchange, which supported indi-viduals' campaigning efforts, though without organising a centralised campaign. There were oral contributions as well as documents placed at the front for everyone to take copies. Cox and Marks, both separately and together, produced superb research findings on key elements of the decline, such as standards and cost.

Baroness Cox is President of the Queen's English Society (QES) formed in 1972, and Joyce Morris is its Patron. QES is concerned with the broad span of language use, not only in schools. Its Silver Jubilee Conference was devoted to "Controversial Issues in English" and the follies of Progressiv-ism were included. Each year it publishes three issues of its journal, *Quest*.

The Campaign for Real Education

The Campaign for Real Education (CRE) was formed in 1987 by a group of 14 parents worried by the decline in state schooling. They were not merely in sympathy with the then government's aim of raising standards and improving parents' choice of schools, but also alert as to how Progressivists had become wall-to-wall educational "experts", so that government could hardly escape their influence, and this meant that many constructive changes were being marred by the incorporation of retrogres-sive elements. The CRE's stand against such wrong-headedness attracted many people who had been distressed but powerless, and today there is a nation-wide network of supporters, working in a broad range of positive ways. There are also strong links with the like-minded in countries such as USA, Australia, Japan and Switzerland.

CRE publishes an incisive termly newsletter and organizes efficient activities such as monitoring educational literature and conferences, attending meetings of other-minded and perhaps deleterious groups, forming working parties to forge and refine logical arguments and pro-posals, and publishing pamphlets for distribution to members and sub-scribers, such as British and overseas teachers, academics, libraries and research institutions.

CRE's intensive voluntary work has won a reputation for honesty, fac-tual insight and effective influence, becoming a fount of information and advice, consulted by parents, teachers, school governors, business people, etc. Contacts are assiduously maintained with opinion-formers: council-lors, MPs, the business world and the media. Information is regularly sent to all the national newspapers, as well as to local and national radio and television programmes, and commentators are provided on request. Journalists frequently ask the CRE for "the voice of common sense" and even the BBC has consulted it, as also have government agencies.

The active and distinguished CRE chairman, Nick Seaton, has important objective investigations to his credit. Although the Campaign is concerned with the whole gamut of education across the age groups and all the school subjects, it also recognises the basic need for phonics and repudiates the harmful guessing inherent in the whole-word method.

The Reading Reform Foundation

While the CRE is concerned with all aspects of education, The Reading Reform Foundation (RRF) focuses specifically on the teaching of reading. It originated in USA when the Wall Street philanthropist, Watson Washburn, wanted to counter the Progressivist approach of the two groups that amalgamated to form the IRA. He declared that his sole aim was "to restore intensive phonics to the teaching of reading throughout the nation." From its start in New York, the Foundation moved to headquarters in Arizona and later to Tacoma in Washington State.

Mona McNee belonged to the RRF for some years and realised that a similar pressure group was needed in Britain, so she spent a week in Tacoma, visiting schools and talking with the directors, Marion and Paul Hinds, to be sure that she was of the same mind as they were.

In 1989, with half a dozen supporters, she set up the RRF's UK chapter and edited 44 issues of its Quarterly Newsletter, reporting and incisively commenting on the various government initiatives and other positive and negative developments in the field of teaching reading. She worked on a shoe-string, distributing copies of each issue to educrats, politicians, public TV figures and others with clout who had the power to work for better literacy. But it was uphill work. The educrats believed the brainwashing of their student days and the laymen inevitably turned to some "professional, qualified" educrat for an opinion, which would always rubbish what she had said. The very words "professional" and "qualified" in this field became a sick joke. Test results, facts and other hard data made no impression. Opinion, fashions, fads and ideology were all. RRF membership during those years ranged up to 200.

As the defects of the whole-word method gradually became recognised, the membership expanded to over 300. The editorship was vigorously carried forward by Debbie Hepplewhite until she became a head with little spare time, and then passed to Jennifer Chew, who had carried out telling research investigations published by the CRE. For example, she compared the spelling ability of Zulu sixth formers learning English as a second language with that of her native-born English sixth-formers and found that the Zulus were much, much better.

In 1990, Mona McNee looked at the available British and American commercial reading schemes for something she could show to parents and say, "Get this to teach your own child." But although some were phonic, e.g. Spalding's *The Writing Road to Reading,* she found nothing that had all the virtues: simplicity, economy, thoroughness and a sufficient range to get children going without being over-comprehensive. In desperation, therefore, she created her own *Step by Step* manual, which will be explained in Part IV, "The Way Ahead".

Step by Step was meant for parents of struggling pupils but it also proved popular for getting younger ones reading before starting school so that they are protected from being harmed by the whole-word method and perhaps having their dyslexia activated into illiteracy. Despite adverse "professional" opinion, it received much word-of-mouth recommendation. Two fathers who had found the book easy to use and effective, wrote "*In My View*" articles in the Daily Telegraph, which helped boost sales.

The method was all there in a single inexpensive book, in sharp contrast to the expensive sequences of material that whole-word schemes spread over years of the child's school life. There was also a range of helpful games to add fun to the learning process and these were reusable over many years. Alice Coleman's assessment of *Step by Step* will be found in Chapter 16, with comments from the numerous thank-you letters from delighted users. These have come from places as diverse as Andorra, Australia, Canada, Japan, Korea, New Zealand, the Philippines, Russia, USA and Zimbabwe.

The RRF is making headway, despite continued resistance from the various watchdogs and voluntary organisations opposed to phonics, and at last the government has included it on its consultation list.

In conclusion we may mention the many well-meaning people and groups whose contacts with would-be recruits to business, universities and also with prisoners, alerts them to the fact that poor literacy is now a national disaster. Understandably, they still turn to the "experts", who unitedly defend the poor practice of the status quo. In spite of the Conservative government's attempt to create improvements in 1988, Progressivism continues to prevail in many ways, and questioners feel constrained to back down, though still with an uneasy feeling that something is wrong.

Part III of this book is entitled "The Struggle for Reform" and will outline attempts to improve education and also the backlash obfuscation by the Progressivist educrat establishment, which still retains all the key positions and fiercely condemns any attempt to get rid of the wrong teaching. Before that however, Chapter 14 will outline a wider context related to the rise and decline of civilisations.

Conspiracy Theory?

Is There a Progressivist Plot?

Teachers, lecturers and gurus, heads, inspectors and advisers, LEAs, government civil servants and ministers, committees of enquiry, quangos, the media, publishers, unions, professional associations . . . So many levels of watchdogs and so many people at each level pushing the sacred name of Progressivism for what has proved worse education with appalling illiteracy. Was their mutual support just self-deception or has there been an organised conspiracy, deliberately using unwitting supporters as their tools?

Reader, before you laugh the conspiracy idea out of court, please try the following exercise in imagination. Imagine that such a conspiracy exists and that you are a member of its inner cabal. You are one of the drivers of a movement that brings you immense kudos and influence as well as a large income from your books and public appearances, etc. Influence is power, money is power, and you naturally want to protect your power from attack. So you use your power to protect your power by manipulating a wide range of sticks and carrots. And as your field is education, you invent and exploit the concept of politically correct language.

Words are the vehicles of ideas, so if you shut out certain words and substitute others, you muffle the excluded ones and introduce those that are more favourable to *you* but which blind most of the people most of the time.

You begin your political correctness campaign with widely acceptable items. You complain about the use of "he" to include "she" and ban the word "nigger" as offensive. These changes are willingly espoused by people in general, and pave the way for further items, such as "chairperson" and the banning of lovable golliwogs.

The substance of such changes is just froth to you. Its underlying aim is to give the thought-police a foothold. Your fundamental manipulations are not stated explicitly but disseminated with imperceptible cunning. You divert attention away from them. You en-courage people to strain at a gnat and swallow a camel, and have arranged it that questions about that unnoticed camel would be unthinkable—literally, not even thought about.

One unquestionable idea is that any suggestion of a conspiracy is automatically ludicrous and the last resort of the unhinged. You have made this so widely accepted as common sense, that if anyone hints at what you are up to, you need only whisper "conspiracy theory" to have him branded as bizarre.

This ploy minimises the possibility of exposing a conspiracy by a dispassionate examination of the facts. Progressivists with their disdain for facts and knowledge have long been educating children to trust imagination more than hard evidence and to confuse the difference between them. So fact can be dismissed as sheer imagination and sneered away, as beyond the bounds of serious consideration. All the firepower of the conscious and unconscious conspirators would concentrate on gunning down any brave individual who protested, before the protest could make a lasting impact.

But conspiracies do exist and we make a small digression to note one that *was* laughed out of court twenty years ago, but is now accepted, with incontrovertible evidence.

The Paedophile Ring

A conspiracy progressively uncovered in Britain, and also worldwide, is an organised network of child abusers who support each other in securing positions of authority in children's homes or other social-work situations that have a supply of captive child victims.

Even Frank Beck, the first mass-molester arrested, trailed ample evidence of not being an isolated case. He had appointed other paedophiles as his colleagues in Leicestershire, where he secured responsibility (or irresponsibility) for *three* children's homes and could call on their support to decry complaints by abused children and even by one untainted staff member. And he had references that helped him win posts in two other areas. The paedophile ring is now known to have infiltrated at least 36 local authorities and further investigations continue.

Moreover, such rings are widely international. Tours are organised in Britain and Japan to visit paedophile hunting grounds in the orient, where sex entrepreneurs provide child wares. One Italian ring, broken in 1997 was traced through ten countries. The first predominant use of the Internet was subscribers' pursuit of illicit sexual interests and there have been so many cases of Internet predators "grooming" children to lure them for sexual abuse that warnings have become commonplace.

The paedophile conspiracy is no longer in doubt but the reader may ask, "What has it to do with education?" The answer is, "Quite a lot".

Firstly, teachers' easy access to children has attracted a number of paedophiles to join their ranks. Our records show that those convicted of pupil abuse include teachers of art, music, physical education, English,

French, Maths and science, as well as heads and deputies. Their attacks have occurred in nursery, primary, secondary and boarding schools as well as units for problem and disturbed children. School caretakers have also offended.

Paedophile abuse is no longer a rare and almost unheard-of practice. In 2000 a police report noted that there were about a quarter of a million paedophiles in the United Kingdom and in 2006 it emerged that there were some 90 teaching in British schools. Ruth Kelly, the Education Secretary of State had actually exonerated one herself.

Secondly, there is a parallel between the sexual abuse organised by a paedophile ring and the intellectual abuse organised by the educational establishment. Both accord with the spirit of the times, as also does the architectural abuse that produced the misery estates. The nature of this trend is supported by the scientific evidence presented below.

The third link is causal. It is now well established that intellectual deprivation in childhood can have devastating effects. Physically, unused parts of the brain atrophy. Mentally, the intelligence quotient is depressed. And emotionally, lack of mental interests cause a child to focus too heavily on other aspects of life. In some cases this is sex, so future paedophiles may be being bred by intellectual abuseas well as by sexual abuse.

The Spirit of the Times

Civilisations rise, peak and fall, and many signs suggest that the West is now in a state of decline. Of course, we are reluctant to accept the anxiety inherent in facing that idea, so readers may find themselves reacting against it. That, alas, will simply assist the downwave of civilisation, of which the educational downwave is an integral part. So please keep an open mind and read on. We need to become alert to the threat if we are to avert it.

The rise and fall of civilisations is well documented. Some, such as ancient Egypt and ancient Greece, had a single brilliant flowering and never rose to pre-eminence again. Lightning does not strike in the same place twice. But occasionally it does. Britain is exceptional in having had two great surges. The first was the Elizabethan age of achievement, in literature, the theatre, global exploration, etc. The second brought the agrarian and industrial revolutions and was characterised by mechanical inventiveness, exploration and trade, the largely peaceful growth of empire, the establishment of hygiene, sanitation and medical advances, great poetry and art, the spread of the Anglican communion, etc. We badly need a third great surge but how can we achieve it?

C. Northcote Parkinson took a broad view of civilisations and charted the alternating ascendancy of East and West. Others have noted similarities that characterise the declining phases of different cultures. Official handouts, for example, took the form of bread and circuses in ancient Rome, while in modern Britain they are parallelled by a wide range of state benefits and multiple forms of amusement: television, theme parks, sports centres, youth clubs and, in the context of this book, the play way in education.

Head and shoulders above other analyses is D. C. McClelland's 1961 book, *The Achieving Society*. As a psychologist interested in economic growth, McClelland was intrigued by calls for government policies based on different, and sometimes contradictory, hypotheses. For example, some groups pointed to hunger and overpopulation in much of the Third World and urged birth control as the key to economic advancement, while others, such as France, argued that all the great upsurges of civilisation have been accompanied by population growth and that economic development should be stimulated by promoting larger families.

McClelland decided to test a range of economic hypotheses against growth or non-growth, to find the best fit. He also included a psychological hypothesis that he thought might be germane, i.e. that growth and decline depended on a nation's dominant motivation and how it changed over time. He recognised three basic types of motivation: *achievement, affiliation (friendliness)* and *desire for power*. Money was not considered a basic motivator as it could help drive any one of the three. It transpired that the motivation theory explained economic trends better than any of the economic hypotheses.

Before discussing the effect of each motivational type, it is necessary to outline its scientific measurement by objective analysis of its literature and/or art. These methods are sufficiently precise to enable different psychologists to produce closely agreeing scores from the same material. One standard technique is to show a picture of a boy sitting at a desk with a man standing beside him, and ask the person being tested to describe the situation that the picture might represent.

Someone motivated mainly for achievement is likely to respond along the following lines. The boy is doing his homework and wants to excel. The man is explaining how he can hone his skill and apply himself better.

Someone motivated mainly for affiliation would perceive the man as friendly to the boy and trying to make things easier for him. He may praise the work as quite good enough, or say it does not matter about working any harder, or even supply the answers himself, to relieve the boy of pressure to find his own solutions.

Someone who is mainly power-oriented may see the man as scolding the boy to make him feel inferior or submissive. Or the boy may be obstreperously lording it over the man.

The imagined scenarios may vary widely but whatever the subject's motivational mind-set, it automatically influences his interpretation along the lines of "try to do better" or "make it easier" or "boss him about". The subject's relative frequency of the three types of response allows the psychologist to produce scores for each component.

McClelland applied such measurements to the literature of past civilisations, using several independent assessors for each sample tested. He also adopted other safeguards. For example, he quoted Berlew's use of ancient Greek literature divided into six categories: man and his gods, estate management, funeral orations, poetry, epigrams and war speeches. These came to the assessors as translated passages in undated random order. When the results were rearranged by date, all six categories revealed high achievement motivation during the civilisation's growth period, a lower score around its climax and a still lower one during the decline. Dominant achievement motivation in the growth phase gave place to dominant affiliation over the peak and dominant power orientation during the decline and fall.

The same motivational sequence emerged with every civilisation tested, even those without literature, which had to be assessed by a different technique based on their art.

McClelland also identified the three types in 40 modern civilisations in 1925 and used them to predict how their economies would change over the next quarter-century up to 1950. He used two measures of economic change: electricity generation, which was precise but rather narrow, and gross national product (GNP), which was broader but less precise. All this assiduous work proved that the predictions based on motivation fitted the 25-year facts better than any of those based on economic hypotheses.

The 1950 measurements singled out Britain and Israel as the two countries most outstanding for affiliation, which implied that both would move on to power motivation next. To understand how this phasing fits conspiracy theory, we must define each type more fully.

Motivation For Achievement

Motivation for achievement characterises people who are dedicated to some goal outside themselves, pursuing it for its own sake and not for any glory it may bring them. It may well bring glory but that is just incidental.

Both the great British upsurges were triggered by a religious revival: first the coming of Protestantism and then of Non-Conformism. Religion is not always achievement-motivated; the Spanish Inquisition was definitely power-oriented. But the British revivals were genuinely productive of achievement. They inspired people to praise and serve God through all their works and actions and strive for excellence in every sphere. Whatever their field of endeavour, from the humblest to the loftiest, they wanted to improve things for the glory of God, and at the lowly end of the scale we are reminded of the words of the old hymn:

> Who sweeps a room as in Thy sight
> Makes that and the action fine.

Excellence develops in whatever fields the individual achievers espouse: arts, literature, crafts, science, technology, business, exploration, etc., and their achievements greatly boost culture and civilisation. They are the driving force of the upwave. Achievers in different fields often know each other and like to learn of each other's work. But they do not depend on each other and are sufficiently motivated to go it alone, *independently*. Difficulties do not deter them, nor does lack of money. If they have money or achieve it, they value it, not for self-indulgence but as a sign of success and a means to further success, ploughing much of it back into the enterprises to help continuing progress.

They raise their children in a God-fearing way, holding it more important for them to be good than happy. Goodness is essential for their eternal salvation whereas any happiness that conflicts with goodness is paving the path to hell. The children are taught to take a pride in work well done, a neat appearance, orderly behaviour and a courteous attitude. The parents want the very best for the next generation but know it comes only to those who *earn* it, so they try to ensure that their children are also motivated for achievement. Thus, the upwave of civilisation sweeps on its way to greatness.

Upwave triggers need not be religious and the whole upwave population is not necessarily achievement-motivated. But the achievers are dominant and they help society to cohere, as their ideals become the accepted social mores. There is a confident social direction and the crime rate is low. Anti-social deviants are not tolerated. Criminals are social lepers, sometimes forced to become outlaws beyond the pale.

As the upwave continues, some achievers turn towards improving the lot of genuine unfortunates and, instead of merely dispensing charity, they achieve laudable reforms, such as the abolition of slavery or taking children out of the mines and sending them to school. But over the generations the idea of making things easier becomes more widespread and ushers in the next phase: motivation for affiliation, or friendliness.

Motivation For Affiliation (Friendliness)

Thanks to the achievers, civilisations come to ride easily on the crest of the upwave. Success abounds, affluence is assured, and self-denial begins to seem superfluous. A new ideal of making life kindlier comes to dominate — an outgoing spirit of goodwill to others and an inner need to attract goodwill towards oneself. People want to like and be liked; they value happiness more than goodness. As affiliators, they are alert to ways of securing happiness. They strive to be "regular guys" — one of the crowd.

They are not independent but *interdependent*. They are affable and participate in group activities. They lend a helping hand, which is genuine altruism but also has its payoff in bringing them affectionate regard. They do not want to exert pressure on others or stir up resentment. Their noblest aim is to serve others.

If they have money, they are generous with gifts and hospitality, which, consciously or unconsciously, are ways of buying friendship. They may spend freely on their own lifestyles, to keep up with the Joneses and maintain a position as a fit member of the community. They support charities and establish new ones. They may disparage achiever attitudes as goody-goody and stress the superiority of their own do-gooder approach. They espouse the ideal of equality and want everyone to be equally accepted and catered for. They generate the welfare society, with public benefits to help compensate for the inequalities of poverty, disability, ill-health or old age. They see criminals as victims of their upbringing, who ought to be helped and redeemed rather than punished or ostracised.

Thus, they generate the permissive society. A little permissiveness can be an excellent leaven for an achieving society but when it becomes dominant, it no longer has an achieving society to leaven and begins to go over the top, sowing seeds of its own decay. This comes about as a result of changes in child-rearing practices.

Affiliators want to be kind to their children and so they give in to their demands. They pamper and cosset, and cannot bring themselves to apply discipline, so children who are testing for the limits never find them and go on pushing their parents harder. At first, the occasional child reared over-permissively is considered *spoilt*, i.e. good material ruined by poor processing. But as affiliator motivation becomes dominant, more families over-indulge their children and the effect is reinforced by child-centred education without proper correction of mistakes. Problem children and problem adolescents are so numerous that they are no longer considered spoilt and are seen as normal.

Achievers would see this as undesirable, and apply negative feedback to create prevention. But the affiliators' reaction is just the opposite: positive feedback that accentuates the trend. Parents blame themselves for failing their difficult offspring and try to be even kinder, which rewards bad behaviour. They may deplore the behaviour consciously, but unconsciously they may even welcome it, because it harmonises with their motivation to give help. The problem child is perceived as disadvantaged by an inadequate upbringing, which is true, but the disadvantage is misinterpreted as repression rather than spoiling and the remedy is wrongly seen as more lenient pampering, such as giving young delinquents trips to Africa, etc., at public expense. This often fails, so delinquency and crime multiply.

Progressivism brings a similar failure to schools for the same affiliator reasons: the cult of kindness that stresses the play way in everything and fails to build backbone, as well as the cult of equality which respects poor work as highly as good work. There are misconceived remedies that do not work and still produce illiterates, together with a complete disregard for the principle of *prevention*, which in this context would be prevention of illiteracy by teaching phonics-first as a way of outflanking the dead-end route into crime.

Motivation For Personal Power

The children of affiliator homes, schools and society grow up into power-motivated adults. From their infancy, they have experienced success in manipulating over-kindly, over-permissive parents and teachers, and success breeds more success. They have never learned that they cannot have all their own way and continue to demand it. Their motive is self-aggrandisement and not some worthy end outside themselves.

They often have an uncanny ability to sum up other's weak points and know just where to exert pressure most effectively. They may be school bullies, intimidating younger or gentler children to extort money or possessions, or pushing them into taking risks as front men in mayhem or crime. They enjoy having victims in their power, to control, harm and humiliate. A research psychologist has noted that these ruthless characters may become successful businessmen, able to thrust ahead regardless of others' needs. Their use for money is to enhance their power and they like to boss their employees about. But this may prove counterproductive in the long run as their ablest staff move to less stressful jobs. Similarly, door-to-door cowboys enjoy power through defrauding people but this becomes known and leads to their downfall and imprisonment.

Other power-people are more subtle and dominate with the aid of charisma. Their huge self-confidence attracts adherents and they feed their drive for domination by seeking ever wider influence, as well as manipulating their followers into ever more loyal bondage.

As power motivation becomes prevalent, not everyone with this drive can become a leader. Some share in the leader's power by being loyal lieutenants or outpost officers carrying the banner into fresh colonies. Others merely shelter under the umbrella of the power organisation, perhaps being obsequious to those above them and bullying to those below. Affiliators also gravitate towards the power structure because it is now the obvious home of the regular guys. The few remaining achievers are sidelined and politically correct language is used to imply that *they* are now the social lepers, treated as figures of fun. Mary Whitehouse, with her campaign for higher moral standards, is an example, and the protagonists for phonics to end illiteracy have been subjected to similarly abusive labelling.

Because power motivation is egotistical, it has no real concern for improving the civilisation or even maintaining its peak. Some groups are unashamedly out for all they can get. Organised crime has followed on from the rare and mostly petty offences of the achieving phase and the multiplying felonies of the affiliation phase. Crime becomes more vicious and ruthless, and foreign organisations find fertile recruiting fields. The headmaster, Philip Lawrence, was stabbed to death by a teenage member of a Triad-type gang. And offences that used to be secretly committed by lone individuals are now more often joint activities. Rape, for example, carries so little shame for its perpetrators that it is no longer surprising to read of another gang-bang. For them this nauseating crime is just a jolly social occasion for exercising their power. And still more unspeakable is the case of the Belgian, Dutroux, who kidnapped young girls for use as sex objects, and killed them when he wanted a bit more variety. One he even did not bother to kill before burying her, but nevertheless he was protected from justice for a whole decade. Kidnapped sex slaves are no longer exceptional and the mind boggles at what worse things may ensue as civilisation plunges still deeper.

Even those supposedly on the side of right may pay only lip service to their duties. Too many Welfare State employees are no longer the nation's friendly servants and have become officious seekers of power. The TV series "Yes, Minister" and "Yes, Prime Minister" exposed an all too truthful conspiracy among civil so-called servants with well developed ploys for outwitting the country's elected representatives. And the recommendations of repeated enquiries into paedophile scandals have not led to effective action.

Not surprisingly, McClelland found that dominant power-motivation accompanied the decline of civilisations. The independence of the achievement phase and the interdependence of the affiliation phase gives place to *dependence* in the power phase. The dependency culture is welcome to power-hungry leaders as it facilitates their control. Their pledges to empower the underdog are superficial ploys to win votes and slow to come to fruition. This may create despair and a search for comfort in various forms of addiction, which means that dependency is joined by *co-dependency* within the addicts' families.

The spirit of achievement spreads naturally and openly. Training colleges did not suppress either phonics or whole-word methods, but recommended phonics on the factual evidence. But it is in the very nature of power motivation to direct its energy into securing a power base through an organised network of allies, protected from attack by their secrecy. And even if their conspiracy is discovered, it is further protected by the politically correct ridicule that has been attached to any idea of a conspiracy. This is exemplified by the ridicule of phonics in the colleges and the brain-washing that made the whole-word method and its derivatives the only thinkable approach.

Implications For British Education

The upwave in British education fitted the upwave of our civilisation as a whole. Progressivism then stood no chance but found its hole in the dyke at about the time that motivation for friendliness became dominant. Schonell's seminal book came in 1945, shortly before the UK was rated as having an outstanding national affiliator score and so it was a time when the greater ease of learning claimed for whole-word methods appealed to a nation that wanted everything to be easier and kindlier.

But affiliation bred power motivation and educational standards declined in concert with rising crime and many other signs of a civilisation beginning its downwave. All the evidence showed that the whole-word approach and related methods, together with Progressivism in general, failed abysmally. In an achievement-oriented society they would have been abandoned forthwith but in a power-oriented society the top priority is hanging on to one's power base. And if that base is one's reputation as a whole-word guru, it is not to be jettisoned because of "minor" allegations about falling standards.

Progressivists easily convinced themselves that such allegations were false. They believed that testing was undesirable, which insulated them from the evidence and let them to deceive themselves that the claim of declining standards must be untrue. Even if they could acknowledge a soupçon of truth, they still believed it was misguided because it ignored the intangible, and greater, benefits that they thought modern methods bestowed. Once again, when Progressivism defended itself, it suspended its own principle of all things being equally good and claimed superiority. It condemned others' facts as "value judgements" while continuing to judge itself as valuable and right.

It was this blind eye for facts that made Progressivism such an abomina-ble vehicle for seizing educational power. Achievers like testing because it reveals their success and illuminates the path to further improvement. Power-seizers hate it because they know, consciously or unconsciously, that any exposure of failure would threaten their ascendancy. Affiliators may not be against tests; they just want more people to pass them so that there is less sense of failure. This aim was embodied in the 1944 Education Act, which provided for more pupils to pass for the grammar schools and for the non-passers also to enjoy secondary education — a term previous reserved for the grammar schools.

Who introduced the idea of not testing at all? It was not Schonell, whose 1950 book was entitled *Diagnostic and Attainment Testing.* He was more an affiliator but his misconceptions led to the later power-motivated decline. It was not then known how inevitably the loosened attitudes of motivation for friendliness paved the way to the downwave, and before it *was* known there was a vested interest in suppressing the knowledge.

It was the 1963 Newsom Report, *Half Our Future,* that pushed anti-testing that extra notch ahead. Investigating the plight of the less able secondary pupil, it argued that failure to pass the 11+ exam for the grammar school had a disastrous effect, and advocated abolishing it and sending all children to comprehensive schools in the name of equality. It did not detect the real problem as defective methods in the teaching of reading and therefore the comprehensives did not stop the rot. Newsom could only have embraced non-testing so easily because it was already being strongly promoted by Progressivists.

Power-oriented people are naturally deaf to any suggestion that they are agents of decay, and their opposition to testing also probably created a disregard for measuring motivation. Motivational analysis became a victim of the spirit of the times just as much as the 11+, the grammar schools and streaming by ability within comprehensives.

All these circumstances and many more fit together to show that our present declining civilisation fits the characteristics of others that have fallen in the past. Motivation for personal power has emerged at the predictable time and in the predictable sequence, accompanied by a predictable failure in many fields of endeavour, including education, where soaring illiteracy has been accompanied by an escalating dependency culture. And unless there is some new revival, it will go from bad to worse.

Progressivists may argue that this evidence of a conspiracy is just circumstantial but there is also direct proof in the way the "entrenched educational establishment" (sometimes called the EEE) reacted to the first real government attempt to halt and reverse the decline.

This attempt was made by the Conservative administration led by Margaret Thatcher. It defined a National Curriculum demanding more structured knowledge and also a national testing scheme. After the defeat of power-motivated non-educational unions, the EEE was naturally apprehensive and geared itself up to beat off the threat to its hegemony. A "green paper" was prepared for circulation to its troops, to reassure them that their interests would be protected, and a copy of it fell into the hands of Baroness Cox's information exchange group, run for achievers. Quite unashamedly it said:

> We have people in place at every level of education to subvert the National Curriculum.

So behind the apparently spontaneous spirit of the times there was a secret and subversive organisation, planning to harm the Conservative government's legitimate policy for educational improvement. This activity agrees exactly with the dictionary definition of a conspiracy: "A secret plan to carry out an illegal or harmful act, especially with political motivation." The conspiracy theory is not far fetched after all.

To conclude this chapter, we mention the parallel situation that existed in USA and produced at least 27 million adult illiterates there. The 1983 Report of the government's National Commission on Excellence in Education made the following point:

> If an unfriendly power had attempted to impose on America the mediocre educational performance that exists today, we might well have viewed it as an act of war.

PART III

THE STRUGGLE FOR REFORM

Chapter 15

Reform and Backlash

The unchallenged downwave has been followed by a period that we term "reform and backlash". It has been presided over by three Prime Ministers, each with a different type of motivation—achievement, affiliation and power-seeking—respectively related to the three phases of civilisation noted in Chapter 14.

Initially we had no idea of the political aims lurking within education; our own training had instilled the principle of not seeking to influence pupils politically. Schooling was to equip people for fulfilling lives and not to help boost political power. However, we gradually realized that a strong party-political element had crept in. Progressivism repeatedly claimed to be the infallible enlightenment of the Left and castigated traditional teaching as the stupidity of the Right. It took longer to understand that this was no mere contrast of views on how to improve education. Teachers in training, and thus pupils, were also being programmed to accept leftism as the ideal and repudiate the political right as "nasty"—a bias quite unrelated to any facts, which, of course, Progressivism condemned as pointless.

This sinister deterioration was foreshadowed by the quasi-innocent approval of dumbing down expressed in the Hadow Report of 1931:

> The curriculum is to be thought of in terms of activity and experience rather than of knowledge to be acquired and facts to be stored.

This made no apparent impact during the upwave but worked behind the scenes during the downwave to undermine standards for political gain. In 1989 Dennis O'Keefe wrote:

> . . . there has been far too much political ideology disguised as education and training . . . . This process continues even now, despite an official government drive in the other direction.

And three years later, George Walden noted that the structures of totalitarianism were endemic within state education, and although not everyone was subversive, all had had their ways of thinking programmed during teacher training. A careful choice of language by the trainers enabled them to promote their extreme ideology without its being recognised for what it was. Leftist supporters of Progressivism had infiltrated all the high positions in the educational bureaucracy and it was difficult, even for the Conservative government, to perceive the magnitude of the educational reform that was needed.

Margaret Thatcher

Margaret Thatcher's motivation for achievement meant a genuine desire to raise educational standards. She had already tried to tackle illiteracy through the Bullock Committee but was foiled from taking action because Labour was in power when it reported, after being captured by the forces of decline.

Back in power her approach to reform was delayed by other political priorities and Progressivist civil servants thrive on delay. Most governments last only a few years but the civil service is permanent and if reform could be fended off for a while, rescue could be expected from the next Labour administration. This almost succeeded as the Conservatives' major Education Act was delayed until 1988.

Once she grasped the educational nettle, Margaret Thatcher launched radical reform, tackling several counterproductive watchdogs. A top priority was concern for children, to enable them to achieve higher standards and lead more fulfilling lives. Ostensibly, this had also been the concern of the architects of comprehensivisation and it carried weight as long as the claims were untested. But once these schools existed, the covert motivation was gradually exposed — not educational improvement but political egalitarianism. The theoretical levelling up was actual levelling down.

Proof of levelling down was presented by Caroline Cox and John Marks in *Standards of English Education* (1983, 1985). They analysed O-Level and CSE results to compare fully comprehensivised LEAs with those that still sent the brightest to grammar schools and the rest to secondary moderns. The findings were unequivocal. The comprehensives dumbed pupils down right across the ability range. At the top end, full selection produced 13-20% more high-grade passes and at the bottom end, the secondary moderns' national average exceeded that for totally comprehensivised London, even though the latter included all the grammar-standard pupils.

Clinching the conclusion was the fact that partly selective, partly comprehensive LEAs scored lower than the fully selective ones and higher than the fully comprehensivised.

The same findings emerged from parallel research within the Department of Education and Science but Progressivist civil servants, with their usual contempt for facts, hounded Cox and Marks with stinging disparagement. The Secretary of State, the clear-headed Sir Keith Joseph, forced them to make a public apology.

Why did secondary-modern pupils excel those in the much glorified comprehensives? Possibly it was because their smaller school size allowed all the pupils to be known to all the staff and hence encouraged more personally than in a vast comprehensive mob. And those who narrowly failed to reach grammar schools would be more stimulated by being top in a secondary modern school than floundering at the bottom of grammar-school classes or in the anonymous middle of comprehensives.

A return to full selection would have been beneficial but also fiercely opposed and the Conservatives helped bright children more quickly through the Assisted Places Scheme. They diverted their state-school funding into fees at independent or grant-maintained schools with their higher standards. LEAs were encouraged to create new grammar schools but as most were strongly Progressivist, only 14 were established.

Progressivist LEAs were outflanked by the Opt-Out Scheme, which freed schools from bureaucratic expense and delays, and let them manage their own affairs, with a share of central government's local subvention. Unlike the wholesale comprehensivisation, progress was slow, to ensure that the effect was as positive as hoped. Applicant schools were examined for suitability and had to be large enough to employ a bursar. Small primary schools were later made eligible if they shared managerial costs. The scheme proved successful and applications for it increased.

Drawing the teeth of LEA watchdogs included strengthening school governing boards, with fewer political Councillors and more parents and successful people from various walks of life, to promote more businesslike management. Governors had responsibility for selecting head teachers, but as they might not understand either the causes or the cure for the decline, some tended to usurp the power needed by heads.

Progressivist training problems led to a commission for NFER to investigate *What Teachers in Training are Taught About Reading*. Unfortunately, the Report was not ready until 1992, when Margaret Thatcher was no longer Prime Minister.

Subversives tried to avert further effort by claiming that phonics *was* being taught. *Analytic phonics* was a term devised for another top-down approach which, like look-say, told children the word first. "Analytic" means breaking down a larger item (a word) into its components (syllables, letter clusters and letters). Another idea was *phonemic awareness*, not an actual method in itself but claimed as an essential prerequisite. Like analytic phonics it proved much less effective than true phonics; both are really pseudo-phonics. They necessitated a new term for true phonics and because it built up (i.e. synthesised) letters, it was renamed *synthetic phonics*.

The implications of these three methods will be detailed later but meanwhile here is a brief outline of their differences. Each starts with a different element of the three needed in learning to read: letters, sounds and words.

- Synthetic phonics begins with letters, attaches a sound to each one and blends them to build words. It introduces the commonest spelling rules first, to give confidence, and saves rarer alternatives until later, to avoid confusion.
- Analytic phonics begins by telling pupils what the words are; its concern for letters is secondary. It may mention just letter groups, or syllables.
- Phonemic awareness begins with sounds only, listening for them as parts of words. It precedes and delays the beginning of reading and also notes varied spellings for the same sounds, which creates uncertainty.

Reading Recovery

Reading Recovery was the 1980s brainchild of New Zealander Marie Clay. Its blaze of publicity for rescuing strugglers commended it to British reformers, but it was another look-say variant, with large bright pictures dwarfing just a few words. It claimed to have been tested, with promising statistics, but the figures had no scientific validity. They were not based on standardized tests before and after the remedial period but only on how many small storybooks the children had mastered—by rote parroting without any ability to tackle unknown words. It was not a true test of reading ability.

Reading Recovery was independently researched, both in New Zealand and in 16 American universities. All proved that it did not deliver success and, even worse, had massaged its statistics in a bogus claim. Some 25-40% of failing children had been dropped from the programme and their records excluded from the figures.

In a few cases the scheme worked 30% better but only when combined with synthetic phonics. However, the *Reading Recovery* establishment refused to sanction phonics as an addition and one can see why. If phonics were the essential ingredient, there was no need to have *Reading Recovery* tacked on to it.

Reading Recovery cost $8,000 per child in USA, partly a teacher-training fee but largely due to its one-tutor-one-child ratio. It rejected research showing small groups did as well as single tutees. In the UK, central government dropped it, though many LEAs continued squandering local tax money on it.

National Curriculum Documents

The government did not realise that many Progressivist "experts" helping the reform were undercover enemies bent upon subversion. When the Reform Act was inevitable, they appeared compliant and in 1987 produced a harmless document that reassured teachers. But while Parliament was closed during the run-up to the 1987 general election, they completed a 100,000–word document couched in such abstruse language that it needed a glossary for 34 new terms. Teachers wading through it were aghast and protested that they needed more time to get to grips with its demands. Opposition had been fomented. Teachers had been lured into a trap and wanted out.

Crypto-Progressivist "experts" appeared the natural choice for top jobs. Duncan Graham was appointed as both Chairman and Chief Executive Officer of the National Curriculum Council (NCC), with responsibility for restoring traditional school subjects and discontinuing politicized ones — just the opposite of what he was covertly aiming for. However, protests were noted and he was replaced by David Pascal, who knew what was wanted and urged the restoration of Religious Education, with its ethical influence upon outlook and behaviour. Philip Halsey of SEAC (Schools Examinations and Assessment Council) built up a big bureaucracy instead of producing worthy exam papers and good marking standards. He was replaced by Lord Brian Griffiths.

Progressivists in subject committees also undermined the government's aims and the CRE censured the Marxist distortion in English and History. Ken Jones had described our language as "one part of an emancipatory and combative politics". The English Committee chairman, Brian Cox, was especially disappointing, as he had earlier called for reform but now supported the "new orthodoxy" that had caused the decline. He rejected true phonics, grammar and good literature and termed Standard English just a dialect. He deemed discussion more important than teaching — a familiar tale that has made education the "messy business" one Progressivist still urges it should be.

John Major

Major was motivated for affiliation. He aimed for popularity, as "Mr. Nice", avoiding the uncomfortable wrenches needed for raising standards. Thus, he delighted the polytechnics by declaring them universities at a stroke, which in no way improved higher education. He had left school at 16, and though his quick mind helped him achieve political leadership, it was not honed into the keen analytical ability that made Margaret Thatcher's insight so penetrating. He also tended to appoint advisers and Ministers who did not outshine him and who might be prey to Progressivism.

Alice Coleman wrote about the ill effects of look-say, asking him to side-step Progressivism and consult enlightened sources, such as Baroness Cox. But he shuffled off her letter to an adviser who simply consulted those she had warned against.

Tim Eggar was appointed Minister for Schools and in 1991 granted Mona McNee and Alice Coleman a brief audience in the presence of Jim Rose. After hearing our careful explanation of the contrast between phonics and look-say, Eggar dismissed it with a highly illogical non-sequitur:

> My son is a backward reader and he was taught by look-say. I was a backward reader and I don't remember how I was taught, so it proves that no method is effective.

A few weeks later, an Evening Standard leader called him "the idiotic Eggar" and we could not find it in our hearts to disagree. He was also deaf to a Dorset deputation begging him to save Sherborne's grammar schools and he did nothing to dissuade Kenneth Clarke from sanctioning their closure.

Secretary of State, John MacGregor, was also insufficiently aware of Progressivist deviousness to know when he was being conned. After Duncan Graham was ousted as NCC supremo, he continued to advise the Department of Education and boasted that he had fooled MacGregor into "saving" politicised subjects and cross-curricular studies, although employers deplored them.

This came about through the Dearing Report. The government was concerned by the protests against the National Curriculum, and also by how it had been escalated into an elaborately prescriptive straitjacket. Subjects were divided into ten levels, each with various attainment targets, which John Marebon described as atomising them into discrete bits lacking the value of a more integrated approach, and totally losing sight of the need to impart a love of learning. Secretary of State John Patten asked Sir Ron Dearing to produce a review based on consultations.

Dearing recommended that National Curriculum material should be reduced, leaving teachers a choice for 20% of the time. This seemed to suit the Conservative principle of greater freedom but it also meant that the choice could be exercised by slipping back into the old familiar ruts of politicised and cross-curricular teaching.

Dearing also advised that the National Curriculum should not operate after age 14, when pupils could select subject options. Some could drop History and Geography, which in our opinion should be continued up to the school-leaving age of 16. But Dearing was not concerned with age 16 and lumped 14–19 together as a unit, thus foreshadowing the Labour party's aim to extend compulsory schooling until age 18.

The National Curriculum did not introduce the simple paper and pencil tests envisaged by Margaret Thatcher and Sir Keith Joseph, but substituted checking of all the different sub-levels of attainment targets. Dearing noted that this could make assessment "a meaningless ticking of myriad boxes" and that " the award of the level relates to conceptual skills and understanding that are *independent of the body of knowledge taught*", but in the interests of compromise with the unions and other Progressivists, he did not recommend the dismantling of this unsatisfactory system.

"Compromise" must be among what John Humphrys has called "hurrah words", used to give a positive "feel" regardless of their actual meaning at the time. Alice Coleman met it in her DICE Project, when architects demanded she should add some of their ideas to her own. But as hers were scientifically proved to reduce the crime and malaise caused by theirs, she refused. They then labelled her with the character flaw of "inability to compromise", which in her own view was resistance to *being* compromised" and "concern for the occupiers". Dearing did not resist, and his compromise has subsequently been criticised as failing to remedy the situation.

Also appointed to the educational helm was Gillian Shephard, whose blinkered resistance to phonics as a Norfolk Councillor has been exposed in Chapter 10. She was not an arch-Progressivist dedicated to extending left-wing despotism but as a teacher she seems to have been infected with Progressivism and was supportive of the status quo rather than opening her mind to how phonics could both prevent and redeem illiteracy. Like Major she was motivated for affiliation and did not want to offend teachers by pushing ahead with reform. Instead, she declared her aim was merely to consolidate. To her credit she ordained a return to the teaching of grammar, but in general there was only the bogus improvement of softer marking causing grade inflation, which she assumed was genuine and to her Ministerial credit.

She was shocked by Chris Woodhead's data on the ILEA's appalling reading standards (see below) and embarked upon activity — not addressing direct improvement through synthetic phonics but planning greater control over schools. An unfortunate result was that it served as a Conservative stepping stone to the still more oppressive control subsequently introduced by the Labour Government. Later she urged "choice" as the great panacea. All parents should choose their children's schools, expanding good ones and shunning poor ones into closure. She seemed unaware that "choice" is only a sound-bite without a variety to choose from and did not mention new grammar schools. Alice Coleman reflected that many good schools' pupils would have learned to read at home so illiterate ones from elsewhere would not necessarily be helped.

However, she knew that mention of phonics would cut no ice, so she questioned school size instead. Andrew Smith's research on 763 Kent schools had found that larger numbers on roll brought disproportionately more school crime, so the effect of choice in enlarging good schools might bring undesirable consequences. Gillian Shephard did not enquire the safe size limit (often exceeded already), but said there would be size control, i.e. choice for some but not for all. And such a limit, like her offer to send Alice Coleman a document on choice, would probably be forgotten.

Teacher Training

The 1992 publication of NFER's report, *What Teachers in Training are Taught About Reading* revealed little readily available information; college documents proved to gloss over the subject. Students' book lists showed that the top four recommendations were all Progressivist: Liz Waterland's *Read With Me*, R. Beard's *Developing Reading, 3-13;* Margaret Meek's *Learning to Read;* and Frank Smith's *Reading.*

A questionnaire to practising teachers enquired about the training they had received. More had been taught about the totally useless real books method than any other and 60% said they had heard little or nothing about phonics. A further 19% had heard of it but only in the context of mixed methods. Twelve per cent of primary teachers could not recall being instructed in any method whatsoever. Another questionnaire elicited views on how satisfied teachers were with the reading instruction they had received. The recently qualified were the most dissatisfied and the satisfaction level rose to 59% among older ones, some of whom may have trained before all the colleges became addicted to look-say.

Despite its somewhat sketchy nature, this report increased unease about the training establishments' role, and this was strengthened by a further report edited by Sheila Lawlor (1990). It seemed a Herculean task to eradicate the lecturers' deeply entrenched Progressivism and so a small pilot scheme for outflanking them was launched instead. This was *training on the job.*

Certain good schools took on apprentice teachers to by-pass Progressivist indoctrination and absorb good practice from supervised lesson presentation and class management, and from experiencing the schools as good working models. This was a great success. Sharon Shrills were not recruited and some other apprentices realised within a few weeks that teaching was not for them and withdrew. This made them a minimal cost as compared with the three-to-four year grants for college students, and also spared other schools the harm that they might do when qualified.

School Inspectors

In this sphere it was decided on a clean sweep of the counterproductive HMIs, which could have been a great step forward. It was costly, as under the leadership of Stewart Sutherland, formerly Principal of King's College London, all the inspectors were given their congé with redundancy payments of up to £150,000. A recruitment drive was launched but Sutherland did not understand the subversives' determination to make the new team just as Progressivist as the old one, and did not keep a sufficiently hands-on control of the new appointments.

Potentially ideal candidates were rejected out of hand, e.g. Jennifer Chew with a commendable record in spelling research and Anthony Freeman, who had been sacked for criticising low standards in GCSE History. Civil servant Anthea Miller urged LEAs to provide a dozen applicants each and these were the majority of those appointed. The CRE noted that not a single acceptance was anyone outside the Progressivist establishment, confirming how thoroughly the LEAs had been infiltrated. And certain displaced inspectors set up Crown Education Associates using civil service contacts to ensure that most of its 31 members were selected to head the new inspection teams. The intention of a clean sweep was totally outwitted.

More constructive was Chris Woodhead's promotion as Senior HMI. A Progressivist before seeing the light of phonics, he was equipped with insight into both sides of the conflict. Knowing the ILEA had the nation's worst record, he ordered an inspection of the teaching of reading in 45 of its primary schools, with very dismal findings. He then set about genuine improvement, identifying bad schools and chivvying them to change their approach. This disturbance caused consternation among teachers, especially as he estimated that 15,000 of them were unfit for the profession, doubtless the Sharon Shrill element. That made him unpopular and many teachers mistook unpopularity for rudeness and wrong-headedness, but among the enlightened he commanded great respect. Judgements within the ring-fence of Progressivism are often quite different from those of people with a wider view.

The problem of LEA advisers was not addressed and some continued to create havoc. A particularly distressing case occurred in the London Borough of Southwark when a primary-school teacher, Vera Conway, found 19 complete non-readers in her new class. Using phonics to rescue them brought condemnation from an adviser, who ordered her to take retraining, to be able to see that the children really *could* read. She lost her job and her pupils lost their chance of becoming literate. Measures needed to oust such intellectual abuse were not forthcoming under John Major.

Coursework

A useful improvement was reducing the percentage of coursework marks contributing to pupils' final grades. Initially, some working parties stipulated that 100% of the mark in their subjects should be derived from work done during the year and assessed by the teachers themselves. This, as we shall show in Chapter 17, is susceptible to various kinds of unfairness, including cheating. It was decided that in future coursework should contribute no more than 20% of the final mark.

But the lesson was not fully learned and completely reversed in the new NVQ, National Vocational Qualification, for which the instructors issued competence certificates to their own students. There was no official check on whether the instructors were themselves competent nor on whether the students had performed each task without help. Another criticism was that they did not repeat tasks to acquire expertise. All the problems of more coursework were resurrected.

Testing

More details will appear in Chapter 17 but meanwhile we note that though testing at age seven was instituted, there was still a skirmish over whether the results should be published. The NAHT union advised head teachers to withhold them, for fear that some schools would be shown up as inferior. In the event, however, the results were much better than expected — suspiciously so, as closer inspection revealed that achievement did not match them. Instead it became clear how very little was taught in some infant schools. The high marks stemmed from easy papers and soft marking, a combination that promoted grade inflation.

Further information was forthcoming after the defeat of resistance to publishing independent schools' results separately from those of state schools. It then became apparent how far the latter were lagging behind, as only 30% of their pupils achieved A-Level grades A-C, as compared with 80% in the independents. This did not spring from family wealth as the Progressivists claimed, as an even higher percentage, 85%, was achieved by the remaining state grammar schools. The active factor was traditional teaching built on a phonics foundation of good literacy.

There were many criticisms unleashed by Progressivists in an attempt to create a backlash in public opinion, and also a few more unwise appointments. For example, Sue Horner of NATE, which was strongly in favour of whole language, was accepted by the NCC as its professional officer for English.

Tony Blair

Tony Blair's motivation was the desire for the personal power that has characterized the declining phase of every civilisation. This took two years to reach public awareness and attract the description "control freak" but to a graphologist it was obvious long before and Alice Coleman noted it in a 1997 article, together with all the pleasing traits that had enabled him to propel himself into a position of power.

Blair asserted that his priority was "Education, Education, Education" and it was assumed he meant raising standards. But higher standards are an unlikely goal for control freaks, who do not welcome well honed minds that may criticize or challenge them. They are more likely to see education as a way of increasing their political support and if we entertain this possibility, we find that the lack of improvement since Labour's 1997 return to power fits in with it. This lack is covered up by false impressions such as grade inflation of GCSE and A–level marks, which during an unbroken rise over 24 years have become annually less believable.

Another cover-up is the idea that not all children should reach even the incomplete stage in learning to read specified for age seven. Contrast phonics, which creates readers for life for almost all at that age. Look-say's slower teaching has been given congratulations for poorer results. As Education Secretary, David Blunkett seemed less concerned with prevention than remediation, and set up summer schools for eleven-year-olds to help them catch up. To parade their success, a boy was chosen to enthuse on television that the course had enabled him to read four more books — a dead giveaway. Reading progress is not measured in book units and it sounded as if he had just learned to parrot four more little storybooks.

The best index of progress is increased reading age (RA) and remedial teachers' ability is measured by their improvement ratios, (IRs), which show how many RA months are gained in one month of remedial work. Mona McNee reckons that the IR should be at least 3, and her own records show that she well exceeds that minimum.

David Blunkett then seemed to espouse prevention of reading failure through a National Literacy Strategy (NLS) with a daily literacy hour. It was not mandatory, but its flow of official instructions gave the impression that it was. It stipulated the use of four "searchlight" techniques, claimed as the high road to fluent reading but really just an elaborate dumbing down. They were cues from context, semantics, syntax and phonics. Only the fourth could possibly be related to *learning* to read, and even that was flawed in the NLS.

Cues from context are plausible. Fluent readers absorb new words in their stride because the context makes their meaning obvious. If not, a dictionary is consulted and only if that fails is the passage scrutinized more laboriously. Usually, unexplained neologisms and words clouded by turgid text reveal bad-mannered writers who lack the courtesy to serve their readers' needs. Pupils should be trained not to *write* in such a sloppy way, so it is desirable always to present them with lucid reading material as models of excellence that they can soak up.

Some languages have features that compel searches for contextual clues. Semitic scripts, written from right to left, have no letter symbols for vowels so words pronounced differently may have the same consonant sequence on paper and the context is vital for identifying them. Tonal languages may show all their sounds but not the pitch of each syllable, leaving meanings to be discerned from the context.

English also has diverse meanings for the same sound but early lexicogaphes tried to be helpful by varying their spelling, e.g. "rite", "write" and "right". Today such variations are more hindrance than help, especially as words with one original meaning have evolved into multiple connotations. There may seem little connection between taps on the door and taps in the kitchen sink, but there is a developmental link between them. A barrel was tapped (knocked) to make a hole through which its contents could be tapped (drawn out) and the flow controlled by a tap (a faucet).

Different words with the same sound and spelling are termed *homonyms* and English now has many. But it also has such a huge vocabulary that writers have an abundance of ways to indicate meaning, so good writing does not necessitate a hunt for contextual clues. The NLS did not need to make a big thing of the context mechanism.

So who does use it? Not learners, who cannot identify the context words either. And not fluent readers, who simply read what is there, without groping for contextual cues. Research by Stanovich finds that only poor readers resort to it, as they can decipher many words but not all and must struggle to get the full meaning. But even they probably abandon this onerous task when no longer prodded in school.

Cues from semantics seems rather a hair-splitting way to stress words versus meanings, as the two are inextricably bound up together at the primary school stage. *Cues from syntax* are also divorced from learning to read. Children are not ready to assimilate grammatical principles until after they have mastered reading, and in any case it is rare to be able to read a difficult word simply because of a grasp of sentence structure.

Cues from phonics might seem a revolutionary retreat from look-say but this is misleading and possibly designed to fend off further phonicist criticism by suggesting that there is nothing further to fight for, which is far from being true.

Phonics is best taught uncontaminated by look-say. When it follows the other NLS cues that have inculcated a guessing habit, it is necessary to break that habit before children can settle to the patient blending and word-building foundations of fluent reading. That would be so even if NLS phonics were the true synthetic brand, which it is not. It is analytic, giving priority to words and still closely related to look-say. For example, it imposes initial sight words to be recognized from their shape.

Thirty sight words are more than enough to establish guessing and the NLS asks for 45, on the argument that these are the commonest words in the language and therefore the most useful for children's composition exercises. The larger number engrains the guessing habit more deeply, making it harder to break, which slows the path to true reading even more and sometimes brings it to a complete stop.

The sight words are also wrongly chosen. Certainly it is logical to replace rarely used words such as "elephant" and near-archaic ones such as "aeroplane" by those used most frequently but spelling-wise they are a motley collection, involving a multiplicity of rules that are not explained. There is not even any grouping of similarities such as "he", "me", "she" and "we". Synthetic phonics, by contrast, introduces the rules one at a time and builds the child's confidence by giving practice in each one's similar words before going on to the next,

National Literacy Strategy Sight Words

I	said	cat	all
up	go	to	get
look	you	come	in
we	are	day	went
like	this	the	was
and	going	dog	of
on	they	big	me
at	away	my	she
for	play	mum	see
he	a	no	it
is	am	dad	yes
			can

The NLS needed the rote learning of sight words because of its slow rate of progress. Pupils reached the age for writing compositions before they had mastered reading, and it saved teachers many a spelling question if the children had these 45 words pre-stocked in their brains.

Synthetic phonics solves this problem in quite a different way. It perfects the art of reading more quickly, well before the age of free composition is reached. Early writing has two objectives: good penmanship, achieved by careful copying, and the translation of spoken language into written, achieved by taking dictation. These are best learned without the distraction of simultaneously having to invent a text. As synthetic phonics develops reading and writing skills first, pupils can later concentrate on the creative aspect of composition without constant distraction by spelling problems.

The slow NLS took the whole reception year for learning the alphabet plus three digraphs, "ch", "sh" and "th", to reach ability to read three-letter words. Compare Mona McNee's *Step by* Step, which covers all these, plus "ee" and "oo" in a single term and also includes longer words with these letters and sounds.

The fact that the NLS included letters was an advance on pure look-say, which considered letters irrelevant. But the improvement was tiny compared with the great leap that comes from introducing synthetic-phonics-only from the start. The scheme's inadequacy led to successive tinkerings, with barrages of instructions.

Furthermore, the NLS's progress beyond the initial sight words and the alphabet was still whole-word based, in the form of analytic phonics, which tells pupils the words before breaking them down into their elements. It adhered to the doctrine of mixed methods but the mix did not step outside the array of variants devised in the hope of overcoming the failures of look-say.

The Clackmannan Research Project

A complete contrast to the government approach was a 2005 report on a remarkable piece of scientific research in Clackmannan, Scotland, led by Joyce Watson of Hull University and Rhona Johnston of St. Andrews University. In 1997-98, thirteen Year 1 classes were pre-tested and divided into three comparable groups to be taught reading by the three allegedly phonic methods. Synthetic phonics used Sue Lloyd's *Jolly Phonics* scheme (see Chapter 16). Analytic phonics used the NLS and the third group used phonemic awareness, with half its time in analytic phonics in order to give testable results in reading progress after six months. The synthetic phonics classes averaged a slightly more disadvantaged socio-economic background than the others, so if the social class factor were valid, they might have lagged somewhat behind. But they did not. Instead they proved to be streets ahead in all four tests made after six months.

First, The British Ability Scales for Word Reading showed that the synthetic phonics classes had advanced their reading ages by an average of 13 months during the six months of teaching, whereas the other two had advanced by an average of only five months, less than expected by natural maturation during that period.

Secondly, Clay's Ready to Read Test also showed that synthetic phonics was the best but gave worse results for phonemic awareness than for analytic phonics.

Thirdly, Schonell's Spelling Test again found the synthetic phonics group had advanced by 13 months and the phonemic awareness group by only five, but here the NLS analytic method was the worst, giving only 3-4 months advance in spelling age.

Lastly, the Yapp-Singer Test of Phonemic Awareness measured ability to recognise separate sounds in words. This should have been an advantage for phonemic awareness and did raise it above the analytic method but still left synthesis well in the lead. Clearly, better phonemic awareness *emerges* from understanding letters and their sounds than from direct prior training in the sounds themselves.

NLS analysis produced the greatest number of under-achieving pupils while synthesis produced the fewest. Lest the difference stemmed from the analytic method's slower pace, a faster form was tested, both alone and with phonemic awareness. There were fewer under-achievers but synthesis was still the best.

Synthetic phonics continued beneficial and gave pupils over three years' superiority at the end of the seven years of the study, whereas the NLS still kept many children's reading ages below their chronological ages. The best results emerged when synthesis was introduced by itself right at the beginning, with no distraction from other methods. "Synthetic phonics first, fast and only" is the constructive approach.

The problem of boys' educational lag, so marked with the NLS, completely vanished with synthetic phonics, and some boys shot right into the lead for both reading and spelling. This reflects the fact that the synthetic approach is directed to the left brain-hemisphere and outflanks boys' lesser facility for transferring material across from the right brain.

The problem of disadvantaged homes also disappeared, which seems a natural result of teachers engaging in effective teaching and not offloading it on to parents, regardless of whether they are likely to be more competent than trained staff.

The Clackmannan research also illuminates the effect of synthetic phonics' modern refinements. In 1955 Rudolf Flesch reported it took over six months' teaching to show its superiority over look-say, but now it is over twice as good within that period.

This research triggered an Inquiry by the House of Commons Education and Skills Committee and a 2005 report, *Teaching Children to Read*. The text was fair but the front summary did not do it justice, exhibiting signs of Progressivist reluctance to accept the clear findings. It typically kept a foot in the leftist camp by means of a "balanced" statement that while some people leant towards synthetic phonics, others thought otherwise. "Balance" has usually been a Progressivist cover for not changing course, as it allows the critics' method to be kept too tiny a part to be effective. Another sign was the dogma that the acquisition of reading is extremely complex and influenced by socio-economic factors, despite the Clackmannan evidence that synthetic phonics makes the acquisition simple and causes the socio-economic influence to disappear.

It is well known that MPs like even the most complex information reduced to one side of a page, so perhaps the summary writer thought that Secretary of State, Ruth Kelly, would read only his front page. It did seem at first that she had not absorbed the full message, as there was talk of repeating the research for verification. Repetition is indeed a standard scientific way of confirming or disproving new concepts, but the Clackmannan conclusions are not new. They are themselves a splendid verification of a method that has been successful for over 3000 years and confirmed by dozens of findings over the last half-century. To repeat it now would be very unfair to two-thirds of the children involved, forcing them into backwardness by the two inferior methods.

Ruth Kelly proved cautious and asked Jim Rose to enquire further. Sue Lloyd, delighted that *Jolly Phonics* had performed so well, went to see him but reported that he did not seem enthusiastic. It must be difficult for someone respected within the Progressivist ring-fence to feel enthusiasm for a method he had hitherto rejected,

While he was enquiring, Progressivists tried to whip up a backlash by framing inaccurate criticisms. One wrote to the press that all the children needed was "praise", despite the fact that Progressivism already doles this out lavishly, with ill effects when it is not deserved. Synthetic phonics is a way to make it deserved.

Dr. Solity of Warwick University said synthetic phonics would be very boring because of all the repeated words. But repetition is *look-say's* attempt to drill children in memorising word shapes. Synthetic phonics gives a strategy for tackling a great variety of words.

Bethan Marshall alleged cruelty in forbidding children to guess the word "elephant" from a picture. She was too blinkered by look-say to know that synthetic phonics neither uses pictures as vehicles of reading instruction nor introduces "ph" words until after children can read quite well. Real cruelty lies in her own substitution of guessing for reading, which condemns so many to illiteracy for life.

Jim Rose's report, *Independent Review of the Teaching of Early Reading*, was eagerly awaited to see which way the chips would fall. Would he invoke Clackmannan evidence to launch a climb back to educational excellence? Or would his engrained Progressivism beat off the evidence and allow the decline to continue?

In the event the report was a step in the right direction. It recognised that children cannot work out the reading code for themselves and must be specifically taught. It stressed the importance of blending letters to form words and appreciated the reinforcing effect of phonics' multi-sensory technique. Ruth Kelly's response was to ordain the universal teaching of phonics and this has been welcomed as ending the long-standing intellectual abuse of our children.

We should like to have seen the report go further and condemn the failed methods; the NLS would be better terminated than renewed as he advocates. It could have mentioned the nine genuine synthetic phonics schemes assessed in the next chapter, to ensure that teachers are not sidetracked by new pseudo-phonics schemes.

Arrangements for retraining teachers leave much to be desired. Two hundred staff have been appointed, but not to give mass retraining. Instead they are to go into individual schools to attempt a remedy there. This seems rather a small number for the 22,400 primary schools with classes of traditional ages for learning to read by the phonic method, let alone those dealing with older illiterates as well, and it does not suggest that there is any sense of urgency in rescuing those now at risk of illiteracy. Even worse, the 200 do not seem to have been drawn from the ranks of known phonics experts, so there is still a big question mark about what they will actually do. Are they look-say wolves in phonics sheep's clothing, like those to be noted in Chapter 16, and is this just another Progressivist device to appear to be reacting to pressure for improvement while really maintaining their own status quo?

Mona McNee found her offers of phonics help in backward Knowsley were vigorously rejected. Eventually she was fobbed off to teach one unintelligent illiterate, whom she made a fluent reader in five months and found he was actually very bright. If this is a typical local reaction, switching over to phonics will not happen at all easily.

Distraction from Teaching

Quite apart from its long-sustained animosity to synthetic phonics, Labour has eroded standards in other ways, one of which was to occupy teachers' time with non-teaching activities. Diversion into an extra examination between GCSE and A-Level has attracted a great deal of attention but the diversion at age seven is even more serious. Primary school teachers must test and probe in order to produce reports listing no fewer than 117 items for each child. Most of them are nothing to do with education *per se* but focus on social engineering. This work is said to subtract a minimum of 40 hours from teaching time—two whole school weeks.

Similarly with five-year-old testing. After a year in the reception class, children are expected to have learned very little of the art of reading but to have absorbed a great deal of social engineering and the ability to display sympathy for other cultures.

Another distraction is the intense battery of initiatives emanating from the Department for Education and Skills (DfES). In *The Third Way: Where To and Between Which?* Professor Anthony Flew noted that 4,400 A4 pages were fired at each school in the year 2001-2002—17 pages for each working day. These had to be pondered with a view to implementing their recommendations, which further diverted time and energy from the basic teaching task, and would involve a rate of change undermining stability.

All the extra pressures were accompanied by apparent concern for teachers' welfare. Small classes were to be a benefit for them as well as for their pupils but as noted earlier, London schools with larger classes attained higher standards than those with smaller ones, and it has subsequently transpired that larger classes in overseas countries result in higher standards than British classes.

A further appeasement was a 2005 decree that 10% of a teacher's week should be "non-contact time", attending to work outside the classroom. Free periods for marking, etc., have always featured in secondary schools but extending them to primary schools has caused a crisis. Who copes with the class when the teacher is out? In some cases it is the teacher's aide but other schools must try to stretch their budgets for extra staff.

None of this creates job satisfaction for teachers. That would come from methods that enable children to do well and love school. Seeing them achieve as a result of one's work is rewarding. Living with dumbing down is not.

Reducing Family Influence

The motivation behind Progressivism is not achievement but desire for power, and that also takes the form of trying to insulate pupils from counter-influences, including the family. NAHT's demand that school starters should already be able to read makes parents a scapegoat for the teachers' own failure to produce a 100% literacy rate but in other respects parental influence is unwelcome to the political left, because it can sometimes counter Progressivist indoctrination. So as well as restoring politicised courses, Labour has also sought other ways of reducing the family's child-rearing role.

Labour knows the value of getting hold of children young and made four the starting age instead of five, in reception classes that precede Year 1. This was presented as a benefit for mothers, who were urged to get jobs and further shrink the time available for interaction with their children. It is also planned to have crèches and nursery schools to care for them from birth, with official advice on what they should be taught at each stage, which takes little heed of individual rates of development. One idea is to encourage them to express emotions such as fear, but who will terrify them so that they know what fear is? This is all contrary to their need to learn how to control the expression of feelings and not always give vent to them. Further domination, masquerading as generosity, is a statement that the government will supply books for these pre-school establishments, probably choosing those that foster left wing attitudes. Jill Kirby has described the whole proposal as "nationalisation of childhood".

There are also indications of a wish to extend the compulsory leaving age to 18 or 19, with at least 50% attending university until 21, or perhaps 22.

Another way to separate children from parents is to lengthen the school day and this, too, has been paraded as a kindly virtue. Working mothers could be helped by school breakfasts as well as school dinners, and delivering children by 8 am. would shift journey-to-school traffic out of the rush hour. The earlier start would be supplemented by a later finish. Some schools already act as paid child-minders for working parents who cannot collect their children until 5.30 pm, but it is now suggested that after-school activities until 6 pm should be the norm. A ten-hour day from 8 to 6 would reduce parental influence nicely.

Dumbing Down

We should ask whether Progressivists' denial of evidence has been the stance of fools or knaves. We know that many teachers are neither, but simply the victims of indoctrination at college. However, the writers of recent whole word schemes cannot be absolved, They arrogantly assume that just because the ideas are *theirs*, they are bound to work well, and they do not bother to test whether this is so before unleashing them into schools. This is typical Progressivist self-justification.

So, too, was David Blunkett's refusal to co-operate with Chris Woodhead, who was working hard to get at the root of educational decline and reverse it. He was so obstructive that Woodhead felt he had no option but to resign, which left him free to speak out against the abuses in the state system in a more forthright way and to a more extensive audience.

Many Ofsted inspectors reverted to their former counterproductive attitudes, paying more attention to social engineering than to progress in the three "R"s. Knowsley is Britain's third worst LEA academically, but a recent inspection report on one of its schools hardly seemed to notice that it had 83 children (20%) with special needs and many more also backward, and praised it to the skies for one kind of social engineering practice after another. How can the LEA see that it is failing its children if it receives such a glowing eulogy from inspectors?

We now pose a more fundamental question. "Does Progressivism merely seek to *sustain* its power or does it try to *increase* it by deliberately dumbing down potential opposition?" Power may corrupt and lead to a pursuit of absolute power, a context that seems to fit the official intellectual abuse in our schools. We have already noted that in USA it has been recognized as tantamount to an act of war. Deliberate dumbing down seems likely in the UK because the Labour government has not stopped at making it difficult for infants to read, but has also attacked three other vehicles of educational excellence: the grammar schools, the independent schools and the universities.

The Grammar Schools

Almost at once the 1997 Labour government banned that substitute for grammar schools, the assisted places scheme that sent bright pupils to fee-paying schools that their parents could not afford. It also spent £1 million to persuade parents to vote for the demise of the remaining 164 grammar schools and when this failed began piecemeal abolition. For example, despite league table evidence that selection benefits pupils right across the ability range, four Gloucestershire grammar schools were closed and the selective system that maintains high standards in Northern Ireland is also being abolished. But those at the top of the power structure evaded the dumbing down for their own families. Ministers, one after another, including Blair, shunned their local comprehensives and sent their children to better schools elsewhere.

Dumbing down by destroying grammar schools was presented as constructive by repeating the hoary old argument that selecting out the brightest children depressed standards for the rest. Let us translate this claim into plain-speak. It is saying that a few bright eleven-year-olds can stimulate their peers to higher standards more effectively than teachers who have had at least ten more years of education, including training for the job. The truth is that the Labour government continues to ignore the levelling-down effect proved by Cox and Marks, and also by Fred Naylor and Roger Peach in *The Truth About Grammar Schools* (2005)

The opposition to grammar schools has been masked by a policy of establishing specialist schools for those gifted in fields such as music, art, sport and technology. Academic talents were mentioned as a kind of afterthought, with references to mathematics *or* science. But the concept of specialism seems being used as misleading spin. It would not restore the all-round merit of the grammar schools but quite the reverse — splitting it into narrow opportunities, so that children cannot match excellence in one aspect with excellence in others. It seems just a more sophisticated way of dumbing down.

Another quite extraordinary attempt to devalue academic excellence was Ruth Kelly's ordinance that GSCE results in single practical subjects should each count as equal to four in traditional subjects.

The first specialist schools, the technological city academies, mostly had better examination results than the comprehensives, because they were selective and given more freedom from LEA interference. Blair was reported as not altogether happy with them but his reason was not educational. He was merely disappointed that the business sector had not produced as much funding as he had hoped.

Another obstacle was created by denying a second choice of school to parents who opted for grammar schools, so that if borderline children were rejected, they would be shunted into the worst local comprehensive. This deterred some parents from applying, which could be interpreted as a falling demand for grammar education. It was an especially nasty device because the 11+ exam marks were already known by the application date and could have been given to parents to inform their choice, but instead they were held back and later, to avoid this criticism, the application date was made unnecessarily earlier.

The Grammar Schools Association has launched a campaign for more of this kind of school—a better provision of choice than Gillian Shephard's plan for bursting the seams of present schools only. It would also benefit those who still narrowly miss acceptance, as they would be at the stimulating top of smaller comprehensives.

In 2005, the Labour government used the concept of choice to mask a blatant piece of social engineering. It claimed choice would be widened if schools had to accept pupils in bands across the ability range—allegedly fairer than letting middle-class children dominate good local schools. Less able ones would be bussed in. Parents protested that the less able (often the less disciplined) would undermine the high quality of local education and create levelling down. Nothing was said about the reciprocal bussing to poor areas of the children displaced from the good schools by those brought in, but that would also mean dumbing down. So, too, would the fact that journey fatigue might leave less energy for learning. Faith schools with their high placement in the league tables have been similarly threatened, and how long would it be before grammar schools also had to accept ability banding? As the government could not oust them by external edict, it might well seek to create their decay from within.

Another failed promise of comprehensives is the assertion that bigger schools would permit an expansion of subjects. In the event soft options such as sociology have driven out the more rigorous ones. Mathematics teaching is at a parlous low ebb; mathematicians are like gold dust in the state system. A shortage of science teachers has ousted the more demanding subjects, physics, chemistry and biology, in favour of a softer General Science course for GCSE, and as this cannot adequately prepare for A-Level courses, these too are shrinking. Latin has been so shrivelled away that one examining board has excised it from its curriculum. The former more numerous grammar schools kept these disciplines healthily alive. But to retain or reinstate them would frustrate the clandestine aim of dumbing down, and so they are sacrificed.

Nor has there been the greater social cohesion expected from educating all pupils together, without streaming by ability. Quick ones were held back and became bored; slow ones had their shortcomings spotlighted and felt humiliated. Some of the latter tried to restore the balance by substituting power for competence and bullying became rampant (See Chapter 18). School selection and streamed classes actually did prevent the invidious contrasts that the all-in-together policy was supposed to do.

The Independent Schools

Labour seems to abhor independence as unpalatable in two ways: freedom not to respond to government directives and retention of traditional methods that create high standards and enviable positions in the league tables. The independents put many state schools to shame and remain a warning against the dumbing down process.

The power motive for gaining control over them was carefully hidden. Instead socialist eglitarianism was invoked to imply that they allowed the rich to purchase an advantage denied to the poor and should be barred from doing so. If not all could have a good education, then none should — levelling down with a vengeance.

It is not only the rich who send their children to independent schools. Many less affluent parents make big sacrifices to do so. They spend their money on education rather than lush living, such as keeping up with the Joneses by constantly redecorating and re-furnishing their homes, eating out at ever more expensive venues, drinking and gambling, taking increasingly exotic holidays and frequenting health spas instead of eating and exercising sensibly. Those choices are rarely criticized. Only the choice of better education is considered reprehensible.

Unfairness is also blamed on the independents' smaller classes. We know these do not guarantee excellence but the idea excuses Labour for not raising standards and arouses socialist envy among teachers. They would be less envious if they had to work the longer hours of independent school staff, especially in boarding schools. And class size differentials are often more than offset by state school provision of teachers' aides.

Labour expressed an intention of cancelling independent schools' charity status and tax their profits but such "profits" as there are go into reserves for specific projects or contingencies. More successful was the raising of state-school salaries, forcing the independents to raise theirs to compete for staff. Another ploy offered benefits for co-operating with local schools, e.g. sharing playing fields. This has gone sour as the independents incurred costs without the supposed reciprocal benefits. Back to the destructive fray, however, is a Charities Bill proposing the cancellation of the independents' charity status unless they can prove they sufficiently benefit the community beyond their own pupils. This surely means to pile on external expenditure, necessitating a large fee increase and fewer parents able to pay it. Failing this outgoing they would doubtless be financially penalized by the loss of VAT exemption.

No opportunity is lost to label independent schools as unfair but actually the unfairness is on the other side. Ofsted charged one independent nearly £5000 for inspecting it because "independents do not contribute to teacher training and inspection". This is a twisted argument. State schools do not contribute either. The funding comes from the taxpayer and independent pupils' parents average more tax than state pupils'. They contribute fully to the state system and take nothing out; in fact they subsidize it. Would the vast aggregate subsidy contributed to the community through these taxes save the independents' charity status or would it be discounted?

Labour, seeking power rather than excellence, would not admit that the true need was more independent schools. Many parents yearn for the independents' higher standards but cannot afford their higher fees. The good news is a trickle of small new private schools with annual fees of £3000–£3500 — little more than one-third of the present non-boarder average. In 2004 the New Model School opened the first of a planned national network. The bad news is that Labour had wind of the trend and seemed to want to stamp it out. It said that any further new schools must be accredited. Would accreditation depend on Progressivist methods, submission to inspectors and a crippling fee?

There is no need for such interference. Independent schools have automatic safeguards. Fee-paying parents can remove their children if they are not being well taught, forfeiting only that term's fee. That is true choice and vastly better than being locked in to an unsatisfactory state school for years on end. In fact, there is a good case for making all schools independent and giving all parents educational vouchers which they could use as whole or part fees for any school that would accept their children. This would remove interference right across the board.

In 2005 Blair announced an apparent *volte face*, namely that state schools could become independent and decide their own character — a complete opposite to the compulsory ability banding proposed not long before. As independent schools are respected for their high standards, the theme of "independence for all" could bestow an enormous benefit. However, Blair's vision of "independence" was unlike ours. Far from removing interference, he would increase it. He advocated parental choice in the sense of empowering parents, and others, to decide curriculum changes and other aspects of running the schools. The staff could have constantly shifting ground beneath their feet, and not the stability needed for excellence. It would be particularly destructive in bad schools where parents have physically attacked teachers. We believe parents should be free to change from one school to another but not to change the nature of the same school. Good schools need inspired heads with power to manage freely. This destructive aspect escaped notice as legislation went through Parliament, when attention focused on rebel Labour MPs' insistence that independence should not mean freedom to select pupils and that LEAs should still enforce ability banding.

The government alleges that British education still outshines that of other countries, but it lags way behind non-Progressivist ones. A single example will be cited. One family moved to France and although school-ing in French was a challenge, they at least expected their daughter to excel in English. But she was bottom of the class. Her English lessons in this country had not taught her enough about her mother tongue to bring her up to the standard of the schoolmates for whom it was a foreign language.

Independent schools know that grade inflation at A-Level has made sixth-form syllabuses too mushy for good education and they are increas-ingly abandoning the British exam in favour of the stable standards of the International Baccalaureate.

The Universities

Grade inflation gave the impression of a steady advance in A-Level achievement, which was used by government to ordain an increase in uni-versity admissions. The present aim is for 50% of each year group to be accepted but even the current figure of 42% has proved far too many for true university standards. Despite the introduction of elementary reme-dial classes, tens of thousands of students have dropped out each year because they could not cope, before even reaching the final examination. The 2005 estimate was 71,000 drop-outs — an arrant financial waste. Nev-ertheless, there is talk of raising the undergraduate proportion of each age group to 70%.

Bludgeoning universities to accept under-qualified entrants not only created drop-outs. It also lowered standards. One of John Major's new-at-a-stroke universities reduced its pass mark to a ludicrous 17% — strong evidence of the adage that "more means worse". The aim of dumbing down is affecting even the academic elite.

It was decreed that universities must take more state-school applicants. Some of these do get better degrees than some independent-school appli-cants with the same A-Level grades, since the latter are fully educated while state education has left the former with untapped potential that blossoms in university conditions. But that is not true of all. Moreover, to reach the state/independent proportions now demanded by government, many state-school products with lower grades must be preferred to inde-pendent-school products with higher ones, and they may not all have uni-versity potential. Hundreds of thousands have already demonstrated that they do not.

Universities are much exercised to identify those state pupils who could genuinely succeed, and meanwhile 48% of them report having to intro-duce remedial coaching. And of course, highly intelligent dyslexics may not even be considered at all if the tyranny of whole-word teaching has robbed them of the ability to read.

Some universities are rebelling against this straitjacket. They have Royal Charters and have come under the heel of government only because they have been nationalized by stealth through financial grants. Nineteen of them, the Russell Group, are trying to extricate themselves through independent funding. One aim is to attract overseas students who pay the full cost of their courses, but this does not help British students. Those with International Baccalaureate qualifications could also be favoured. There are still well over a hundred universities outside the Russell group to meet the government's dictates.

The Present Challenges

So what is the situation at the time of writing?

The training establishments remain almost wholly dedicated to Progressivism, still selecting Sharon Shrills as students and still indoctrinating them in ways that prevent their teaching children to read.

Teachers seem a long way from having their burden lightened by synthetic phonics. They are so heavily oppressed by bureaucracy and indiscipline that a recent enquiry showed nearly three-quarters of them are considering leaving the profession. So many have already left that Labour has launched its own version of teaching on the job, in order to get more rapid replacements, but without the safeguards introduced by the Conservatives. Instead of having the trainees learn wholly from immersion in excellent schools, it subjects them to a summer of preliminary indoctrination and attaches them to Progressivist schools that reinforce the dogmas. Training is very slow; one apprentice told Alice Coleman that even in his third term, he still taught only one lesson per day, and his next year is to be spent in the same school.

Possibly some better heads are being appointed by governors' selection committees, especially as they are advised by consultancies such as the Association of School and College Leaders. There is no guarantee that they understand the risks explained in this book, although the consultants have a constant inflow of up-to-date information and may see the importance of ensuring that new heads will introduce synthetic phonics to put a stop to illiteracy at all stages in school life.

Inspectors, with a few notable exceptions, seem worse than ever, doling out high praise for social engineering aspects and showing little concern about appalling academic standards. The same is true of the grade inflating examiners.

LEA bureaucracies are still largely oriented in favour of Progressivism, while the present counterproductive role of central government has been outlined above.

There are rays of hope in the publishing world as more phonics schemes are appearing. Chris Jolly has been an energetic hero in marketing Sue Lloyd's teaching material. Newspapers are much more open in mentioning phonics teaching in a respectful spirit and even the BBC has taken a step in the right direction. Despite the unpromising title of its *Words and Pictures Plus*, it does in fact trace out letters with a "magic pen" and introduces a little slow blending. It needs to build further on this small foundation.

The campaigning organisations, CRE, RRF and QES, are vigorously active and making an increasing mark, boosted by the Clackmannan research findings, but there is still a long way to go and a wilful backlash to beat.

Methodology, testing, discipline and cost still present many problems, which will be discussed in the next four chapters. Then in Part IV, we shall outline simple and practical ways of redeeming the various difficulties that beset education.

Chapter 16

Progress Towards Phonics

How far has sabotage of the reform drive suppressed the resurrection of phonics? This question will be answered mainly through comments on new reading schemes. The word "phonics" has made a sufficient impact to attract mention and it is encouraging that even the schemes emerging from Progressivist stables have given something of a nod in its direction. The word is no longer totally taboo, although it is often only an adornment of schemes still firmly rooted in look-say. But there are also a number of genuine phonics schemes, which do not merely recapture upwave efficiency but advance beyond it with refinements that bring unprecedented ease and speed to the learning task.

Start to Read

This is a new departure in the *Mr. Men* series, now written and illustrated by Adam Hargreaves. It has 46 small storybooks, each with ten colourful pictures facing a text page. The tales are interesting and word repetition is skilfully handled to avoid being blatantly boring. The letters a and g are sensibly formed as children write them.

These little books have been welcomed for early learning but they exemplify the apprenticeship approach, restricted to the enjoyment of being read to. The words are bunched in whole sentences and short paragraphs, the letters are too small for beginners and their grey colour makes less impact than strong black. The words are completely ungraded and there is no guidance as to the learning process.

Start to Read's 2004 series has Betty Root as its educational consultant. It spaces out certain look-say words to show their shapes clearly, but that still does not create an efficient path to learning. The main innovation, following sight words, is separate letters — probably to meet the NLS requirement for children to know the alphabet There is a demand for sheer memorisation of 26 letter shapes, 26 letter names and 26 letter sounds. Progressivism claims relevance and meaning but how can children find these 78 bits of memory work relevant and meaningful when there is no blending into words? Such a long list carries a high risk of forgetting some of them before actual reading begins.

Start to Read is a very slow start and does not get beyond noting that certain letters begin certain words – a warning that many more books will be needed. The slow pace stems from time-wasting activities such as colouring pictures, circling them and drawing lines to connect them, which can all be done without noting the words they are supposed to be teaching. The illustrations detract attention from real reading and some children may outgrow the books' babyish style before acquiring any useful reading skill.

It might seem encouraging that such a stalwart Progressivist as Betty Root has also been tempted to write a little book for four-to-five-year-olds entitled *Phonics* but the title is misleading. The book begins with words not letters and has absolutely no grading from simple to more difficult ones. "Clean" and "dirty" appear only two pages after the contents list and the next page has "elephant", "guitar" and "ice cream". The book is a typical example of claims to be using phonics made by people who do not understand it.

Phonic Code Cracker

Phonic Code Cracker, costing £40, was produced in 1992 by Sylvia Russell of Jordanhill College in Glasgow. Scottish reading standards have declined less than English ones but this scheme is not the best phonics and has the following defects.

- It is a remedial scheme, for pupils aged seven or older. It accepts that backwardness can persist throughout school life and seems unaware that phonics taught to school starters can *prevent* illiteracy in the first place.
- It is very long-winded; 323 "levels" form 12 "books" in a ring-bound cover.
- Pupils must learn all 26 letters plus 76 "helper sounds", e.g. "ba" and "fe", before meeting words at the 43rd level. This seems boringly repetitive and meaningless, which the book admits, by warning of the difficulty in memorising so many letter shapes and – yes! – word shapes. Real phonics does not involve word shapes as it *codes* letters to build words, so the word "code" in the scheme's name is off-track.
- The slow learning speed is reinforced by repeated testing. Pupils must read each set of letters, helper sounds, syllables and words on three days running, before going on to the next set.
- Tests are timed. Pupils must gabble the sounds in a given number of seconds, and there are 1140 timings per pupil. But timing is misconceived. The need is to get it right and not be flustered by pressure to think faster. Speed for details and slow overall learning is the wrong

way round. Pupils need time to get details right and an efficient set of tasks that speeds the total learning period.

- Pictures are another time-wasting ploy. Pictures of objects starting with each letter sound are to be cut out of something else and pasted into the scheme's spaces, while some exercises require drawing. But pictures and drawing activate the right brain hemisphere and distract attention from the reading process that needs the left brain.

- *Code Cracker* demands much teaching time but teachers are not expected to use it. It is for parents, which ignores the fact that many non-readers are dyslexic children with illiterate dyslexic parents unable to rise to this challenge.

- Sounds are translated into letters, which is phonemic awareness, known to be less effective than starting with letters and then noting their sounds. Guessing at initial, medial or final sounds, as here, merely delays the stage at which children are actually reading words and not just playing about with them.

- *Code Cracker* neglects to impart the *joy of reading,* which comes from immersion in interesting stories. There are no stories here. Even at Level 265, the exercise is still reading a list of nonsense syllables.

Onset and Rime

Onset and Rime is an analytic method first studied by Lynette Bradley and Peter Bryant of Oxford University and promoted by Usha Goswami in *The Journal of Experimental Child Psychology*. It breaks words down into their beginning and end sounds, as being the easiest to hear. An example is "st-op", where "st" is the onset and "op" the rime. Middle sounds can be added in. It does not distinguish between single letters, digraphs and tri-graphs; they are all sounds to learn separately and there are 1493 of them. This is far more complex for children to learn than synthetic phonics, with only 26 basic symbols to learn and to blend logically.

Phono-Graphix

Phono-Graphix (1977) is an American method devised by C. and G. McGuiness, who considered it foolproof. Katy Dias and Lynne Juniper, reporting in *Support for Learning* in 2002, described how Bristol LEA used it for a scientific comparison. Three groups of children were taught by differ-ent methods for seven months. The first group of 17 used *Phono-Graphix,* 14 used a mixture of *Phono-Graphix and Onset and Rime,* and 34 used the *National Literacy Strategy.* All the participants were of similar ability and all were close to 5 years and 3 months old at the start. Table 16.1 shows the scores for the following four aspects, tested at the end of the experimental period.

- Blending series of sounds enunciated at one-second interval
- Segmenting words into separate sounds

- Reading nonsense words
- Coding knowledge, i.e. saying letters pointed out.

Table 16.1: Comparison of Three Reading Approaches
(Results converted to percentages to aid comparison)

Method	Phono-Graphix Only	Phono-Graphix + Onset and Rime	NLS
Blending	69	36	27
Segmenting	85	44	35
Nonsense words	50	14	11
Code knowledge	49	36	36

The *Phono-Graphix-only* method clearly produced better scores than the other two. Its percentages were dragged down when it was used as a mixed method with *Onset and Rime* and there were even lower results for the NLS, which is a mixed method in itself. The table appears to support our own observation that mixed methods muddle the child. The right method needs to be unitary and not contaminated with something different.

Dias and Juniper were encouraged by *Phono-Graphix* but also cautious. The small numbers tested and the narrow range of abilities did not ensure that it would suit all children. It was also disconcerting that it produced only half marks for two of the test items. *Phono-Graphix is* far from being foolproof and appears to have three defects.

Firstly, it is phonemic, beginning with sounds and working from them to letters instead of vice versa. It claims this goes from the known to the unknown, an adage that is not always justified. Children talk before they read, so it is plausibly argued that they should study their known speech sounds before tackling unknown letter forms. But children think in words not sounds, so sounds are *not* known and have to be worked on. Reading needs both visual and auditory skills but approaching it from the auditory side does not seem to facilitate the visual side. The low figure of 49% for code knowledge is a clear danger signal. After seven months' teaching, the children could not name half the letters pointed out to them. Starting with sounds causes delay.

Sounds may not be adequately identified where there are regional accents or sloppy speech and they may also defeat hard of hearing pupils if they are not tied down to a visible letter. There may also be difficulties when children are expected to pick them out of whole words. By contrast, starting with letters enables each one to be isolated individually and presented in large display print so that it is unmistakable. The related sounds can then be made equally specific and hence more available for blending, with the result that an understanding of sounds emerges as a natural by-product.

A second defect is that *Phono-Graphix* is not as graded as it claims. Its Level 2 is more difficult than its Level 3. Certainly the latter has longer words, but their polysyllables obey the same simple rules as in Level 1 and allow early, confidence-inspiring mastery. *Phono-Graphix* urges the need for confidence but does not optimise it in practice, as Level 2 loads the learner with all the different and confusing ways of spelling the same sounds. True grading teaches each major way first so that learners can advance much further on a regular-spelling basis before meeting the alternatives where choices have to be made.

The third defect is actually paraded as a virtue: "no rules and no exceptions". This is back to look-say, requiring all words to be learned individually. Thus, teaching that long "a" can be spelt "ai", "ay" or "a-consonant-e", deprives children of the clear rule for using "ai" in mid-word and "ay" as a word final or before a suffix beginning with a vowel, e.g. "plain", "play", "playing". Such rules speed the acquisition of both reading and writing skills, especially when they are shown to recur with other sounds, e.g. "oi" and "oy" as in "toil" and "toy", or "ei" and "ey" as in "their" and "they". So while *Phono-Graphix* was a marked advance upon look-say and the National Literacy Strategy, it still fell short of what synthetic phonics can achieve.

THRASS

Though later than *Phono-Graphix*, this 1992 scheme is further from true phonics. *THRASS* stands for "The Handwriting, Reading and Spelling System" by Alan Davies and Denyse Ritchie. The 2002 edition had pretentious language and a hard-to-handle A3 format.

THRASS claimed to be synthetic phonics but if it was phonics at all, it was analytic, giving precedence to words over letters, which like phonemic awareness, was conclusively proved inferior by the Clackmannan Report. It seems that *THRASS* saw an advantage in appropriating the *term* "synthetic phonics" while remaining ignorant of its substance.

It ignorantly contrasted an alleged "old phonics" with its own, supposedly superior, "new phonics". It mistook old phonics as confined to one-sound-one-letter, while new phonics had digraphs, etc. This grandiose "invention" of what is actually a centuries-old system showed just how far the full scope of phonics was lost to the look-say generations.

The re-invention fell far short of true phonics. Because the 26 letters could not provide a one-to-one correspondence for all sounds, THRASS devised a new alphabet of 120 items, beginning "b", "bb", "c", "k", "ck", "ch", "q" . . ., but it still left gaps, e.g. soft "c" and "g" were represented only by "ce", "ge" and "dge", omitting "ci", "cy", "gi" and "gy". The authors insisted that "c" in "city" was *not* soft "c" but just a different way of sounding hard "c".

THRASS claimed to suit the whole age range from pre-school to university. It ignored young children's need for small digestible items and presented all 120 at once, on a chart. This would be overwhelming for infants. And is learning to read really a university pursuit?

The scheme also combined pictures and words in the same way as look-say. The pictures were essential for identifying the 120 alphabet items. "b" was represented by a picture of a bird with the keyword "bird" beneath. There was no insight into the confusion caused, especially to boys, by demanding the use of both sides of the brain at once.

The 120 keywords included nearly all our spelling complexities with no simplification for beginners. Learners were thrown in at the deep end, with no initial stage of being taught to swim. "From the outset, both lower-case and capital letters are always identified by name—as is expected of good readers and spellers, whether they are children or adults." This echoes the real-books concept of pretending to be readers in the hope that pretence would become reality. It is absolutely non-phonic to deny beginners the *sounds* of the letters.

The first of *THRASS's* ten stages located and named the 120 chart pictures—a right-brain activity delaying the left-brain activity of reading. Stage 2 located and named the standard alphabet's 52 lower case and capital letters plus 26 letter names, just another rote learning exercise. The two stages together made children learn 198 items without building up a single word. Stage 3 consisted of learning to write the 52 lower case and capital letters.

Stage 4 continued routine memory work: naming the 120 new alphabet items and locating them on the chart, while Stage 5 named and located the 120 keywords as sight-words. Even 30 sight-words in other schemes have proved enough to inculcate the harmful guessing habit that obstructs systematic phonics, so 120 must be even more destructive.

Stage 6, at last, related letters to sounds, making the learner locate the 120 items and classify them by their sounds, grouping the diverse spellings into 44 phonemes.

Eventually, at Stage 7, blending was introduced but only for the 120 irregularly spelt keywords, while Stage 8 demanded spelling them from memory. Stage 9 consisted of three tests and only at Stage 10 were there any additional words. These made up THRASS's final word bank to 500, which is very few—often exceeded in the vocabulary of a two-year-old.

THRASS's delays were quantified by its record sheets, which allocated ten weeks for each of the ten stages—two-and-a-half years in all, or nearer three with gaps for sports days, Christmas parties, etc. So after nearly three years the children have not mastered even the 850 words of Basic English, and are clearly well behind their chronological age.

Compare this with a four-year-old class taught for 32 weeks by Mona McNee, using her *Step by Step* scheme, with phonics instruction, exercises and games. Her successor did not advance them further in the scheme during the remaining two months, although an assistant kept them in touch with what they had already learned. When the headmaster tested them in late June, no child had an RQ of less than 100 and their average reading age was ten months ahead of their average chronological age. THRASS does not begin to measure up to that in nearly three years.

A major reason is that THRASS omits the helpful rules of logic and pattern in reading and spelling. It merely advises children to make new words like some of the old, not enabling them to work out which alternative should be copied in any given case. Its whole background explanation shows that it cannot be a recipe for success, but neither is it cheap. Its core cost is £310 plus other specified but unpriced items. Each child needs £8. 40p worth of equipment, which is £252 for a class of 30, and at least part would have to be tripled for the three years of the scheme. There is also £123 charged for each set of reading books and CDs.

These false stabs at phonics use pretentious language, probably to conceal their inadequacies, even from their authors. The true phonics schemes are a refreshing contrast, expressed with lucid directness and explicit instructions on how to achieve success. Eight of them will now be discussed: *First Aid in Reading, Writing and Spelling, Sound Discovery, Sound Foundations, Read Write, Toe by Toe, Butterfly, Jolly Phonics and Step by Step.*

First Aid in Reading, Writing and Spelling

Theodore MacDonald is to be congratulated on his brave attempt revive phonics in 1984 — the dark days before the 1988 Education Act made mention of it respectable again. His book begins with clear and helpful advice to parents teaching their children to read and this is followed by 21 chapters explaining the whole system, right up to the rudiments of grammar. There are then 208 instructional exercises including 45 passages for reading.

This scheme is workable. The instructions are precise and easily understood, and it is stressed that the order of the exercises must be adhered to strictly. Given the recommended daily lesson, the average child should become a fluent reader in six or seven months — a vast improvement on the years demanded by non-phonics programmes.

However, the scheme lacks certain refinements that have been worked out for later neo-phonics systems. In particular, the child has to learn 174 two letter blends such as "bl", before progressing to the first whole word.

These blends are essential knowledge, but it speeds the learning process if they are taught in the context of actual short words.

Sound Discovery

This 2001 manual by educational psychologist, Marlynne Grant, is phonics-based and successfully teaches children to read. It begins logically with short vowels and regular consonants, which are blended into words of up to five, or even six, letters, e.g. "crisp" and "sprint". The letters are synthesised into words and then the words analysed back into their letters as spelling exercises. Analysis is considered useful for spelling but to be efficient it must come *after* synthesis, as here. When introduced first it retards mastery of reading.

There is then a shift to phonemic awareness, not always teaching the commonest spellings first. Most long vowels are formed by adding "magic e", e.g. "pal – pale", "met – mete", "slim – slime", "rod – rode" and "cub – cube", which creates thousands of words and is the same for all five vowels. However, Ms Grant advocates that words such as "late" should merely be acknowledged as existing but "parked" for attention later. Long "a" is taught using the digraphs "ai" and "ay", which occur less frequently. For long "o", she introduces "oa", "ow" and "ost" (as in "post") and includes the magic "e" without parking it. This phonemic-awareness use of different spellings for the same sounds can be confusing at this early stage.

In 2003 *Sound Discovery* was tested as a remedial exercise for 17 backward primary-school children aged 4–11. They were tutored in small groups of similar attainment instead of with others of the same age, and assessed by means of several tests.

The Salford Sentence Reading Test gave no reading age for six and a seventh had slipped back a little but the other ten had gained an admirable average of 13 months during the ten weeks of the experiment. Only two reading ages had risen to match chronological ages, but the test gave great hope if the method were continued for longer.

Young's Parallel Spelling Test obtained scores for 16 of the children, showing an average gain of nearly six months during the ten weeks.

Level 7 of the Basic Literacy Assessment Test required decoding of five-letter words with the consonant-vowel pattern, CCVCC. Four were already at this level before the research began and four more reached 100% through the tutoring, while the remaining nine had lower scores up to 80%. Two further levels of the Basic Literacy Assessment Test showed that several children were already up to the 100% standard initially. All the rest except one made gains in reading sight vocabulary and spelling high-frequency words.

The scheme has merits but as we shall show, others have more.

Sound Foundations

In 1990 Tom Burkard saw how Mona McNee taught his struggling son to read and after some years as a teacher himself, he and his wife Hilary decided to publicize phonics' virtues more widely. They founded The Promethean Trust as a registered charity to tutor children handicapped by the inefficient teaching of the look-say approach and they currently have about 50 on their books. Some parents pay the modest fees but if they cannot afford even that, they are funded by the Thomas Anguish Trust. Wider interest is gradually being aroused and free phonics seminars are offered. In 2005, Tom Burkard's pamphlet, *After the Literacy Hour*, was published by the Centre for Policy Studies in its "*Pointmaker*" series.

In 2002 the Trust produced its three-volume *Sound Foundations* for £54. It was at pains not to crib Mona McNee's *Step by Step* but lost something in the process. It is very useful for individual remedial work, as it gives look-say victims the confidence of being able to decode a reading vocabulary of some 5,500 words. "They love it!" say the authors.

Sound Foundations stops word-guessing by using a "cursor card" to uncover one letter or digraph at a time, in the left-to-right direction. This simple device prevents reversion to seeking whole-word shapes and guides sequential blending to build up each word.

There are question pages with six or eight sentences to be read aloud for meaning. Each sentence uses spellings already learnt and has its last word missing. Below there are three words, only one of which makes sense, and the child has to draw a ring round the right one. This is helpful but does not afford practice in writing to match progress in reading. It would be better to have them write the correct word in the space at the end of the sentence.

Sound Foundations advocates timing children's answers and if they do not respond within three seconds, telling them the word. This is to forestall guessing, but strugglers have been confused by poor teaching, and need time to work things out at their own pace. Being cut off without enough time to think may seem like yet more failure.

There are also timed tests, which break the rule that it is better to be right though slow than rapid but wrong. And frequent pauses for time recording may delay progress even with a single pupil.

Tom Burkard is aware that long concentration on single words and short questions can delay reading for pleasure and the Promethean Trust has been developing storybooks graded to use the same rules learnt at each successive stage. This grading is a vital requirement, neglected during the period of Progressivist tyranny.

Read Write

Ruth Miskin is known as a superb teacher and her synthetic phonics scheme, *Read Write,* incorporates all the basic criteria of relating letters to sounds, blending them and progressing through words of graded difficulty. It also covers writing and talking. The system has its own trainers experienced in teaching it, and when a new school embarks upon it, its teachers and classroom assistants are trained in how to use it. Each day, two 20-minute periods are devoted to literacy development in the reception class and an hour in subsequent classes. The time is broken up by questions to be answered and activities.

The wasted "down-time" of group-working is reduced by pairing children who have reached the same stage and setting them to practise together, answering the questions and engaging in the activities. Those with learning difficulties are given individual attention every day from the start. This arrangement avoids overt comparison of quick and slow learners, which can give the latter a sense of failure, but it also retains the disadvantages of grouping — the need to repeat instructions for those who reach the same stage at different times and the necessity for extra paperwork in order to keep track of each child's progress.

In her submission to the House of Commons Committee on *Teaching Children to Read* (2005), Ruth Miskin cited favourable OFSTED reports from nine schools using the *Read Write* method and provided statistical tables quantifying the higher standards reached. The table for a one-year pilot study at Bow Boys' School in Tower Hamlets was most impressive. The Suffolk Reading Test showed an average gain of 22 months in reading age, almost twice the 12 months expected by natural maturation. One pupil actually advanced by nearly 3½ years, although three had a small relative slip back, gaining only 11 months.

This scheme could be improved further by teaching the spelling rules in a more integrated order. For example, children are helped when taught that "ai" and "oi" in mid-word are replaced by "ay" and "oy" at word ends but *Read Write* teaches "ay" and "oy" in Set 2, defers "oi" to Set 3 and does not list "ai" at all, unless in the final "red card" stage of irregular words. The "magic-e" rule is deferred until after an assortment of ten vowel digraphs used in far fewer words.

Read Write has different schemes for infant beginners and older strugglers. Both include a fair amount of equipment and their cost for classes is £465 and £682 respectively. There is a separate writing scheme (£55) and a comprehension programme (£490). In addition there are seven school packs of storybooks costing £1050 in colour and £560 in black and white. This system appears very successful but we criticise its emphasis on "speed cards". This runs counter to our belief that children should not be hustled while getting to grips with the art of reading and that speed should be allowed to develop naturally.

Toe by Toe

This remedial scheme is based on the teaching success of Keda Cowling, who worked in Bradford where English was often not the mother tongue. When she retired she produced a remedial system for those aged over seven and her son Harry managed its desk-top publishing side (1995). The scheme was entitled *Toe by Toe* because it was structured in the tiniest phonic steps, in an order carefully arranged to promote progress.

Toe by Toe is taught on a one-to-one tutor-to-pupil basis and the pupil's book is designed to record progress so minutely that learning can continue perfectly smoothly when the tutor changes, for example when parents take over during holidays. Each tutor can immediately see the exact point reached and each double page carries a "coach box" giving clear instructions on how to teach it.

The scheme is very businesslike. There are no games, lest they distract pupils from the aim of mastering print, so lessons last just 20 minutes per day. They embody the multi-sensory technique, "See it, say it, write it", to build up blends, syllables and words under the tutor's direction. Each item must be read correctly on three consecutive days before being ticked off as learned. The ticks are treated as commendations for successful achievement to raise learners' self-esteem and help them to stop seeing themselves as stupid. Their reading and writing improve dramatically by up to one year of reading age during the first three months, and then even faster. The whole scheme takes five months on average, except with the very hard-of-hearing and poorly sighted, and at the end the pupils take great pride in being able to read words such as "philately".

Toe by Toe is seriously concerned to quell the guessing habit inculcated by the failed look-say methods that have necessitated its remedial programme. To achieve this, it uses nonsense syllables to stop the learner expecting a word and jumping to the wrong one. Nonsense syllables go on a long way through the 287–page book.

The scheme is effective for all children with learning difficulties, especially dyslexics, and can be used by statemented children's support assistants. Its prospectus notes its adoption by 300 schools and 70 language support schemes, as well as being taken into many individual homes by parents and tutors. It is also suitable for adults with weak reading skills and enables parents failed by the education system to learn alongside their children. It has proved successful in prisons, which is of vital national importance in view of the fact that so many offenders seem to have been drawn into crime because their lack of literacy has denied them the opportunity to earn an honest living.

The course-book costs £25 plus p & p, which is less than the fees for two private lessons. Greater expense is incurred by the need for five months of one-to-one tuition, though one tutor can give 20 minutes to quite a few students in a day.

The Butterfly Project

Irina Tyk is headmistress of the primary Holland House School, which, like other independent schools, cannot afford to lose custom by producing that Progressivist hallmark, a high illiteracy rate. For a few years from 1991, she offered a summer school, *The Butterfly Project*, for less fortunate pupils from elsewhere, in three classes of 20: total non-readers, unacceptably backward strugglers, and fair readers needing help with comprehension. They attended for three hours each school-day morning for three weeks, receiving a total of 45 hours teaching. Before and after testing revealed an average gain in a whole year's reading age, which is equivalent to a week's progress for each hour.

Butterfly rejects pictures entirely, stressing that it is *letters* that enable children to read — not external cues of any other sort. The focus is entirely on learning letters and blending them to represent 44 English sounds. To expedite progress, blending was introduced right at the start. Lesson 1 presented short "a" plus five consonants, showing how eight three-letter words could be assembled. There was no question of sight words; the eight were genuinely read by building up their sequences of letters and their sounds.

The speed at which the children reached meaningful whole words gave them confidence but care was taken that this acquisition should not be superficial and forgettable. *Butterfly* impressed memory through a multi-sensory approach. The children saw the symbols, said them aloud, learned to write them, listened to words dictated for them to write and undertook a number of systematic exercises involving word completion, where one letter was omitted for the child to supply. There was no consumption of printed books by using them as worksheets. Each whole word was written out in a lined exercise book, which enhanced learning much more than simply inserting a single letter into a gap.

Lessons 2 and 3 added twelve more consonants, creating a total of 44 three-letter words with short "a". Short "e" was covered more quickly, as 17 consonants were already known, and "a" was kept under revision, including a neat exercise to change just the vowel in ten words, e.g. "bat/bet" and "tan/ten". The other short vowels followed and also the capitals for proper nouns and the pronoun "I". The long vowels were dealt with first by their main spelling, using magic "e" after an end consonant, before introducing digraphs such as "ai", "ay" and "ey". The trickiest consonants, "c", "k", "q" and "x" came separately.

The *Butterfly* programme continued logically and showed pupils the spelling regularities that gave them true mastery and ability to tackle unknown words. It had no truck with guessing or telling them words they were stuck on, but made the instructions so simple and straightforward that there was little occasion to be stuck or tempted to guess. These essentials also underpin other phonic systems, such as Spalding's *The Writing Road to Reading* and Rudolf Flesch's *Why Johnny Can't Read,* both in USA.

The summer schools were discontinued but the method remained in use in Holland House School where yearly records show remarkable results. The official average score of 100 is routinely exceeded by a very large margin, even up to 139. The children's reading ages are all well above their chronological ages and illiteracy is entirely prevented.

In 2004 *Butterfly* was selected for use by the New Model School, a charity aiming to serve families dissatisfied with state education but unable to afford normal independent school fees. It provides much cheaper private education by cutting overheads. Its first school, Maple Walk, rented a church hall and used an adjoining green as a playground, which enabled it to keep its charge down to £2,700 per year for mornings only and £3,300 for whole-day tuition. There are many state schools absorbing a far bigger per capita sum, even without counting their share of LEA administration costs and if vouchers were issued to allow a genuinely free choice, there could be a growing national network of independent schools providing an excellent education based on synthetic phonics and 100% literacy.

Jolly Phonics

As an infant-school teacher, Sue Lloyd wanted to *prevent* illiteracy and not just rescue strugglers let down by the system. She benefited from i.t.a. but at first combined it with look-say, which always left a sizeable group of children finding it hard to remember words. Then she introduced a little phonics and as it brought improvement, gradually added more, with remarkable success. Average scores of 102 on Young's reading test rose steadily, stabilizing at 110-116, depending on the children's ability. Because phonics enabled them to blend letters and work out words for themselves, they learned to read much more quickly.

When i.t.a. was strangled by Progressivism, Sue Lloyd retained its benefits by converting its symbols to standard digraphs, e.g. "ch" and "ng". She kept "y" as a consonant, used "oo" for both its short and long sounds, and did not distinguish "au" from "or". For long vowels she used "ai", "ee", "ie", "oa" and "ue", which are more complex than the magic "e" for all five and may make her method rather slower than *Butterfly*.

Sue Lloyd found a publisher in Chris Jolly, who has been most enterprising in promoting her manual, *The Phonics Handbook,* as far afield as Lebanon, Nigeria and Australia. He has contributed towards defeating illiteracy, with a sale of over 100,000 copies, plus supporting materials. The whole system is known as *Jolly Phonics.*

Jolly Phonics gives great attention to perceiving sounds but not in the counter-productive phonemic way. Each sound follows its visual letter or digraph right from the outset. Five letters are taught each week in an order that separates those that might be confused with each other and multi-sensory reinforcement is interestingly applied.

Each letter and digraph has a handbook page to be photocopied for each child. It shows capital and lower case forms, with several words containing the letters, and an excellent arrangement for developing writing skill. Within double guidelines there is first a bold letter annotated with arrows showing how to write it, followed by five repeats in faint broken lines for the children to trace over and get the feel of how they are written. The rest of the double line is a space for writing the letter a few more times without guidelines to trace.

There is a large picture to colour and a small one showing an action devised to impress each sound on the memory. This reveals the author's splendid insight into children's minds. For example, short "a" has a picture of two angry ants and the activity is to think of them crawling up one's forearm, scratching at them and uttering a horrified "a — a - a!" Some pictures do not represent anything beginning with the letter concerned but elicit the sound in a different way. For example, "m" is illustrated by an empty plate with a knife and fork at the ready. The children draw their favourite food on the plate and the class activity is to rub their tummies and say an appreciative "mm", "mm!" All great fun.

Photocopiable flash cards show letters, *not* words. The latter are provided in sets of ten on 48 strips of increasing difficulty, to be read to parents, giving vital blending practice. There are also ingenious exercises and games, such as dice games to give progress along a track, with words to be read out when a counter lands on them.

The text is excellent. Lucid language reflects Sue Lloyd's clear insight into infant learning and her ability to cater for those with poor memories. A Devonshire teacher reported, "I have been using the scheme for six weeks and I'm really surprised with the results. The children are so enthusiastic and so are the parents. I feel very positive."

Chris Jolly, unlike other publishers, did not fear testing but actively sought willing research experts. One, Professor Dale Willows of the Ontario Institute for Studies in Education, wanted to package a reading and writing programme that would stimulate both teachers and children. She arranged a trial in poorly performing schools with children handicapped by family poverty, unemployment, single parenthood, homes without books and a foreign-language mother tongue. Eighteen classes of five- and six-year-olds using *Jolly Phonics* were matched with another 18 using the accustomed teaching strategies.

In a standard test, barely 20% of the control group recognised the first four words while 60% of the phonics group did and also made a reasonable attempt at the next five. Dale Willows concluded that the plausible excuses so often claimed as responsible for learning difficulties are not valid and that the true cause is the wrong teaching method. After her findings, three large education authority areas in the Toronto region endorsed *Jolly Phonics*. Unfortunately, Canadian contacts report, the area was so steeped in look-say that they would have needed more training to use the scheme to best advantage.

Proof of phonics' superiority needed to be followed up by research into the relative merits of the three supposed phonics alternatives: phonemic awareness, analytic phonics and synthetic phonics. This was the objective of the Clackmannan research described in Chapter 15, where *Jolly Phonics* was the synthetic element and eminently proved its worth.

Jolly Phonics is clearly an excellent form of synthetic phonics and has made a commendable contribution. It is believed that *The Phonics Handbook* is in some 12,000 British schools. It now needs equally scientific research to compare it with other synthetic methods, notably *Butterfly* and *Step by Step,* and not just with the proven inferiority of the analytic and phonemic awareness approaches.

Step by Step

Mona Mcnee's *Step by Step* serves both strugglers and beginners of any age, either for private tuition or class teaching. Its focus upon just *what* to learn is simple enough for pre-schoolers without being too babyish for adults. It immediately filled a new niche as a parents' manual for "school-proofing" children by making them readers before the schools' illiteracy-inducing methods had a chance to bite. Its lucidity enables untrained users to produce rapid results and it also teaches writing. It creates self-confidence by presenting the commonest spellings first, to bring thousands of regularly spelt words within the child's orbit before meeting rarer alternatives.

Step by Step was long rejected by downwave publishers. When, at last, one issued it as "*c – a – t = cat*", only 2000 copies were printed and after no serious publicizing, it was pronounced dead from lack of demand. There immediately followed a rush of 700 orders for the privately published version when John Clare, Education Editor of the *Daily Telegraph* commended it as "excellent" and "the best". Its sale of 21,000 copies, partly through word-of-mouth recommendations from satisfied users, and partly because some of them wrote to the press, is a remarkable testimony to its quality. It is also the least expensive scheme.

Alice Coleman is deeply impressed by the wealth of detailed thought that went into it, beginning with a simple but effective test of whether a child is reading-ready. Whereas Progressivist teachers label pupils as unready when look-say fails them, *Step by Step* uses a simple test. A child is given a succession of 12 letters on small cards to see if (s)he can recognize the same letters on a panel. Ability to recognise them all identifies reading readiness and in at least two cases it has been clearly evident in children as young as two years and nine months.

Step by Step does not rush or hassle learners but it has an organized structure that permits rapid progress. This means that children are able to read *before* they reach the stage of needing to use unknown words for compositions, with all the risk of spelling errors. By the time it comes to creative writing, the child already has a basic accuracy, so errors are fewer and do not overwhelm but act as stepping stones to further achievement. Learners quickly reach the level of fluency at which they independently read for pleasure and are guaranteed not to relapse, as is so often the sad case with look-say.

At this point in Alice Coleman's assessment, Mona McNee commented that Progressivists would accuse us of self-justification, without independent back-up. This is an example of their propensity for "projection", a mechanism that denies one's own defects but projects them on to others with fierce criticism. Progressivists are arch-self-justifiers and reject anything that might prove their claims invalid. But when they consider others' achievements, self-justification becomes a crime. So we need to show that *Step by Step* is based on solid experience and not just plucked out of the air as Progressivism was.

Mona McNee's patient investigation of dyslexia has been explained earlier as one of the foundations of her system, and also one of the reasons for its success. We now add evidence of that success, both from her own teaching records and also from the testimony of other people who have used her method.

She has taught some 360 dyslexic strugglers to read, keeping meticulous lesson records of their progress. These show that the average improvement ratio (IR) has been 3.7, i.e. well over three-and-a-half months advancement in reading age (RA) for each month of instruction. The magnitude of IR 3.7 can be better appreciated by comparing it with the IR of 2.1 achieved for synthetic phonics in the Clackmannan project.

The figure of IR 3.7 might be an overestimate, as the Clackmannan children were learning from scratch while the *Step by Step* strugglers may have retrospectively benefited from their earlier exposure to print, once *Step by Step* helped its mysteries to fall into place. Conversely, however, it may be an underestimate, as Mona McNee saw most pupils only once a week instead of daily, as in primary school. Whatever the finer points, her IR has been a substantial improvement for pupils whom others had failed and it is four-and-a-half times as rapid as the NLS method used in the Clackmannan research.

She took a 6.9-year-old non-reader as a boarder for a week's intensive teaching, with several daily lessons plus activities such as catching a ball to help counter dyslexic problems with direction. After one day she took the child for an independent reading test, which showed her reading age had risen from the notional non-reader value of 5.0 to 5.9. Four days later a second test yielded an reading age of 6.3 — a remarkable IR of 47 between the two tests.

Progressivists dislike IRs that exceed their own values of 1.0 or less and attribute them to oppressive "hot-housing". But Mona McNee's hot-housed pupil did not feel oppressed. On the contrary, she was delighted that the teaching was *freeing* her from the stress of illiteracy and said she wished she could stay for another week. This makes it clear why hot-housing in the United States completes the task of teaching to read within three months, after which the young readers benefit much more from *all* their schooling.

Mona McNee's own records were corroborated by endorsements from others. In her correspondence file, Alice Coleman found well over a hundred letters of heartfelt gratitude for the help afforded by *Step by Step*. Frequent eulogies such as "delighted", "excellent", "impressive", "miraculous" and "wonderful" were not mere effusions but backed up by objective accounts of the writers' experiences.

Particularly heart-warming were letters from the parents of pupils whose sustained whole-word failure had convinced them they were hopeless and robbed them of self-esteem. A private tutor commented on a boy who trembled as soon as a book was opened because he had so often been denounced as stupid. Switching strugglers over to *Step by Step* not only gave them the ability to read but also restored their emotional stability. Many were said to have become a different child, often within a very short time.

> . . . he neither understood nor enjoyed reading but after a few months with Step by Step he became a bookworm.

> . . . in three short weeks his ability has soared and with it his confidence.

> After one month the improvement in his reading, spelling and all-round confidence is impressive.

> School and remedial help both failed and he was struggling emotionally. But after learning from Step by Step he achieved full marks in a school spelling test and read himself to sleep with Brer Rabbit.

One child was completely given up by the school.

> Well, guess what? He loves working from your programme. Thank you for a wonderful tool.

One mother wrote that the claim "Teach Your Child to Read in 90 Days" seemed an unrealistic gimmick but her husband persuaded her to give it a try and she found that it was true. Of course, the actual time varies with individual children's ability, parental aptitude and the time devoted to teaching, but most families are amazed by its rapidity.

The scheme helps strugglers of any age. B. could hardly read a letter after his reception year but with a summer of *Step by Step* he could blend three-letter words. A seven-year-old

> just could not master reading in school but after 46 days with Step by Step he could read almost everything and called it "the magic book". At nearly eight, S. was terribly lost and frightened, with no confidence even to try and had developed the art of switching off when anyone tried to teach him. But with Step by Step he managed a breakthrough and learnt how to make a real effort.

A non-reader of nine was extremely embarrassed and described by his teacher as "totally submerged" in class. His parents then kept him home, where he made "fantastic progress with Step by Step. It opened up a whole new world for him." And an 11-year-old with an RA of only 7.6 picked up interest with Step by Step and read a bit each night, without any of the previous hassle.

Step by Step was used for backward 12–16 year-olds "who had wasted years of learning because they were given no knowledge of phonics". All made very good progress as well as feeling more secure when they had no pictures to guess from. They also appreciated not having to memorize words. One school-leaver still could not read or write properly but then found *Step by Step* very helpful. And a teacher of both child and adult dyslexics said that no struggler was too old to benefit from it.

From adults we turn back to the very young, and move from the need for rescue to the aim of prevention. Many correspondents told of their success in school-proofing their children and grandchildren and many wanted extra copies of *Step by Step* for relatives, friends and neighbours. It is easy to believe that this scheme has played a large part in the rise of literate school starters to 20% of the intake.

The creation of reception classes at age four seems to have pushed the age of pre-school reading instruction down to three, but there is still a harvest of success stories. One remarkable parent began teaching her little girl at the age of two years and nine months and completed the course in ten months, "much quicker than I would have believed possible." Another case concerned two adopted children with a history of abuse and neglect. The new parents were warned that one of them would tear any book up but with *Step by Step* he came to love them and was confidently working on blending letters to make words.

Comments on the scheme included those by John Clare, Education Editor of the Daily Telegraph. Although commending other phonics schemes, he reserved his highest praise for *Step by Step*, partly because of its success-ful use by parents and partly for its straighforwardness and speedy results. Others appreciated its clear explanations, practical common-sense guidelines, organized structure and graded steps, declaring it attractive to novice teachers and popular with children, both for its can-do ethos and "brilliant" games. Martin Turner, when the Dyslexia Institute's psycholo-gist, recommended it to parents as exceptionally user-friendly and to the point. A further advantage is having the full gamut of teaching to read within a single, low-cost book.

Progressivist methods have never won such fulsome praise from those at the receiving end. They have plenty of self-justification but few satisfied users. Mona McNee's correspondents were aghast when they discovered the "terrible "standards" of state schooling. One said of her daughter, "She has been given books with five-words phrases which she proudly reads with her eyes closed." Another was frustrated because "this simple, com-mon-sense way isn't being taught at school to give every child a chance."

How far did the success of *Step by Step* and other synthetic phonics schemes make inroads into the monolithic stranglehold of the watchdogs criticised in Part II? Mostly there was little or no effect within the state sys-tem but only a few encouraging nibbles round the edges. Teachers who had always retained their faith in phonics were delighted by the emer-gence of new phonics programmes and one wrote to Mona McNee, "Your scheme develops my own ideas, only better."

Remedial teachers are more receptive than class teachers; the latter cre-ate the problem while the former must try to solve it. Many welcome *Step by Step* as the best approach and regret that it had not been mentioned in courses on how to teach children with learning difficulties. One described it as "a breath of fresh air in a world in great need of it" and others, includ-ing private tutors, are trying to pass on its message as widely as possible.

One tutor, Evelyn Freeman, wrote of her many adult students who broke down in tears when explaining how they felt about their poor read-ing, writing and spelling, for which they blamed themselves. Such deep feelings seemed insurmountable but *Step by Step* helped them learn quickly and grow in confidence and self esteem. Once given a system that provided a strategy, they made steady progress. Ms. Freeman met it when her dyslexic son was rescued by her mother, so after taking up a college post to target poor basic skills, she introduced it to her colleagues. In gen-eral, however, colleges still turn a deaf ear to the case for synthetic pho-nics, as shown by their production of new pseudo-phonics schemes.

Many parents found teachers hostile to the idea of private tuition to res-cue the children that the school had left backward. They felt this was a reflection on their professionalism so although tutors are now engaged by one family in four, this is kept a big secret from the schools. One parent who contrived to introduce *Step by Step* by the "back door" was pleased to learn that the school was actually using it, but most teachers who give it a welcome are in independent schools. One, concerned with teaching English as a foreign language, extolled its structured approach as a great help.

If teachers could cast off their unjustified distrust of the phonic method they would find several great benefits for themselves. The first would be increased professional pride in making the whole class literate and improving test results.

The second would be a huge reduction in paper work. Used from the start, *Step by Step* enables all the children to advance through all its steps together. There are activities to deepen the understanding of fast learners while slower ones are becoming well grounded in the basics at the same stage. So instead of having to record immense detail for each child, it becomes sufficient just to note the step-number reached by the class as a whole.

Thirdly, teachers in poorer schools would be relieved of much of the burden of stress due to insubordination. There would no longer be humiliated illiterates seeking self-esteem through rampant bullying or brighter ones bored to distraction by the slow overall pace, so behavioural problems would be reduced to manageable proportions.

"A prophet is not without honour save in his own country", and *Step by Step* is beginning to make an impact overseas. A family in Washington D.C. reported that the difference in accent on the video did not detract from its effectiveness and a Californian was so impressed that he offered to sell it across the States on his website.

Because it has so much to offer, the actual content of *Step by Step* is reserved for explanation in Part IV, "the Way Ahead".

The campaign for universal literacy still has a long way to go but at government level it is encouraging that Ruth Kelly recommended phonics in all state schools. That does not mean that the campaign has been won. On the contrary, the most recent Department for Education and Skills statistics reveal that the figure for illiterate school leavers, i.e. those not reaching Level 2 literacy, is now 42% — worse than ever. More pressure is needed to secure adequate re-training. It would be easy to use the coming year's "Baker Day" in-service training to ensure that *all* teachers absorbed the synthetic phonics methodology, both to prevent future illiteracy and also to remedy it at any age before backward pupils leave school.

This cannot be done by the established "expert" subversives who have constantly sabotaged any such reform. They have repeatedly condemned phonics and there is no way that they can re-train themselves so fundamentally. Instead, care must be taken to appoint trainers who understand the full scope of the synthetic phonic method. To rescue adults it would be necessary to appoint genuine phonicists to teach evening classes that shrink the backlog instead of letting it increase as the BSA has done.

If this challenge were properly met, it would totally eliminate the worst scandal of our state schools.

Chapter 17

Testing:
A Pyrrhic Victory

The battle to establish testing was won but that did not end the war. One excellent effect was to make everyone conscious of the need to improve standards but the tests themselves, at every level, have been subverted, precluding a true picture of attainment and progress, and impeding real reform. Most attention has been focused upon GCSE and A-Level, which Labour massively expanded, with exams in all three of Years 12, 13 and 14. This required a huge marking workforce and immense co-ordination to achieve fair grades — an elusive goal.

Progressivism has such a spurious belief in equality that it assumed *any* extra hands with red-ink pens could do the work, but this is not so. Marking has been extensively botched and calls for checking have escalated. By 2003, no fewer than 18,000 examinees had to have their scripts remarked and in 2004 one head reported that 313 of her students had had their grades increased with others still to come. And serious re-marking delays have cost some sixth-formers their university places.

The test at age 14 fared even worse. In 2004 there were so many thousands of complaints of erratic marking of the English exam that the situation was considered a fiasco and no league table was published. To speed the issue of results, the two parts of the exam had been sent to different markers and the ensuing discrepancies for individual pupils were described as "haywire". The term "rogue markers" appeared in the press and the chief examiner resigned in despair.

Apart from unfair inconsistencies, there have been continuously rising marks, which the government claimed as proof of educational enhancement but which others criticised as unmerited grade inflation — higher marks stemming from softer marking and not from truly improved performance. By 2006, the percentage of passes at A-Level had been increasing for 24 years continuously and becoming more suspicious every year. Particularly suspect was the fact that the successive percentages plotted on a graph formed a fairly direct line rising toward a 100% pass rate within a very few years. Will no-one fail then, even with a blank script?

Like the passes, the higher rankings have also increased and so many now receive straight A marks that at least one university found it too difficult to select students from the solid mass of top-grade applicants and rejected A-Level marks in favour of college entrance exams. And some independent schools have decided to abandon A-Levels altogether and switch over to the more stable International Baccalaureate.

These problems are not irrelevant to our concern with primary school teaching, as it is the lack of literacy created there that is the main cause of the later troubles. Unfortunately, there has been less of a spotlight on tests for younger pupils and in 2004 the government chose to ease the marking burden by decreeing that formal testing at age 11 should cease, leaving it to their teachers to assess them. There is also talk of banning the seven-year-old test, and certainly much of its present form is unhelpful. Teachers are expected to record 117 kinds of information about each child, most of which have no educational significance but are part of the social engineering programme. They sterilize a great deal of teaching time and seem to do more harm than good.

But this should not be an excuse for throwing the baby out with the bathwater. A test of infant-school reading is vital for detecting backwardness, as the earlier it is identified, the sooner remediation can ease the child's anguish. Though this book aims to restore effective teaching at the outset and completely obviate the need for remediation, testing is still essential to ensure that this is achieved. And the results should be published, to inform parents when choosing the vital first school.

In this chapter we do not hesitate to comment on tests and examinations throughout the age range, to draw attention to the fact that the whole system needs a radical overhaul. In Part IV, we shall suggest a better form of test for infant reading and hope that it will also inspire simplification throughout education.

A prime testing criterion is fairness but the present system is unfair in many ways. For example, it was a facile solution to the examiner shortage to make teachers responsible for assessment, as it is impossible to ensure that they all mark to the same standard.

The extent to which marking can be a lottery was brought home to Alice Coleman at a prestigious overseas university. Students in the English department were distressed by what seemed wild variations in marks given by different tutors and concocted a communal essay to hand in to seven of them. Their fears were justified. The grades for this identical piece of work ranged from A- to D+. If this can happen within a single reputable department, how much more likely is it in all the diverse schools of a nation? Poor teachers may rate their top pupils as excellent even though their standard is what good teachers would consider mediocre. NFER, in conjunction with Brunel University found that science and mathematics teachers disagreed on how to measure their pupils' achievement and even on what constituted achievement. Yet these are the subjects in which it is easiest to be objective.

Apart from purely incompetent variations in standards, the test set-up is an open invitation to either conscious or unconscious dishonesty. Teachers marking their own classes are also providing assessments of themselves and their schools—a patent temptation to err on the side of generosity. Those who adhere to objective standards may find their schools slipping in the league tables below those with more liberal marking, which may lead parents to prefer the latter. Although a false guide to school quality, it can cause diminishing rolls and possibly school closure and is particularly serious in independent schools where healthy numbers are essential for financial viability. One governing board reacted to a small slippage in the league tables by sacking the head. Had he really worsened from one year to the next or was it a case of that year's children being a little less able than the previous year's?

Coursework is even harder to mark fairly and a Herculean task to monitor. Some National Curriculum options were originally based on 100% coursework, with grades awarded entirely on the teacher's say-so. The manifest disparities led to a coursework limit of 20% but that was still enough to affect the final grade.

One abuse has been described as "legal cheating". First drafts of essays, etc, are inspected by teachers, who explain how to improve them to get full marks. Learning to improve is educationally vital but its use in examination coursework makes it dishonest. Similarly, parental help is a constructive addition to schooling but becomes unfair when parents' education creates examination differentials. Calling it a "rich cheat's charter" is no solution. It would be better to keep the educational value of such help and strip out dishonesty by banning coursework from exams.

A worse trend is plagiarism, aided by demands for typed coursework. Candidates can download appropriate passages from the internet. Teachers cannot check everything and may detect the cheating only if two students in the same class have copied the same piece. Still less detectable are custom-written essays, for which there is a growing market. These can be submitted without even being read by the plagiarists. Qualifications can be awarded partly for "original" material that has not actually passed through the minds of those adjudged worthy and such cheating has even become a problem among Oxford undergraduates.

Despite public concern about coursework ethics, the government called for more—a 4000-word A-Level dissertation to identify the best among the undifferentiated A and A* mass. Yet such dissertations could attract the same "help" as existing coursework and impose an extra burden upon the examiners. Only unseen questions, as in traditional examinations, can separate out the real high-fliers.

Nor is the non-coursework element immune to cheating. Test papers are sent to schools in advance and may be opened to make enlarged photocopies for poorly-sighted pupils. Some have been opened by unscrupulous, or desperate, teachers to instruct their classes in the answers. One head found a teacher drilling her class in the words set for the spelling test. Another resigned after confessing she had altered test scripts to improve the marks and the school's standing. We have also heard of a teacher who dictated the test with the answers up on the board. With job prospects at stake, it is not surprising that a few exploit these loopholes but it is grossly unfair for the honest majority to have their classes outshone by those of less merit.

Exam papers have been stolen for sale to candidates. The Edexcel Examining Board reported that two mathematics questions were publicized on an internet revision website. This necessitated identifying those who performed much better than expected and establishing whether they had seen the purloined papers. An American study developed a method of identifying which teachers were cheating in the national SATS tests and found they were numerous. We should obviate the need for a similar exercise here by overhauling the whole present testing structure.

One attempt to minimize unfairness is the so-called *objective test*. Group reading tests, like the television show *Who Wants to be a Millionaire?* provide each question with several answers for the child to pick the right one. There are marks for correct answers but, unlike *Millionaire*, no penalties for wrong ones, so there is every incentive to guess. Those who can answer every question score 100% but for those who cannot, the score is in the lap of luck. Someone ignorant of just one answer may guess it right and receive an undeserved top score, while an equally knowledgeable child may guess it wrong and score less. Greater ignorance means more scope for guessing, so scores can differ widely for children who ought to be adjudged equal.

Those who know nothing ought to score zero but rarely do. They can work through the questions, underlining answers at random and get some right purely by chance. Statistical theory shows that with four alternative answers, examinees probably choose a correct one, on average, once in four, scoring 25%. With three alternatives, they probably get one in three right and score 33%. But many make either fewer or more correct guesses and win lower or higher marks accordingly.

So "objective" tests do not give equal marks for equal real attainment but award higher scores for lucky guesses, which defeats the aim of finding the true picture. False results are greater for those who know less and guess more, which conceals deficiencies at the low end, where there is most need for remedial action.

The unfairness is greatest for individuals. As progressively more test results are averaged, for whole schools or whole LEAs, positive and negative errors tend to cancel each other out, so comparisons made with these averages can point to year-on-year changes. Even so, these averages are themselves inaccurate. For example, those who know nothing can never average zero because some score higher through guessing and no-one scores an offsetting negative value. Thus, objective tests do not reveal the true depth of the education abyss.

Another unfairness is age variation. A five-year-old class includes those who have just stopped being four and those about to be six, so the oldest have lived for 20% longer than the youngest and are more able to learn. School reports can reassure parents by comparing their children's ages with the class average but it was felt that younger ones competing with older ones might lose self-esteem. An attempt to remedy the situation was to admit starters in three age groups, in successive terms, but that increased the younger entrants' handicap, as when they came to be in a whole-year class, they were not only disadvantaged on an age basis but had also had two fewer terms in school. The privation imposed by later entry is worse than being in the same class as older ones — an inequality that needs to be rectified.

Much in the content of both syllabuses and tests is educationally counter-productive. After the starting age was reduced to four, there was a test at five, to inform Year 1 teachers about their entrants and also allow calculation of the *value-added* effect of their own teaching. But it is unnecessarily elaborate, while also underestimating what the reception class ought to achieve.

The all-important information at this stage is how far a year of teaching has created the capacity to read. The official expectation for the reception year is knowledge of the whole alphabet and ability to read three-letter words plus a few consonant digraphs — a stage that Mona McNee achieves in one term. Again we stress that the official prescription seems a dumbing-down delay of potential achievement.

There is no question but that testing is necessary and equally no question that its present form falls far short of any optimum. It needs to be made consistent as between individuals regardless of the school they attend and also consistent over time so that any improvement or decline can be observed accurately without the smokescreen of grade inflation. A better alternative along these lines is possible and will be explained in Chapter 21. It is based upon the principle of *preventing* problems in the first place instead of the present practice of first creating them and then trying to offset their harm by tinkering about with them.

Chapter 18

Disintegrating Discipline

During the downwave, lack of discipline frequently brought lapses in behaviour unheard of during the upwave. One extreme instance occurred where neither the teacher nor an inspector could prevent several outbreaks of fighting during a single lesson.

Initially, the reform drive seemed to assume that restoring traditional teaching and testing would spontaneously resurrect better discipline and, indeed, the self-esteem bestowed by literacy and the motivation awakened by testing might have gone far towards doing so if the subversives had not prevented their fruition. As it was, the government overlooked the need to re-educate teachers on discipline and so much misconduct went from bad to worse. It was debated during John Major's premiership but not remedied. .

In 2005, David Bell, head of OFSTED, reported further deterioration over the eight years of Labour government. Problems appeared even in nursery schools, some having up to 40% of their children disruptive. This was due to home influence and probably reflected the presence of local problem estates. When Margaret Thatcher commissioned Alice Coleman to redesign several such estates, the head of the primary school serving the worst one said that the design improvement had made her pupils much calmer and easier to teach. The tenants were the same; only the criminogenic architecture had changed.

So architecture can be the initial cause of indiscipline, not teachers or parents, and since 1997 Labour has allowed even worse designed homes to be built. Some tenants are strong enough to protect their children from this powerful influence but many are defeated, especially if their own upbringing was tainted in similar estates.

Teachers need to counter this initial indiscipline but many compound it by failing to set behavioural boundaries. Class control becomes easier if the synthetic phonic method gives all pupils the satisfaction of good reading progress. Conversely, illiterates created by the whole-word method cannot be set to read quietly and they probably become increasingly disruptive as they pass up from class to class.

When they reach the secondary school and cannot cope with its work, they may become thoroughly disaffected. The huge size of comprehensives allows many such pupils to join forces and develop a gang culture that is now a curse in 50% of English secondary schools. In 20% the gang culture is *constantly* oppressive and the other 30% suffer at least one aggressive incident each term. Bell gave various reasons for this unrest, including the big increase in autism but found the main factor to be reading failure. Two-thirds of those suspended or expelled were seriously backward readers.

He also mentioned that many pupils prefer strict teachers and clear disciplinary boundaries, to define unacceptable behaviour that will not be tolerated. They do not find this oppressive but welcome the safety it offers. What is truly oppressive is the stress that is suffered as a result of Progressivism's unfettered "freedom".

Three aspects of indiscipline covered here are bullying of other children, insubordination to teachers, and delinquent behaviour both in and out of school. Certain psychological explanations follow and we also touch on reasons why attempts at improvement mostly fail. Our own suggestions for good discipline are in Part IV.

Bullying

Bullies usually come from dysfunctional families. Some have been so pampered that they expect everyone to bow to their commands and know how to pressure them into doing so. Others have been bullied themselves, with a behavioural model to imitate. They do not retaliate against those who harm them but vent their spite on smaller, weaker children. They are extraverts. Their outgoing nature makes them keenly aware of their environment and its people. They hone their antennae to become adept at recognising a wide range of vulnerabilities that can be mocked as a means of dominating their victims, e.g. pimples, sticking-out ears, a slight physique and any personality traits that they can exploit to get their victims on the raw and in their power.

The taunts need not be related to facts. Bullies have fertile imaginations and use them to spread false rumours. They may constantly jeer at girls for being fat, even while driving them into anorexia. A five-year-old was made to hate her body, and a 13-year-old asked for cosmetic surgery on her nose, eyes and thighs. One girl was declared a lesbian and then cornered and groped by a gang. A boy was called gay and accused of stripping others for sex. His friends were bullied into deserting him and expressing revulsion: "Don't infect me, gay-boy! Keep away!" Progressivism's early sex education aimed for tolerance of homosexuality but that has proved just as wrong as its other claims.

Bullies' victims tend to be introverts, lacking outgoing aggression. Two personality types are especially singled out. The first is the "born victim" — children bullied at home but lacking the toughness to fight back and the awareness needed to bully others. They go through life being taken advantage of. The other typical victim is the nice, sensitive child with good family relationships, who has never met aggression and has no idea how to deal with it. If clever, good at games or popular, these children unconsciously emphasize the inferiority of bullies who are trying to compensate, so their subjugation seems essential to feed the bullies' spurious sense of superiority.

Schools and problem estates are the chief venues of aggression and some unfortunate children are victimised in both. There seems no escape from the constant psychological damage. It is no longer a case of "Sticks and stones can break my bones but words can never hurt me." Sustained verbal abuse can cause utter misery and also the intense stress that triggers physical illness. Such illnesses are welcome to the victims because they keep them at home, and are a respite from bullying attacks.

Some victims find refuge in truancy or develop an intense school phobia, refusing to leave home. Others are so traumatised that they take their own lives and during the tenure of the Blair government the rate of suicides due to bullying has risen to about 20 each year. This is all the more significant in that the total suicide rate has been falling as a result of the ban on selling potentially lethal drugs in large quantities.

Nor are sticks and stones lacking. Jostling and shoving creates the fear that excites bullies to worse things: arm-twisting, punches and kicks, and resort to bats, broken bottles, knives, machetes and guns. These weapons were first intended to frighten rather than harm but later they came to inflict harm in order to frighten. The notorious killing of 10-year-old Damilola Taylor resulted from the same sort of broken-bottle stab that the North Peckham Estate gang habitually used to break in their victims but in his case it severed an artery and he bled to death. The teenager who murdered Luke Walmesly protested his innocence by saying that he meant only to scare him, yet he stabbed with such force that the knife went right through his breastbone before piercing his heart. And it is frightening that a growing number of violent attackers believe that their terrorism deserves neither blame nor punishment.

Escalating violence has included sexual attacks and also a few deliberate murder plans. One boy took a gun to school with a hit-list of those he meant to shoot. Multiple shootings are no longer isolated incidents in US schools and could come to Britain, like other transatlantic trends. Yesterday's exceptions become today's norms.

Bullies pick unobserved venues and victims do not reveal their weakness by telling parents or teachers. There is a moral code of not sneaking, which bullies reinforce by threats that tale-tellers will receive even worse treatment. The persecution may not be realised by adults until the victims' health and personality have broken down.

Parents' complaints are often disbelieved. Teachers have not seen the bullying and deny it exists. Heads may fear for their schools' reputation if they admit there is bullying and disclaim responsibility if it happens outside the school gates. Denial may persist even after the facts are known. One teacher quelled the bullies but when her class moved up, the torment resumed and the new teacher refused to believe it.

Esther Rantzen established Childline to help children who were physically or sexually abused at home but school bullying problems emerged as rampant. This brought the subject out into the open and generated a spate of media attention. However, schools were cautious, as some bullies accused their victims and complaints could not be taken on trust. Moreover, some teachers acted in a foolish way that allowed bullies to identify complainants and inflict merciless reprisals.

A better approach was a "bully box", where victims could post anonymous details about their tormentors. This gave a clearer pattern of information and, when acted on, the bullying virtually ceased. But even more than a cure we need *prevention*.

Some letters to the press dismiss concern by saying that bullying has always existed and is a useful way of toughening children up. One suspects that their writers have been the bullies rather than the bullied, and they clearly have no compunction about the way it is causing lifelong harm and a growing number of deaths.

Social workers brought into cases of physical injury may ineptly compound the damage. One terrified child was forcibly dragged to school where the bullying continued. It was threatened she would be taken into care if her parents kept her home and the sexual abuse now common in care homes seemed an even worse evil. The parents were not informed they could have educated her at home and others who did so were told that home education damages social development. It does not. Some parents have even been accused of inflicting the bullies' injuries themselves. The concept of Munchausen's-by-proxy has been flung at them without evidence and the victims added dread for their parents to that for themselves. Bullying has hideous ramifications and an effective solution is desperately needed.

Insubordination

It is not only children who are victimised by the aggressors. Teachers, too, are abused. Even some three and four-year-olds hurl degrading remarks at the staff. The worst form of disruption used to be talking in class. It was rarest where pupils had individual desks separated by gangways but when two shared a table, the congenitally talkative found it hard to resist commenting, though usually in a whisper to avoid attention. This was stamped on at once and the talkative ones accepted blame quietly. .

Progressivism destroyed this disciplined atmosphere. Children were seated round tables to face inward and encouraged to chat in order to develop social interaction. They could walk across the room to collect materials and equipment. And teachers' authority was diminished. Children were to set the agenda and teachers were to be only facilitators — servants or slaves. Talking and walking came to be free activities, not necessarily connected with schoolwork and class control became very difficult.

Bad behaviour was contained by the threat of the cane but when corporal punishment was banned, covert disruption gave place to overt insubordination. The self-righteous supporters of STOPP were great exponents of the crooked thinking that claims "some means all" or "a little is the same as a lot." For them a single slap on the hand or a few strokes of the cane were child-beating just as much as long-continued torture, with physical injury. Their intervention has led to bullies causing far more, and far worse, child-beating than the cane, which did not drive its recipients to suicide as does the incessant bullying practised since the ban. The dogma that not spanking a child means he will not become violent has been conclusively disproved.

Many teachers say their authority is a joke. Asking children to pick up the litter they drop may result only in swearing. Telling them to sit down and get on with their work may simply elicit jeers. Disobedience, aggression and violence have become the norm in some schools and if a teacher even touches a child, it can provoke an accusation of assault. This happened to one who simply pushed a shouting boy into his seat. Fortunately that teacher was acquitted but others have been convicted, and those accused may be kept in a state of apprehension for a year before their cases are heard. Louts who perceive how to bully also know what false charges may succeed. One, dragged away from viciously kicking a boy on the ground, accused the teacher of starting the violence, which showed it was unsafe even to protect children. Teachers are now allowed to push or pull pupils — but this is not enough to offset the escalating problem.

Thousands of teachers have been assaulted by pupils and 10% say that they regularly face incidents that make them fear for their safety. A study of 304 primary schools in just four LEAs revealed 838 cases of verbal abuse, 64 cases of non-sexual attacks and 62 sexual attacks — a total of 964. Boys have raped teachers and a 15-year-old girl stabbed a teacher in the neck three times with the points of her compasses. Some teachers were too intimidated to report their injuries and others did not have them taken seriously. Only eight of the 964 incidents were officially logged. The NAS/UWT has said that similar experiences are widespread through the country and increasing each year.

Sydney Matthews of ATL dealt regularly with teachers who had been seriously injured or accused of assault. One teacher won £82,500 compensation after a violent 10-year old left her unable to work and needing a surgical collar for life. Sums up to £330,000 have since been paid out. School cost is increased for no educational return. An extreme case was Heywood Comprehensive, Nottingham, where dire indis-cipline led 30 of its 50 teachers to resign. Its truancy rate is among Britain's highest but if the anti-social bullies were forced to attend, the disruption would be even worse. This school spent £180,000 to call in an American, Professor Freiberg, an expert on saving schools blighted by knives and guns, and six teachers were sent to Texas to learn his CMCD method (Consistency Management and Co-operative Discipline). Freiberg believes poverty is partly to blame, but this is difficult to accept, as indiscipline was rare during the much fiercer poverty of the Great Depression between the World Wars. Much present poverty is located in Nottingham's appallingly designed estates, so, once again, the finger points to Modernist architecture as well as Progressivist illiteracy and indiscipline.

Freiberg's practical measures are sensible and include giving the children responsible tasks as door monitors, register callers or helpers in lesson presentation. This seems to support the idea that children might be better served by leaving school earlier to learn from life through the responsibility of a job. However, the Labour government has the opposite aim of extending compulsory schooling up to age 18. This has the political advantage of reducing unemployment and also gives longer for leftist brainwashing, a process illustrated by the teacher who asserted that Left is good and Right bad, but could not identify Left and Right or define their good or bad points. Was she one of the Sharon Shrills favoured for acceptance by her training establishment?

Teachers are already being raped by disaffected 15-year-olds so how much worse would the sexual assaults be if schools have to cater for scores or hundreds of illiterate and disaffected older youths whose only aim is to cause trouble?

Bereft of the cane, schools fell back on suspension or expulsion. These were given the politically correct name of "exclusion", presumably under the misapprehension that a skunk by some other name would smell sweeter. Once exclusion became the sole means of relief, it skyrocketed. By the year 2000, no fewer than 13,000 disruptive yobbos were excluded – decisions not made lightly as they lost the schools money. However, the Secretary of State took fright and ordered a one-third reduction in the number. Disruptive pupils were not to be expelled right after their outrageous acts but kept in school for several months of pastoral help. This was a heavy burden, as there was nothing to stop them from continuing to wreak havoc during that time. And parents could appeal against exclusion with the result that, all too often, the appeal panel ruled that violent pupils must be reinstated. In one case the teachers voted to go on strike rather than accept back a thoroughly vicious boy. He then sued them on the grounds that a strike would deprive him of his education but the House of Lords ruled that the strike was legal.

Furthermore, even successful exclusion might not alleviate the situation, as goodbye to one's own louts might mean being forced to accept those from neighbouring schools. A teacher has described how one such transferee knew exactly how to cause complete chaos in her classroom for a whole year, carefully going just as far as not justifying a call to the police to arrest him. For all that time he robbed his classmates of their education. A log was kept of his antics to justify excluding him after the third term but then he went to another school to steal another class's education for a year.

When special schools were introduced they were meant for slow learners, mostly made slow because of the indigestible look-say foisted upon them. At that time it could be argued that these children should remain in local schools to have local friends but successive generations of slow learners became so disillusioned that they were also highly disruptive, and returning them to local schools was no longer seemed beneficial — except to the government. Labour ordained the closure of the special schools to "re-integrate" their pupils into the mainstream, bringing all their problems with them. This has proved disastrous. Insubordination, injuries and deaths have reached new levels.

There is also a completely different source of disruptiveness in some children — "attention deficit disorder". This is treated with the drug Ritalin, which effects a miraculous transformation in behaviour but must be taken long-term and ultimately has serious health effects. In many cases there is an alternative solution, as junk foods have been identified as one of the causes and a dietary change can cure.

Junk foods are labour-saving for working mothers, and the Labour government has urged more mothers to get jobs. Less understandable is the school's abandonment of nutritionally balanced dinners in favour of a cafeteria choice that includes junk foods. And when children's palates have been trained in this way, they tend to spend pocket money on yet more junk food, which may be available for purchase in schools.

Crime

Bullying and insubordination are mainly power-motivated but another cause is covetousness. Theft and burglary are rife. Even by the mid-1980s,

Andrew Smith found these crimes in 368 state schools in Kent (47%). Possibly there were more, as those losing less than £200 were not counted. Today's percentage is probably greater.

Covetousness might be combined with the power motive in the form of robbery with violence, taking other children's dinner money and leaving them to go hungry. It also resulted in a huge wave of mobile-phone theft, which was eventually stopped by deactivating 400 phones reported as stolen. Extortion with menaces induced some frightened children to part with their savings or steal from their relatives because they were threatened with a beating or stabbing if they did not pay up. One terrified boy was coerced into giving two teenage bullies £5580—his grandmother's life savings—and was only rescued when he was found searching her house for more.

Another motive is destructiveness. Vandalism seems to be a matter of letting off steam or vindictively punishing the school that is the scene of so much humiliation. Criminal damage occurred in almost 30% of the Kent schools and 9% were set on fire. Insurance companies say schools are the Number 1 arson target.

The areas surrounding the school are also vulnerable. Shops may at first replace broken glass but after further damage insert metal "panes" instead. Shoplifting is usually prevented by not admitting more than two children at the same time and using closed circuit television to observe what they do behind the stacks of goods.

Local adults at first, and then those further afield, are also mugged, burgled, wounded, raped and killed, often just to have a bit of fun. The boy who raped a 94-year-old in a churchyard, laughed as he committed the outrage, as also did two schoolgirls who killed an old lady and took her body in a wheelie bin to tip into a canal. A recent murder was committed by boys who decided to enjoy themselves by going out to find a stranger to kick to death, and there are increasing numbers of vicious "slap-happy" episodes, at least one of which has killed the chosen victim.

Because Heywood Comprehensive in Nottingham suffered from extreme indiscipline, it is not surprising that the Nottingham police force is also seriously plagued. In 2005 it announced that it could not cope with the local spate of murders and other serious crimes, and pleaded both for more funding and for help from other forces. A powerful drugs ring had taken out a contract to have the CID head killed, and he and his family had to be moved to a secret, police-guarded dwelling. Nottingham's bad housing design is a powerful trigger but the failure of Progressivist education is also to blame.

Psychological Explanations

Freud inspired the twentieth century with a fear of disciplining children lest it should create harmful repression and the trend was reinforced by Dr. Spock, through his multi-million sales of child-care books. Progressivism was in sympathy with both and donned a halo of freeing children from oppressive discipline, though it did not shrink from oppressing them in the other ways we have described.

Later in his life, Spock recognised the harm he had done but his attempt to reverse it had little effect. Freud never developed any such hindsight but most of his tablets of stone have now been proved speculative misconceptions. Progressivism still goes to great lengths to preserve its hegemony.

Carl Jung's psychology proved sounder than Freud's but Progressivism ignored it. Jung said that both introversion and extraversion were needed to balance an active inner life with outgoing relationships. He also noted four mental functions: thinking, feeling, sensing and intuition, which again should be balanced, as if one were badly neglected, it would become a repressed "shadow", causing problems.

"Balance" does not mean that everyone must develop all six aspects equally. Different emphases are in harmony with the adage that it takes all kinds to make a world. Nevertheless, education should try to provide rounded development and traditionalism did so. Progressivism, by contrast, is intolerant of balance and powerfully points along a narrower path. John Dewey rejected the rich inner life of introversion as something futile and rotten, and advocated forcing children into constant extraverted interaction. Progressivism also tragically narrows development of the four Jungian functions.

Thinking is the brain's latest-evolved, most human function—the least instinctive and the most in need of explicit teaching. It depends upon accurate analysis of true facts but Progressivism reviles facts and praises false opinions, to give "encouragement". This pseudo-compassion saps thinking and robs pupils of their educational birthright.

Progressivism also emasculates *Sensing*. Pop music is preferred to classical, though it tends to arouse aggression while the latter has a calming effect. Crude children's art has been elevated to the honour of appearing on national stamps while the brilliant innovations of past masters are neglected. Taste buds have been perverted by school-dinner junk food and muscular development damped down by banning sports as harmfully competitive. The lack of behavioural boundaries has also done sensuous harm by unleashing the pursuit of ever more dangerous thrills, not excluding the sensual descent into rape and murder.

Still more nonsensical is the idea of teaching children differently according to which sense is their natural avenue to learning. Would visual ones benefit from excluding music and auditory ones from using voice in lieu of text? This would make Progressivism even more lop-sided. For six decades look-say has restricted reading to the visual recognition of whole words, suppressing the vital auditory input of letter sounds, which phonics keeps in balance, as well as having a broader multi-sensory approach.

Intuition is also ill served by Progressivism. It is the pattern-recognition ability of the right brain hemisphere and needs to be checked by the left brain's logical thinking, so that valid ideas are distinguished from simply weird ones. Different people gravitate to different types of pattern skills, such as reading maps, perceiving body language, understanding machine operation or building construction, or gaining insight from putting information into new contexts, but even such natural tendencies need to be developed by teaching. All children can learn them to some extent and they should not be denied to those who lack a natural flair. After all, the whole raison d'être of education is to furnish something over and above the natural and instinctive.

The one intuitive aspect prized by Progressivists is imagination. They consider it a leading virtue and the sole mechanism of creativity. Though "It's all your imagination" means "It's a pack of lies", this does not matter to them as they scorn facts and truth. It was imagination that led a pack of 14-year-old girls to control access to the school lavatories and prevent those they did not like from using them. Some creativity! Imagin-ation is useful in some fields but harmful in others. Even where it is essential it needs to be supported by thought and knowledge. Imaginative fiction would be unintelligible without a thoughtful command of language, while the creativity of the Jubilee Bridge over the Thames revealed the cost of ignoring established know-how. It wobbled dangerously because the designer had neglected the problem of resonance and expensive remedial work was needed to make it safe for public use.

Too much imagination, and too little science, now go into science-fiction violence and tales of black magic. The boy who cut out a woman's heart to eat did so because the dark side of imaginative writing had convinced him that this was a sure-fire recipe for immortality. The Progressivist contempt for the factual was thus responsible for a cruel murder. Progressivism boasts of being "relevant" but it is actually just the opposite. It insulates children from realities and there can be dire consequences.

The Jungian *feeling* function has been mistreated differently. Progressivism leaves it free to fill the thinking gap. Thinking and feeling both offer criteria for making decisions and exercising judgement, and either may be more appropriate in given circumstances. But even when feeling is relevant, some degree of thinking is needed as a check, which cannot be done properly when thinking is undermined by Progressivism. The result has been a growing frequency and intensity of impulsive emotional behaviour.

Feeling was glorified in Daniel Goleman's book, *Emotional Intelligence*. This introduced rich scientific insights, in a thesis that the idea of IQ predicting success in life is false and that emotional intelligence is a more powerful asset. He assumed that the IQ concept was simply mistaken but there may have been a change over time as Progressivism undermined thinking ability and befouled it with emotional indiscipline Letters to the press showed that some interpreted Goleman's thesis as licence to let uncontrolled emotion "hang out". He himself was much more disciplined and described five learning stages needed for the acquisition of full emotional intelligence.

Stage 1 involves recognizing one's own emotions. Wife-beaters usually fail to see their own anger and blame their violence entirely upon the women's supposed provocation, so they need constructive self-observation. Stage 2 is control of the feelings recognised, and this is where discipline at an early age is effective. Anger control needs both stages. The idea of anger control has been in the air and may be what the former Education Secretary, Charles Clarke, meant when he urged that four-year-olds should spend less time learning to read and write, and more time discussing their emotions. But this would be doubly counterproductive. Discussion without control could be a dead end and control would be harder without the thinking enhanced by reading and writing.

Stage 3 consists of using one's disciplined emotions as motivation to achieve one's goals in life and Stage 4 involves developing empathy to understand others' feelings. This leads to Stage 5, handling relationships, the pinnacle of emotional intelligence, which underpins management and leadership success by deploying others most effectively. It is claimed to be the fundamental way of getting on in the world.

Alice Coleman added two types of emotional *unintelligence* preceding Stage 1 — the cold-blooded, or cruel, and the hot-blooded, or violent. Bullies may have either. More surprisingly, she also recognized that the peak achievers at Stage 5 can be bullies as well. "Deploying" others can also mean "manipulating" or "exploiting" them.

Emotional intelligence, like the intellectual kind, can be either positive or negative. Managers need to perceive others' feelings to oil the mechanism of their work but that may be close to the perception used by bullies to distress their victims. Bullies' emotional intelligence may smooth their path to top-dog positions, where they gratify themselves by heartless bossiness. This has led to a surge of staff complaints, so they may not win in the end, as good workers escape to less stressful posts and the business suffers. Scandalous bullying in the army drove four recruits to their deaths.

So again it is clear that prevention would be better than cure. Bad schooling is opening up a massive can of worms. Trying to cure bullies by making them understand their victims' terror is not always a sound approach. The worst ones already understand it very well and delight in their power to use their understanding to create the suffering.

Emotional intelligence is not the last word. We also need moral intelligence to ensure that both thinking and feeling are applied to ethical ends and not distorted for the sake of power or self-aggrandisement. This is a major raison d'être of discipline.

Progressivism narrows Jungian aspects of child development and enlarges the corresponding shadow areas that cause psychological harm. Its misconceptions are a gross element in the UK's present troubles. Fortunately, it is not always applied to extremes but it needs to be fully sloughed off and discipline is essential to its defeat.

Self-esteem is also a vital trait undermined by Progressivism. George Bernard Shaw rightly declared that eroding it is an enormous abuse but recent public discussion has confused it with conceit and arrogance. It is neither, but just the basic faith in oneself that we all need in order to live our lives constructively. It means feeling comfortable with oneself and coming to terms with who one is. The cry "I don't know who I am" was never heard during the upwave but became accepted as normal during the downwave. Progressivism systematically destroys self-esteem by insisting on the look-say method that leaves so many people humiliated by illiteracy and confused about themselves.

Ability to read helps enhance the child's growing self-esteem. Withholding that ability works to destroy it. The child is made to feel inferior and of little worth. This is a completely undeserved misery that may last for life. It also brings distress to many who do learn to read, as illiterate bullies try to boost their own self-esteem by establishing a cruel ascendancy over those who appear cleverer. The ineffective whole-word method is a misery-making machine on a grand scale.

Good schools can provide self-esteem for those who are deprived of it in inadequate homes but, though this aim is adopted, it is often counterproductively applied. Teaching all pupils to read is a good start but, beyond that, teachers must insist that children toe the disciplinary line and acquire an ongoing habit of reasonable behaviour. This gives them freedom from criticism and helps consolidate their feel-good factor. Failure to discipline for fear of bruising their self-esteem leads them into further extremes, which beneath their cocky facades bruise it still more.

Self-esteem is not inborn and needs to be developed, together with esteem for others, i.e. respect. Four combinations of these two aspects were explored by Thomas Harris, who used the term "OK" for esteem and wrote the book "I'm OK, You're OK". As babies are totally dependent upon adults, they perceive the world as "I'm not OK, You're OK", and need good parenting to lift them into the "I'm OK" state, while retaining the "You're OK" element and extending it to more other people.

The other pairs are "I'm not OK, You're not OK" — a bleak outlook on life — and "I'm OK, You're not OK" — a dangerous outlook. This last group feels entitled to gratify themselves in any way, regardless of harm, or even death, to those nonentity others. There seems no way to redeem them because they find everyone else inferior, with nothing to teach them. The Progressivist dogma that teachers are mere facilitators to serve pupils reinforces the ugly "I'm OK, you're Not OK" personality, as it does not equip children with respect for others. This group is usually small but over time the disaffected yobs have reached the point where the police find them beyond control.

Another mistake is excusing anti-social behaviour on the grounds that bad homes, and not the miscreants themselves, are responsible. This effectively gives them a licence to misbehave, knowing that they will not be blamed. Such pleas have sometimes prevailed in court cases, sparing the offenders a prison sentence and freeing them to repay the judges' mercy by committing further crimes. This simply creates more victims without reforming the criminal. The pleas should be translated into "plain-speak": "This offender's background has made him irresponsible and he cannot help committing crimes. Public safety requires he should not be left free for repeated offending." It is sad and it reflects the failure of schooling as well the home.

Still more counterproductive are attempts to raise self-esteem by making offenders feel special and taking them on costly holidays. This has been criticised as just a means of free exotic travel for two accompanying staff. Claims that it works may apply to certain borderline cases but it leaves hardened cases laughing up their sleeves. One boy on such a trip sneaked out of his motel room at night to go burgling and the notorious "Safari Boy" taken to Africa continued a serious offender. He said that he found Africa boring.

Such rewards for bad behaviour are doubly counterproductive. In the first place they do not instil the message that wrong is wrong and can have unpleasant consequences that ought to be avoided. And secondly, they do not restore self-esteem. They may give a temporary impression of being esteemed by others, but self-esteem is something that has to be earned by the self and inwardly engrained if it is to carry one through life. Learning to read fluently is one sure component that also opens up others through at least a degree of school success and access to special interests and abilities.

Moral Intelligence

The 20th century has been a time of modernisms. Some, such as electricity, have brought even greater benefits than was envisaged but others have not lived up to their promise, as is abundantly clear of Modern Movement architecture and Progressivism.

Psychology is another modernism. Despite the positive contributions of great men such as Carl Jung and H.J. Eysenck, its early vision of more stable and mentally healthier communities has proved not merely false but actively counterproductive. Who can doubt that Psychology's century has ended in a far worse state than it began? The serious-crime rate is nearly 50 times as high now as it was then and the crimes themselves tend to be more callous, with a large increase in serial rapes and murders. Marital breakdown is common, with its destructive effect upon children, and violent hooligans have multiplied out of control in many areas.

The reason is that Psychology has progressively replaced religion as a power in our lives. Christianity and its Judaic ancestor promote a strong sense of responsibility for one's actions, while Psychology fosters irresponsibility. Nothing is the fault of the perpetrator; everything has been inflicted upon him by his defective upbringing. So he has no sense of blame or shame.

Psychology did not denounce religion as explicitly as Progressivism denounced phonics, but it nevertheless contrived to edge it off-stage. At the time of the 1988 Education Act, the Conservative government wanted to ensure that religious assemblies should start each school day and that there should also be Religious Education lessons.

The Labour government has quite opposite ideas. Nick Seaton, in his 2001 paper, *Free Our Schools*, explained how religious education had been replaced by Personal, Social and Health Education (PSHE) plus Citizenship. This sounds as if it teaches moral values but in reality it offers a mish-mash of mixed moral positions from which children are to take their own choice. Quite recently it has been announced that schools are no longer to teach "right and wrong".

The hidden aim is to convert all children into little socialists but the overt aim, as expressed by Blair, is to inculcate "respect". This it has signally failed to do, leading to the introduction of Anti-Social Behaviour Orders (ASBOs). These are rarely accompanied by effective action and in many areas have become just a joke among the hooligans and vandals, who continue to make our streets unsafe. Religion actually did inspire the respect we so badly need, and could do so again, given sincere teachers.

Segregation

Despite the policy of returning disrupters to the classroom, at least the worst ones are sent to special institutions. These may not be successful in rehabilitating their inmates and the disorder at Feltham Young Offenders Institution has included murder.

It was decided to establish four Secure Training Centres as expensive boarding schools run by the private sector. The press calls them "child prisons". The first one, Medway, was the responsibility of "Rebound", which like Securicor is a subsidiary of Group 4 Total Security Ltd. It opened in 1998 with 100 staff to cater for 40 offenders aged 12–15, each of whom had committed at least three crimes that would have meant jail sentences if they had been adults.

Rebound completely failed to understand how very anti-social these young delinquents were and the staff were quite inadequately trained to deal with them. Within a matter of weeks they had smashed windows, doors, and kitchen equipment, etc., to the tune of £100,000. Police in riot gear had to be summoned to quell the troublemakers and the Home Secretary wanted prison officers to be available to use their training in tough control-and-restraint techniques when there were any further crises but the warders could not be spared from their demanding work in the jails themselves.

After the rioting, the inmate roll was reduced from 40 to 30 and class size from five to two. This seems still one too many as it continued to provide each delinquent with an audience and accomplice to spur him on to further unruly behaviour.

Seeing is Believing

Despite press accounts of indiscipline, it still needed more impact upon public consciousness if it was to generate constructive action. This came from a television programme, *Classroom Chaos*, based on films taken by Sylvia Thomas (a pseudonym). Back in 1970 she had taught in a large secondary school, where the pupils had started school in the 1960s and "being cheeky" meant nothing worse than whispering in the back row. She had never needed to shout to keep control. But when she returned as a supply teacher after 30 years, she was appalled by the deterioration in discipline. After her very first day, she recalled, "I sobbed my heart out, thinking, "Is this what education has come to?" And the same disintegration characterized all 14 of the schools where she had to teach. A quiet class was so rare that it seemed quite eerie, and most teachers told of her experiences replied, "I am not surprised; that is my life".

She decided to film her days in these schools by fitting a secret camera to her briefcase and wearing a jacket-button microphone. The resulting film was described by Becky Barrow in the *Daily Telegraph* as "a withering portrayal of the education system." Pupils were noisily swearing, using mobiles, uttering obscenities and dire threats and fighting each other. They felt free to walk about or hide under the desks and also eat, which was not allowed in the classroom. One greeted an attempt at discipline by saying, "I'll come to your house and blow you up." Another said, "Don't talk to me like that—I've got my rights you know." One boy was searching for pornography on the internet—"I just typed in anal, didn't I?" This was a school where there was a policemen stationed on the premises and he was called in to deal with the young paedophile, who had obviously taken in two school subjects—sex and computer science—if nothing else.

Chaos it was, and an insight into what many teachers are expected to endure. No wonder their profession proves to be one of the worst two for the generation of stress, and no wonder there is such a high staff turnover.

Conclusion

Discipline and learning go together. Many teachers may spend more lesson time trying to secure order than is left for actual teaching. This is part of the reason why today's expensive twelve-year school span from 4–16 is producing worse educated products than the upwave's more economical nine-year span from 5–14. It also indicates the futility of creating a further increase to a compulsory fifteen years, from 3 to 18.

Even at age four or five there are disciplinary problems and the latest ploy has been an anonymous attempt to incite five-year-olds to refuse to obey orders to sit down, be quiet and listen, on the grounds that this infringes their human rights accorded by European law. It is clear that the growing trend towards indiscipline needs to be countered and a brief hope was raised in 2005 when Ruth Kelly mentioned zero tolerance when setting up a Committee to report on the disciplinary problem. This Committee might have had a brighter future than some of its predecessors (Chapter 11) as its Chairman, Sir Alan Steer, had been a head teacher but he immediately ruled out punishment and protested that not all children were horrid. True, but it is precisely the horrid ones that were to be his committee's concern. One wonders whether he would have been able to make a success of Medway if he had been in charge there?

Ideas for a positive approach will be discussed in Part IV.

Chapter 19

The Price We Pay

No-one who has read thus far with an open mind can doubt that the tyranny of look-say and associated methods, and of Progressivism in general, have imposed an enormous national cost in terms of human misery. This chapter now turns to the financial cost involved.

Shoddy Goods

People pay local and national taxes for a vast school system to deliver teaching and teacher training that fit children to live healthy, cultured, ethical and self-supporting lives. Far too often it manifestly fails to do so, not even teaching the basic skill of reading, or teaching it so defectively that it is virtually lost soon after leaving school. And those who do learn to read may have such poor standards of spelling, syntax and rational use of language that they are far from valuable to many employers. S. Parsons recently calculated that the overall cost of poor skills to business is some £10 billion each year, for further training to bring under-educated staff up to the basic standard that should have resulted from adequate schooling.

If similar breaches of faith occur with goods and services in the private sector, purchasers can have recourse to the Trades Descriptions Act to obtain reimbursement from suppliers. There is now a trend for ill-educated pupils or their parents to sue for compensation but, even if they win, it is not the supplier who pays. It is the taxpayers, already defrauded once, who are forced to pay again so that public funds can meet the further cost of the system's inefficiency. Some, indeed, pay three times. Those parents who make sacrifices to secure enlightened private education, are not spared from forced contributions to state-sector schooling and training, nor from meeting a share of the penalties imposed by lawsuits.

In environmental cases it is recognised that using public money to clean up pollution has little effect and this has led to the principle that *the polluter pays*. We need a parallel principle in education — *the intellectual abuser pays*.

We need a way to ensure that the failed watchdogs, who are salaried to provide education but produce intellectual cripples instead, should find that litigation affects them personally. Obviously they cannot compensate all the illiterates who have been robbed of employment by their promulgation of Progressivism but, as we shall see, there is a case for arranging for the abusers to lose their own employment so that they can no longer damage others' lives with their harmful theories.

Teacher Training Costs

We start with the training establishments, which first indoctrinate their students and then certify them as fit to unleash into schools, which makes them doubly responsible — or, more aptly, doubly irresponsible. There are nearly one hundred of them. It is said to cost as much to train a bad teacher as a good one but that is a grossly over-optimistic view. The switch from good training to bad brought immensely escalating expenditure.

During the upwave the training period was two years, with a minority taking a one-year diploma after university graduation. Most were largely or entirely self-funded. Until 1942, the maximum support was a £25 grant and a £35 loan for each year. There are now many more university-trained teachers, most of whom were until recently state-funded for both tuition and maintenance over four years, while College of Education grants grew from two years to three and often four. Today, intending teachers receive £6000 annually, i.e. £24,000 for a four-year course.

This longer and costlier training is still thought inadequate and in need of in-service supplementation. Certainly some upwave teachers went *at their own expense* to summer schools designed to enhance their knowledge and skills but today these extras are financed by the LEAs and often provide additional income for the training gurus. Even so, when Kenneth Baker was Secretary of State for Education and Science, he set aside five more training days each year for all teachers. The combined length of initial training, in-service courses and Baker Days may average twice as long as the upwave course that produced effective traditional teachers.

It is not only the cost of student grants that has multiplied. The increased training time requires perhaps twice as many staff, together with the capital and maintenance costs of additional buildings and additional colleges. As these institutions are attached to different universities, we have not been able to assemble their total cost but Jim Rose has recently stated that it is probably the largest element in the total education budget.

The value received for this vastly increased investment has declined, not only in falling educational standards but also in a lower ratio of training years to teaching years. The two-year training produced teachers at age 20 with retirement at 65 — a maximum ratio of investment-to-returns time of 1: 22.5. Today, the starting age is usually 22 and any thought of working beyond 60 has vanished, so the maximum ratio is only 1: 9.5 and even this is not often achieved.

Before World War II, women teachers had to resign on marriage but replacement was easy and there was no staff shortage. Even during the war, when many men teachers were in the forces, there was no staffing crisis, partly because the retirement age was raised to 70. Today married women teachers are acceptable but the high wastage rate means staff vacancies are chronic in some areas.

It is no longer the norm to love the work and want to stay in it for life. Teaching is now so stressful that only 19% stay in post until 60. Frequent early retirement, from age 50, imposes the cost of early pensions, plus successors' salaries. At one point, this expenditure became so great that there was talk of banning subsidised premature retirement. A still greater loss is that some 40% of teachers leave the profession during their first year and 18% more within three years. So over half do not even repay their training investment with an equal number of teaching years. And some time ago it was found that over 85,000 qualified trainees had never taken any school job at all and as that number will have been added to subsequently, it may now be approaching 100,000. The system seems to pour taxpayers' money into a vast sieve that leaks it out faster than it flows in, creating a severe teacher shortage.

Some of those who do not stand the pace may be the Sharon Shrills accepted for training in lieu of better applicants but many of those do cling to their jobs, contributing to the decline of standards. Chris Woodhead found an accumulation of some 15,000 sub-standard staff, who should not have been in teaching at all.

It also seems possible that potentially good teachers are so switched off by their experience as pupils that they do not apply for training. Labour has enticed more applicants with larger annual grants but that does not guarantee that the recipients will actually teach. Some seem to see the course simply as a way of deferring the prospect of unemployment, so much of this incentive money may merely be pouring more into the top of the sieve without plugging the holes at the bottom. In any case, an increased college intake does not relieve the teacher shortage immediately. There is a delay over the three or four-year training period.

College lecturers are the chief recipients of research grants and, given their contempt for facts, it is not surprising that they rarely produce useful results. In 1998, Chris Woodhead found £70 million had been completely wasted on projects masquerading as research, and this has since built up further. Professor James Tooley showed that nearly two-thirds of recent projects did not even meet minimum academic standards of honesty and impartiality. The most genuine research was by people who were not paid for it but who had education's well-being sincerely at heart.

So the present training system is immensely wasteful. It funds many students who do not teach for more than a few terms, if at all. It instils methods that promote illiteracy. It dictates classroom layouts that undermine learning and allow distracting noise to penetrate to other classes.

And it engages in bogus research to prop up bogus Progressivist methods. The financial tragedy is that these methods cost vastly more than the tried and tested upwave methods wherever they survive today. It has many serious national repercussions and needs total replacement.

Fortunately a better alternative was explored by the Conservatives: *learning on the job*. Selected good schools recruited apprentices to initiate into the art and science of teaching. These observed excellent teachers at work and discussed successful lesson construction. They perfected their own presentations with the teacher present and no indiscipline distractions. They learned whether children absorbed enough from their lessons for true development. And they soaked up knowledge of how a good school is run.

The realistic experience of learning on the job soon convinced some apprentices that teaching was not for them and they dropped out within a few weeks instead of incurring three or four years' abortive training costs. The "training schools" were obviously those that provided good models of achievement and discipline, and infant schools would be those where children learned to read the first time round and did not incur remedial costs later. As such trainees spread to other schools, infants' ability to read would become general and a broad wave of literacy would advance steadily up the age range. Junior schools would be able to achieve more when receiving 100% literate pupils, and so would secondaries, so that more schools would reach the standard needed to give training to apprentices.

Labour's similar scheme does not dispense with Progressivist trainers in the same way. They provide a preliminary summer of indoctrination and also supervision during the year on the job in schools they have chosen. The probationary year that follows is in the same school.

Both approaches cut the lead time from acceptance to qualification from three or four years to one, and provide more in-school teaching during that one, but this is still too long a wait for the many school-children launched upon illiteracy. They need immediate rescue and teachers should be able to provide it. In the next chapter we shall explain Mona McNee's *Step by Step* scheme as a useful tool for salvaging betrayed pupils of all ages. Meanwhile, the closure of the education colleges would bring a huge saving in staff salaries and property upkeep.

Teaching Costs

The teacher-to-pupil ratio has also become costlier. This is not to condemn teachers. Most work hard but faulty training and bureaucratic pressures undermine their effectiveness. Even those OFSTED deems incompetent were led by their trainers to think themselves worthy and some might have been so if properly trained.

As so few teach for long, the best cost comparison is the starting salary. When Alice Coleman began her teaching career in 1943, shortly before the downwave began, her annual salary was £162. In 2004, inner London teachers began on £20,733, which was 128 times as much, far more than inflation over the same period.

For greater accuracy, the salary should be related to the number of pupils taught. Class size in 1943 was often up to 50 and Alice Coleman's school was fortunate to have only 40, so her salary was £4 per pupil per year. Today, average class size is 29 so inner London's per-pupil pay is £714, or 178 times greater. But this is not the whole story. Today's larger schools have more supernumerary staff, giving an overall teacher-pupil ratio about 1:18, so pay per-pupil is more realistically £1152 or 228 times greater.

Actual classes are often smaller because of the high truancy rate. Fear of bullying, avoidance of illiteracy's humiliations, attraction to street crime, family holidays at off-peak times and plain boredom, are among the reasons for unauthorised absences. It is no easier for the teacher when pupils have gaps in their schooling but it does mean that they are delivering less education for the same pay.

Teachers' workload is further reduced by their own absences. These were extremely rare during the upwave but recently the annual average was said to be 14 days, which must reflect stress and eagerness for relief to the tune of a 7% decrease in the total of working days. This adds the cost of supply teachers.

The story continues with remedial teachers, visiting schools to relieve part of the class workload by abstracting illiterates for special reading instruction. In 1985 this added 10% to Norfolk's education budget, a cost still escalating when Mona McNee left the county. Some older remedial teachers scored successes by supplying the phonics missing from infant schools but those steeped in look-say continued using the same methods and failed to assuage the distress of children floundering in every subject that required reading. The ineffectiveness of the remedial costs is clear from the fact that about half of school leavers are still illiterate or semi-literate, but such factual evidence did nothing to deter Progressivism's blinkered dominance.

As education came to absorb over half of some local authorities' tax levy, it would have been logical to cut out remedial costs by means of the phonic principle of *prevention is better than cure*. But Progressivism was impervious to logic and continued to believe that throwing money at a problem was the only route to improvement. So there was increased expenditure for more of the same. Because of backward children's failure to read, it was argued that the one-to-one remedial periods were too short and more permanent provision was needed. Non-readers were "statemented" as having special needs so that they could be allocated individual aides. As this brought more money to the schools, the numbers labelled as having special needs tended to increase and even reached 40% in some schools. Officialdom resolutely ignored pleas to compare the efficacy of different teaching methods and closed its mind to the *absence* of high-cost special-needs pupils in schools where phonics teaching precluded the creation of illiterates.

We have seen that Labour's flourish of remediation through three-week summer schools appeared to be merely more look-say but in the second year a Coventry school seemed to make a real advance. It raised the reading age of eleven year-olds from 8 or 9 years to 11 by "supplying the knowledge of the alphabet that the children had somehow missed at the infant stage". A hopeful picture! But then look-say was back and Alice Coleman's meeting with the new instructors got nowhere. They understood too little to have even a glimmering of their own incomprehension. The earlier success was just a flash in the pan.

Teachers also shed work to classroom assistants. At the last count there were 96,000 in England and Wales — 23% of the 410,000 teachers. It was hoped that their presence, for chores such as cleaning paint pots, would help deter bad behaviour and many also contributed to actual teaching, e.g. taking one small group or covering for absentees. The unions felt this usurped professional skills and Nigel de Gruchy of the NAS/AWT protested against using these "pig ignorant peasants". A storm of counter-protest came both from the "peasants" and from Dave Prentis, General Secretary of Unison, the public service union, which had some 50,000 of them as members. He defended them as hardworking and dedicated, and de Gruchy apologised. "Classroom assistants have indeed graduated to more demanding professional roles. I made a grave mistake in employing the language I did."

It was not taken kindly that the aides' initial salaries were higher than those of teachers outside London. So for nearly a quarter of classes the salary cost is slightly more than doubled. Teachers need help in view of the administrative burdens imposed upon them but teaching to read is still largely far below the standard of the upwave.

Classroom aides are not the only assistants. Teachers have relinquished playground duty in breaks and lunch hours at a cost of £50 million for special supervisors. Older children have been conscripted into mentor roles for younger ones and it has been suggested that higher education students should be paid to work in schools in part of their vacations.

Responsibility has also been externalized on to parents. It was mentioned earlier that teachers had so far forgotten their educational role as to be indignant that not all school starters could already read. Pupils were sent home with books for reading lessons with parents — a practice reinforced by Labour's rigid homework schedule across the subject spectrum. Parents are not paid for this but it does mean that the teachers are providing less value-added schooling than during the upwave.

The home contribution may also involve financial outlay. To avoid illiteracy, some 10% of parents buy independent primary education while at a further 20% have ensured that their children can read before entering state schools. *Teach your pre-school children to read and make them schoolproof* is one aim of Mona McNee's *Step by Step*. Many other parents, once the children are in school and the educational defects become clear, incur the expense of tutors. One providing company estimates that at least a quarter of families now employ tutors at various stages, beginning with six-year-olds when reading backwardness becomes apparent. This is further evidence that state schools are doing a lesser job despite all the extra money poured into them.

Parents have also given voluntary help in schools as "Mums' Army". This does not increase educational expenditure but it does relieve teachers of part of their work and affects the pay-per-pupil ratio. However, this contribution has now been undermined by delays due to the Labour government's anti-paedophile decree that not only teachers but volunteers also, must be vetted at length.

A further externalisation is Volunteer Reading Help, which provides aides to hear children read in schools. Their training consists of the same old counterproductive method and we have not met any who understand the phonic principle. One found it amusing that a small boy in her remit was groping after the use of alphabetic sounds to decipher words but when Alice Coleman urged her to encourage this, she drew in her horns and said she must consult her advisers. One can imagine their negative response. ALBSU (now BSA) has spent many millions on trying, but failing, to repair the deficiency that should never have been created in the first place. In 1995 it decreed that its volunteers must take a City and Guilds course, which was very politically correct and ignored phonics.

Despite all the increased funding, the teacher's lot has not become happier. The state-school system is still haemorrhaging its staffing life-blood and the government has attempted to stem the flow. One offer is £5000 each, (£20 million in toto) for high-flying university students to train during their summer vacations, and thus be qualified to teach as soon as they graduate. Much depends on how high-fliers are identified. Some brilliant people cannot slow their thinking sufficiently to comprehend children's learning processes so here, too, the cost of training may be wasted.

Ideas for enticing teachers to stay longer in post were a bonus for those completing five years and an opportunity after seven years to apply for a £2000 salary increase for competence. Of 200,000 applicants, 90% received the award, adding an annual cost of £36 million. This does not suggest very stringent competence assess-ment. The increment scale was also extended over more years to a top rate of £35,000 and special rates were introduced for those in subjects having the greatest teacher shortages. Some heads now receive £100,000 per annum.

Greater expenditure seems the only solution the establishment can envisage but there are alternatives. Learning on the job, mentioned above, would allow the training institutions to be closed, releasing their numerous lecturers to help staff the schools. There need be no redundancy payments as other teaching jobs would be available. Of course, these might carry lower salaries but the higher rate could be offered for posts in the schools with the worst problems. After all, these people claim to be experts and might be expected to apply their expertise where it is most needed.

All teachers should be trained in the phonics principle, to rescue non-readers of any age. Baker-Day phonics courses could bring illiteracy to a speedy end. Tutors should be true phonicists and should also re-train college staff returning to school careers. The resulting decrease in illiteracy would end the need for aides, and some of these could also become teacher apprentices.

The Duration of School Life

A third cost factor is the learning to earning ratio, which compares the length of schooling to that of working life. The learning years are not used to best advantage for all the reasons explained: the whole word method that creates illiteracy and the classroom arrangement and indiscipline that waste so much learning time. To compensate for the lower attainment, massive expenditure has added more school years, which also camouflage unemployment figures. Keeping school-leavers out of the job market can be made to seem an employment achievement.

In the late upwave, state schooling was funded for nine years, from 5 to 14. Raising the leaving age increased it to 10 years in 1945 and 11 in 1972, while the earlier starting age made it 12 years. None of this has improved education, but the false meme of "more means better" persists and in 2005 Labour floated the idea of three more compulsory years, from 3 to 18—a 25% increase with commensurate costs. It would be extended to 21 for the 50% planned to go to university (and a whisper of 70% despite the 71,000 undergraduate drop-outs in a single year). Some universities say they cannot bring such badly educated students up to degree level in three years and need four, up to age 22. This would mean an 18-year learning period.

Starting work at 22 and retiring at 60 gives a working life of 38 years for the majority, a learning-to-earning ratio of 1: 2.1, as compared with a ratio of nearly 1:6 for the majority in the late upwave. Obviously, the employment return for educational time-investment was almost three times greater before the onset of Progressivism and there has been an enormous change in the relative numbers of the education-subsidised and the tax-payers who subsidise them.

The reduced learning-to-earning ratio has caused a dearth of skilled craftsman who would once have become apprentices at 14. They were then satisfied learners in trades suited to their talents instead of failed under-graduates as so many are now. This mistaken policy increases everyone's home-repair costs and also supports Labour's welcome of massive immi-gration to fill the employment gap, at a cost as yet incalculable, especially as some are serious criminals. All this reflects Progressivism's failure to make the most of the years best suited to formal learning for the majority, before many children mature to the age of needing to enter the adult work-ing world and begin learning from life rather than the artificialities of the classroom. Once in work, they can go on learning in a variety of other ways if the schools have performed their prime duty of equipping them with reading fluency.

The Labour government became devoted to keeping children in the school environment regardless of whether it was past the sell-by date for them and decided to pay them £30 per week for staying on after the pres-ent compulsory leaving age of 16. This did not guarantee that they learned anything further. One sixth-former wrote to the press explaining the coun-terproductive reality of this policy. Instead of the relief from disruption which the sixth-formers had anticipated when those uninterested in learn-ing left school at 16, they still had them there, creating havoc. These unruly conscripts were attending purely for the money, which they were using to procure tobacco, alcohol and drugs. The taxpayers being soaked for these weekly payments were thus being forced to pay for junkies' drug supplies.

These facts point to a solution. A return to phonics teaching for all infants would have everyone, apart from the blind, profoundly deaf and brain-damaged, reading fairly fluently within two years. They would still need instruction in spelling rules, syntax and vocabulary but mass illiter-acy would be over, together with the epidemic of dyslexic problems. Learning would become more effective each school year and many would be sufficiently educated at 14 to enter the world of work. Those who could obtain an apprenticeship at that age should be allowed to take it up, and 15 could be the end of compulsory schooling for others. Such an approach would eliminate the cost of trying to make up for earlier deficiencies by keeping so many children in school longer than is psychologically appro-priate for them. Of course, those genuinely interested in learning would be able to stay on.

Reducing the school population thus would reduce the number of teachers needed and help solve the staff shortage. It should also make teaching a more attractive career again as the current proliferation of humiliated illiterates would be succeeded by greater school satisfaction for all and more co-operation in learning.

Local and Central Government Costs

A further cost factor is the teaching-to-administration ratio. How much is spent on management as compared with actual education? LEAs are funded from local taxes and also central government grants, and retain a proportion for their own staff and offices, often wastefully. Gerry Bowden MP cited an example of ILEA waste concerning a broken washbasin, which the school could have quickly replaced for £70. However, ILEA did not allow independent action and imposed a chronicle of form-filling, inspection visits and other delays, which escalated the cost to £500. As Britain's highest-spending and lowest-achieving authority, the ILEA may have been atypical but many others are also an expensive way of administering education.

LEAs were targeted for reform by the 1979–1997 Conservative government. The *Opt-Out Scheme* invited secondary schools to apply for freedom from LEA control, and if they were deemed capable of self-management, they received a share of their authorities' administrative funding. This halted interference and opt-out applications increased. Although primary schools particularly needed freedom in order to restore phonics, they were initially thought too small to qualify but were later accepted in groups sharing bursar services, etc. Other funding went on assisted places in independent schools for bright children, elite City Technology Colleges partly sponsored by business, and national examinations to create awareness of the need for high standards.

There were frequent protests against Conservative "cuts" in the educational budget, described by the NAHT President as "verging on the criminal". In reality however, the Conservative government, 1979–1997 made increases in real terms of 51% for nursery and primary schools and 49% for secondary schools. The alleged "cuts" were simply how far these increases fell below the extreme demands of the unions. Nevertheless, the increases were not wholly admirable as there could have been large savings if the government had recognized Progressivism's flagrant wastefulness.

After 1997, the Labour government ended the opt-out and assisted places schemes, which triggered a closer look at what the LEAs were withholding from the schools. Nick Seaton, of the Campaign for Real Education, produced two reports. In 2000/2001, the total budget for the English LEAs was over £23 billion, of which under £17 billion went to the schools. The difference of £6 billion (26%) was complex to account for. Some of it, such as capital for school buildings, was obviously justified, but it emerged that over £180 million had been unjustifiably diverted from education to finance highways, social services, etc.

After these initial deductions, which Seaton described as "opaque", there remained the General Schools Budget (GSB, 1998-1999) and the corresponding Local Schools Budget (LSB, 2000/2001), which allow comparison of further withholdings (Table 19.1). In each of the table's three rows, the most extravagant councils withheld at least twice as much as the most prudent. The third row, which includes the opaque initial deductions, shows that the worst authority withheld nearly 44% of the entire budget, which was well over twice the percentage of the best one. There is undoubted room for greater efficiency and saving.

Table 19.1: Percentage of Funding Withheld by LEAs
(taken from Nick Seaton's lists)

Year	Best 10 LEAs	Worst 10 LEAs
1998/99	13.7–21.7	33.6–38.7
2000/2001	15.9–19.8	27.2–38.3
2000/2001 (gross)	19.2–23.0	32.6–43.8

If opting out and other measures had been taken to their logical conclusion, all schools would have taken charge of their own budgets and the LEAs would have become redundant. Many of their staff, especially the advisers, could have gone back into the teaching workforce to help eliminate the shortage.

In 1997, the Labour government pleased the unions by announcing an educational budget three times as large as the last Conservative one but this proved to be misleading "spin". It was not an annual sum but had to cover three years, so it was actually a three-year freeze, with no increase for inflation and thus a real cut. The most economical LEAs found it hard to cut administrative costs and the table shows they had a slight rise in 2000/2001, whereas the most profligate ones had plenty of waste to trim and somewhat reduced their still high percentages.

Labour later became spendthrift, apparently aiming to spend as much on education as any other country, still insisting that money would buy excellence. It was commented that "No child left behind" really meant "No cheque left unsigned". Prime Minister Blair had a vast stock of initiatives but little follow through. The schools groaned under a torrent of fresh criteria to be applied but new edicts streamed in before the earlier ones could be implemented. This not only diverted attention away from the teaching task but also led to expenditure without results. Some further examples of generosity with taxpayers' money include:

- £1 million annually to ten heads, each to save 20 failing schools in action zones

- City academy heads' salaries to be £100,000.
- Bonuses for teachers in the worst 500 schools; rewards for the best achievers
- Free £1000 laptop computers, eventually for every teacher (£410 million)
- £2000 per school for books—a low figure in comparison with computers.
- £20 million to help schools speed up the sacking of incompetent teachers
- £170 million per year for national literacy and numeracy studies.
- £5 million for expansion of literacy summer schools
- £19 billion for nursery school places, smaller classes, better buildings, etc.
- £450 million to prevent 5-13-year-olds from turning to truancy, drugs and crime.
- Multi-millions for extracurricular activities for 60,000 pupils in schools with a high proportion receiving free meals. £80 million for after-class clubs.
- £5000 extra salary for maths teachers.
- Government to pay off student loans for teachers of shortage subjects: (maths, science, English and modern languages).
- £227 million per annum for eight agencies giving career advice and trying to dissuade those wanting to drop out of sixth forms.
- £540 million: Sure Start nursery schools, play schemes, child and health care.

The total cost of school education in 2005 was £36 billion—a shocking sum, especially for a product that is unnecessarily substandard and still in decline. Greater effectiveness, founded on synthetic phonics, would slash the cost enormously.

PART IV

THE WAY AHEAD

Chapter 20

The Best Way to Teach Reading

The True Way Out of the Wood

We have shown how look-say, etc., created mass illiteracy and foiled efforts to redeem it, and we now turn to the positive side — how the power Mafia can be defeated. Until we have a government that whole-heartedly desires better education and also knows how to overcome the Mafia's ploys, we need an outflanking strategy.

Parents can outflank the look-say disaster by teaching their children to read before starting school, and thus prevent their ability from being mangled. The number of parents who have succeeded in this role has been multiplying and may now exceed the 20% figure cited a few years ago. Other parents may also have tried to schoolproof their children, but without success because they did not escape the sticky flypaper of look-say schemes. This chapter explains how to streamline the teaching both for beginners and for trapped strugglers.

It can also help teachers slough off their faulty look-say training and switch to effective synthetic phonics. They need to be warned, however, of the Progressivist backlash that misrepresents what the phonics method actually is and substitutes false models.

Authors of reading schemes naturally believe that they have devised the best one possible but that is often not the case. Even those that shine in scientific trials may not be the last word as there may exist better schemes that have not yet been tested. Mona McNee has pleaded to have her *Step by Step* scheme tested against others, but to no avail, though the evidence discussed in Chapter 16 leaves no doubt of its value. It underpins a smooth and rapid acquisition of reading skill and also prevents gender-lag in boys, socio-economic lag in poor areas, and dyslexic lag everywhere. Children taught by this method from the start never discover whether they are dyslexic because they are not handicapped by the problems generated by look-say.

When Alice Coleman assessed recent schemes for Chapter 16, she found no weaknesses at all in *Step by Step*. It embodied the full range of phonic strengths, together with many thoughtful refinements that ease and accelerate the learning process. These are clear enough to help untrained parents teach their own children unless, of course, their own schooling has left them illiterate. Some parents have been taught by Mona McNee alongside their children and one mother who learned in this way said it was her greatest bliss to be able to leave a note for her husband, "Dinner in the oven."

So we make no apology for using *Step by Step* as the model, though we still hope a qualified researcher will test it scientifically and add an extra dimension to its accreditation.

If you intend to teach from *Step by Step* you should begin by preparing your mind. Your own experience as a proficient reader is not a safe guide to a beginner's needs. You may unconsciously make assumptions that confuse your child. Starting from the adult position is precisely the mistake made by the "experts" who urge that children should guess words from their context, when the context leaves them equally at sea. You need to understand that it is all Greek to young learners, so try to step into their minds by making sense of this passage.

دِرَختهای باغ به خوبی مُواظِبَت میکُنَد . أَصغَر دَر

آبیاری و سَمپاشی درختها به پِدَرِش کُمَک میکُنَد .

وَقتی که میوهها میرسد، أَصغَر وَ پِدَرِش میوهها

Unless you know Persian, you will soon give up the hopeless effort, and that is exactly the lesson you need. A page of English is as much gobbledygook to your child as this Persian is to you and that is why the gimmick of learning from real books converted look-say reading ability from a low standard to a no-standard.

Remember, too, that children have very short attention spans; their minds flit like butterflies from one thought to another. Do not concentrate on one thing for longer than seems natural to the child, as that would turn reading into a chore instead of a rewarding fun experience. Mona McNee's *Step by Step* reading scheme takes such needs into account and she explains below just what is involved.

Step by Step

When I, Mona McNee, retired from six years of teaching strugglers in a Norfolk middle school, I was besieged by requests to tutor children who were having problems with reading. To find the best method I looked at every available commercial reading scheme and found that most were either look-say, or an unhelpful mix of methods, or far more comprehensive than most learners need.

I wanted a system I could put into the hands of parents and say, "Do it yourself." It had to be cheap, practical, graded, thorough and simple, so that they would not need training, and to achieve all that, I had to write and publish my own scheme. I called it *Step by Step* and arranged everything the beginner needed in a logical order, so that easy stages came first as foundations for the more advanced ones to build on. The *Royal Road* scheme by Daniels and Diack pointed me in the direction of phonics-first, starting with the letters of the alphabet.

Steps 1–26: The Letters of the Alphabet

For the first six letters and their sounds I use c-a-t and d-o-g. I have found that many pupils confuse d with its mirror image, b, which begins at the top, so from the start I aim to get the d right and leave the b till later. I show a round clock and say that c begins at 2 o'clock, backs up to 12 o'clock and then continues round and down to 6 o'clock and up to 4 o'clock. a is the same but continues on straight up and down. d is also the same but goes up tall and then down again, while g begins like a and then adds a tail.

The pupil first practices these letters with a big arm movement from the shoulder, "drawing in the air" to get the feel of it, and then makes the smaller movements needed to join up dots in a large letter outline provided in *Step by Step*, before going on to smaller writing. The c, a and o are made to fit exactly the right height between parallel lines, while t and d each have a "tall" and g has a "tail".

The work with these first six letters is vital. The children learn how to hold a pencil with the thumb and first two fingers, not pressing too hard and making the letters sit on the line to be read from left to right. They are taught that a group of letters can make a word. They learn that words depend on which the letters are and also their order, so that even the first three can make four words: "a", "at", "cat" and "act". Most importantly in today's world of reading failure, they learn that they can get it right first time, carefully, even slowly — that *they* can read it from the letters they see and sound, and *not* by being told what the word is or what the letters say. I do tell them, however, that the same letter twice — "ff", "ll" and "ss" at the end of one-syllable words — is sounded only once.

If they have learned to sing an a-b-c song, they know there are a fair number of letters but only so many. One little boy, trying to learn by look-say, asked his mother how many words there are. When she replied, "Oh I don't know—thousands", he gave up. Learning to use just 26 letters is far easier than trying to guess innumerable words.

If pupils know á-b-c as "ay-bee-see", I say that this is the alphabet of letter *names* but reading uses letter *sounds* to build up words: "á, buh, kuh". "Kuh-a-tuh", for most children, blends to say "cat" but a few need the sounds without the "uh" at the end. We aim to learn at least one letter a day, although some children can absorb two, or even three, and there must be some work *every* day. This first stage is vital. My most recent printing of *Step by Step* added 24 extra pages, mostly for three-letter words formed of consonant-vowel-consonant (CVC). This easy material has only three sounds to glue together and helps to make sounding out and the left-to-right direction become automatic.

The main look-say schemes since 1945 have little or no reference to letters, sounds and blending. They are the publishers' gravy train, commercially successful but educationally not. They neglect the foundations and steer infants towards pictures and guessing, instead of to the safe phonics-first method used in *Step by Step*. Their dozen levels, each with some ten story-books, are profitable precisely *because* they keep progress very slow and extended over years.

By contrast, *Step by Step* is designed to be much quicker. Although the child must not be hurried impatiently, the overall progress is fast. This is made possible by providing a great variety at the first CVC stage—*seeing* the correct letter formation, *hearing* how to spell it, *feeling* how to write it and *practising* through supplementary exercises and games. Direct teaching is kept within the bounds of the child's attention span and extended by means of the different approaches of the games and exercises. These seem an enjoyable switch of activity but they are nevertheless revising and reinforcing what has been learned.

One exercise uses *anagrams*; it gives a picture and three jumbled letters for the pupil to write in the correct order. Or there is just the picture for the pupils to write the matching three-letter word. There is never a relevant word beneath a picture for the child to guess. Some of the work is in the form of puzzles, and children love puzzles.

When the pupils know all 26 letters, they can play more word games and exercises. One exercise uses small "*Is it?*" booklets, where they read a word on a right-hand page and then turn over to a picture on the back to see if they got it right. There is no seeing the picture first and then guessing a word below it. But after working through the booklet two or three times, they can use it back to front for spelling, by looking at the picture, writing the word and then turning back to check whether they have spelt it right.

The challenge of Fig. 20.1 is to produce as many three-letter CVC words as possible, using the vowel in the middle and any two consonants from the outer squares. The example here yields "ban", "bap", "bat", "cab", "can", "cat", "ham", "hat", "mac", "man", "map", "mat", "pan", "pat", "sap", "sat", "tan" and "tap". Then a new card gives a different set of letters to yield a new set of words, such as "hen", "peg", etc. The various versions of this puzzle and all the games are fresh every time, unlike re-read story books.

For the *bingo game*, the teacher has a set of 32 words and each child has a card with an individual selection of 16, arranged in squares, four across and four down. They also have 16 small blank squares. The teacher calls a word and the children search their cards to find it. If it is there, they cover it with one of the small blanks. There is anticipation to see who can cover a whole line first and the teacher then checks that all the covered words have been called. There are five "wins", three for the first horizontal, vertical and diagonal lines, a fourth for all the words round the outside and a fifth for a full card.

t	b	p
c	a	s
h	n	m

Fig. 20.1.

The *pairs game* is played with 52-card packs of playing card-size, either specially printed or home-made. They are made in sets of four, two for pictures of the same object and two for that object's name. For beginners 12 or 16 cards (three or four sets) are placed face down on the table and players take it in turns to pick up two. If both belong to the same set, they are shown and placed at the player's side as a trick. The player then has another turn. After eight cards have been won, eight more are taken from the pack to join those face down, while the players close their eyes, not to see where they go. If the two picked up are not a pair, they are laid back. Players try to remember where they put them so that if in a later turn they find a pair to one they have picked up previously, they can find it again to score a trick. The winner is the one who scoops the most tricks. Pairs assist reading by making it necessary to decode a word to see it if refers to the picture, or to see when two words are the same.

Another simple item is a *roller*. Using the inner cardboard cylinder of a toilet roll, I write, in a column round it, six words with a space for something missing. Then I take a strip of paper and write on it in red, either a single vowel or a letter group such as "ee", "oo", "au" or "sh", and staple the ends to make a band which is slipped over the roll and moved down to bring the red letters into the space in each word in turn. For example, to practise a short "á", I write six words on the roll with the "á" omitted, such as "c t", "r n", "h m", "f t", "h t" and "s d". As I slide the strip round, the pupil can "make" the words, "cat", "ran", "ham", "fat", "hat" and "sad", to practise blending and the short "a" sound in CVC words. I thread string through the roll and tie it, so that if the strip slips off it is not lost.

Slides and ladders is a dice-throwing game like snakes and ladders. The squares are large to accommodate words big enough for children to read easily and a space between rows gives greater clarity. Squares may be blank or contain pictures or instructions such as "Run on to a hat" or "Run back to a dog". Forward jumps are small so that players do not miss reading many instructions and fall-backs are short to avoid discouragement. Teachers may be able to devise other games, perhaps helped by craft lessons for older pupils who can make sets that will be useful and not end up in the bin a week later. Making them gives practice in measuring, precise cutting, handwriting and careful clipping round pictures from mail-order catalogues. They would also provide a sense of purpose in the work.

Games manufacturers produce materials like Stott's *Programmed Reading Kit*. My own games are available, commercially printed on fairly substantial card, which can be used again and again. I am still using some I made in 1975. They are much cheaper than the elaborate look-say reading schemes. *Step by Step* has hitherto been priced at just £5 for the complete scheme up to established reading skill, while the full set of games for each reading stage and videos cost £80. They can be used for class after class.

Many of *Step by Step's* varied activities can be whole-class and blackboard work, as different worksheets prevent copying from a neighbour. Faster pupils are kept constructively busy with the games—not just "colouring cherries red". Thus occupied, they give the teacher time to check or help the slower ones. So though quick ones go ahead with extra activities, the group is kept together at each stage and, apart from the deaf, blind and brain-damaged, no child fails. The method is safe for dyslexics, now the majority of reading strugglers, and because they keep up, they may never know that they are dyslexic.

Praise is constant throughout *Step by Step* but only if deserved. I present work to do and if pupils pay attention they can get all of it right. For strugglers who have suffered so much failure, this really matters. Nothing succeeds like success and nothing kills enthusiasm like failure. When I first meet individual strugglers of any age, I give them a 20–minute check on what they already know. Can they distinguish "b" and "d"? Do they look at all the letters? Do they realise that the "y" in "yellow" also occurs in "happy" and "fly". I do not waste time re-teaching what they know but start at a later step, to fill the gaps.

In a class, however, children knowing some or all letters do the same exercises as beginners but with more emphasis on correct letter shapes and sizes to fit the guidelines, and not pressing too hard. They can all improve in some way while the beginners catch up.

Strugglers' chief bad habit is guessing. I combat this with a long list of words laid out like the sinuous mouse-tail in *Alice in Wonderland*. When pupils read the first word, "fox", I uncover the next word "fix" and ask, "Which letter have I changed?" This directs attention to the individual letters and slows down the fast guess. Only when they have identified the changed letter do I let them say the whole word. Then I expose the next word, "six", and so on.

This is an exercise they can get completely right if they slow down and think what they are doing. And at this stage they can read the early Primary Phonics storybooks.

Stages 27–35: Blending Consonants

When the CVC stage is firmly established, pupils move on to blending more than one consonant together, to create four-letter words such as "crab" with a blend at the beginning or "vest" with a blend at the end. Some children take this in their stride and hardly notice the progression. It leads on to words such as "crust", with blends both fore and aft, and eventually to words of more than one syllable, if they still have just one letter per sound as in "hospital".

More advanced games and exercises keep pace with the reading range (Fig. 20.2) and there are also *Make-a-word* boxes of letters, a few sentences to read, with a spelling follow-up, e.g. Pam drinks a glass of m - - - , and some "Yes/No" questions.

These lessons — developing an automatic left-to-right direction, concentrating on each letter, sounding out, listening to the sounding, *not guessing*, and learning new words all the time, constitute the first third of learning to read.

Steps 36-62: Digraphs

In Step 36 I explain that the 26 letters of the alphabet are not enough for the 52 sounds in English, so some are shown by two. Two "e"s saying "ee" is simple but "oo" needs two columns, for the short sound in "book" and the long sound in "food".

p	nt	mp
f	a	st
l	c	r

pant
past
fast
last
cast
lamp
camp
ramp
stamp

Fig. 20.2: A slightly more advanced version of Fig. 20.1.

For "sh", "th" and "ch", I remind the children that "h is the blowy letter". I blow on my hand for an unvoiced "h" and they do the same. Then I present "sh" as in "hush" and "th" and again they feel the blow. For "th" I give two short lists, one for the voiced sound ("this", "them" and "the") and the other for the unvoiced sound ("bath", "think" and "thunder") and they put a hand against their throats to feel the tremble with the former and its absence with the latter.

For "ch" I sneeze and they copy, feeling the rush of air on their hands. "Ch" words have three columns, one for word beginnings ("chin" and "chop"), one for ends ("much" and "rich"), and one for "tch" ("fetch", "match" and "stitch"). The written work for these digraphs is a listening exercise. From a picture of a fish, the children have to hear the "sh" sound and then write the word in the "sh" column. This gives them practice in listening, writing and spelling.

By now my pupils are accustomed to the pattern of the lessons. They learn a new letter group and do one or two examples of an exercise, which they take home to complete. Then they finish with a game. The programme is cumulative. The games become more demanding as their reading skill advances. For bingo I use more advanced words, for example, the names of football teams, towns, countries, cooking ingredients, flowers, trees, simple boys' and girls' names, and names with soft "c" and "g" and the Greek "ph" and "ch". (Oddly, a bingo with pop-group names fell flat!).

In the most advanced pairs game (Packs 11 and 12), one words in each pair is in capitals and the other in lower case. And more cards are put face down at the start. I also have different slides and ladders games for each reading stage.

The established lesson pattern is next applied to letter groups formed by adding "r" to a short vowel: "ar", "er", "ir", "or" and "ur". Then I introduce the "magic e" to show that when it comes at the end of a word it changes each short vowel sound to a long vowel sound, e.g. "cap/cape", "them/theme", "pin/pine", "rob/robe", and "cub/cube".

Many schemes omit the "e-consonant-e" as it is rarer than "ee", but it does occur, e.g. "eve", "these", "serene", "extreme", "compete" and "complete".

Steps 63-70: Hard and Soft "c" and "g"

Soft "c" and "g" are omitted from some supposed phonics schemes. The rules are clear but pupils have become so used to hard "c" and "g" in the earlier steps, that changing to the soft sounds, "s" and "j", needs a lot of practice. And these spellings are found in many "grown-up" words — unfamiliar vocabulary for a young child.

The soft sound "s" occurs in the letter name "c" and the soft sound "j" in the name "g". Both these consonants have their soft pronunciations if they are directly followed by the vowels "e", "i" or "y", e.g. "ice", "city", "fancy" and "gentle", "gipsy", "energy". If the pupils can understand the reasons for the spellings "lack", "lake", "lace", "lacking" and "lacing", and similar differences with "g", they are doing well. I usually leave it at that but give four pages of written work for soft sounds. There are a few words where "ge", "gi" and "gy" have to be broken apart by inserting a "u" to keep the "g" hard, for example, "guess", "guitar" and "guy".

Steps 71-75: "Ou" and "Au"

These steps illustrate the rule that the only English word to end in "u" is "you". Others are foreign borrowings. When the sound in "cloud" comes at the end of a word, it is spelt "ow", as in "cow". Similarly, when the sound in Paul comes at the end it is spelt "aw" as in "claw". But "ow" and "aw" can be used in mid-word as well, e.g. "owl" and "lawn". "Ou" and "ow" can also say other sounds such as short "u" in "cousin" or long "o" in snow" or "yellow".

Pupils can now see from *Step by Step* that there are only a few more letter groups to learn, so the games are no longer needed for motivation. Most are ready to read short stories with large print and good line spacing. I use the *Trog* series and James Webster's *Shorty* books.

Steps 76-96: Foreign Influences

When the Vikings came to England, their language had a gutteral sound made in the back of the throat and spelt "gh". The Anglo-Saxons could not pronounce it, so although they kept the spelling, they left the sound out, or in a few words they turned it into a more pronounceable "f". The silent "gh" might be the end of a word as in "high", or it might be followed by "t", sounded as if the "gh" did not occur, as in "light". The "igh" is one way of spelling long "i" but only in a few words.

Inserting "ei" makes the long "a" sound, as in "weigh" or "eight". Inserting "au" makes the ordinary "au" sound, as in "caught", but has an exception in "laugh" and "laughter". But when "ou" is inserted, the fun begins, as "ough" can say seven different things. Two of them reflect Anglo-Saxons' efforts not to leave "gh" silent. They translated it into what they thought was the nearest sound in their own language: "f", but they did not always stick to the same vowel in front of it. So we have either "-off" or "-uff", as in "cough" or "tough". Sometimes they left it silent but sounded a different vowel: "ow" as in "bough", "oh" as in "dough" and also the "er" sound in "thorough". In just one word, "through", it is an "oo", and when it is followed by "t", it is sounded like "au", as in "bought", and "fought".

The multiplicity of "ough" pronunciations is used by look-say protagonists to "prove" that phonics does not work. But in *Step by Step* children do not meet "gh" until they are 80% of the way through learning to read, so although it is a hard challenge, they have then become confident enough to work at it. And there are actually very few words with this spelling.

From French we have inherited a few unusual pronunciations, such as "sh" for "ch", as in "machine" or "chute"; "een" for "ine", as in "Pauline" or "marine" and "k" for "que", as in "antique" or "oblique". From Greek, we have the use of "ph" for "f", as in "elephant" or "phantom", and "ch" pronounced "k", as in "echo" or "school". Some foreign words break the English rule of not ending in "i", "j", "q", "u" or "v", for example, "ski", "raj", "menu" or "Slav".

Though English uses the Roman Alphabet, it has three more letters than Latin. One, "w", creates irregular effects. It was pronounced "v" where the Anglo-Saxons came from but they did not get their tongues round an initial "vr" sound for "wr", so although they left "w" in the spelling, they omitted it in speech and sounded only the "r". "Rong" is the wrong spelling but the right pronunciation for "wrong".

"W", including the "w" sound in "qu", affects the sound of "a", "ar" and "or", if they immediately follow it. Short "a" is pronounced as short "o", as in "was", "swamp", "twaddle" and "squat". The digraph "ar" turns into "au", as in "war", "dwarf", and "quarter", while "or" is sounded as "er", as in "word" and "worth".

Steps 97–100: Four Miscellaneous Spelling Rules

1. "-ti" as in "initial" and words ending in "-tion"
2. The suffix "ture"
3. The rule "i" before "e" and its exceptions: (i) after "c"; (ii) when "ei" is not pronounced "ee", as in "rein" and "leisure"
4. The prefixes "be", "de" and "re"

The spellings taught in *Step by Step* enable pupils to take off and read books at their own level of interest, absorbing new words and widening their vocabulary through reading.

All these steps and activities are designed to prevent guessing, sight-word memorisation, boredom, failure and other miseries. The use of phonics is a far cry from Schonell's description of it as "deadly drill . . as dull as ditchwater". It is purposeful, intensive and satisfying, and it boosts the child's self-esteem. The variety of activities extends the span of attention happily and an hour's lesson flies by. Thousands of children have been taught to read using *Step by Step* and its phonics method. The essence is sounding out, blending and grading. It shows that learning to read does not have to be rocket science, and there is no cheaper scheme.

The *Step by Step* book includes an exposé of the myths propagated by Progressivism and the resulting widespread illiteracy epidemic. It has references for further reading and a list of helpful material, such as the related games and DVDs (See Appendix 2).

Chapter 21

Truly Objective Testing

We have seen how standards plummeted during Progressivism's ban on testing and also how restored testing has been overdone by the subversives to the point of sickening people against it and paving the way for abolition of tests at ages seven and eleven. This is a devious approach to throwing the baby out with the bathwater, so we clearly need a better way ahead for testing as well as teaching. The complex overkill of recent years should be replaced by a more streamlined system that is honest and fair, sensible and effective, educationally informative and capable of relieving both teacher stress and pupil stress.

This chapter presents our proposal for the improved testing of reading ability in the light of these various desiderata. A similarly simplified numeracy test could also be devised but that is not within the remit of this book.

Stable Standards

Both the content of the test and the system of marking it should remain at the same standard each year to avoid the misleading effect of grade inflation. This poses a double challenge, continuity with the past and continuity into the future.

Only existing tests can provide continuity with the past but we have seen that their results can be flawed and also that their variety prevents any valid comparison of different areas. We therefore recommend that each school should retain its existing reading test purely to give in-house information in relation to the past, and use a new, foolproof national test as a basis for future league tables.

We propose a new literacy test after two years of schooling, the period needed for pure, untainted, synthetic phonics to make readers for life of all children in ordinary schools. The blind and profoundly deaf would be in their own special schools, and brain-damaged children are very rare. We should no longer be satisfied with the low aim of bringing only 75% up to standard and failing the other 25%. Dyslexia would be no problem as phonics does not activate it into illiteracy.

Now that children start school at age four instead of age five, the test could take place at age six. The earlier illiteracy is detected, the more easily it is remedied, and any school that does not achieve a complete success rate should be carefully inspected for lingering look-say methods and incompetent Sharon-Shrill teachers.

A Simple Spelling Test

Testing should no longer steal forty hours of teaching time for recording 117 aspects of each child's personality. Most of these are probings related to social engineering and can be dropped forthwith, while the genuinely educational ones — listening, reading, writing and spelling — can be integrated into a simple spelling test.

The test words would be dictated orally, thus ensuring the need to listen with care. The answers would have to be written down, so legible writing would be required, as also would correct spelling. Reading would be tested indirectly, as poor readers would not be able to translate spoken words into their letters and spell them correctly.

Fairness

A simple spelling test could be made rigorously fair. Writing down dictated words would eliminate scope for the chance underlining of correct alternatives, so every mark would be honestly earned. Children taught by look-say would be penalised by words not on their flash-card list but those taught by synthetic phonics would be able to use their systematic strategy for tackling unknown words and representing their sounds by letters. Thus, the test would yet again highlight the superiority of true phonics and help to spread it as the most effective way to teach reading.

Another aspect of fairness would be the grading of the test words in strict order of difficulty, so that if children spell correctly up to the nth word, it can reasonably be assumed that they are able to spell most words up to that level. This would be true of pupils taught by Mona McNee's *Step by Step*, which has carefully formulated gradations, but it would not be true for look-say pupils. They might know "elephant" and "aeroplane", which are taught early for their distinctive shapes, but still be completely flummoxed by much simpler words that they have not specifically learned.

To assist the choice of correctly graded words, Alice Coleman is preparing a handbook entitled *Streamlined Spelling*. It follows *Step by Step's* order of progressively greater difficulty so if the test words were always drawn from the same specified sets, they could be different each year but maintain the same standard over time.

Teaching For The Test

Teaching just the test words (illicitly obtained) is cheating and gives a false impression that pupils have also mastered all similar ones. But teaching *for* the test is quite different and a legitimate part of the teacher's role. Those using *Step by Step* and *Streamlined Spelling* would be equipping their pupils to spell many words that they have never encountered but which follow the same straightforward rules as those they have met and can therefore be accurately written down from dictation. For example, there are 300 three-letter words with a short vowel between two regular consonants, which are easy for a well-taught child to work out correctly.

Streamlined Spelling explains each rule and illustrates it with many words. Those suited to tests at age six are asterisked. Others could be suitable for older ones. The book is too solid for child learners to study directly as it might intimidate them but it can help teachers' and parents' preparation. It would not cut corners but be basic education, and could be tackled by older secondary pupils.

Test Impartiality

Teachers should not have to produce test results that could condemn their own competence. Nor should the word list be lodged in the school beforehand. All suspicion of cribbing would be avoided if external examiners brought it with them on the test day.

There are some 22,400 state and independent schools with six-year-olds and if there is more than one class of that age, they could be jointly tested in the school hall. If each external tested two schools a day, the ideal of having all testing on the same day would need 11,198 examiners. However, if tests were spread over four days, the number would be 2,800 — a manageable average of 24 for each local education area.

The examiners could include all inspectors regardless of their subject specialisms. An advertisement could invite retired teachers and others to apply, and after winnowing out applicants making spelling errors, the likely ones could attend an LEA centre for spelling and voice tests. Any misspelling would disqualify them and they should be able to speak clearly and audibly in a large school hall. Those accepted would not need subsequent retesting and only replacements would be checked. There should also be a few extras to cover for cases of illness.

Test Administration

Where two or more classes take the test together, they would use the school hall and also have a mock test there so that the children would not be distracted by unfamiliar conditions on the day. A sample word list could be issued for the first year's rehearsal but thereafter the previous year's test list would be available.

Test-setting would be streamlined. Words would be chosen from pre-scribed parts of the source, each with a very brief context sentence or defi-nition. This would be much quicker than a completely open choice of sentences to read, which involves a great deal of conferring on phrasing, choice of alternative words for underlining, the design of layout and illus-trations for the test paper, and arrangements for printing individual cop-ies for all the children being tested. The envisaged list could be typed on a single page and copies given to each examiner.

The schools would prepare answer papers headed by code numbers for the school and class, plus each child's name and date of birth, with a list of numbers from 1 to 25 at the beginning of successive lines where the answers are to be written. The code numbers, names and dates could be supplied in advance to the test marking centre, to be entered in a computer file with the birth date translated into months of age at the test date. That should be as late in the school year as possible to allow maximum time for teaching and learning.

The externals would meet on Monday of the test week to collect the sealed test paper and practise the procedure. For each item the examiner would say the question number, the test word, a short context sentence and the test word again, e.g. Number 1 [pause] "had" [pause] "I had a birthday surprise" [pause] "had".

They should speak in standard English but with some acknowledge-ment of local accents, e.g. a short "a" in words such as "grass" for schools in the north. Hard-of-hearing children would sit in front. Deaf ones would receive the words in sign language and blind children would answer in Braille, both deaf and blind in their own schools. Testers should ensure that all the children have finished writing before going on to the next word.

The testing would occupy Tuesday to Friday of the test week and scripts would be taken straight to the test centre on each day. The school would retain photocopies, to guide correction of children's mistakes and also act as a check if inaccurate marking is suspected.

Communal marking would begin the following Monday, awarding one mark for each correct answer out of the 25 and quadrupling the total to give a score out of 100. Each script would take no more than one minute to mark, so some schools' results could be entered into the computer as early as the first day and printed out to send to the head with a request to raise any objections by return.

After any corrections the computer could calculate average ages and median scores for each class, school and wider area. The arithmetic mean is a suitable average for the ages but not for the scores, because they are

ordinal data, i.e. it is not possible to establish whether the increasing difficulty is of exactly the same amount between all successive pairs of words.
For ordinal data, the appropriate average is the median, the mark of the
middle child, halfway between the top and bottom of the total list. The
median is not distorted by any exceptionally high or low mark, nor
affected significantly by any zeros accorded to absentees.

Class medians would enable head teachers to pick out weaker classes
and probe how far how far the differences reflect pupils' ages and intelligence, or the method or quality of the teaching. The school's median could
be compared with those of other schools, and ultimately with the national
median. Inspectors would also have more precise information as to failing
schools, which they could then check for any adherence to the inferior
look-say method.

Research

Merging spelling results in a national data bank would produce more
accurate league tables than at present and also facilitate two pieces of
major research. Firstly, the medians of individual classes could be related
to the teaching methods used. This might be possible only during a very
restricted time slot, as if synthetic phonics came to be used universally, the
evidence on look-say, etc., would become unavailable.

The kind of methodological information needed initially is shown in the
questionnaire below. It would give more precise data than the crude and
useless four categories in the Bullock Report. Different methods may have
varied with successive class teachers, so a complete picture of influences
would need separate forms filled in by all who have taught the class before
the time of the six-year-old test. The influences may have been varied and
complex, so a highly skilled researcher would be needed to formulate a
classification for computer use. Where there is a high teacher turnover it
may be impossible to secure data from all concerned, and these cases
should be analysed in a category of their own.

Some research results could be obtained very quickly, for example, how
many schools use each reading scheme, either exclusively or as part of a
mixed method system. Key findings would be the medians achieved by
schools using exclusive methods, how these aggregate to a national
median, and how that median compares with the overall national median
to be obtained from all the test results.

Methodology Questionnaire

School Code Number - - - - - - - - - Class Code Number - - - - - - - - - - -

1. Do you use a phonic method at any stage?   Yes/No
    If yes, go to Question 2. If no, go to Question 5.

2. Do you use phonemic awareness, analytical phonics or synthetic
    phonics? Delete the type(s) you do not use.

3. Which phonics reading scheme(s) do you use?- - - - - - - - - - - - - - - - - -

4. When do you introduce phonics?
      (a) Right at the start?   - - - - -
      (b) After a number of sight words?   - - - - -
      (c) After sight words and sentences?   - - - - -
      (d) Later   - - - - -

5. If you use initial sight words, how many do you use?   - - - - -
    Please append a list of these on the back of this page.

6. When do you introduce sound-blending?
      (a) Along with the letters right from the start?   - - - - -

      (b) After the whole alphabet has been learned?   - - - - -

      (c) After some but not all letters? How many?   - - - - -

      (d) Not at all   - - - - -

7. How long does it take for children to learn the whole alphabet?

    - - - - - weeks   - - - - - months   - - - - - terms

8. How long is it before children can read all CVC words?

    - - - - - weeks   - - - - - months   - - - - - terms

9. If you use any of the following methods, mark them 1, 2, 3, etc., in
    order of importance.
      (a) Look-say/whole word   - - - - -
      (b) Paired reading   - - - - -
      (c) Shared reading   - - - - -
      (d) Apprenticeship   - - - - -
      (e) Reading recovery   - - - - -
      (f) Real books   - - - - -
      (g) Other non-phonics? -

10. How long does your preferred method or mix of methods take before
      (a) The majority can read?   - - - - -
      (b) All can read?   - - - - -

11. How many children are there in your class?   - - - - -

12. How many special-needs children are there in your class? - - - - -

13. How many children could read before starting school?   - - - - -

A second research aim would use the computer data to establish standard new spelling ages (SAs), on the same principle as reading ages (RAs). This investigation should take five years after the introduction of universal synthetic phonics teaching, to ensure that the rising standard due to phonics efficiency has stabilised.

The data base for the six-year-old test would allow identification of national median scores for each monthly age group: 5.11, 6.0, 6.1, etc. Knowing individuals' scores would indicate their spelling ages and these could be related to their chronological ages, to show whether they are ahead, backward or average. Spelling age (SA) can be divided by chronological age (CA) and multiplied by 100 to obtain a spelling quotient (SQ) in the same way as the reading quotient (RQ).

$$\frac{SA}{CA} \times 100 = SQ$$

SQ 100 would mean average spelling ability and higher or lower scores would give precise indications of how far children were shooting ahead or lagging behind.

As spelling ages would be established only for six-year-olds, some children might be off the scale, either at the top (splendid!) or the bottom (a cause for concern). The reason for researching over five years is that the first phonics spelling testees would have reached age eleven and a further test then could extend the spelling-age scale, based on the scores of those taught purely by synthetic phonics from the start.

Relief of Stress

The proposed test would relieve teacher stress in two ways. The obvious one would be relief from the burden of recording 117 items about each child and relinquishing the testing task to external examiners. The preparation of spelling answer forms and photo-copying the completed scripts would be done by the school secretary, and teachers would only have to fill in the methodological questionnaire above, for the one year before the synthetic phonics method became universal. This arrangement would release a great deal of tedious pen-pushing time and allow teachers to concentrate on the professional work that originally attracted them into the profession.

Less obvious is the fact that stress can change from negative frustration to positive stimulation when one can do something constructive to resolve it. Today's teachers often find reading problems insoluble but switching to synthetic phonics would be constructive, rewarding the teacher with higher literacy levels. And *Streamlined Spelling* would be a sourcebook for the spelling rules needed to excel in the test.

The blossoming expertise of both teachers and children would make test results depend much more on the children's different abilities and less on teaching defects, so the stressful elements of blame and anxiety would be removed from teachers.

Children's stress would also be alleviated, as the *Step by Step* approach spares them the pressure of trying to run before they can walk. It does not ask for free composition before they can read fluently, so they do not experience the constant setback of wanting to use words they cannot spell. Instead, they write short, humorous passages dictated to them to reinforce what they have just learned and get them right. These dictations also function as frequent mini-tests that inoculate them against test anxiety. And less anxious teachers also communicate a less stressful attitude.

Children can be told not to worry if they cannot spell all the test words, as some are for older children. This allows high fliers to show their paces while removing the stigma from those who fail to score full marks. Test-consciousness could be restricted to less than one hour each for the practice run and the actual test. There would be no suspenseful wait for results as teachers could mark their classes' scripts in half an hour or so, and pursue corrections in the next spelling lesson, while the externally marked results would not take much longer. And children would gain confidence from being able to read and from practising the graded spellings needed for the test.

The league tables would still show some schools well ahead and some in the tail. But the tail would no longer be shameful, as the present dreadful illiteracy rate would have been shed and the worst schools would not be so very far below average.

Economy

The cost of this kind of testing vis-à-vis the present system would have to be explored but there would be clear savings in the setting, printing and postage of test papers. The substitution of one six-year-old test for the present two — one on entry and the other at age seven — would also be an economy. The army of external examiners would be an expense but only for a brief period each year. There would be relatively few full-time salaries for peak and slack times alike and a great saving in the permanent overheads of office space: heating, lighting, cleaning, redecoration, repairs, etc. And as the testers would largely be inspectors, retired people or the self-employed, there would be no call for employers' contributions towards national insurance or superannuation, nor for sick pay or holiday pay. Travel expenses would mostly be for short distances.

There would also be many indirect savings after removal of the stress inherent in the present testing overload, such as lower rates of teacher absences and staff turnover.

Conclusion

The testing method advocated here is radically different from the current one and should solve all the latter's problems. It would bring into play the paper and pencil tests that were envisaged at the outset of the struggle for reform and make only a brief incursion into the year's educational work. The test would cease to be a massive bundle of oddments but would substitute integrated literacy fundamentals, and give teachers a clear target for this vital foundation.

Other advantages would be systematic records of attainment standards, fully comparable over area and over time, made possible by fair and accurate assessment using logically graded test questions delivered in a tamper-proof way. Teachers would be relieved of their stressful overload and pupil stress would also be avoided.

Chapter 22

Restoring Order

There are five main reasons for the breakdown of discipline. Two are architectural, bred by the stranglehold of Modern Movement design, two are educational, bred by the stranglehold of Progressivism and the fifth is the effect of junk-food.

Architectural Influence in the Home

Behaviour, like character, is mainly formed during the first few years of life and children in the misery estates designed by Modern Movement architects, are subject to multiple assaults upon their early development. They are exposed to many models of bad behaviour and may be forced into allegiance to estate bullies or delinquents, while parents are robbed of essential design aids to good child rearing. For example, fenced and gated front gardens train children to walk along the footpath and not trespass into other people's property, but communal greens directly abutting ground-floor flats afford no concept of trespass. They may encourage knocking at doors and running away, peering through windows, and breaking in to burgle. Other defective designs also inhibit growth of a healthy social structure.

There are up to 16 design defects in blocks of flats, 12 in houses and 10 in other aspects, such as parking provision or refuse storage. The more there are, the worse the hooliganism and crime. Even in the same estate, blocks with fewer design defects have better socialised children and less crime than those with more. The Broadwater Farm Estate, where a tenant mob murdered a policeman, had worse design than Alice Coleman has seen anywhere else.

Design affects how many families go off the rails. Parental strength or weakness varies and worse design means a worse cut-off point in parental control, with more children succumbing to yobbishness. Alice Coleman's DICE Project redesigned nine horrendous estates and achieved a large immediate drop in crime, because the changes enabled residents to create a better social structure naturally.

Schools serving bad estates find school starters much more difficult to manage than those from well designed houses. The problems have been ascribed to socio-economic factors but the true cause is misconceived architecture – a finding that gives rise to optimism, because bad design is much easier to change than socio-economic conditions, and design improvement has demonstrated that the anti-social effects are reversible.

Design improvement needs investment up front, but more than pays for itself as it creates cost savings in 13 areas of government expenditure, including education. It was on an estate redesigned by DICE that the primary school head found the children's behaviour noticeably better. Discipline improved, teacher stress decreased and there was scope for achieving higher standards. The tenants were freed from the miseries of loutism, crime and a sense of parental failure. There are multiple reasons why there should be massive design improvement throughout the country. The government owes it to the residents themselves, who have been victimized by official Modern Movement planning and also to all the other victims of its ramifying ill-effects, as well as to taxpayers forced to subsidise all these evils.

Architectural Influence in the School

The second architectural obstacle to good discipline is the fact that school buildings often embody the same Modernist mistakes as the misery estates. Andrew Smith's study of 763 state schools in Kent identified 17 harmful design and layout features, mostly the equivalent of those that had been proved damaging in housing. His test measures were the incidence and cost of theft/burglary, criminal damage and fire, and, as already mentioned, schools are the Number One target for arson.

Modernism seems to breed such arrogance among its practitioners that they ignore common sense. A school caretaker, formerly a police officer in the Royal Marines, explained how the architect of his school disregarded a dozen agreed safeguards. He left pipes exposed instead of behind walls and, as predicted, the boys stood on them and bent them. He placed a sash window above a catslide, although asked to avoid ways for pupils to get on to the roof. He gave the engineering room an ordinary door, despite a request for a double one to admit large machines, which had to be dismantled to get them in. He created spaces between staircases and walls after being asked not to, because pupils would drop litter through the gap. And he did precisely what was not wanted by putting entrances to pairs of classrooms in a deep narrow recess where streams of pupils coming and going physically clashed. At just six weeks old, this grimy school looked ready for major refurbishment.

Smith's advice for schools echoes that for housing, stressing that "small is beautiful". The crime-free 42% of schools did not exceed 400 on roll for primaries and 700 for secondaries. Small size helps discipline because all the staff know all the children, who cannot use anonymity to shield them from the consequences of bad behaviour. It also means a lout is less likely to have allies to back him up than in a large school, and is therefore more likely to accept the rules of good conduct.

Schools are larger than homes and have to be shared but the ideal is just one building, so that children cannot lurk out of sight among an irregular scatter of blocks that screen the activities of graffitists, vandals and bullies. Nor should there be an elaborate ground plan of wings and bays that also screen anti-social behaviour. Andrew Smith measured this latter feature by counting the number of outside walls between changes of direction, and discovered that they ranged up to 100 in a single building. In the language of the architects, this directional complexity is intended to avoid "blandness" but it blithely disregards the discipline problems it creates.

Some LEAs are still increasing school size; one London Borough recently closed ten large secondary schools and created four monster ones. As well as multiplying discipline problems, this increased journey-to-school distances at a time when the government was urging that children should walk to school.

We have mentioned the counter-trend that is now developing, of establishing small new independent schools to provide a low-cost market niche for parents seeking higher standards and better discipline within their budgets. For example, the New Model School Company now plans ten new schools in London as part of its projected national network.

We advocate that state schools should reduce excess size by selling mobile classrooms for off-site use by new independents and walling off some on-site buildings to form small new schools accessed from a different street. Once existing state schools are left smaller, their other design defects would be easier to tackle. A system of vouchers, cashable at state or independent schools alike, would help provide the spur of competition and highlight the design defects that need to be changed.

Margaret Thatcher launched design improvement by sponsoring Alice Coleman's DICE Project but Labour boycotted her work. Michael Howard, as Leader of the Opposition, was interested but not returned to power, so at present only local councils can make architectural inroads into indiscipline.

The Role of Phonics Teaching

We need to conquer illiteracy so that all children can enjoy school satisfaction instead of humiliation and resentment. Synthetic phonics gives all children a sense of reading progress and equips them for further scholastic achievement—a powerful factor in winning good-conduct co-operation. We need say no more.

Discipline in the Infant School

The Progressivist concept that self-discipline is better for children than discipline by adults is a complete fallacy. Children do not know intuitively how to behave well and must be taught. Letting them roam round the classroom and chat to others unchecked does not teach them to concentrate on learning and can waste over half their time. It also presents school as a place where they can do as they please, so that they see subsequent disciplinary effort as criticism and punishment. Then, especially if they are failing to read, they may become frustrated and antagonistic. The seeds of unruliness have been sown.

Reception-class teachers should recognize the trouble they may be laying up for later colleagues if they fail to create a calm, co-operative atmosphere right from the start. They should oust the false idea that children are socialized by their peers and listen to psychologists who find that there is better maturation in the company of adults. Teachers' influence should pass civilisation down the generations.

The Plowden Report gave official blessing to the time-wasting class layout of separate in-facing groups, and we now need the better alternative that has the whole class facing the teacher.

Infants have very short attention spans, for good physiological reasons. A change of focus diverts the blood flow to a different part of the brain and assists its balanced development. So every day's teaching programme should include a sufficient variety of mental and physical pursuits to promote whole-brain health. However, this variety should not involve simultaneous demands upon the left and right brain hemispheres, which would cancel each other out and result in non-progress, as so often happens with the look-say method. It is one of the benefits of Mona McNee's *Step by Step* reading scheme that it keeps the reading lesson going on for an hour by varying the types of left-brain activity that are brought into play.

It is desirable to leave space for physical activity at the front of the infant school classroom and this can be achieved by arranging two rows of tables round three sides of a square, i.e. along the left, back and right sides of the room. The tables should be for individual reading, writing, number work and artwork, and not for lazy riding on the coat-tails of others in a group. The children must be kept too busily engaged to play up and not left at a loose end for idle chatter. For older children, it is better to have single desks one behind the other and interspersed with gangways, as this cuts out the temptation to talk illicitly with another pupil sharing the same table.

It is important to make pupils feel that they are being drawn into a friendly place. With small classes there can be a smiling "Good morning, X", for each one as they file in, and training to respond with a smiling "Good morning, (teacher's name)".

Pupils and parents should know the school rules, such as not speaking without raising one's hand to be chosen, and not leaving one's seat without permission. Some schools ask parents to sign an agreement before accepting their children.

Ongoing encouragement comes from friendly words and gold stars for good work and good conduct. Praise is essential but must be deserved. The Progressivist ploy of indiscriminate approval must be halted. It is unfair to praise false information as true, to let careless work pass muster and to reward bad conduct. These attitudes "educate" children to do all the wrong things instead of equipping them for success and fulfilment, and they generate stress later through incompetence in the workplace.

When children do wrong they should be corrected but without damaging their self-esteem. They need to know why such conduct is unacceptable and shown a constructive way to do better. Sitting them by themselves for a while to think it over may help. One bully-gang leader was horrified to learn that her behaviour was bullying and her interval of solitude showed her she had no real power without her cronies. She resolved to be nicer to other children in future. Such a volte-face is rare but younger children are often responsive to being asked whether they would rather have a gold star, or how they themselves would feel if to "be-done-by-as-you-did". There is no need to make a big meal out of a lapse from grace, nor should it be referred to again.

Leaving misconduct unchecked is also bad for the rest of the class. Children are great imitators and if unruly conduct is left on show and not controlled, it may become a spreading infection. This is especially important for those school starters from problem estates who have not been socialized during their formative years.

A few extreme extraverts cannot respond to simple admonition and a spanked hand may be the most constructive way to help them. For older ones the cane may need to be restored, as less damaging and more effective than constant futile nagging.

Over and above the technical approaches, we urge a return to the religious background that played an important part in creating good behaviour in the past. Many parents have demonstrated a wish for this by seeking to enrol their children in church schools. At present the church would need financial help to establish enough schools to meet the demand, but there is no reason why government funding should not be directed to giving that choice instead of being restricted to purely secular establishments. In the long run it would prove a public saving as it would help prevent many of the behavioural and criminal problems that are a cost to the state.

Eliminating Junk Food

So far we have referred to normal bad behaviour and will now take more serious cases. One that is easily manageable is the behavioural effect of junk food This can be cured by healthy menus for school dinners.

In 2005, chef Jamie Oliver, launched a crusade to use his own dietetically balanced recipes in school dinners. Cafeteria junk food would be replaced by cooked meals with healthy nutrients and junk would be banned from school vending machines. Fizzy drinks are a leading junk element and Yorkshire Water is installing water coolers in every primary school in its area, so that children can quench their thirst without having to buy a drink. During the upwave water fountains were automatically present.

Oliver's initiative evoked enthusiasm from the media and also by Ruth Kelly, but not always from pupils. It must be resolved *which* foods are junk, as some formerly so labelled have since been exculpated. The question was raised as to whether better school food can offset the effect of continuing junk at home, but there is proof that it can. Menus by the chef of the Savoy Hotel had already been used in one Hertfordshire school for four years, where they led to rapid, sustained improvement in conduct and also in exam marks. Nor did the pupils rebel, so it could be constructive to compare his menus with Jamie Oliver's.

Elsewhere, a fish-oil supplement so transformed an 11-year-old's conduct and concentration that the head participated in a scientific trial. Teachers said the oil improved memory and made reading progress much faster than in the control group. Pupils no longer gave up in the face of slight obstacles but persevered and achieved. Dietary improvement should be required immediately in all schools, to put a stop to much unruly conduct without the unpleasantness of censure and punishment.

Progressivism's Tearaway Legacy

After 60 years of Progressivism there is much aggressiveness that resists simple measures. A BBC programme, *The Tiny Tearaways,* showed a child psychiatrist diagnosing and curing the problems of violent children by addressing their parents' defective behaviour, but that does not let Progressivism off the hook, because its effect upon former pupils has produced poor parents.

Perhaps educational psychologists could be trained by *The Tiny Tearaways* psychiatrist, to use her technique in infant schools, so that little children are not punished for their victimization by bad parents but can benefit from a change of regime at home. Similarly, victims of look-say teachers who react aggressively should not be severely punished without first changing to synthetic phonics. If, however, gentle methods prove inadequate because too much damage has already been done, then a real deterrent is needed to stop them from going from bad to worse and sink-ing into the irredeemable "I'm OK, You're Not OK" mode. The cane formerly prevented this worst-case scenario and the role of isolation will be discussed later.

One helpful approach in difficult schools is a ban on items that support unruliness and if they are brought from home, they should be taken away at the entrance, preferably by the school policeman if there is one. Sources of noise distraction, including mobile phones, should not be allowed in the classroom and many London schools have banned them. Knives and guns should be confiscated with a threat of prosecution, since the law does not allow them to be carried. A sniffer dog could be used to detect pupils with drugs, which should also be confiscated, and these culprits should be kept in isolation away from other children for fear of spreading the drug habit.

Hoodies are another problem that leapt into prominence in 2005. Hooded coats concealing the face were hooligans' answer to closed circuit television surveillance, as they made the perpetrators unidentifiable. One big store banned hoodies from entering and found it attracted significantly more customers when these menacing figures were absent. At least one school followed suit.

Passing to more extreme problems, we note a Dutch solution applied to tearaway families who were wrecking their own flats and creating havoc for other tenants. When they were moved out into a group of indestructible steel houses, they settled down peaceably and did not impinge upon the apprehensive households nearby. This seems to be a DICE-type solution, showing the superiority of single-family homes over shared apartment blocks and it has attracted interest in British housing circles. There might also be an application in schools.

We recall the excluded boy who was recycled into another school where he ruined his classmates' education for a whole year. This should never be allowed to happen and failing commitment to an improved Medway-type unit, one or two solitude cells within the school might be the answer. Schools might find it safer to have rather larger classes and one or two supernumerary teachers to deal with problem pupils individually, leaving them for periods to work by themselves. Even when the teacher is present for instruction, (s)he should simply walk out if the pupil begins to play up. The teaching priority would usually be synthetic phonics to help restore confidence in education and provide scope for earning privileges and a trial return to the classroom.

Another advantage of the solitude solution is that the culprit is not on show, attracting imitators and extending the indiscipline. Nor need it occasion constant carping and blame. It must be emphasized that the aim is to help these youngsters develop better self-esteem by commending more mature behaviour when they make greater efforts.

Future secure units like Medway are still needed for those already severely criminalized, and they could be built with indestructible steel rooms for individuals. The current prison philosophy keeps inmates interacting with others, as they will need to socialize after their release, but this is putting them into bad company, just what good parents try to avoid, and they teach each other even worse forms of crime and violence, as well as conspiring to supply drugs in prison.

Instead, they should gradually work up to interaction after a preliminary taming period. As they are mostly extraverts, they would hate being alone, and initial solitude might be just the thing to make them realize the seriousness of their behaviour.

Each one-man room would be equipped for its inmate to sleep, bathe, eat and be taught. He would quickly come to value the teacher's advent as a diversion and co-operate in learning, because otherwise (s)he would walk out and leave him alone again. Teaching him to read could engage his interest in suitable books, and as his attitude changed, he could graduate to a class of two, and then more, and also to eating in the canteen, as well as assisting in the vegetable garden, the kitchen or other aspects of maintenance required for the establishment. This approach would defer interaction until the inmates have passed out of the stage of infecting each other with even worse intentions than they had when first committed to the secure unit.

They would need daily exercise but again they could start alone and graduate to something more sociable, as their behaviour merited. It might be a while before they could join a group big enough to play football, but that would be something to aim for.

The scheme of privileges should be carefully graded and the grades should be known to each inmate to enable him to see how he is increasingly rewarded in logical accordance with his improvement in behaviour and work. This would make a constructive impression upon him and afford opportunities at each stage for the praise that increases self-esteem and reinforces good conduct. The present system has a more negative focus on withholding privileges as a punishment for lapses, when recrimination undermines self-esteem. Backsliding in a positively graded system would probably be rarer and any downgrade could be applied with just a brief statement of why, without corrosive disparagement.

Some such effective method is essential, to satisfy the call of Lord Stevens, the former Metropolitan Police Commissioner, for a new level of law to deal with 14-18-year-olds who are "knowing, active criminals". Current methods have failed abysmally and something else is needed for these and even younger ones of the same ilk.

The Restoration of a Religious Ethos

Over-arching all of these techniques is the role of religion in creating a sense of individual responsibility for behaving well. This is a strong reason why church schools do so well, both academically and in terms of good conduct. This is a Christian country and state school pupils should not be deprived of the advantages of being immersed in Christianity.

The Labour government wants children to understand other cultures and faiths, but it needs to recognise that foremost in such an aim should be ways of familiarizing children with the ethos of the country where their parents have chosen to live.

Chapter 23

Conclusion and Recommendations

Summary

This book addresses the sixty-year train of events that replaced rising standards of education with falling standards. It aims to support the struggle
for recovery by paving the way to universal literacy and it tries to clarify
four parts of the problem and its solution.

Part I explains what is at stake. The dispute between traditional and
Progressivist education has lacked a proper analysis, leading the public to
believe "Nothing is fully black or white; there are only shades of grey".
That is not true here. Educational decline has directly resulted from the
damaging dogmas of Progressivism, and we have shown *how* its look-say
method of teaching reading creates a widespread illiteracy that undermines the very foundation of learning. Its many alleged benefits are all
injurious false fronts and basic impediments to literacy. We have also
exposed the erroneous Progressivist allegations about phonics and shown
that the true phonic method is highly beneficial.

Part II offers insight into the mechanisms of the Progressivist takeover.
We trace how its agents infiltrated every watchdog meant to safeguard
standards and enticed them to lick the hands of the intruder instead. We
concluded the dismal story by noting the repeated pattern of civilisations
going through the same motivational stages of achievement, affiliation
and the self–aggrandising desire for personal power that causes decline.
Progressivism's ring-leaders work to gain exclusive power and are determined to hang on to it, come what may.

Part III, "The Struggle for Reform", traces the Conservative government's recognition of the decline and its attempts to remedy it through the
1988 Education Act, and also the way all its efforts were dogged by
Progressivists' undercover subversion. Four aspects have been accorded
their own chapters.

- Teaching methods, where some progress is emerging through the
  backlash smoke-screen of bogus assertions, more in spite of state
  schools than because of them.

- Testing, which evoked awareness of the appalling standards but produced false evidence through grade inflation, and a sense of revulsion through overkill.
- Discipline, which has been in increasingly disastrous decline.
- Cost, which has been soaring horrendously.

Part IV, "The Way Ahead", outlines how the struggle for reform could be shorn of its subversive backlash in each of these fields. Chapters 20 to 22 offer constructive ideas for teaching, testing and discipline, while the present concluding chapter summarises our recommendations and also indicates how they would be enormously cost-saving.

Recommendation 1: Synthetic Phonics for All

Synthetic phonics should be re-introduced immediately as a sure-fire way of achieving literacy for all. This task is two-fold: outlawing every trace of the counterproductive obstacles imposed by Progressivism and filling the resulting educational vacuum with training in the straightforward phonics method that prevents illiteracy from developing in the infant school and remedies it among all older strugglers and illiterates. If these goals are to be achieved, it will require more than the present simple exhortation to resort to phonics.

Outlawing Progressivist impediments to reading means ridding ourselves once and for all of the idea that children must be clever enough to teach themselves a skill that teachers have been taught it is impossible to teach. All the props supporting this stupid attitude must be banned, and they are many, as the failure of one led on to invention of the next, no more successful. So out with look-say, whole word, paired and shared reading, the apprenticeship method, real books, whole language, psycholinguistics, analytic "phonics", the National Literacy Strategy, phonemic awareness and the restriction of sense inputs to the type favoured by the child. These and their ilk should forthwith become no more than historical curiosities and the reading schemes that embody them should be named and shamed.

The reading vacuum should be filled by advising all state schools to buy one of the true phonics schemes noted in Chapter 16. Publishers would fall into line automatically as falling sales of non-phonics schemes alerted them to the need for change. They might call on their accustomed authors to provide new ones but such dyed-in-the-wool leopards are not likely to change their spots efficiently, so their stabs at phonics would attract heavy criticism.

Broadcasting is a different matter and because reading is visual as well as auditory, television would be the target for reform. The BBC, in return for its license fee, should be instructed to employ leading synthetic phonicists as advisers on effective programmes for both young beginners and adult illiterates. It is not enough simply to recommend their taking BSA courses. Direct television teaching could be of greater help.

Face-to-face retraining of teachers is also essential and could be achieved in a single year at no extra cost by using the Baker Days, which all state-school teachers must attend. The five days would be ample for instruction in synthetic phonics, which, despite the denigration invented for it, is far simpler than the snarled-up complexities that look-say adherents boast of. Again, there should be genuine phonics experts as tutors and not the same old gurus who have perpetuated illiteracy in previous Baker Days. Capable people could be recommended by the Reading Reform Foundation and the Campaign for Real Education.

We recommend including synthetic phonics in courses for intending head teachers. Mona McNee's DVD, presenting the whole *Step by Step* course in action, should be available in all schools as a refresher for teachers and heads, as well as being ideal for recruits to the profession. Grammar-school staff have no need to teach synthetic phonics but they do need to understand the nature of the reform. Others would almost all have at least some illiterates in their schools and could participate in a national rescue campaign for pupils of all ages.

The USA hot-housing approach teaches beginners to read in three months and the time might be even less for strugglers if a logical remedial scheme let previously confusing information fall into place. Schools could plan a one-term structure for synthetic-phonics teachers, putting non-readers and poor readers into a hot-house class of their own. If there were enough of them, they could be divided into illiterates and semi-literates, or perhaps into those willing to learn as against the more obstreperous. Pupils who master reading could quickly return to mainstream classes to start benefiting from the rest of their schooldays, and their success might act as a spur to less co-operative ones.

The reform would create an initial upheaval but would soon bring benefits right across the board — better teaching, better test results, better discipline and lower cost. Because synthetic phonics keeps the whole class together, teachers are saved the repetition involved in dealing with separate groups, and this could foster a general return to efficient whole-class teaching. Time wasted in the group system would be cut and learning progress accelerated.

The cost of reading schemes would be reduced instantly and there would no longer be a need for outside remedial teaching, which may absorb at least 10% and perhaps 20% of the total schools budget. Dyslexia would revert to its upwave condition when it was not activated into illiteracy, so the cost of statementing and classroom aides would cease. A further saving would be in adult illiteracy classes, as synthetic phonics would provide a cure instead of letting the problem escalate as the BSA has done.

The BSA itself could be wound up, and the Baker Days could be discontinued, again with financial savings. There would also be a brake on the cost of compensating former pupils who sue because they were left illiterate.

Reading fluency enables school leavers to obtain, and succeed in, employment, which could spare the nation the high cost of the dole and the even higher cost of government make-work jobs created to disguise the unemployment figures.

Illiteracy is a major factor in high crime rates, so its eradication would cut felonies, saving schools the heavy cost of theft, burglary, criminal damage and/or arson, and also reduce the cost of the whole law and order system. We should need fewer police, probation officers, law court officials and prison staff. There would also be savings for crime victims, while less stress and violence would reduce demands upon the National Health Service.

Teaching Children to Read (2005) urged further methodological research. This need not cost extra as it could use existing funds, now thought to be mainly wasted on useless work. Further waste could be avoided by focusing on advancement. Synthetic phonics' superiority is well proved, so the next step should compare different synthetic brands, to see which are best in which conditions. The Chapter 21 questionnaire would afford interim hindsight, comparing phonics with non-phonic methods before the latter are swept into history.

There is still a powerful Progressivist Mafia that has constantly protected its own destructive methods and beaten off the evidence for true phonics. There is no reason to believe that they have had a change of heart. They can still grossly interfere with the re-introduction of synthetic phonics, so we have explored whether they are capable of reform or whether they should be excised from the educational system. Much greater freedom for schools would ensue from the closures advocated in Recommendations 2–4 and the reform in Recommendation 5.

In place of these burdens there would be a more constructive set of constraints that would genuinely lead to better education for pupils and a greater choice of schools for parents.

Recommendation 2: Closure of the Training Establishments

Progressivism with its core effect of illiteracy, has its source in the teacher-training establishments, many of whose leaders have invented faulty hypotheses to parade as infallible theories, without a shred of proof. We have highlighted the not rare practice of some of these institutions of accepting substandard students who are more susceptible to the brainwashing. The result has been the appalling decline of educational quality not only in state schools but also in the support systems that take former teachers into their employ.

Plummeting standards have been paralleled by soaring costs. The two-year training period has been increased to three years and often four, and the number trained massively exceeds those who make teaching a life-long career. Possibly 100,000 qualified trainees have never embarked upon a school job at all and nearly 60% of those who do start teaching leave the profession within four years. A business conducted upon such lines would soon be bankrupt and the training system must be adjudged educationally bankrupt.

Training gurus seem so self-righteously impervious to evidence and so set on dominating the whole educational scene that one cannot conceive how to wean them from their counterproductive role. Reform seems impossible and the best solution appears to be complete closure of the present training system.

Fortunately a more effective and economical alternative has already been tested — learning on the job. It has been introduced by both Conservatives and Labour, and the former completely by-passed the training establishments. Good schools could select suitable apprentices to train in teaching, good discipline and aspects of school management, while immersed in an excellent working model of what a school should be. They would need only one year instead of three or four.

The apprentices' qualification would be a Diploma attested by three arbiters: the head of the training school, the head of the different school where they spend a probationary year in their first post, and an inspector who has observed them teach three lessons.

The Diploma would cover practical aspects of teaching. The academic content of school subjects would be covered separately. Many applicants would already have a degree or licentiate and others might need to take evening classes. Separating the academic side in this way should make it less prone to Progressivist distortion or politicization.

One aspect to be resolved is the question of numbers. At present the training establishments qualify numerous graduates but so many do not teach for long, if at all, that far fewer truly suitable trainees are needed. Even so, there seem too few good schools at present and although they should multiply after our Recommendation 1 made synthetic phonics universal, a supplementary source of new teachers would be needed at first.

One such source might be older, experienced teachers, now retiring at age 60. There is talk of raising the general retirement age and some teachers might like a few more salaried years before their income drops to pension level. Other sources would be remedial teachers, teachers' aides and the supposed education experts of the training establishments.

A second question is cost. Enormous redundancy payments were made to HMIs in the hope of reform, but to no purpose as their places were filled with like-minded Progressivists, and that mistake should not be repeated.

Training college staff would not be made redundant but moved sideways into school posts, normally with a lower salary, although those opting for bad schools could keep their present rate. This fits Labour's proposal to pay more to teachers in such schools. If any of them found they could not cope, they could leave, but that would be voluntary, not enforced redundancy, so the cost would be kept down.

The training establishments' buildings and grounds would no longer incur upkeep costs and could be sold, giving income that, together with ongoing savings on staff salaries and student grants, would assist a substantial reduction in education costs. Apprenticeship schools would need remuneration for their training role, but the rate need not be high, as there would also be the benefit in kind afforded by extra bodies to help around the school.

Recommendation 3: Abolition of LEAs

Local education authorities are also counterproductive watchdogs that combine the power of Progressivism with high expenditure. They may control as many as 40 aspects of local schooling and absorb up to 44% of the total schools budget. Both Conservatives and Labour have seen benefits to be derived from extricating the schools from their manipulation. The former's Opt-Out scheme created more independence and gave the schools concerned a share of LEA funding. The latter's scheme retains various aspects of LEA control. But both show that the idea of abolition is neither undesirable nor unworkable.

It was thought that only large schools could cope with taking over LEA services, but many small independent schools do so without difficulty. Small size means a lesser task and a clearer purview. It is large comprehensives that usually have the lowest standards and worst indiscipline, as well as the high cost of crime. We advocate universal opting out.

Gerry Bowden MP told how the huge Inner London Education Authority spent six times more on a simple repair job than the school would have needed if it had commissioned the work directly instead of going through ILEA channels. This means it would not be necessary to divert the whole of LEA budgets to schools; there could also be a substantial saving.

We advocate that schools should be funded by vouchers, to emancipate them from LEA control. At present, on average, only £3330 of the £5500 annual cost per pupil reaches state schools and small private schools survive on fees of under £3500, so we suggest that the vouchers should have a value of £3750 at the primary stage and £4000 at the secondary stage. The extra amount would allow the building up of contingency funds.

The vouchers would be issued to parents to maximize their choice of school. They could be presented in part payment of fees at expensive independent schools, full payment at less expensive ones or used in any state school. Real choice involves having a larger and more varied group of establishments, and the availability of vouchers would give a boost to the founding of new independents. This has been a slow process all the time that parents have had to find fees in addition to paying taxes for state education.

How would the various services fare if the LEAs were abolished? Which ones would become unnecessary and which ones could be adequately provided in other ways?

Schools know their own needs and potential and should be free to develop their own character without the type of impediments imposed by the LEAs. They should appoint their own Boards of Governors from among respected people whose merits would be noted in their prospectuses and who would co-operate with in-house responsibility. There should also be in-house decisions on class size and (within limits) school size, the type and degree of selectivity, grounds for expulsion of pupils and dismissal of incompetent staff, and so on. Schools can make their own arrangements for the midday meal, any after-school activities, and the care and maintenance of their premises.

There would be no need for LEAs to handle educational budgets, as vouchers and student grants would come from central government directly to parents, universities and evening-class colleges. Vouchers would create a fairer system as they would eliminate any LEA bias in the allocation of funds. They would also spare schools the time and effort that must now be invested in the protracted process of going cap in hand to the authorities and negotiating at length for what is needed. Schools would have to cut their coat according to their cloth but should find that quicker and more economical. It would also end the practice of *having* to spend everything within the financial year for fear of a grant reduction, so contingency funds could be accumulated.

School doctors, nurses and educational psychologists could be attached to the District Nurse set-up, although the last would be less needed as the synthetic phonics method eliminated illiteracy and its attendant emotional disturbance. A specialist truancy officer could be attached to the Social Services.

Some LEA services could be dispensed with altogether. Rising standards resulting from Recommendation 1 would make local advisers an unnecessary duplication of Her Majesty's Inspectorate, and as mentioned above, the Baker Days would be discontinued.

Freedom from LEA interference would be more satisfying for schools and also less of a tax burden. Again, there need be no redundancy payments as LEA staff could be offered posts as teachers, school bursars, etc. At present the greater part of educational spending is met by central government and we recommend that it should all be transferred there. Nationally it would be a rather small item but in local budgets it is the heaviest one, so its transfer would permit a welcome drop in the local tax levy and bring local Councils closer to raising and disbursing the whole of their funding. This idea — "localism" — is currently attracting a great deal of attention as a way of helping local authorities become financially more responsible.

Recommendation 4: Streamlining in Central Government

Our radical conclusions as to the dispensability of training establishments and LEAs have prompted us to take a critical look at central government's education arm. This has grown from a Board to a Ministry to a Department within the authors' lifetime – ever more expensive. How far is its operation constructive and how far is it mere meddling?

Of late there has been a constant barrage of meddling related to both teaching and testing, virtually on a day-to-day basis. This has done nothing to raise standards but much to divert teachers' efforts out of teaching and into administrative chores. In addition, financing has been grossly unfair, for example, the large shift of funding from some authorities to others, not because their educational needs had changed but because some had lost their Labour majority on the Council, for which financial punishment was inflicted.

Educational vouchers would not only be more equitable but would also eliminate lengthy Ministerial and Civil Service deliberations on differential funding. Consequently routine voucher issue could be undertaken by the Treasury. A new Education Act could embody stable requirements for schools and put a stop to continual meddling in school life.

Another shrinkage in the DfES's role would result from the rising standards of literacy guaranteed by synthetic-phonics. This would obviate the need for the constant stream of Committees of Inquiry that has been triggered by falling standards and other Progressivist problems. Inspection and examining would still have a place but these could be respectively made by an independent HM Inspectorate and universities, not necessitating an expensive elephantine central Department. We dare to suggest that this could be closed and its staff transferred either into teaching or other government departments.

Recommendation 5: Her Majesty's Inspectorate

It should be made clear to inspectors that the days of treating education as a field of social engineering are over and that their future duties should be as follows.

Firstly, they should revert to the HMI's original aim of promoting high standards through testing. They should participate in test procedures, not only that advocated here for literacy but also those for other subjects and other ages below GCSE level.

Secondly, they should observe three lessons by each probationary teacher, in order to decide whether to co-sign the Diplomas of those learning on the job and thus endorse the views of the heads of the training schools and the schools providing the first job.

A third role would be assessment of incompetent teachers, as a back-up when schools already wish them to leave the profession or find a different post, e.g. with younger children. There should be no more threatening of teachers with lack of promotion for using wrong methods. In fact the tables could be turned and complaints of unprofessional conduct by inspectors could be registered with the Inspectorate.

Care should be taken to appoint an overall Chief Inspector who, like Chris Woodhead, fully understands what is needed to restore British education to its former pre-eminence.

Recommendation 6: Requirements for Schools

There would be two natural constraints upon the schools. One would be educational achievement, publicized in the league tables, and the other would be parent satisfaction. If parents were dissatisfied, with standards or their children's happiness, they would be free to withdraw and take their vouchers elsewhere. If this happened on a sufficient scale in any school, it would be left under-financed and automatically driven into closure.

Withdrawal of pupils should not be frivolous and a small deterrent would be non-returnability of the voucher for any term the child has started. The parents should feel that the problem is serious enough to justify their paying another school for the rest of that term.

A nationally imposed constraint would be an upper school- size limit, to avoid the rise in crime characterizing larger establishments and the resulting non-educational costs. At first, limits of 400 on roll in primaries and 700 in secondaries would apply only to new schools, but larger existing ones with academic or disciplinary problems should also work towards size reduction within a specified period.

Small new primary, especially infant, schools should be encouraged, to boost the incidence of synthetic phonics. Smaller schools would also bring other advantages. There would be more of them so they would be closer together, cutting journey-to-school distances and costs. They would bring educational provision closer to the ideal of parents who have said "Choice is less important than certainty that the nearest school is of a high standard."

Official bussing could be replaced by private mini-bus firms, responding to schools' data on numbers on roll and places of pupil origin. These could compete to charge reasonable fares, with no obligation to transport unruly or bullying children. Parents choosing inconveniently located schools would be responsible for individual travel but in time there would be enough new schools to give a good choice within easy reach. Some secondary schools might develop grammar-standard streams and perhaps become grammar schools completely.

Insisting that new schools remain small means that they can more easily find suitable sites and there should be no fussy insistence on doctrinaire perfection, such as large playing fields. Many splendid upwave schools had only asphalt playgrounds. Some new private schools have rented church halls for the first year-class or two and worked up to large detached houses or portakabins on small vacant sites as the age range expanded. Two important criteria would be fire-service approval of safety precautions and police approval of building and site security. Given these, and neighbours' acquiescence, planning permission should be granted immediately.

It is important to avoid a multiplicity of buildings or single buildings with tortuous outlines, which create concealed spaces where bad behaviour may develop, including graffiti, vandalism and bullying. These are among the reasons why certain large schools with multiple buildings should be encouraged to reduce their numbers on roll. They could, for example, sell their "temporary" classrooms for new schools to re-erect on other sites. Or they could wall off part of their grounds to enclose a building for a new school, with access from a different street.

At present the financial advantages of large schools militate against size reduction. Heads' salaries are logically related to having to cope with more pupils and staff, and a flat-rate value for vouchers would give monster schools disproportionately more money to play with, even if much of it goes on rectifying problems. A disincentive to sizes over the suggested limits might be a reduction in the redemption value of excess vouchers presented to the Treasury.

Educationally, schools should be required to return to traditional teaching practices with their high standards. Teachers should cease to be Plowdenite facilitators and resume the role of disseminating true knowledge and national culture. Classes should face them and be trained to listen attentively and work individually. The subjects earmarked in the 1988 National Curriculum should be restored and vapid ones with a politicizing content should be dropped.

Recommendation 7: Testing

Testing is vital both for teachers, as a check on whether they are truly achieving high standards, and for parents, as a basis for choosing their children's schools. Progressivists have made testing a bogeyman said to inflict intolerable stress on children, which is doubtless true where Progressivist methods have left them too ignorant to excel. With proper teaching, stress is rare and pupils can be inoculated against it by habituating them to frequent small tests and giving help rather than criticism when there are errors.

There have been so many appalling blunders in testing at all levels that a complete overhaul is needed. The Treasury could commission responsible universities (preferably the Russell Group) to set up and run a simpler new system for all testing. More demanding past syllabuses and marking standards could be reinstated to improve A-Levels and GCSE. In this book we are concerned with the first national test for literacy, hitherto at age seven. We have made detailed recommendations in Chapter 21, including the reduction of the test age to six, now that children start school at four. In two years or less they should have finished learning to read and the test could take place near the end of their second year (Year1).

In place of the 117 largely social engineering aspects that have to be reported at present, there could be a simple spelling test, dictating 25 words to involve listening, writing and sufficient reading ability to be able to address spelling. Sets of words at the same levels of difficulty each year could be selected from the successive lists in Alice Coleman's forthcoming *Streamlined Spelling*, which was originally created for just this purpose. The present scope for cheating would be obviated by having external examiners take the test papers into schools on the test day and return the scripts to a centre for communal marking. As each one could be marked in less than one minute, the results could be supplied to all schools within two weeks.

The marks would be accurate assessments of each candidate's ability, without the luck factor inherent in "objective test" guessing and would therefore be comparable for every school in the country. Photocopies of the scripts could be retained in the schools to allow immediate corrective work as well as checking whether the official marking has been faultless. Another advantage would be to relieve teachers of the present marking burden and give them more actual teaching time.

Earlier testing and generally rising standards would justify bringing GCSE down to age 15 or even 14 and letting those who pass leave school and go into employment. This is an age when many youngsters are more ready to learn from life than from yet more classroom experience, and being both literate and in a job would help prevent hooliganism. It would preserve schools from much of the appalling violence committed by older pupils over the last decade or two and also protect younger ones from seeing bad examples to imitate.

Recommendation 8: Improving Discipline

Synthetic phonics creates job satisfaction for teachers, school satisfaction for pupils and family satisfaction for parents, and also, allied with whole-class teaching, helps to ensure orderly classrooms. But indiscipline has other causes, which should also be tackled.

The first cause is Modern Movement architecture in the home area. Children from misery estates with a broken-down social structure may create disciplinary problems that can steadily worsen if they not taught to read. These estates should be tackled without delay. Alice Coleman's *Utopia on Trial* identified 38 design defects that impede child-rearing, and her DICE Project re-design of nine notorious estates showed that removing these and adding single-family houses, allowed residents to develop a good social structure naturally. Most children's behaviour improved quickly and spontaneously, creating safer places to live and endowing the schools with calmer atmospheres and easier teaching. This allows synthetic phonics the best chance of improving education in areas that are now the most disastrous.

Many estate improvement schemes let anti-social behaviour persist because they do not remove the precise impediments to child-rearing. Only DICE has carried out the research that supports a sustainable new footing, as it identifies and reverses the *causes* of the problems. It leads to 13 kinds of cost saving including a 95% reduction in housing upkeep.

There is a second architectural obstacle to good discipline. For six decades, new schools have also been designed by Modernist architects, with many of the same defects as problem housing. Andrew Smith's Kent study revealed 17 common features that fitted the statistics on school theft, burglary, criminal damage, and fire. The school-size reduction recommended above would make the re-design task more economical.

Reducing the number of buildings has been mentioned and another aspect is the site perimeter. It should not have entrances on different sides to allow intruders to cross it. Entries for staff and pupils should be on the same side, with high railings to allow surveillance, and gates should be lockable. The other sides should have high walls to keep intruders out, reduce playground noise for neighbours and minimise the nuisance of balls going over into adjoining property. The head's room and caretaker's office should afford a view of who is entering.

Thirdly, poor discipline is generated in the schools themselves, by Progressivism. Letting children roam around on the pretext that it makes them responsible, should be rejected from the outset. Becoming able to sit and listen or do individual work should be one of the main learning priorities from the children's first day at school, although adapted in duration to children's short attention spans with frequent changes of focus.

We believe also that religious education can be a potent factor in creating good behaviour and should be restored in its traditional form.

Despite these recipes for better discipline, some behavioural problems may still be inherited from Progressivism for a while yet. We recommend vetting the children as they arrive at school, partly to habituate them to good-mannered greetings but also, where necessary, to confiscate weapons, impound mobile phones and, with the aid of a sniffer dog, isolate any with drugs to keep them away from drug-free pupils, and inform their parents.

We urge that schools should not be forced to reinstate excluded troublemakers nor keep those from other schools if they misbehave and undermine other children's education. We advocate the return of the cane to prevent degenerating behaviour in unruly extraverts and suggest that teacher members of STOPP should be drafted for a spell in the worst schools to see how far they can make their own solutions work.

There should be an explicit school-rule book given to parents before their children are accepted. This should make it clear what kinds of misbehaviour would be treated by isolation, graffiti-cleaning, caning, suspension or expulsion. Most parents would sign such an agreement chit, probably convinced that their children would not offend in these ways, but if they were unwilling, the schools should be free not to accept their children.

For incorrigible pupils we advocate sin-bins, with staff trained to re-integrate them into the mainstream. They would be taught synthetic phonics in individual cells with no other child to impress or egg them on to play up. They would mix with more other children only as their work and conduct improved, and should have strenuous exercise to absorb their energy and dampen their aggressiveness. They should be protected from television models of undesirable language and activities, and not progress to team games until they seem capable of good sportsmanship. There should be clear rules explaining the graded steps of conduct improvement that would earn graded rewards, such as associating with one or more others.

Conclusion

Our proposals for releasing schools from most of their present government control may seem draconian although most of them, individually, have been recommended by others also. Critics should pause to consider that freedom was the natural state of education during its long historical upwave. Despite there being little or no official influence, progressively more children were taught to read and the residual 5% illiteracy rate was still spontaneously falling at the time of the 1870 Education Act. Today's independent schools continue to demonstrate that the virtual absence of government interference allows higher standards. These facts justify our call for a return to near independence for all, to support enhanced learning at lower cost. If all our eight recommendations were implemented it would definitely be

"GOODBYE TO ILLITERACY".

Postscript

While this book was in the press, the Department for Education and Skills issued a new reading scheme, *Letters and Sounds*, which has enough of a phonics flavour to have evoked a mistaken headline, 'Back to Basics'. It claims to impart reading ability in three years but it has not been tested so there is no evidence that it can. On the contrary , it wastes the whole of the first year and parts of the other two on 'phonemic awareness', a pseudo-phonic method that has been proved to hold children back. See Chapter 15 of this book. There are also recurrent exercises in 'analytic phonics', another counterproductive technique.

The genuine phonic method does make an appearance but is marred by an inadequate knowledge of the spelling rules and a failure to adopt a graded order from simple to more complex. Some words are introduced as 'tricky' exceptions, despite the fact that they exemplify the same rules as hundreds of others.

It would have been quicker, cheaper and more effective to have simply recommended the eight successful schemes discussed in Chapter 16, especially the original *Step by Step* outlined in Chapter 20. This delivers reading ability within two years and often in as little as three months with a private tutor.

Appendix 1

Acronyms

AEP	Association of Educational Psychologists
ALBSU	Adult Literacy and Basic Skills Unit (Now BSA)
AMMA	Assistant Masters and Mistresses Association (Now ATL)
ATL	Association of Teachers and Lecturers (Formerly AMMA)
AUT	Association of University Teachers
BBC	British Broadcasting Corporation
BDA	British Dyslexia Association
BECE	British Early Childhood Education
BERA	British Educational Research Association
BILD	British Institute for Learning Disabilities
BSA	Basic Skills Agency
CA	Chronological Age
CLPE	Centre for Language in Primary Education
CRE	Campaign for Real Education
CVC	Consonant — Vowel — Consonant
DES	Department of Education and Science (1979–1997)
DfEE	Department for Education and Employment (1997–2001)
DfES	Department for Education and Skills (2001–)
DIY	"Do it yourself"
ESN	Educationally Sub-Normal
GCSE	General Certificate of Secondary Education
GMC	General Medical Council
GNP	Gross National Product
GTC	General Teaching Council
HMI	Her Majesty's Inspectorate
HSC	Higher School Certificate
ILEA	Inner London Education Authority
ILTA	Inner London Teachers Association
IRA	International Reading Association

i.t.a.	Initial teaching alphabet
IQ	Intelligence Quotient
LATE	London Association of Teachers of English (Now NATE)
LEA	Local Education Authority
MP	Member of Parliament
NACRO	National Association for the Care and Rehabilitation of Offenders
NAGM	National Association of Governors and Managers
NAHT	National Association of Head Teachers
NATFHE	National Association of Teachers in Further and Higher Education
NAPE	National Association for Primary Education
NAS/UWT	National Association of Schoolmasters/Union of Women Teachers
NASEN	National Association for Special Educational Needs
NATE	National Association for the Teachers of English
NCDS	National Child Development Study
NFER	National Foundation for Educational Research
NIACE	National Institute of Adult Continuing Education
NLA	National Literacy Association
NLS	National Literacy Strategy
NUT	National Union of Teachers
PAT	Professional Association of Teachers
QES	Queen's English Society
RA/RQ/ARQ	Reading Age/Reading Quotient/Average Reading Quotient
RRF	Reading Reform Foundation
SEO	Society of Education Officers
STOPP	Society of Teachers Opposed to Physical Punishment
UKRA	UK Reading Association (Now UKLA—UK Literacy Association)
VRH	Volunteer Reading Help

Step by Step Materials

Step by Step

This is a basic reading scheme, a work-book for children with simple instructions for parents and other untrained people teaching children to read and write. Its synthetic phonic method is now recognised in the government's Rose Report (2006) as the best way to learn reading, and is effective for all, including dyslexics. It does no harm and facilitates rapid progress. It lays foundations for good spelling and helps develop healthy self-esteem. A somewhat changed version is now available from Galore Park Publishing, 19/21 Sayers Lane, Tenterden, Kent, TN30 6BW (£13.49 plus £2.75 p & p), or from any bookseller. See galorepark.co.uk

Games

Currently available from Mona McNee, 2 Keats Avenue, Whiston, Merseyside, L35 2XR, at the prices below. Cash with order. Prices include p & p in the UK. (To be produced eventually by Galore Park Publishing).

Pairs	12 levels, 12 packs of cards	£12
Bingo	12 levels, 12 game boards	£12
Slides & Ladders	12 levels, 12 game boards	£12

Books

Is it?	Reading and spelling books at 12 levels	£12
Dot to Dot Books	Learn your letters	£0.75
	Write a Story	£0.75

Videos

Especially valuable for those who are moving into phonics from the whole-word and related methods. Available from Renaissance Videos, Norwich. Tel: 01603 767 272

First Steps	A one-hour video teaching the 26 letters, three-letter words and blending.	£10
Teaching Reading: The Phonics Method		
	A one-hour video for teachers	£20

Reading Reform Foundation's Newsletter

Annual subscription	£10

Bibliography

Adams, M.J. (1990) *Beginning to read: thinking and learning about print.* Massachusetts Institute of Technology Press, Cambridge, MA, USA.

(1990) Why not phonics *and* whole language? Orton Dyslexia Society, Minneapolis Symposium , USA.

(1998) The three-cueing system. *Literacy for all: issues in teaching and learning.* Editors: F. and J. Osborn, Guildford Press, New York, USA.

Adams, M.J. & Bruck, M. (1993) Word recognition: the interface of educational policies and scientific research. *Reading and Writing,* 5(2),

(1995) Resolving the great debate. *Network News and Views.* October 95.

Adams, M.J., Foorman, B.R., Lundberg, I. & Beeler, T. (1998) The elusive phoneme: why phonemic awareness is so important. *American Educator,* Spring /Summer.

ALBSU (1991) *Extending readings skills.* Adult Literacy and Basic Skills Unit, London.

(1992) *The basic skills of young adults* The Social Statistics Research Unit, London.

(1994) *Making reading easier.* Adult Literacy and Basic Skills Unit, London.

(1995) *Read and write together: BBC Education,* London.

Alexander, R., Rose, J. & Woodhead, C. (1992) *Curriculum organisation and classroom practice in primary schools.* Department of Education and Science, London.

Atkinson, D. (1997) *Toward self-governing schools .* Institute of Economic Affairs, London.

Augur, J. (1981) *This book doesn't make sens cens sns scens sense.* Amethyst Books, Bath.

Bald, J. (1994) *Phonics arising.* Times Educational Supplement, 8th July, London.

(1997) *The literacy file.* Self-Published, Linton, Cambridgeshire.

Baldwin, G. (1967) *Patterns of sound.* Chartwell Press, Heinemann Medical Books, London.

Barrs, M. & Thomas, A. (1991) Editors. *The reading book.* Centre for Language in Primary Education, Southwark, London.

Bartholomew, J. (2004) *The welfare state we're in.* Politico's Publishing, London.

Beard, R. (1987) *Developing reading 3-13,* Hodder and Stoughton, London.

(1994) *Teaching literacy: balanced perspectives.* Hodder and Stoughton, London.

Beard, R. & Oakhill, J. (1994) *Reading by apprenticeship?* National Foundation for Educational Research, Slough.

Beck, I.L. & Juel, C. (1995) The role of decoding in learning to read. *American Education,* 19(2).

Bell, D. (2004) *The notion that children learn to read by osmosis . . . was plain crackers.* Speech at Chester-le-Street, October 2004.

Benn, C. (1975) The size of schools. *New Society,* 6th March, 75.

Bennett, J. (1975, 1988) *Learning to read with picture books.* Signal Press, London.

Bennett, N. (1976) *Teaching styles and pupil progress.* Open Press, London.

Bishop, M.M. (1986) *The ABCs and All Their Tricks.* Mott Media, Fenton, Michigan, USA.

Blachman, B.A., Ball, E.W., Black, R.S. & Tangel, D.M. (1994) Kindergarten teachers develop phonemic awareness in low-income, inner-city classrooms. Does it make a difference? *Reading and Writing,* 6.

Bloom, A. (1987) *The closing of the American mind.* Penguin, London.

Blumenfeld, S. L. (1973, 1988) *The new illiterates.* Paradigm Co., Boise, Idaho, USA.

(1975) *Why America still has a reading problem.* Reading Reform Foundation, Massachusetts Branch, USA.

(1983) *Alphaphonics*. Paradigm Co., Boise, Idaho, USA.

(1983) *A premier for beginning readers*. Paradigm Co., Boise, Idaho, USA.

(1997) *N.E.A.: Trojan horse in American education*. Paradigm Press, Boise, Idaho, USA.

(1996) *The whole language/O.B.E.fraud*. Paradigm Press, Boise, Idaho, USA

Bowey, J.A. Vaughan, L. & Hansen, J. (1998) Beginning readers' use of orthographic analogies in word reading. *Journal of Experimental Child Psychology*, 68.

Bowis, J. (1988) *ILEA: The closing chapter*. Conservative Political Centre, London.

Bradley, L. & Bryant, P. (1983, 1985) Onset and rime. *Journal of Experimental Psychology*.

Brett, D., King, M. & Wertheimer, Michael (2005) *Max Wertheimer and Gestalt theory*. Transaction Publisher, London.

Brice-Heath, (1989) *Ways with words*. Cambridge University Press.

Brooks, G., Gorman, T., Kendall, L. & Tate, A. (1991) *What teachers in training are taught about reading: the working papers*. National Foundation for Educational Research, Slough.

Brooks, G., Gorman, T., Harman, J., Hutchison, D. & Wilkin, A. (1996) *Family literacy works*. National Foundation for Educational Research/ Basic Skills Agency, Slough.

Brown, I.S. & Felton, R.H. (1990) Effects of instruction on beginning reading skills in children at risk for reading disability. *Reading and Writing*, 12(3).

Bruck, M. & Treiman, R. (1992) Learning to pronounce words: the limitations of analogies. *Reading Research Quarterly*, 27(4).

Brunner, M.S. (1993) *Retarding America: the imprisonment of potential*. Halcyon House, Portland, Oregon, USA.

Bruton-Simmonds, I. (2002) *Mend yourEnglish or what we should have been taught at primary school*. Queen's English Society. London.

Bryne, B. (1988) *The foundation of literacy*. Psychology Press, Hove, East Sussex.

(2000) Acquiring the alphabetic principle: what children contribute and what needs to be taught. *British Journal of Educational Psychology: Cutting Edge Conference*.

Bullock Report (1975) *A language for life*. Department of Education and Science, HMSO, London.

Burchill, J. (1991) *Inspecting the schools: breaking them monopoly*. Centre for Policy Studies, London.

Burghes, D., Marenbon, J., Moon, B., Smithers, J. & Woodhead, C. (2004) *Comparing standards :teaching the teachers*. Editor: S. Lawlor. Politeia Education Commission Report, London.

Burkard, T. (1996) Phonological training in reception year. *British Journal of Curriculum and Assessment*, 6(3)

(1999) *The end of illiteracy? The holy grail of Clackmannanshire*. Centre for Policy Studies. London.

(2006) Sound Foundations — the intensive synthetic phonics programme for the slowest readers. *Reading Reform Foundation Newsletter*, 57.

Burkard, H. & T. (2002) *Sound Foundations*. The Promethean Trust, Norwich.

Burt, C. (1917) *The backward child*. University of London Press.

Bynner, J. & Parsons, S. (1997) *It doesn't get any better: the impact of poor basic skills on the lives of 37-year-olds*. The Basic Skills Agency, London.

Cane, B. & Smithers, J. (1971) *The roots of reading: a study of 12 infant schools in deprived areas*. Ed. Gabriel Chanan. National Foundation for Educational Research, Slough.

Carnine, D., Grossen, B. & Silbert, J. (1992) *Direct instruction to accelerate cognitive growth*. ADI Press, 3343.

Carnine, D. (1995) *Using high-performance schools to improve student academic achievement*. National Center to Improve the Tools of Educators, (A direct instruction course). Eugene, Oregon, USA.

Cary, L. & Verhaeghe, A. (1994) Promoting phonemic analysis ability among kindergartners. *Reading and Writing*, 6(3).

Cassidy, K. (1990) A is for the alphabet. *Guardian*, 20. 3. 1990.

Cato, V. & Whetton, C. (1991) An enquiry into LEA evidence on standards of reading of 7 year old children. National Foundation for Educational Research for the Department of Education and Science. Slough.

Cato, V., Fernandes, C., Gorman, T., & Kispal, A. (1992) *The teaching of initial literacy: How do teachers do it?* With an appendix on children's writing at age 7 by White, J. National Foundation for Educational Research, Slough.

Chall, J. (1967, 1983) *Learning to read: the great debate.* McGraw Hill, New York, USA.

(1997) *The great debate: ten years later.* L. Erlbaum, New Jersey, USA.

(1997) Learning to read: the great debate 20 years later. A response to "Debunking the "great phonics myth" *Phi Delta Kappan,* March, 97.

(1997) The new reading debates: evidence from science, art and ideology. *Teachers College Record,* 94.

Chapman, J.W., W.E. Tunmer & J.E, Prochnow (1998) *An examination of the effectiveness of Reading Recovery.* Massey University Report to The Ministry of Education, New Zealand.

Chew, J. (1990) *Spelling standards and examination results among sixth-formers, 1984-1990)* Campaign for Real Education, No. 7.

(1992) *Literacy, Leeds, LINC and the mixed methods myth.* Campaign for Real Education. No. 11.

(1994) *Professional expertise and parental experience in the teaching of reading, or mother often knows best.* Campaign for Real Education, No. 22.

(1997) Initial literacy and the phonics controversy. *Controversial Issues in English,* Proceedings of the Queen's English Silver Jubilee Conference.

(1997) Methods of teaching reading: a guide for the layman. *Quest* 66.

(2001) Analytic phonics makes a come-back – but where is synthetic phonics? *Reading Reform Foundation Newsletter,* 45.

(2001) The RRF calls for the withdrawal of ELS programme, [Early Learning Support]. *Reading Reform Foundation Newsletter,* 47.

(2006) Phonics: the holy grail of reading? *Reading Reform Foundation Newsletter,* 57.

Clark, M. (1976) *Young fluent readers.* Heinnemann, London.

Clarke, M. A. &. Cummins, N. L. (1993) Whole language: reform and resistance. *Language and Education,* 7(2).

Clay, M. (1979) *Reading: the patterning of complex behaviour.* Heinemann Educational, Auckland, New Zealand.

(1984) *The early detection of reading difficulties.* Heinnemann, Auckland, New Zealand.

(1987) *Reading recovery: a handbook for teachers in training.* Heinnemann, Auckland, New Zealand.

Cohen, D.K. (1995) What is the system in systemic reform? *Educational Researcher,* 24(9).

Coleman, A. (1985) *Utopia on trial: vision and reality in planned housing.* Hilary Shipman, London.

(1997) Tony Blair. *The Graphologist,* 15(4).

(1997) Dumbing down. *The Salisbury Review,* 24(1).

(In preparation) *Streamlined Spelling.*

Collins, J. (1997) How Johnny should read. *Time,* October 97.

Collins, M. & Tamarkin, C. (1982) *Marva Collins' way.* Jeremy P. Tarcher, Inc., Los Angeles and New York, USA.

Cowling, K. (1994) *Toe by Toe.* Cowling, Baildon, West Yorkshire.

Cox, B. (1991) *Cox on Cox: an English curriculum for the 1990s.* Hodder and Stoughton, St. Albans.

(1997) Editor. *Literacy is not enough.* Manchester University Press.

Cox, C., Douglas-Home, J., Marks, J., Norcross, L. & Scruton, R. (1986) *Whose schools? a radical manifesto.* The Hillgate Group, London.

Cox, C. et al (1989) *Learning to teach.* The Hillgate Group. The Claridge Press, London.

Cox, C. & Marks , J. (1981) *Real concern.* Centre for Policy Studies, London.

(1982) Editors: *The right to learn.* Centre for Policy Studies, London.

(1990) *The insolence of office: education and the civil servants* .The Claridge Press, London.

(1997) *Voluntary Schools Threatened.* The Free Nation, September.

Cox, C., Marks, J. & Pomian-Srednicki (1983, 1985) *Standards in English schools.* National Council for Educational Standards.

Crosby, R.M.N. (1968) *Reading and the dyslexic child.* Souvenir Press, London.

Crouch, W. (1991) *Mr. Wordmaker and the V Team; Shorty Stories.* Wordmaker Bookers, Waterlooville, Hampshire.

Cunningham, A.E. & Stanovich, K.E. (1993) Children's literacy environments and early word recognition skills. *Reading and Writing*, 5.

(1998) What reading does for the mind. *American Educator*, Spring/Summer, 98.

Daniels, J.C. & Diack, H. (1954) *The Royal Road Readers,Teachers' book.* Chatto and Windus, London.

(1956) *Progress in reading.* University of Nottingham Institute of Education.

Daniels, J.C. (1966) The place of phonics. *The First International Reading Symposium, Oxford, 1964.* Editor: J.A. Downing. Cassell, London.

Davies, A. & Ritchie, D. (2002) *THRASS (The handwriting, reading and spelling system)* . Chester.

Dawkins, R. (1976) *The selfish gene.* Oxford University Press.

Department of Education and Science (1990) Fourth Edition. *Why teaching? TASC (Teaching as a career).*

Department for Education and Skills (n.d.) *The NationalLliteracyStrategy: Key stages 1 and 2.*

Deuchar, S. (1989) *What's wrong with ours schools?* Campaign for Real Education.

Devlin, A. (1995) *Criminal classes: offenders at school.* Waterside Press, Winchester.

Dewey, J. (1910) *The school and society.* University of Chicago Press, USA.

(1938) *Experience and education.* Collier, New York, USA.

(1956) *The child and the curriculum.* University of Chicago Press, USA.

(1964) *On education.* University of Chicago Press. USA.

Diegmuller, K. (1996) A war of words: whole language under siege. *Education Week*, March, 96.

Dombey, H. & Moustafa, M. (1992) *Words and worlds: reading in the early years of school.* National Association of Teachers and Advisers in English, London.

(1998) *W(hole) to part phon'ics.* Centre for Language in Primary Education, London.

Donaldson, M. (1989) *Sense and sensibility: some thoughts on the teaching of literacy.* Occasional Paper No. 3, Reading and Language Centre, University of Reading.

Downing, J.A. (1964) *The initial teaching alphabet.* Cassell, London.

(1997) *The i.t.a experiment.* Evans Brothers London.

(1997) *The i.t.a. symposium.* National Foundation for Educational Research, Slough.

Drake, W.E. (1968) *Journal of Learning Disability,*

Eakman, B. (1991) *Educating for a "new world order"* Halcyon House, Portland, Oregon, USA.

Education Acts

(1870) (Forster)

(1944) The Education Act (Butler)

(1976) Establishment of Comprehensive Education.

(1981) Special Needs

(1988) The Education Reform Act

Ehri, L.C. & Robbins, C. (1992) Beginners need some decoding skill to read words by analogy. *Reading Research Quarterly*, 27.

Ehri, L .C. (1995) The emergence of word reading in beginning reading. *Children Learning to Read.* Falmer Press, Canada.

(1998) Grapheme-Phoneme Knowledge is Essential for Learning to Read Words in English. Editor with J. Metsala, *Word Recognition in Beginning Literacy.* Erlbaum, New Jersey, USA.

Elkin, S. (1998) Reading is the right of all. Quest, 69

Elkonin, D.B. (1963) The psychology of mastering the elements of reading. *Educational Psychology in the USSR.* Stanford University Press, USA.

(1973) USSR methods of teaching reading. *Comparative Reading.* Macmillan, New York.

Ellis, A. (1994) *Reading, writing and dyslexia.* Open University, Milton Keynes.

Ellis, E.W. (1979) *Illustrated spelling.* Stanley Thornes, Cheltenham.

(1979) *Find the Words.* Stanley Thornes, Cheltenham.

Engelman, S. (1969) *Preventing failure in the primary grades.* Science Research Associates. Eugene, Oregon, USA.

(1997) *Teach your child to read in 100 easy lessons*. Science Research Associates, Distar, Eugene, Oregon, USA.

Flesch, Rudolf (1955) *Why Johnny can't read*. Harper Row, New York, USA.

(1997) *Why Johnny STILL can't read*. Harper Row, New York, USA.

Flew, Anthony (1981) *The politics of Procrustes: contradictions of enforced equality*. Maurice Temple-Smith, London.

(1991) *Empowering the parents: how to break the educational monopoly*. Institute of Economic Affairs, London.

(1994) *Shepherd's warning: setting schools back on course*. Adam Smith Institute, London.

(1995) *All the right places*. Adam Smith Institute, London.

(19xx) *Power to the parents: reversing educational decline*. Sherwood Press, London.

(1997) The third way: where to and between which? *Libertarian Alliance*, February., 97.

Foltzer, M. (1965-89) *Professor Phonics gives sound advice*. St. Ursula Academy, Cincinatti, Ohio, USA.

(1976, 1985) *A sound track to reading*. St. Ursula Academy, Cincinatti, Ohio, USA.

Foorman, B.R. (1995) *Early intervention for children with reading problems*. Draft, University of Houston.

Foorman, B.R., Francis, D.J., Novy, D.M & Liberman, D. (1991) How letter-sound instruction mediates progress in first-grade reading and spelling. *Journal of Educational Psychology*, 83(4).

Foorman, B.R., Francis, D.J., Fletcher J.M & Schatschneider C. (1998) The role of instruction in learning to read: preventing reading failure in children at risk. *Journal of Educational Psychology*, 91(4).

Freedman, J. (1993) *Failing grades: Canadian schooling in a global economy*. Video, Society for Advancing Educational Research.

Froome, S.H. (1970) *Why Tommy isn't learning*. Tom Stacey Ltd, London.

Fry, D. (1985) *Children talk about books: seeing themselves as readers*, Oxford University Press.

Gagg, J.C. & M.E. (1955) *Teaching children to read*. Newnes Educational, London.

Gaines, C. &. Wray, D. (1995) *Reading issues and directions*. National Association for Special Education Needs/ UK Reading Association.

Garfield, A. (1992) *Teach your child to read*. Vermilion Press, London.

Garsten, R., Darch, C. & Gleason, M. (1988) Effectiveness of a direct instruction academic kindergarten for low-income students. *Elementary School Journal*. 89(2).

Gatto, J.T. (1992) *Dumbing us down :the hidden curriculum of compulsory schooling*, New Society Publishers, Philadelphia, USA.

Glass, G.V. et al (1982) *School class size: research and policy*. Sage, California, USA.

Glynn, T., Bethune, N., Crooks, J., Ballard, K. & Smith, J. (1989) Reading Recovery in context: implement-ation and outcome. *Educational Psychology*, 12 (3/4).

Goleman, Daniel (1996) *Emotionalintelligence: why it can matter more than IQ*. Bantam Books, New York, USA; Bloomsbury, London.

Goodman, K.S. (1970) Reading: a psycholinguistic guessing game. *Theoretical Models and Processes of Reading*. Edited by Singer and Ruddell. International Reading Association., USA.

(1986) *What's whole in whole language?* Scholastic Educational, Bright Ideas Series, USA.

(1992) I didn't found whole language. *The Reading Teacher*, 46(3).

(1996) *Ken Goodman on reading*. Heinnemann, Portsmouth, New Hampshire, USA.

(1997) Phonics phacts. *Nebraska Language Arts Bulletin*, January.

(1997) NOT! an attempt to centralize power. *Education Week*, September.

(1998) Comments on the Reading Excellence Act (US). *Readingonline*. (Website).

Goodman, K.S. & Y.M. (1977) Learning about psycholinguistic processes by analyzing oral reading. *Harvard Educational Review*, 47(3).

Gorman, T. (1989) *What teachers in training read about reading*. Occasional Paper No. 4. Centre for Research in Language and Communication. National Foundation for Educational Research., Slough.

Gorman, T. & Fernandez, C. (1992) *Reading in recession: 1987-1991 trends*. National Foundation for Educational Research, Slough.

Goswami, U. (1990) *Phonological skills and learning to read.* Erlbaum, New Jersey, USA.

Goswami, U. and Bryant P. (2002) *Phonological skills and learning to read.* London.

Gough, P.B. (1993) The beginning of decoding. *Reading and Writing,* 5(2).

Grant, M. (2000) *Phonics first books.* Ridgehill Publishing, Bristol.

(2000) *Sound discovery.* Ridgehill Publishing, Bristol.

(2004) Raising literacy attainments of all pupils in a mainstream primary setting with particular reference to boys' writing – a six-year longitudinal study. *Reading ReformFoundation Newsletter,* 52.

Gray, E. & Burn, J. (1983) *Reading matters.* Christian Institute, Newcastle.

Groff, P. (1982) Sight words: the major myth of reading. *Reading,* 16(3).

(1987) *Preventing reading failure.* National Book Co., Portland, Oregon, USA.

(1991) Teachers' opinions of the whole language approach to reading instruction. *Annals of Dyslexia,* 41.

(1996) The rise and fall of whole language and the return to phonics. *Journal of the Simplified Spelling Society,* 22.

Hadley, H. (1994) *The phonics book.* Stanley Thornes, Cheltenham.

Hadow Report (1931) *The Primary School.* The Consultative Committee on Education.

Hall, S.L. & Moats, L.C. (1999) *Straight talk about reading.* Contemporary Books, Chicago.

Hall, N. (1987) *The emergence of literacy.* Hodder and Stoughton, London.

Halsey, A.H. (1972) *The trends of reading standards.* National Foundation of Educational Research, Slough.

Hampshire, S. (1990) *Susan's story.* Corgi, London.

Every Letter Counts. Sphere, London.

Harris, T. (1992) *I'm OK, you're OK.* Jonathan Cape, London.

Heaton, P. & Winterson, P. (1990) *Dealing With dyslexia.* Better Books Publishing, Bath.

Hegel, G.W.F. (1803) Published in English (1942). *The philosophy of right.* Oxford University Press.

H. M. Inspectorate (1978) *Primary education in England.* HMSO, London.

(1989) *Reading policy and practice at ages 5-14.* Department of Education and Science, London.

(1990) *The teaching and learning of reading in primary schools.* Department of Education and Science, London.

Hester, H. (1983) *Stories in the multilingual classroom.* Inner London Education Authority.

Hirsch, E.D. (1996) *The schools we need and why we don't have them.* Doubleday, New York.

Hogenson, D.L. (1974) Reading failure and juvenile delinquency. *Orton Society Annual Bulletin.*

Hogg, M.C. (19xx) *Patterns and sequences.* Oliver and Boyd, Edinburgh.

Holdaway, D. (1979) *The foundations of literacy.* Ashton Scholastic, Australia.

Holland, R. (1995) *Not with MY child, you don't.* Chesapeake Capital Resources (Citizen Projects Publishing Division), Richmond, Virginia, USA.

Holt, M. (1999) The phonics scandal *or illiteracy can seriously damage your health. Quest* 71.

Honey, J. (1997) *Language is power: the story of standard English and its enemies.* Faber and Faber, London.

Hooton, M. (1976) *The first (and second) reading and writing book.* Heinnemann, London.

Hornsby, B., Shear, F. & Pool, J. (1974) *Alpha to omega.* Heinnemann, London.

Hornsby, B. (1995) *Overcoming dyslexia.* Heinemann, Oxford.

Huey, E. (1908) *The psychology and teaching of reading.* MIT Press, Cambridge, Mass., USA. Reprinted 1958.

Humphrys, J. (2004) *Lost for words.* Hodder and Stoughton, London.

Hunt, R. et al (1986) *Oxford reading tree.* Oxford University Press, Oxford.

Hyams, D. (1994) Through a Glass Darkly. *Salisbury Review,* 12 (3).

Hynds, J. (1984) *Recent developments in reading.* Avery Hill College, London.

(1988) *Primary language record handbook for teachers,* Avery Hill College, London. UK.

Isaacs, S. (1932) *The children we teach.* University of London Press. UK.

Ivens, K. & Seaton, N. (1990) *Operation whole curriculum – a tangled web*. Campaign for Real Education, No. 6.

Johnston, R.S. & Watson, J.E. (1997) What sort of phonics? *Literacy and Learning*. Autumn 97.

(1999) *Accelerating Reading Attainment: The Effectieness of Synthetic Phonics – http://scre.ac.ukspotlight/index.html*.

(2001) A long-term follow-up of the effectiveness of synthetic phonics teaching in Clackmannanshire. *Reading Reform Foundation Newsletter*, 45.

(2003) Accelerating the development of reading, spelling and phonemic awareness skills. *Reading and Writing*,

(2004) *A seven-year study of the effects of synthetic phonics teaching on reading and spelling attainment*. Scottish Executive, Edinburgh.

Jones , K. (1992) *English and the NationalCurriculum*. Institute of Education, University of London.

Jorm, A.F. & Share, D.L. (1983) Phonological recoding and reading acquisition. *Applied Psycholinguistics* 4(2)

Juel, C. (1988) Learning to read and write. *Journal of Educational Psychology*, 80.

Juniper, L & Dias, K. (2000) Phongraphix—who needs additional literacy support? *Support for Learning*, 17(1).

Kelly, B. (1993/4) Sacrosanctity vs science: evidence and educational reform. *Effective School Practices*, Fall 93/Winter 94.

Kershaw, J. (1974) *People with dyslexia*. NACRO, Paragraphs 83-86. London.

Khalsa, D.S. (1997) *Brain longevity*. Century House, London.

Kirby, J. (2006) *The nationalisation of childhood*. Centre for Policy Studies, London.

Kline, C.C. (1988) Teaching disabilities. (Review of "The Learning Mystique" by Gerald Coles) *Readings*, December 88.

(1994) Reading, writing and `rithmetic taught without a measuring stick. *Effective School Practices*, Summer, 94.

Kozol, J. (1985) *Illiterate America*. Anchor Press/Doubleday, New York, USA.

Lamb, B.C. (1997) *The opinions and practices of teachers of English: a national survey of teachers of English to 11–18-year-olds*. The Queen's English Society, London.

(1994) *A national survey of communication skills of young entrants into industry and commerce*. The Queen's English Society, London.

Lawlor, S. (1987) *Opting out: a guide to how and why*. Cetre for Policy Studies, London.

(1988) *Away with LEAs*. Centre for Policy Studies, London.

(1990) *Teachers mistaught: training in theories or education in subjects*. Centre for Policy Studies, London.

(1993) Editor. *The Dearing debate*. Centre for Policy Studies, London.

(1993) *Inspecting the school inspectors. New plans, old ills* Centre for Policy Studies, London.

(1992) *Nursery choices: the right way to pre-school education*. Centre for Policy Studies, London.

(2000) Editor. *Comparing standards: the report of the Politeia Education Commission* Politeia, London.

(2004) Editor: *Comparing Standards: teaching the teachers*. Report of the Politeia Education Commission, Politeia, Lodon.

Levine, A. (1994) The great debate revisited. *Atlantic Monthly*, December, 94.

Levinson, H.N. (19xx) *Dyslexia*. Springer-Verlag, New York, USA.

Liberman, I.Y. & A.M. (1990) Whole language vs code emphasis: underlying assumptions and their implications for reading instruction. *Annals of Dyslexia*, 12.

Liberman, I.Y. & Shankweiler, D. (1991) Phonology and beginning reading. In *Learning to read,basic research and its implications*. Editors: Rieben ? & Perfetti, C. A. L. erlbaum Associates, Hillsdale, New Jersey, USA.

Little, J.W. (1993) Teachers' professional development in a climate of educational reform. *Educational Evaluation and Analysis*, Summer, 15(2).

Lloyd, S. (1992) *The phonics handbook*. (& other materials). Jolly Learning Ltd., Chigwell, Essex.

(2001–2) The development of "Jolly Phonics". Parts 1-5. *Reading Reform Foundation News-letter,* 45-49.

(2003) Synthetic phonics — what is it? *Reading Reform Foundation Newsletter,* 50.

(2004) Learning to read and write – fashion or fact? *Reading Reform Foundation Newsletter* 52.

Lyon, R. (2001) *Measuring success.* US House of Representatives.

MacDonald, T.H. (1984) *First aid in reading,writing and spelling: A handbook for parents and teachers.* Hale and Iremonger, Sydney, Australia.

(1992) Much ado about reading (and how to solve the problem). *Campaign for Real Education,* No. 14.

(1998) *The road to reading:step by step instructions on teaching your child to read.* Aurum Press, London.

(2003) Are we disabling our children? *Quest,* 85.

Macmillan, B. (1997) *Why schoolchildren can't read.* Institute of Economic Affairs, London.

(2000) Reading between the lies. *Quest,* 68

(2002) An evaluation of the government's early intervention initiative: the Early Literacy Support Programme. *Reading Reform Foundation Newsletter,* 49.

(2004) *Why boys are different.* Thorson's, London.

Marenbon, J. (1987) *English our English.* Centre for Policy Studies, London.

(1993) *Testing time: the Dearing review and the future of the national curriculum.* Centre for Policy Studies, London.

Marks, J. (1991) *Standards in schools:assessment, accountability,and the purposes of education.* Social Market Foundation, London.

(1993) *Examination results: educational standards and underachievers.* Educational Research Trust, London.

(1996) *Standards of English and Maths in primary schools.* Social Market Foundation, London.

(1998) *Value for money in LEA schools.* Centre for Policy Studies, London.

(1999) *Standards and opportunities.* Institute for Economic Affairs, London.

(2000) *Girls Know Better: Educational Attainments of Boys and Girls.* Civitas, London.

(2000) *The betrayed generations: standards in British schools 1960-2000. Centre for Policy Studies,* London.

(2002) *Standards and spending: dispelling the spending orthodoxy.* Centre for Policy Studies, London.

Marks, J., Cox, C. & Pomian-Srednicki, M. (1986) *Examination performance of secondary schools in the Inner London Education Authority.* National Council for Educational Standards, London.

Marks, J. & Naylor, F. (1985) *Comprehensives: counting the cost.* Centre for Policy Studies, London.

Marsland, D. (1992) *Towards the renewal of British education.* Campaign for Real Education, No. 23.

Marsland, D & Seaton, N. (1993) *The empire strikes back: the "creative subversion" of the national curriculum.* Campaign for Real Education, No. 20.

Martin, R.L. (1968) *Fabian freeway.* Fidelis Publishers, Santa Monica, California, USA.

McGovern, C. (1989) Teacher training (synopsis) *Campaign for Real Education Conference 1989: The School Curriculum and Standards & Multicultural Education and Teacher Training.*

McGuinness, D. (1997) *Why children can't read and what we can do about it..* Penguin, London.

McGuiness, C. & G. (1998) *Reading reflex: The foolproof phonographix for teaching your child to read.* . The Free Press, New York & London.

McIntyre, C.W. & Peickering, J.S. (1999) Multisensory structured language programs: content and principles of instruction. *MSSL Methods,* September 99.

McKenna, M.C., Stahl, S.A. & Reinking, D. (1994) A critical commentary on research, politics and whole language. *Journal of Reading Behaviour,* 26(2).

McKenzie, M. (1986) *Journeys into literacy.* Schofield and Sims, Huddersfield, W. Yorkshire.

McLelland , D.C. (1961) *The achieving society.* The Free Press, New York and Col-lier-Macmillan, London.

McNee, M. (1980) Letter in *Spring Bulletin of the National Council for Educational Standards*.

(1980-81) The chance of a lifetime. *Winter Bulletin of the National Council for Educational Standards*.

(1983) Educational cripples. *Contemporary Review*, No. 1405.

(1986) Back to firm ground. *Education Today*, 36(3) College of Preceptors, London.

(1986) On teaching not to read. *Salisbury Review*, April, 86.

(1988) *Our post-war reading disaster*. Video, McNee.

(1990) *Step by Step. systematic phonics manual for all ages*, McNee, Merseyside.

(2001) Dyslexia: the only way forward. *Quest*, 83.

(2003) Education: reading, Step by Step. *The Lantern*, X(3).

McPike, (1998) The unique power of reading and how to unleash it. *American Educator*, Spring, 98.

Medwell, J., Wray, D., Poulson, L & Fox. R. (1998) *Effective teachers of literacy*. Literacy Study Com-missioned by the Teacher Training Agency.

Meek, M. (1977) *The cool web: the pattern of children's reading*. Bodley Head, London.

(1981) *Learning to read*. Bodley Head, London.

(1983) *How texts teach what readers want to learn*. Thimble Press, Stroud.

(1991) *On being literate*. Bodley Head, London.

Meek, M. et al. (1983) *Opening moves*. Bedford Way Papers.

Meyer, R (2002) *Phonics exposed*. L. Erlbaum, New Jersey, USA.

Milburn, C. (2004) Reading between the lines. *The Age*, November, Australia.

Miles, T. R. (1974) *Understanding dyslexia*. Hodder & Stoughton, Sevenoaks.

Miles, T.R. & E. (1974) *Helpingr the dyslexic child*. Methuen, London.

Mills, C. & Timson, L. (1988) *Looking at language in the primary school*. National Association for the Teaching of English, London.

Minns, H. (1990) *Read it to me now!* Virago, London.

Miskin, Ruth (2002) Ruth Miskin's new literacy programmes. *Reading Reform Foundation Newsletter*, 49.

Moats, L.C. (1997) California reading initiative: a revolution in education policy. *Perspectives*, Orton Dyslexia Society, 23(1).

(2002) Whole language lives on: the illusion of balanced instruction. *The .Ford- ham.Foundation*, October, New York, USA.

Moats, L.C. (2004) *Children of the code: teaching teachers to teach reading*. New Horizons for Learning, Script of interview by Boulton, personal communication to M. McNee.

Moller, D. (1997) Let's get our children reading. *Quest* 65.

Moon, C. (1985) *Practical ways to teach reading*. Ward Lock, London.

Moorman, G.B., Blanton, W.E. & Mc Laughlin, T. (1994) The rhetoric of whole language. *Reading Research Quarterly*, 29 (4).

Morais, J. (1994) Reasons to pursue the study of phonological awareness. *Reading and Writing*, 6(3).

Morris, J.M. (1958) Teaching children to read. 1. The relative effectiveness of different methods of teaching reading. A. The place and value of phonics. *EducationalResearch*, 1.

(1959) *Reading in the primary school*. Newnes, London, UK

(1965) *Report on reading research relating to reading in England and Wales, 1946–60*.

Prepared for the Plowden Committee. Ministry of Education..

(1966) *Standards and progress in reading*. National Foundation For Educational Research, Slough.

(1972) Editor: *The first "R" yesterday, today and tomorrow*. Ward Lock, London.

(1974–1983) *Language in action resource book*. Macmillan Education, London and Basingstoke.

(1975) Language and literacy: spontaneity and contrivance in the learning-teaching situation. *Reading: what of the future?* Editor: D. Moyle. Ward Lock Educational, London.

(1975) Creating more than a basic reading scheme. *The content of reading*. Editor: A. Cashdan. Ward Lock Educational, London, UK

(1976) Mother tongue and father tongue. *Reading: research and classroom practice*. Editor: J. Gilliland. Ward Lock Educational, London.

(1978) Children's reading achievement in relation to their teachers' attributes. *Reading: implementing the Bullock Report*. Editors: E. Hunter-Grundin and H. U. Grundin. Ward Lock Educational, London.

(1979) New phonics for old. *Growth in reading*. Editor: D. Thackray. Ward Lock Educational, London.

(1979) New phonics: a development from the teaching research connection. *The reading connection*. Editor: G. Bray. Ward Lock Educational, London.

(1979) Stylistic variation in texts for young children. *The reader and the text*. Editor: L. John Chapman. Heinemann Educational Books, London.

(1979) Diagnosis in the classroom. *Teaching reading: the key issues*. Editor: Alistair Hendry. Heinemann Educational Books, London,

(1979) The early reading curriculum and the problem of vocabulary. *Reading through the curriculum*. Editor: Bruce Gilham. Heinemann Educational Books, London.

(1979) Children like Frank, deprived of literacy unless . . . *Reading: meeting children's special needs*. Editor: D. Dennis. Heinemann Educational Books, London.

(1979) *United Kingdom Reading Associatoin's first twenty-one years*. Macmillan Education, London and Basingstoke.

(1983) *Phonics 44*. Macmillan Education, London and Basingstoke.

(1990) *The Morris Montessori word list*. The London Montessori Centre, UK

(1993) Texts for reading assessment. *Literacy text and context*. Editor: D. Wray. United Kingdom Reading Association

(1994) Editor. *Professional writers support the cause of literacy*. Society of Women Writers and Journalists Seminar, Beresford Business Centre, London.

Mosse, H.L. (1982) *You can prevent or correct learning disorders*. (Formerly *The complete handbook of children's reading disorders*) Riggs Institute Press, Beaverton, Oregon, USA.

Moyle , D. (1968) *The teaching of reading*. Ward Lock Educational, London.

(1980) *Language patterns*. Holt, Roberts and Winston, London.

(1980) *Pull or push?* Holt, Roberts and Winston, London.

Murray, W. (1969) *Ladybird. Teaching reading*. Penguin, London.

National Grammar Schools Association (2001) *Grammar schools in the twenty-first century*. Oldbury.

Naylor, F. (1991) Higher standards and more choice: a manifesto for schools. *Campaign for Real Education*, Editor: N. Seaton.

(2002) *Comprehensive Ideology: Burns and the Betrayal of Two Communities*. Campaign for Real Education, No. 30.

Nevola, F., (2002) Why are so many of our children failing to learn to read? If the NLS is flawed what can we do about it? *Reading Reform Foundation Newsletter*, 49.

Newsom Report (1963) *Half our Future*. Ministry of Education.

NFER (1972) *The Trends of Reading Standards*.

(1991) *Reading Report to CATE*

Nicholson, T. et al. (1988) Have we been misled by miscues? *The ReadingTeacher*. 42.

Nicholson, T. (1989) A comment on Reading Recovery. *New Zealand Journal of EducationalStudies* 24(1).

(2000) *Reading the writing on the wall*. Dunmore Press, Auckland, New Zealand.

Norcross, L. & Brown, P. (1990) *GCSE: The egalitarian fallacy and the lost battle*. The Claridge Press, London.

North, M.E. (1992) The Writing Road to Reading: from theory to practice. *Annals of Dyslexia*, 42.

Nugent, C. (1983) Method and mythod in modern reading philosophy: the handicapping effect of clichéd theory in schools. *Proceedings of the UKRA Conference1983*. Heinnemann, London.

OFSTED (1993) *Boys and English: a report from the office of Her Majesty's Chief Inspector of Schools*. HMSO, London.

(1993) *English key stages, 1, 2 and 3: fourth year, 1992-1993*. .

(1994) *Primary matters: a discussion on teaching and learning in primary schools*.

(1995) Class size and quality of education.

(1996) Reporting pupils' achievement.

(1996) *The teaching of reading in 45 inner London primary schools: a report of HerMajesty's Inspectorate in collaboration with the LEAs of Islington, Southwark and Tower Hamlets.*

(1998) *The NationalLiteracy Strategy: an HMI evaluation.*

(1999) *The National LiteracyStrategy: an interim evaluation.*

(1999) *The National L iteracy Strategy: the second year.*

(2000) *The National Literacy Strategy: the third year.*

(2003) *The National LiteracyStrategy*: The FirstFourYears

(2001) *Teaching of phonics: A paper by HMI.*

O'Hear, A. (1987) The importance of traditional learning. *British Journal of Educational Studies*, 35(2).

(1988) *Who teaches the teachers?* Social Affairs Unit, Department of Education and Science.

(1991) *The father of child-centredness,:John Dewey and the ideology of modern education.* Policy Study No. 12, Centre for Policy Studies, London.

(1991) *Education and democracy.* The Claridge Press, London.

(1992) *Empowering parents: how to break the educational monopoly.* Institute of Economic Affairs,London.

O'Keeffe, D. (1989) Introduction to teacher-training session. *The school curriculum and standards & multicultural education and teacher training.* Campaign *for* Real Education 1989 Conference.

(1986) *The wayward curriculum.* Social Affairs Unit, Department of Education and Science. UK.

Orton, S.T. (1929) The sight reading method of teaching reading as a source of reading disability. *Journal of Educational Psychology,* 20 (February).

(1937) *Reading ,writing and speech problems in children.* W. W. Norton, New York.

Palmer, S. & Corbett, P. (2003) Literacy; what works? Nelson Thornes, Cheltenham.

Pearson, P.D. (1989) Reading the whole language movement. *Elementary School Journal,* 90(2).

Peers, M. (1972) *The trends of reading standards.* National Foundation for Educational Research, Slough.

(n.d.) *A comparative study of the spelling errors of children who were taught to read and write through the medium of the initial teaching alphabet with those taught through traditional orthography.* Manuscript dissertation.

Perfetti, C. (1995) Recent advances in reading research and their application. *Reading 2000 Seminar,* University of Glasgow.

Pesetsky & 39 others (mostly MIT staff) (1995) *Blasting whole language.* Letter to Massachusetts Commissioner of Education. Endorsed in the Phyllis Schlafly Report, 1996.

Phillips, M. (1996) *All must have prizes.* Little, Brown and Co. London.

Piaget, Jean (1955) (English Translation, 1966) *The growth of logical thinking.* Routledge and Kegan Paul, London.

Pinder, R. (1987) *Why teachers don't teach like they used to.* Hilary Shipman, London.

Pinker, S. (1995) *The language instinct.* Penguin.

Pitman, Sir J. (1959) Learning to read: a suggested experiment. *Times Educational Supplement,* 29th May.

(1961) Learning to read: an experiment. *Journal of the Royal Society of Arts,* 109.

(1966) The initial teaching alphabet in historical perspective. *The initial teaching alphabet and the world of English.* Edited by M. J. Mazurkiewicz, Initial Teaching Alphabet Foundation, New York, USA.

(1967) *An appreciation of the i.t.a. symposium.* The Initial Teaching Alphabet Foundation. *London.*

(1981) The Principle of Initial Learning-Media application for Learning the English Language. *Reading Instruction Journal* 24(2).

Pitman, Sir J. & St. John, J. (1969) *Alphabets and reading: the initial teaching alphabet.* Sir Isaac Pitman and Sons, London.

Plowden, B. (1967) *Children and their primary schools.* A Report by the Central Advisory Council for Education (England). Department of Education and Science.

Pollock, J. (1978) *Signposts to spelling*. Heinemann, London.

Povey, A. (1999) *Plans, plans, plans. An education policy based on central control.* The Point-maker, Centre for Policy Studies, London UK.

Raban, B. & Moon, C. (1992) *A question of reading*. David Fulton, London.

Radford, J. (1989) *Reading the signs: towards a nation of illiterates*. Derbyshire Parents Association, Ashbourne.

Rayner, K. (1993) *Eye movements in reading: recent developments*. American Psychological Society, 2(3).

Rayner, K., Foorman, R.B., Perfetti., C.A., Pesetsky, D. & Sehlenberg, M.S. (2003) How psychological science informs the teaching of reading. *Reading Reform Foundation Newsletter* 50.

Reason, R., & Boote, R. (1986) *Learning difficulties in reading and writing*. National Foundation for Educational Research. Nelson, Windsor.

Reid, J.F. (1967) Evaluations – 10. *The i.t.a symposium,* Editor: J. A. Downing. National Foundation for Educational Research, Slough.

Robinson P. & Smithers, A. (1988)

Rodgers, G.E. (1996) The hidden story. First Books, Boomington, Indiana, USA.

Root, B. (1986) In defence of reading schemes. Reading and Information Centre, University of Reading.

(1989) *Help your child learn to read.* Usborne Publishing, Falmouth.

(200x) *Phonics.* Parragon pub {sic], Bath.

Rose , J. (2005) *Independent review of the teaching of early reading: interim report.* Department for Education and Skills..

(2006) *Independent review of the teaching of early reading: final report.* Department for Education and Skills.

Rousseau, J-J. (1762) *Emile.* Translated by Barbara Foxley, 1933. J. M. Dent, London. Everyman edition 1993.

(1762) *Du Contrat Social* Penguin Edition, 1968.

Russell, S. (1992) *Phonic code cracker.* Jordanhill College, Glasgow.

Sanders, B. (1994) *"O" is for "ox". (Violence, electric media and the silencing of the written word.)* Pantheon Books, New York, USA.

Saudek, R. (1928) *Experiments with handwriting.* Reprinted 1978. Books for Professionals, Sacramento, California, USA.

Schlafly, P. (1994) *What is Reading?* The Phyllis Schlafly Report, Vol. 27, March.

(1997) The fakery of "America Reads". The Phyllis Schlafly Column. A syndicated news column in many newspapers. Washington Times, 7. 5. 97.

Schonell, F. J. (1936) *The essential spelling list.* Macmillan, London.

(1939) *Happy venture readers,* Oliver and Boyd, Edinburgh.

(1942) *Backwardness in the basic subjects.* Oliver and Boyd, Edinburgh. (4th edition, 1961).

(1945) *The psychology and teaching of reading.* Oliver and Boyd, Edinburgh.

Schonell, F.J. & F.E. (1950) *Diagnostic and attainment testing.* Oliver and Boyd, Edinburgh.

Schools Council (1981) *The practical curriculum.* Working Paper No. 70. Methuen Educational, London.

Seaton, N. (1992) Editor. *Reading, spelling and sex education.* Campaign for Real Education, No.14.

(1993) *Teacher training: public funding for progressivism.* Campaign for Real Education, No. 18.

(1994) Developments in Education. *The Lantern, 1(4).*

(1997) *School funding: present chaos and future clarity.* Centre for Policy Studies. London.

(1999) *Fair funding or fiscal fudge? Continuing chaos in school funding.* The Pointmaker, Centre for Policy Studies, London.

(2000) Unfair Funding. *The Pointmaker.* Centre for Policy Studies, London.

(2001) Free our schools. *Freedom Today,* July.

Sexton, S (1990) *Our schools – future policy.* IPSET Education Unit, Warlingham, Surrey.

Shanker, A. (1995) Classrooms held hostage. *American Educator,* Spring 95.

Share, D. (1995) Cognitive processes in early reading development. *Issues in Education,* 1(1). JAI Press, Greenwich, Connecticut, USA.

Sielaff, M. (1991) Reading: why ignore the evidence? Editorial, *Phoenix Gazette,* Arizona, USA.

Slavin, R. (1999) *Success for all.* Fordham Foundation, New York, USA.

Slough, E. (1997) *The grammar book.* National Association for the Teaching of English, London.

Smith, A. E. (1997) *Educational land use in Kent.* University of London, PH. D, Thesis.

Smith, F. (1971) *Understanding reading: a psycholinguistic analysis of reading and learning to read.* Holt, Rinehart and Winston, Eastbourne.

(1973) *Psycholinguistics and reading.* Holt, Rinehart and Winston, Eastbourne.

(1977) Making sense of reading—and of reading instruction. *Harvard Educational Review,* 47(3).

(1978) *Reading.* Cambridge University Press.

(1985) Creating worlds. *Conference at Lincoln University, Nebraska,* USA..

(1986) *What's the use of the alphabet?.* Reading and Language Centre, Abel Press, Victoria, B.C., Canada.

(1986) *Insult to intelligence: the bureaucratic invasion of our classrooms.* Heinnemann Portsmouth, New Hampshire, USA.

(1988) *Understanding reading.* Laurence Erlbaum Association, Hillsdale, New Jersey, USA. Fifth edition 1994.

(1989) *Overselling literacy.* Phi Delta Kappan, January.

(1991) Join the company of authors. *Times Educational Supplement,* 23rd August, 91.

Snowling, M. (1995) Phonological processing and developmental dyslexia. *Research in Reading,* 28.

Southgate, V. (1981) *Extending beginning reading.* The Schools' Council., Heinemann, London.

Sowden, P.T. & Stevenson, J. (1994) Beginning reading strategies in children experiencing contrasting teaching methods . *Reading and Writing,* 6(2).

Spalding, R.M & W.T. (1957) *The Spalding method of phonics for teaching speech ,writing and reading.* Revised 1986. William Morrow, New York, USA.

(1962) *The Writing Road to Reading.* Quill/ William Morrow, New York, USA.

Spock, B. (1946) *Baby and child care.* Parker Books, now Simon & Schuster, London.

Stanovich, K.E. (1994) Romance and reality. *The Reading Teacher,* 47(4).

(1994) Constructivism in Reading Education. *Journal of Special Education,* 28(3).

(2000) *Progress in Understanding Reading.* Guilford Press, New York, USA.

Stanovich, K.E. & P. (1995) How research might inform the debate about early reading acquisition. *Journal of Research in Reading,* 18(2).

Start, K.B. & Wells, B.K. (1972) *The trend of reading standards.* National Foundation for Educational Research, Slough.

Stevenson, H. (1991) Japanese elementary school education. *The Elementary School Journal.* (News and Views, September 1991.

Stone, J.E. (1996) Developmentalism. *Network News and View,* June.

(1998) *Learning requires more than play.* Reprinted on the Internet: Education Matters, August 2004, X(7).

STOPP (1984) *The violent 81%.* The Society of Teachers Opposed to Physical Punishment, London.

Stott, D.H. (1964) *Roads to literacy.* Holmes MacDougall, Edinburgh.

(1974) *The parent as teacher.* University of London Press.

(1981) Teaching reading: the pycholinguistic invasion. UK Reading Association, 15.

Strickland, D. (1995) Reinventing our literacy programme: books, basics, balance. *The Reading Teacher.* 48(4).

Sumbler, K. & Willows, D. (1998) Time management: monitoring activities. *Jolly Phonics and Control Classrooms,* Unpublished paper, Ontario, Canada.

Taylor, Sir C. (1990) *Raising educational standards.* Centre for Policy Studies, London.

Terman, S. & Walcutt, C. (1958) *Reading: chaos and cure.* McGraw Hill, NewYork, USA.

Thackray, D.V. (1971) *Readiness for reading with i.t.a and t.o* Geoffrey Chapman, London.

Theis, D (1993) A whole lotta learning going on. *Effective School Practices,* Summer, 93.

Thomson, G.B. & Nicholson, T. (1999) Editors: *Learning to read.* International Reading Association/ Columbia Teachers' College, USA.

Thouless, R.H. (1930) *Straight and crooked thinking.* Hodder and Stoughton, London.

Tizard, J. (1972) *Children with specific reading difficulties.* Report of the Advisory Committee on Handicapped Children. Ministry of Education, London.

Tizard, B. & Hughs, M. (1984) *Young children learning.* Fontana Press, London.

Tooley, J. (1996) *Education without the state.* Institute of Economic Affairs, London.

(2001) *Reclaiming education.* Cassell, London.

Tooley, J. & Stanfield, J. (2003) *Government failure: E. G.West on education.* Institute of Economic Affairs, London.

Tooley, J., Dixon, J & Stanfield, J. (2003) *Delivering better education.* Adam Smith Institute (Research) Ltd, London .

Toomey, D. (1993) Parents hearing their children read: rethinking the lessons of the Haringey project. *EducationalResearch,* 35.

Torgesen, J.K. (2000) Lessons learned from intervention research in reading: a way to go before we can rest. *Current Trends in Educational Psychology,* London.

(2002) Preventing early reading failure. *American Federation of Teachers,* 28.

Tunmer, W.E. & Hoover, W.A. (1993) Phonological recording skill and beginning reading. *Reading and Writing,* 5(2).

Turner, M. (1990) *Sponsored reading failure.* Ipset Education Unit, Warlingham, Surrey.

Reprinted in *Language, literacy and learning in educational practice.* Clevedon.

(1991) *Reading, learning and the national curriculum.* CPS Policy Challenge, Centre for Policy Studies, London.

(1991) The reading debate: finding out. *Support for Learning.* 6(3).

Tyk, I. (1993) *The Butterfly Book: a reading and writing course.* Irina Tyk, Potter's Bar, Hertfordshire.

(1999) How to teach children to read. *Quest,* 66.

Uhry, J.K., & Shepherd, M.J. (1993) Segmentation/spelling. *Reading Research Quarterly,* July-September.

Underwood, J.E. (1955) *The problem of the maladjusted child.* Ministry of Education Report. U.S. Government, Washington, D.C.

(1979) *Illiteracy in America: extent, causes and suggested solutions.* National Advisory Council on Adult Education.

(1983) *A nation at risk.* National Commission on Excellence..

(1984) *The nation responds.*

(1985) *Hearing: oversight on illiteracy in the USA.*

(1985) *Becoming a nation of readers* R. C. Anderson..

(1986) *What works.*

(1986) *Illiteracy in America: extent,causes and suggested solutions.* National Advisory Council on Adult Education.

(1986) *Oversight on literacy in the United States.* Hearing of the House Senate Sub-Committee.

(1989) *Illiteracy: Incurable Disease or Education Malpractice?* US Senate Republican Committee Statement.

Vellutino, F.R. (1979) *Dyslexia:theory and practice.* Massachusetts Institute of Technology Press, USA.

(1991) Introduction to Three Studies on Reading . . . Code-Oriented vs Whole Language. *Journal of Educational Psychology.* 83(4).

Vernon, A.C. & P.E. (1960) *Intelligence in attainment tests.* University of London Press.

Warnock, M. (1978) *Special educational needs.* Ministry of Education.

Waterland, L. (1985) *Read with me: an apprentice approach to reading.* Thimble Press, Stroud, Gloucestershire.

Watson, J. & Johnston, R. (1999) *Accelerating reading attainment: the effectiveness of synthetic phonics.* School of Psychology, University of St. Andrew's.

Webster, J. (1981) *The rescue handbook* and the *Shorty Stories*. Ginn, Aylesbury, Buckinghamshire.

Wertheimer, M. (1924) *Gestalt theory social research, II*. Lecture at Kent Society, Berlin, Germany.

West, E.G. (1965) *Education and the state* Institute of Economic Affairs , London, UK (See Tooley and Stanfield, 2003). Reprinted by Liberty Fund, Indianapolis, 1994.

Williams, Sean (1998) *Levelling down*. Centre for Policy Studies, London.

(1998) *Freedom for schools*. Centre for Policy Studies, London.

Willows, D.M. (1978) A picture is not always worth a thousand words: pictures as distractors in reading. *Journal of Educational Psychology*, 70 (2).

Woodhead, C. (1995) *A question of standards: finding the balance*. Politeia, London.

(1996) Conspiracy of silence on failing schools must be broken. *The Times*, 7th May.

(2000) Education should be about common sense not cyberspace. *Quest*, 74.

Wu, H-M. & Solman, R.T. (1993) Effective use of pictures as extra stimulus prompts. *British Journal of Psychology*, 63.

Yalon, Dafna, (2003) *Graphology across cultures*. British Institute of Graphologists, London.

Yeo, E. (1991) *The rise and fall of primary education*. Campaign for Real Education, No. 8.

Zollner, J, Harrison, B. & Magill, B. (1996) The hole in whole language. *Australian Journal of Remedial Education*, 27 (5).

Index

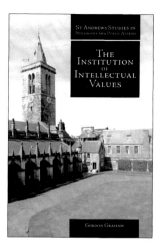

The Institution of Intellectual Values
Gordon Graham

This is a revised and expanded version of the much-praised short book *Universities: The Recovery of An Idea*.

'Graham has written an elegant and extraordinarily refreshing book, with no fudging of his own opinions and judgements ... It deserves a very wide readership and will surely stand as a point of reference for years to come.' **Gordon Johnson**, *Times Higher Education Supp.*

'A short reflective treatise on British university education that deserves to be widely read.' *Political Studies Review*

'This volume ought to be compulsory reading for every government minister or civil servant with responsibilities in this area.' **Margaret Atkins**, *New Blackfriars*

'Though densely and cogently argued, this book is extremely readable'. *Philosophical Quarterly*

290 pp., £14.95 / $29.90, 978-1845401009 (pbk.)

Can Oxford Be Improved? *Anthony Kenny and Robert Kenny*

In December 2006, dons at Oxford University caused turmoil by rejecting a set of governance reforms that were contained in a government white paper and championed by their own vice-chancellor. This book is a response to these events and is essential reading for all with an interest in the future of this great university. **Sir Anthony Kenny** was formerly Master of Balliol College, Oxford and president of the British Academy. He is the author of many books on philosophy and over forty years has held almost every kind of post in Oxford from graduate student to pro-vice-chancellor. **Robert Kenny** is managing director of a consulting firm.

128 pp., £8.95 / $17.90, 978-1845400941 (pbk.)

The New Idea of a University *Duke Maskell and Ian Robinson*

This book is an entertaining and highly readable defence of the philosophy of liberal arts education and an attack on the sham that has been substituted for it.

'A seminal text in the battle to save quality education'. *THES*

'The most important essay on the university system in the past 20 years'. *Cambridge Quarterly*

'This wonderful book should make the powers that be stop and think'. **Chris Woodhead**, *Telegraph*

'A severe indictment of British universities'. *Oxford Magazine*

208 pp., £14.95 / $25.90, 978-0907845348 (pbk.)

Education! Education! Education! *Stephen Prickett (ed.)*

The essays in this book criticise the new positivism in education policy, whereby education is systematically reduced to those things that can be measured by so-called 'objective' tests. Contributors include Libby Purves, Evan Harris, Rowan Williams, Roger Scruton, Robert Grant, Bruce Charlton and Anthony Smith.

'This book is a call to action.' **Antony Sutch**, *The Tablet*

200 pp., £17.95 / $29.90, 978-0907845362 (pbk.)

Values, Education & the Human World *Ed. John Haldane*

Contributors include Bryan Appleyard, David Carr, Mary Midgley, Anthony O'Hear, Richard Pring, Anthony Quinton, Jonathan Sacks, Stewart Sutherland and Mary Warnock.

'A forthright attack on the "empiricist orthodoxy" that, with its disastrous effects on education, permeates the modern world'. **Paul Standish**

274 pp., £17.95 / $29.90, 978-1845400002 (pbk.), St. Andrews Studies, Volume I

Education & the Voice of Michael Oakeshott *Kevin Williams*

An examination of Oakeshott's defence of liberal education and his influence on Hirst and Peters.

250 pp., £30.00 / $49.90, 978-1845400552 (cloth)

The
Salisbury Review
The quarterly magazine *of conservative thought*

No representation without taxation

imprint-academic.com/salisbury

25 Years of Conservative Thought

Friedrich Hayek   Roger Scruton
Ray Honeyford   John O'Sullivan
Enoch Powell   Alfred Sherman
Anthony Daniels
Robert Grant
Tim Congdon